Lectures in

Corporate Finance

Fifth Edition

Revised Printing

Jayant R. Kale
Georgia State University

Richard J. Fendler
Georgia State University

KENDALL/HUNT PUBLISHING COMPANY
4050 Westmark Drive   Dubuque, Iowa 52002

Cover image copyright © Digital Vision

Copyright © 2003, 2006 by Jayant R. Kale and Richard J. Fendler

ISBN: 978-0-7575-5767-5

Kendall/Hunt Publishing Company has the exclusive rights to reproduce this work,
to prepare derivative works from this work, to publicly distribute this work,
to publicly perform this work and to publicly display this work.

All rights reserved. No part of this publication may be reproduced,
stored in a retrieval system, or transmitted, in any form or by any
means, electronic, mechanical, photocopying, recording, or otherwise,
without the prior written permission of the copyright owner.

Printed in the United States of America
10 9 8 7 6 5 4 3

Contents

◆ 6   Time Value of Money: The Basic Concepts   169

◆ 7   Time Value of Money: Advanced Topics   191

◆ 8   Financial Securities   227

9 Valuation of Bonds and Stocks and the Cost of Capital 249

10 Basics of Capital Budgeting 273

11   Advanced Topics in Capital Budgeting   297

Preface

Several years ago, the finance department at Georgia State University, in response to comments and suggestions received from students, recruiters, and faculty teaching finance electives, decided to restructure the department's core undergraduate course. This book is a consequence of that process. All business majors in the University must take the finance core course—annual enrollment averages 1,400 students. Of this number, approximately 20 percent become finance majors; for most of the rest, this is the only finance course that they ever take.

All faculty members who have taught this type of course have undoubtedly heard from students who found the material to be too abstract. Non-finance majors, in particular, often experience difficulty seeing the usefulness and applicability of what they are taught in finance. As a rule, introductory finance courses tend to be too general. And because of this overwhelming and general nature, those of us who teach finance electives often find that students have forgotten many of the basic principles and skills on which advanced courses are supposed to build.

In response to these concerns, we conducted a thorough evaluation of the objectives and content of our existing finance undergraduate core course. The evaluation process at every step kept in view one basic question: what should a student know or have learned at the end of this course? As a result of this process, we realized that the existing course was actually a general survey course, covering twenty-one or more textbook chapters and ten major topics. Fundamental understanding and the development of basic skills were being sacrificed for broad based coverage. Students were being exposed to much more information than was necessary.

Consequently, we redesigned the course according to the opposite, unique principle: *"less is more."* That is, less (in fact, half as many topics) taught in greater detail will produce more understanding, more emphasis on basic skills, and more student excitement and curiosity about the field of finance. Note that less does not imply less rigor; the new course is considered by most students to be the most rigorous course in the undergraduate business core.

The evaluation involved surveying the faculty to identify the five major topics that all students exiting this course needed to know—not just know about but know well. This was deemed the core knowledge necessary for finance electives, and the overview of finance required for non-finance majors to understand the function of finance within a firm. Additionally, we wanted adequate attention paid to the exciting and practical sides of finance so as to persuade the undeclared to seriously consider finance as their major.

The survey produced a strong consensus concerning the following five topics: financial statements and financial reporting, the identification (from accounting data) and analysis of cash flow, the principles of time value of money, stock and bond valuation, and capital budgeting. (A sixth topic would have been the principles of risk and return). Using these topics, we developed a set of learning objectives and a course outline. We then began the search for an appropriate text. The only available option that we could find was to use a financial accounting book, eight chapters from a twenty-six-chapter traditional financial management textbook, and a study guide. This option would have subjected our students to various writing styles, incongruous terminology, formulas and definitions, non-sequential chapters, and multiple text assignments. Additionally, the books for the course would have cost each student more than $150.

Given the unacceptability of these factors, and the fact that we were certain that we could produce a better-focused and integrated product at approximately one-third of the cost, we decided to write this book. To the best of our knowledge, this book is unique in that it was written specifically for an undergraduate introductory course in corporate finance. It contains only the information deemed necessary for a student to know or have learned at the end of such a course. We did not use any existing text as a guide; instead, our only guide was the learning objectives and course outline developed in the evaluation process.

Readers of this text will immediately recognize that it was written primarily for students. Both authors have more than fifteen years of classroom teaching experience and have been ranked by students as some of the best instructors in the University. The writing style of the book reflects their belief that text material should come across as it would in a lecture and not as it often does in a traditional textbook. For example, in most chapters there are several problems that need to be solved in space provided in the text before proceeding to the next section. The objective of this approach is to ensure that the student fully understands the given concept before proceeding to the next concept. In fact, all instructors do this when we teach. Therefore, this book allows the instructors to employ their own teaching styles and at the same time ensures proper student learning outcomes.

Finally, we note that this product has been classroom tested for many semesters, by more than twenty-five different instructors, and by more than 5,000 students. It has been edited and modified in response to feedback from all who have used and read the book. Students have been asked each semester to provide comments on the writing style and readability of the text. These comments have been extremely favorable. We are routinely thanked for writing a readable and intuitive text and for actually being concerned and doing something about the exorbitant cost that students pay for textbooks. Students appreciate the workbook style that encourages them to work problems as they read the chapters. They also like the fact that they are asked to read the entire book in the order in which it was written.

What has been our favorite comment received to date? One student wrote: "this book actually appears to have been written by humans"—implying, we infer, that in the eyes of students most academic textbook authors are aliens (or perhaps something worse)!

Note Concerning End-of-Chapter Assignments and Problems

There are three Assignments at the end of each chapter (with the exception of chapter 1 and chapter 8). These problems and questions are meant to be done as homework and turned in to the instructor for grading. Or, they can be used as excellent chapter summary problems. The assignment problems purposefully span the material and problems in the chapters. Detailed solutions for every assignment problem are available to any instructor who adopts the book, and these solutions can be shared with your students. Our main purpose in all that we do is to promote student learning and understanding. Finance is an analytical subject matter, and working problems is one of the best ways to learn basic subject matter upon which more advanced ideas and topics can build. Seeing a detailed solution soon after working a problem is one of the best methods known for enhancing the learning experience.

Each chapter also contains end-of-chapter questions and problems. These provide additional practice in applying the principles discussed in each chapter. Additionally, as noted above, within most chapters are several problems that should be worked as they are encountered. Blank space is provided for working these problems right in the text as they occur. Answers to these in-chapter problems are listed in the text immediately following the problem. Many of the end-of-chapter problems are similar to these in-chapter problems.

Acknowledgments

The authors wish to thank the following: all of the FI 3300 students who have used the book and have provided "almost always positive" feedback and comments, the FI 3300 instructors who have provided valuable feedback on the original editions of the book (in particular, Pete Dadalt, Jann Howell, Beverly Marshal, Jouahn Nam, Padamja Singal, and John Thornton), Georgia State University, the finance faculty at the University and the Chairman of the Department of Finance, Gerry Gay, for his encouragement, support and guidance.

Chapter **1**

Introduction and Overview

After studying Chapter 1, you should be able to:

- Understand why sound financial management is vital to the survival of a business.

- Identify the three main subject areas in the field of finance.

- Describe different forms of business organization.

- Explain why the goal of a financial manager should be to maximize the wealth of the firm's shareholders and why this particular goal is preferred over other goals.

- Describe the basic difference between Financial Management and Accounting.

- Understand the importance of cash and the basic relationship between cash flow and value.

1.1 The Mysterious World of Finance ....

Most successful business enterprises have the following in common: a product (or service) that people want or need, an efficient method of production and/or delivery, effective marketing, quality managers, a trained work force, and a vision and strategy for future growth. The managers of successful firms also usually possess a thorough understanding of the principles of financial management. In fact, the managers of most of the best corporations in the U.S. devote at least as much time to the finances of their firms as they do to operations. This is probably why so many current top managers and CEOs majored in finance in college or graduate school and/or were promoted out of their (or some other) company's finance department. They know that whereas even the most excellent financial management cannot save a firm with a bad product, poor financial management can cause a firm that efficiently produces, markets, and delivers a high-demand product to fail. The following story illustrates the importance of financial management to a firm.

When at seven years of age, Bennie Feldhaus completely disassembled and then rebuilt his father's riding lawnmower, doubling the mower's top speed and power while reducing its gas consumption by 30 percent, his parents knew that Bennie was destined to be something special. By age ten, Bennie had rebuilt the engines in both the family automobiles, achieving similar results. By fourteen, Bennie had memorized the engine specifications of every car made in the U.S. over the past five years. By sixteen, he knew the specifications of all foreign made automobiles as well.

Bennie, however, disliked school. To him school was boring and a waste of time. He wanted to be working on automobiles. So, after he finally graduated from high school at age twenty, Bennie started working in his uncle's auto garage. Bennie, who was personable and funny as well as talented, soon gained a reputation as a master auto mechanic. Mechanics from all over the city would call Bennie regularly for advice.

After ten years of working for his uncle, Bennie decided that there had to be a better way to profit from his talent. Accordingly, at age thirty, Bennie took all of the money that he had and started an auto parts store. His plan was simple. He would use his reputation and experience among the mechanics in the city to build a solid customer base and he would use his personality and knowledge to provide better instruction and service than any other auto parts store around.

Bennie's Auto Parts and Service Center was an immediate success. Within a year Bennie was making more money than he ever thought possible. He worked twelve hours per day, seven days per week, and even at that rate, he could not keep up with the demand for his products and services.

Unfortunately, Bennie had one, what he considered to be minor, problem. He didn't understand the principles of corporate finance. Approximately 40 percent of Bennie's customers paid with checks. When he received a check from a customer, Bennie would stuff it into a drawer in the counter. Because he was so busy, often he would not deposit the checks for weeks. Another 30 percent of Bennie's customers paid with credit cards. Bennie never verified the credit cards, and in any given month approximately 10 percent of these purchases would be returned by the credit card company unpaid. The rest of Bennie's customers requested that Bennie bill them for their purchases. Again, because he was so busy, often Bennie did not accurately record the credit purchases. Accordingly, any time a customer complained about his bill, Bennie would adjust or wipe out the debt. If a customer did not pay after Bennie sent out a second notice, Bennie would stop sending bills. Collections took too much time and besides, he reasoned, his sales growth would easily make up for a few uncollected accounts.

Bennie did not have an inventory system. He ordered parts whenever it seemed like he needed them, and when they arrived he put them on whatever shelves were mostly empty. Often he would order a part for a customer only to find out later that the needed part was sitting on a shelf in another part of his storeroom. Cataloging inventory took too much time and besides, he reasoned, with the rate his sales were growing, having a few extra parts laying around couldn't be all that detrimental to his firm's health.

Finally, Bennie never paid much attention to the bills he received from his suppliers. He was too busy selling products and making money. He would send payments only after he began to receive threatening letters or phone calls. However, because he was so busy he never bothered to balance his checkbook, and consequently often the checks he sent bounced. In one particularly bad month, his bounced check fees to the bank exceeded $1,500.

Halfway into his second year of operations, Bennie's suppliers began to demand immediate payment for all outstanding bills and refused to ship new parts without first receiving payment in cash or cashiers check. As Bennie began to have trouble getting parts, he started to lose customers. Soon his cash flow dried up and Bennie was forced to go to the bank to seek a loan to consolidate all of his outstanding debt.

Not surprisingly, the bank officer laughed at his request. Bennie had a long history of bounced checks, he did not have any type of financial statements to show to the banker, and he did not have any definite plan for how he was going to repay the loan. Without the loan, Bennie was forced to declare bankruptcy. To make matters worse, one year later he was indicted for tax fraud by the federal government. Because he was too busy to bother with minor details like financial records, Bennie never bothered to send any money to the IRS. Today, Bennie is in jail making license plates pondering, in his spare time, the mysterious world of finance.

A thorough reading of this book will not necessarily qualify you to be a successful financial manager nor will it reveal all of the mysteries of the financial world. It will, however, help you to understand the repercussions of Bennie's actions (or lack thereof) and perhaps allow you to keep from making the same mistakes that Bennie made if you decide to start a business of your own. Who knows—had Bennie read this book before starting Bennie's Auto Parts and Service Center, he might be spending his spare time playing golf instead of making license plates!

◆ 1.2 Finance As a Field of Study ···

Finance is a very broad based subject matter. To organize its study, the (actually non-mysterious) field of finance is divided into three separate, though inter-related, subject areas: corporate financial management, investments, and financial markets and institutions. *Financial markets and institutions* studies the determinants of interest rates, the regulation of financial institutions (banks, savings and loans, insurance companies, pension funds, and so on), the structure and functioning of the various financial markets, such as the stock and bond markets, and the various financial assets (and the secondary markets for the assets) issued by financial institutions (such as mortgages, auto loans, collateralized mortgage obligations, and certificates of deposit).

Investments focuses on how individuals and financial institutions make decisions concerning the allocation of securities within their investment portfolios. The major securities studied in Investments are stocks, bonds, options, and futures contracts. A central theme of this subject area is the determination and management of risk.

Corporate Financial Management, also often referred to as business or corporation finance, involves the actual financial management of a business enterprise. This is the broadest subject area of finance. It includes topics such as financial reporting and financial analysis, cash flow analysis, financial forecasting, the management of inventory and accounts receivable, current liability management, security valuation, the measurement and analysis of risk, capital budgeting under certainty and uncertainty, dividend policy, capital structure, bankruptcy, mergers and acquisitions, and international financial management. Also, because financial managers must deal with investors and financial institutions when they need to raise outside funds, any study of corporation finance must include at least a survey of the other two subject areas. To see why this is so, consider the following.

In the most basic sense, finance is concerned with the process through which funds are transferred from savers to borrowers. Savers, or surplus units, are those households, businesses, and governments whose income exceeds their consumption. Borrowers, or deficit units, are those households, businesses, and governments whose consumption exceeds their income. Although any household, business, or government may be either a surplus or a deficit unit, in the economy as a whole, most deficit units are businesses and most surplus units are households (in this context, surplus units are commonly referred to as investors).

The transfer of funds from surplus units (investors) to deficit units (businesses) takes place in a financial market or through a financial institution:

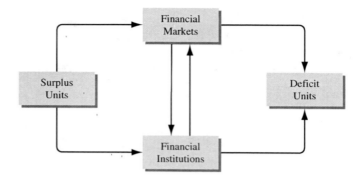

Businesses (deficit units) borrow money to purchase physical assets such as machinery, raw materials, real estate, plant, and equipment. This money is obtained either directly from surplus units through a financial market (such as the stock or bond market) or indirectly through a financial institution. In exchange for the funds they receive, these deficit units issue claims (called financial assets) against the cash flows that the physical assets that they purchase are expected to generate. For example, a firm, which borrows $1,000,000 to purchase a plant, gives to the provider(s) of the $1,000,000, financial assets which promise the owner(s) of these financial assets a part of the actual annual cash flow that the plant produces.

Investors lend money, that is, purchase financial assets, to earn an expected return. This return is a function of the annual cash flow that the physical asset purchased with the investor's funds is expected to generate. As long as the actual cash flow equals or exceeds the expected cash flow, investors are content. If, however, the actual cash flow is less than the expected cash flow, the investor loses. In the extreme, the actual cash flow can even be negative, implying that investors can lose part or all of their initial investment.

The fact that actual cash flows can, and most often always do, deviate from expected cash flows is what causes financial assets to be risky. Identifying, managing, and valuing risky cash flows is the essence of finance. These are the central themes that integrate the three subject areas of finance. Financial markets and institutions, which encompasses the mechanisms that allow businesses to issue and investors to purchase financial assets, primarily concerns the risks that different trading systems add to, or subtract from, financial assets. Investments primarily concerns the manner in which investors evaluate financial asset risk and determine expected cash flows, and use this information to determine financial asset values. Finally, financial management primarily concerns the process whereby business managers apply the same risk measurement and valuation principals used by investors to determine and manage physical asset risk, and to raise the funds necessary to expand their businesses.

The primary purpose of this book is to present an overview of the Corporate Financial Management subject area. In it we outline the basic principles of corporate financial management. All of the topics under the heading of corporate financial management are not covered in this text. However, after reading and working through this book you should know and appreciate the role and duties of a financial manager. And, should you decide to take additional courses in finance, you will possess a solid foundation upon which you can build future knowledge.

1.3 ▸ Forms of Business Organization ....

All businesses must be organized in some legal manner. In the United States, there are three main forms of business organizations: sole proprietorships, partnerships, and corporations. Although other types of business organizations (specifically, limited partnerships, limited liability partnerships, and professional corporations) are growing in popularity, the three main types listed above dominate the business world.

A sole proprietorship is a business that is 100 percent owned by a single individual. In most sole proprietorships, this owner is also the operator or chief manager of the business. A sole proprietorship is simple and inexpensive to establish. In most states, one merely obtains a business license and begins operations. Sole proprietorships require no formal charter and are subject to fewer government regulations, and usually a lower tax liability, than corporations.

There are two drawbacks to the sole proprietorship business organization. First, it is very difficult for such companies to raise large amounts of capital. The main sources of capital for sole proprietorships are the owner, friends and family, and commercial banks. The first source is limited to the personal wealth of the owner, and even in the case of a wealthy owner, the owner might not wish to invest a significant amount of wealth in a single entity. The second source usually involves difficult personal relationships, and identifying an acceptable return to friends and family in the event of success is often tricky. Borrowing from a commercial bank usually requires much red tape, can involve potential intervention in the management of the business, and, most significant, is limited to the amount of money invested in the business by the first two sources. A bank generally will not contribute any more to a business than the owner of the business is willing to contribute. Simply put, if business owners do not believe enough in the potential success of their businesses to invest most if not all of their personal wealth, why should a bank invest in the businesses?

A second drawback to the sole proprietorship business organization is that the owner of a sole proprietorship has unlimited personal liability to the debt of the business. If the business fails, the creditors of the business are entitled to not only all of the assets of the business, they can also take the personal assets of the owner (until the full value of all of their claims are satisfied). Due to this unlimited liability feature, the business bankruptcy of most sole proprietorships usually results in personal bankruptcy for the owner.

Another form of business organization is a partnership. A partnership is essentially the same as a sole proprietorship, except that the business is owned and operated by two or more individuals. These individuals must agree on who will provide the initial start-up capital, who does what work, and how the profits (or losses) of the business will be shared.

Partnerships have most of the same benefits and drawbacks as sole proprietorships, though some differences exist. Multiple partners might be able to contribute more capital to the business than a single owner. On the other hand, unlimited personal liability applies to all owners, regardless of the percent of ownership. Thus, if a business of two partners goes bankrupt and one of the partners with little personal wealth also goes bankrupt, the other owner who might have substantial wealth is responsible for all of the remaining debts of the business. Finally, transfer of ownership of a partnership is often difficult. If one of the owners of the business dies or decides to leave the business, the other owner(s) must buy out the departed owner (or survivors). If the remaining owner does not have sufficient personal wealth to do this, the business usually folds.

In terms of numbers, more than 85 percent of all businesses in the U.S. are organized as sole proprietorships or partnerships. In terms of revenue, however, more than 80 percent of all business in the country is conducted by corporations. A corporation is a legal entity, separate and apart from its owners or managers. Though much more complex and costly to establish, the corporate form of business organization offers three distinct advantages over the other forms of organization:

1. *Limited Liability.* As a separate legal entity, a corporation bears the entire burden of all debt in the event of bankruptcy. That is, the owners (or shareholders) of a corporation cannot ever lose any more than the amount they invested in the company. If a shareholder purchases 1,000 shares of stock in a corporation at $100 per share and that corporation later goes bankrupt, the shareholder will lose only the $100,000 that was originally invested. If in the bankruptcy the creditors are due $10,000,000 and the total value of all liquidated assets of the firm is only worth $6,000,000, then all assets will be liquidated and the creditors will only get $6,000,000. The owners (that is, shareholders) of the firm are not in any way liable for the additional $4,000,000 in claims.

2. *Ability To Raise Capital.* Due to the limited liability feature, corporations are able to attract more investors than unincorporated businesses. In fact, the stock of many corporations is public, meaning that the company's stock trades in an organized stock market, such as the New York Stock

Exchange. Companies whose stock trades publicly have access to almost unlimited capital (of course, the company must provide an attractive potential return to obtain this capital). Also, corporations with large amounts of equity capital can attract large amounts of debt capital. As noted above, banks, and other creditors, view owner equity as a sign of faith in the future prospects of the company.

3. *Easy Transfer of Ownership.* The ownership of a corporation is represented by shares of stock. Owners of corporations who decide to liquidate their interest in the corporations need only sell their shares of stock. If the company is a public company (that is, its shares trade on an organized exchange), this merely involves a call to a broker or a click of the mouse.

The principles of financial management described in this book apply directly to a publicly traded corporation. Sole proprietorships and partnerships have specific management and operational issues that are unique to those organizations. Nonetheless, the basic goal of financial management and the importance and valuation of cash flow expressed throughout the book apply to all forms of business organization.

1.4 The Goal of Corporate Financial Management

The goal of any corporation must be to create value for its stockholders. Stockholders are the owners of the corporation and their basic reason for investing in the company in the first place is to make money. The managers of any corporation are merely the employees of the owners of the firm, the shareholders. As such, managers are sometimes referred to as "agents." Agents are hired by owners to run the company to create as much value for the owners as possible. If the agents do not perform their duties to the satisfaction of the owners, they can be fired or replaced.

To a stockholder, value is represented by the price of the company's common stock. Note that at any given time, the price per share multiplied by the total number of shares outstanding is simply equal to the total value of the equity of the company. This total value is owned by all shareholders in the company according to their percentage ownership (that is, the number of shares they own divided by the total number of shares outstanding). If the price per share increases, the value of each stockholder's stake in the company (that is, their personal wealth) increases. Thus, all else constant, the goal of a financial manager must be to maximize the price per share of the company's stock.

Remember that maximizing the price per share of the company's stock is not necessarily equivalent to maximizing the firm's profit. If you were the owner of a firm, would you rather your firm report profit for the year of $150,000 but have generated no cash, or would you rather have $150,000 in cash and report zero net income? As will be shown in the next couple of chapters, such situations are entirely possible. Likewise, would you rather your firm generate $150,000 in net cash flow this year and $0 thereafter, or generate $30,000 in net cash flow per year for the next five years? As will be shown in the next section of the book, the former earnings stream would usually be preferred to the latter. Although there are several factors that determine the value of a firm's common stock, chief among these factors is cash flow (both for the coming year and in future years). The proper management and valuation of cash flow is the main theme of this book.

1.5 The Relationship between Accounting and Finance

Because much of finance involves the analysis and management of a firm's income statement and balance sheet, it is common to ask: "What is the difference between finance and accounting?" The most direct answer to this question is that whereas accounting is backward-looking (literally, to some of us), finance is forward-looking. Accounting statements present a historical account of the money earned, raised, and spent by a firm from its inception through the current period. It focuses on the book value of the firm's assets. Conversely, finance is the study of all of the future cash that the firm's current and prospective collection of assets can potentially earn. It focuses on the market value of the firm. In essence, though related, the two subjects can be said to be diametrically opposed. The following story illustrates the relationship between book (accounting) value and market (finance) value.

Joe Vitale is a third year business major at Urban University, a 25,000-student campus located in the downtown area of a large metropolitan city. "Urb-U" is not a traditional campus. Instead, it is actually a disjointed collection of university classroom buildings, labs, offices, dormitories, and other buildings that are interspersed throughout the downtown area.

As fate would have it, the two sets of buildings with the greatest distance between them (approximately three miles) are the dormitories and the general classroom buildings. To further complicate matters for students, whereas parking near the dormitories is adequate, parking near the classroom buildings is essentially non-existent. The university refuses to provide a free shuttle service for monetary reasons and is not allowed to run a for-profit service for political reasons. Students are encouraged to walk, bike, or use the public transit system. Most consider the first method to require excessive time and unacceptable effort and the second to be hazardous to life and limb. The city transit system is expensive, slow, overcrowded, and seldom on schedule.

Joe, a budding entrepreneur, realizes that this situation has the potential to earn someone a sizeable amount of money. Following several conversations with his finance professor/consultant, Joe has decided to start a shuttle service between the dorms and the classroom buildings. He plans to use money that his grandfather gave him for MBA school to buy a transport van. The van costs $30,000, has a four-year life, and will be depreciated on a straight-line basis to a zero salvage value. Joe and his consultant estimate that the business is capable of producing the following cash flow series:

Book value = Purch. price − 1 yr. of deprec.

Year	Estimated Cash Flow
1	$20,000
2	$15,000
3	$15,000
4	$10,000

Annual Depreciation = Purch. price − salv ÷ useful Life

These cash flows are the revenue that Joe expects to collect minus the payment of all expenses (gas, insurance, vehicle maintenance, advertising, wages to drivers, applicable taxes, consultant fees, and so on), and a salary to himself as the manager of the operation. These are residual cash flows—those left over after all expenses have been paid. They belong to the provider(s) of capital. In this example, the cash flow series above represents Joe's expected return for providing the $30,000 to buy the necessary asset(s) to start and run the business (that is, Joe's expected return as the owner of the business).

Assuming that Joe starts his business today and that his only asset is the transport van, what is the book value of his firm? The answer is, of course, $30,000. That is, the original purchase price of the van.

What will the book value of the firm be after one year? Note that annual depreciation of the van is:

Annual Depreciation

(Purchase Price − Salvage Value)/Useful Life = ($30,000 − 0)/4 = $7,500 per year for 4 years.

Thus, the book value of the van (and therefore, of Joe's firm) after one year is:

Purchase Price − One year of depreciation = $30,000 − $7,500 = $22,500.

What will the book value of the firm be after (a) two years? (b) three years? (c) four years?

Answers: (a) $15,000   (b) $7,500   (c) $0.

Now for a more difficult question. Assuming that Joe starts his business today, what is the market value of his firm? The answer to this question has little to do with the cost or book value of the firm. Instead, the

Book val.
1 yr. = (30,000 − 7,500) = $22,500
2 yr. (30,000 − 15,000) = $15,000
3 yr. (30,000 − 22,500) = $7,500
4 yr. (30,000 − 30,000) = $0

answer depends on the cash flows that Joe's firm is expected to generate. Specifically, it depends on what someone else would be willing to pay today in exchange for these expected cash flows.

Assume that Joe has a very rich uncle to whom Joe has explained the business opportunity and the cash flow series shown in the table above. Joe's uncle believes that Joe's assumptions and estimates are fair, reasonable, and accurate. In fact, the uncle is willing to give Joe $34,000 today if Joe will agree to sign over to him all of the net cash that the business actually generates for each of the next four years— that is, if Joe agrees to sell ownership of the business to his uncle. If the business generates less cash than expected, Joe's uncle loses. If, however, it generates more than expected, Joe's uncle gets the expected cash plus the extra cash.

Why would Joe's uncle propose such a deal? Is it solely because he is related to Joe? Actually, Joe's uncle is quite shrewd. He is merely investing his money in Joe's firm. He has many alternative investments from which to choose. Instead of investing in Joe's firm, he could deposit the $34,000 into a savings account, buy a CD (certificate of deposit), buy government or corporate bonds, buy publicly traded stock, or invest in some other type of asset. Joe's uncle chooses Joe's firm because he considers it to represent the best expected return available given the risks involved (specifically, the risk that the actual cash flow will be significantly less than the expected cash flow).

Do such transactions actually occur? In fact, they occur all the time. Other than risk, this transaction is not unlike a car loan. The bank gives me $34,000 to buy a car in exchange for my promise to pay $717.41 per month for the next 48 months. That is, an amount today in exchange for a future expected cash flow series. A similar comparison can be made with a house loan, credit card line of credit, stock purchase, and so on.

Obviously, my loan payments to the bank are probably more certain than Joe's cash payments to his uncle. That is why the expected return on the bank loan is substantially less than the expected return on the investment in Joe's firm. Whereas (as will be shown later in this book) the expected cash flow stream on the bank loan represents a 7.5 percent annual return, the expected cash flow from Joe's firm represents a 31.15 percent annual return!

Returning to our earlier question, what is the market value of Joe's firm? The answer is $34,000 because that is what an investor is willing to give Joe today in exchange for all of the future cash the firm is expected to generate. (If Joe can find another investor who will give him $35,000, then the market value of his firm would be $35,000). Note the difference between market value and book value. Whereas the book value of Joe's firm is $30,000, the market value of his firm is $34,000. Whereas book value is what was actually paid for the asset(s), market value is what the asset(s) is (are) worth in ability to produce expected cash flow within the context of a firm.

Recall that the goal of a financial manager is to create value for the firm's shareholders. The most direct way to achieve this goal is to find, purchase, or manage assets so that their market value exceeds their book value. That is, assets would be worth more than they cost. In the example above, when Joe sold ownership of the firm to his uncle, he created $4,000 of wealth for himself. If Joe is able to more efficiently manage his firm so that the expected cash flow for each of the next four years is greater than listed in the table above with no additional risk added, Joe can create even more wealth for himself (or for his uncle if he sells to his uncle).

One final question concerning the relationship between finance and accounting: Given the fundamental difference between the two subjects, why does much of finance involve the analysis of a firm's income statement and balance sheet? Financial managers, outside analysts, creditors, and stockholders analyze accounting data to identify trends concerning, in particular, cash flow. Accounting statements, as shown in the following two chapters, do not specifically list cash flow. However, taken together, income statements and balance sheets provide valuable information concerning the flow of cash during a given accounting period. And, although these are historical values, to the degree that historical trends and relationships will continue into the future, they can be important indicators of future potential cash flow—and thus useful in determining and managing market value. Thus, just as potential employers would use your school records (that is, grade point average, major, extracurricular activities) as indicators of the type of employee you might be for their firms, financial analysts use accounting data as indicators of the potential of a given business enterprise.

1.6 Value and the Importance of Cash ....

Count the number of times that the terms *"cash"* and *"value"* have been used to this point in the book. The answers are cash (forty-seven times) and value (thirty-three times). Obviously, there is an important connection between these two terms. Consider the following.

Suppose that the shares of ABC Co. trade on the New York Stock Exchange (NYSE). At nine o'clock in the morning, the price of ABC's stock is $30 per share. Soon after you observe this price, the management of ABC makes the following announcement: "The company's R&D division has discovered that with a slight modification in its manufacturing process, ABC will be able to generate significant reductions in manufacturing costs." Assume that the cost of modifying the manufacturing process is negligible and that it will take very little time to incorporate the modification into the manufacturing process. In other words, the cost savings will begin to be realized almost immediately. Also suppose that the announcement made by the firm is truthful and completely believable. What do you think will happen to the price of ABC's shares? Will the share price increase, decrease, or remain unchanged?

The answer to this question is obvious—the share price will rise. If your answer was that the share price would increase, you already know the most important concept in finance. Let us spend a few minutes on the obvious reason why the share price will rise. To do this, let us begin by answering the following seemingly simple question. (You must circle the one answer that you think is most correct).

Why does a typical investor buy stock in a firm such as ABC?

A. The CEO of ABC is the investor's favorite uncle.

B. The investor loves the company's name ABC.

C. ABC manufactures products that have great social value.

D. The investor believes that ABC's share price will increase substantially in the future.

Which answer did you choose? Our guess is that you circled D and, if so, your choice was the most correct. Note that answers A, B, and C are not wrong. It is possible that some investors buy shares for one or more of these reasons. However, we are interested in the reason for the *typical investor* and, clearly, the most probable reason why an investor buys shares is to make money. Therefore, answer D is the most correct answer. This is one of the most fundamental rules in finance and it is also a very simple rule. Buying shares is just one form of investment and, in fact, this rule applies to all investments. ***People make investments to make money.***

Let us now go to the next question. Again, you must circle the most correct answer.

What determines the current price (that is, the price today) of a firm's share of common stock?

A. The growth rate of the company's sales.

B. The quality of the firm's products.

C. How much money the shareholder will make from owning the firm's share.

Which answer did you circle? You will notice that, unlike the first question, the answer is not immediately obvious. All three choices appear to be important factors in determining the current share price. Which one, however, is the most important?

Let us consider the choices one by one. Suppose that the sales of a firm increase by leaps and bounds. Although high sales and high sales growth are generally favorable signs, the profits that these sales generate depend upon the firm's costs—high sales result in high profits only if costs are less than revenues. A firm might be better off by reducing sales of products whose production costs are greater than the price that they fetch. Therefore, the volume of sales and/or sales growth is not the most important determinant of the share price.

How about the quality of the firm's products? Again, it depends upon the cost of achieving quality. If the marginal (that is, additional) cost of producing a high quality (as opposed to say an average quality) product exceeds the marginal revenue from the product, then the firm is better off making only average quality products. Thus, product quality alone cannot be the most important determinant of the share price.

That leaves us with the third choice, what the share price will be in the future. Aside from the fact that it is the only alternative left, there is another reason why this is the best answer. Recall that the main reason an investor buys a share is to make money. The money that an investor will make depends upon what the future share price will be—if the price in the future is high, the investor will make more money. We have just argued that increases in sales or product quality do not necessarily translate into more money for the shareholder. Therefore, the most important determinant of the current price of a share is how much money the investor can make from owning that share. This leads us to the next rule.

The price of an investment depends upon how much money that investment will generate.

These two simple rules justify your answer to the original question that the price of ABC's shares will increase as a result of the cost-reducing modification to the manufacturing process. Because the modification reduces costs, the profits of the firm will be higher. These higher profits will ultimately result in more money for the shareholders (for example, in the form of higher dividends). Finally, because the price of the share depends upon how much money the shareholders will make, the fact that they expect to make more money will result in an increase in the price that they would be willing to pay for the share and, consequently, the share price will go up.

This brings us to the fundamental concept (mentioned earlier) in finance:

The value of an investment is determined by the future cash flows that the investment generates for the investor.

The concept above might, at first, appear to be a simple restatement of what we had been discussing before. However, some important words have been changed and added. These are underlined. First, the word price was replaced with value. Second, the fact that it is the cash flows in the *future* that are relevant was never made explicit before. Finally, the term cash flows was substituted for money. There are reasons for these changes.

The terms price and value are usually considered to be equivalent in finance. One way to see this equivalence is to consider an asset, say a share of ABC company's stock. Suppose that this share belongs to you, and that you believe (on the basis of how much money this share is going to generate for you) that this share is worth $30. In other words, you value this share at $30. If you received an offer from a buyer for this share of $35, would you sell the share? The answer is yes. If the offer price were $28? No. In other words, you, the seller, would be willing to sell your share at a price that is no less than $30, the value that you place on the share. Now suppose that the buyer is a person just like you and knows exactly what you know about ABC Co. and, consequently, also places a value of $30 on the share. Would this buyer buy this share at $28? The answer is yes. At $35? Certainly not! In other words, the buyer would be willing to buy this share at a price no greater than $30. Therefore, if a transaction involving this share of ABC did take place between you and the buyer, it could take place only at the price of $30, the value that both you and the buyer place on the share.

Next, let us consider the concept that only the money that the asset generates in the *future* determines its value. The rationale underlying this concept is quite straightforward. When you buy an asset, what the asset generated in the past went to its previous owner, not to you. The only money that you will get is what the asset will generate for you after you buy it, that is, in the future. Therefore, the value that you place on an asset will be determined solely by the money that the asset will generate in the future. This is not to say that the money that the asset generated in the past is not useful information. However, it is useful only to the extent that it might provide you with some idea as to what the asset will generate in the future.

Finally, let us turn to the use of the phrase "cash flows" instead of money. The reason for considering only *cash* flows is simple. The only thing that an investor can spend is cash. Therefore the only thing that the investor cares about is the stream of cash flows that the asset will generate in the future. This fact might seem somewhat trivial at this point, but its importance will become apparent later in the course.

1.7 Careers in Finance

As finance professors, we are often asked the following questions from our students:

1. How much money does a finance major make?
2. What kinds of jobs are available to finance majors?

These are relevant and important questions for anyone considering any major in college. However, as important as these questions are, the answers to these questions should not overly influence your career choices. Be careful to pick your major based on what you like to do as opposed to the job you might desire to have, or how much money you can make. It is much more important to be happy at what you do than to have a prestigious title or to make a lot of money. Your career is something that you will do for a very long time. If you do not like what you are doing, neither a fancy title nor a large paycheck will make you happy.

One way to determine what you like is to keep an open mind about different classes while in college. Take many different courses in different areas. Continue taking classes in subjects that you find interesting and challenging, or in which you do well. Over time, you will begin to differentiate subjects that stimulate your intelligence relative to those that bore you.

If, as we hope, finance turns out to be the former, the following information will provide you with a brief overview of the level of salaries and the different types of jobs that you can expect in the field of finance. As described in section 1.1, the field of finance is divided into three separate, though interrelated subject areas: corporate financial management, investments, and financial markets and institutions. Jobs and career paths exist in each of these areas.

The following table shows average salaries for 2004–2005 based on experience and degree type:

	Average Salary (plus bonuses)		
	Entry	**4–9 years**	**10–15 years**
Undergraduate finance major	$47,000	$ 95,650	$143,350
Finance major with MBA	$56,930	$127,600	$177,550

Sources: *www.jobweb.com/SalaryInfo, www.businessfinancemag.com, www.careers-in-finance.com, and www.jobsinthemoney.com.*

Note that these are average salaries for some of the most popular jobs in finance. Numerous factors influence salaries including position, tenure, specialized skills, geographic location, and size of the employer. Salary ranges around these averages grow with experience. For example, the standard deviations in salaries in the table above is $4,700 for entry-level positions, $37,390 for 4–9 years of experience and $83,850 for 10–15 years of experience.

1.7.1 Careers/Jobs in Corporate Financial Management

As the term implies, financial management is the management of a firm's finances, specifically, the money flow through the company. Firm financial managers determine when and how much money a company needs to begin, sustain, or expand operations. Financial analysts and corporate treasury managers set, alter, and monitor policies concerning a company's cash and marketable security accounts, credit policy, inventory balances, long-term asset purchases and sales, debt market structure, dividend policies, and more.

Entry-level positions involve collecting and analyzing data and identifying strengths, areas of concerns and trends. More senior positions often also include decision making and other management responsibilities. Though much of finance is number-oriented, people skills, the ability to communicate, both orally and in writing, and salesmanship are often the traits that lead to promotions and increased responsibilities.

The most senior financial management position in a company is the chief financial officer (CFO), who is usually second only to the CEO (chief executive officer) in terms of visibility, responsibility, and compensation. The CFO is responsible for every decision in the firm that involves or concerns money—essentially all decisions. The fortunes of many companies rise and fall on the quality of the decisions made by the CFO.

1.7.2 Careers/Jobs in Investments

Investments is a broad-based subject and career opportunities in the area are varied and many. People who work in the investments field help companies, governments and individuals to issue financial assets (that is, raise or borrow money), assist investors to purchase securities and manage their portfolios, and ensure that financial markets operate efficiently. Some of the more popular job titles in investments include Investment Analyst, Asset Portfolio Manager, Investment Advisor/Consultant, Merger/Acquisitions Underwriter, Investment Banker, Securities Broker and Trader.

Individuals entering this field must possess strong analytical and interpersonal skills. This is a high work, high risk and high potential reward profession. Though base salaries in this area are not high, bonuses and commission opportunities can be extraordinary. Very successful individuals in investments can attain annual compensation in the multimillion-dollar range.

Most entry-level positions involve analysis of company financial statements. To succeed and be promoted, you must be skilled in your understanding of accounting, have good spreadsheet skills, and be analytically fluent. Additionally, you must be able to communicate with clients to generate sales and network to expand your business contacts and opportunities. Interest in current events and an understanding of business cycles and macro-economic trends and influences is essential. A fair amount of travel should be expected, and visits to New York, Hong Kong, Tokyo, London, Moscow, and Singapore are common among senior investments professionals.

1.7.3 Careers/Jobs in Financial Markets and Institutions

Most jobs in this area are in some way, shape or form, related to commercial banks. Commercial banking is a rapidly changing and evolving industry and today's banks are more diverse and comprehensive than ever. Job and training opportunities in this area are tremendous. Many finance majors begin in the field of banking, receive training, and make contacts, then enter either financial management or investments.

The most common entry-level jobs in commercial banking are credit analyst and commercial loan officer. A strong understanding of accounting is essential for these jobs. The ability to effectively communicate via writing is also very important, because banking often requires documenting loans or justifying credit analyses.

As the area of financial services has become increasingly more competitive and as federal banking regulations have been relaxed, banks are focusing more attention on marketing their products and services to consumers, and on high-tech applications and procedures. These trends are opening opportunities in banking to finance professionals who can develop and deliver new products or services to the markets. Bank managers and officers must be able to foresee, understand, and take advantage of opportunities and trends in the economy and in the financial markets. Those who do so will find a career in banking to be exciting, challenging and rewarding.

1.8 Purpose and Organization of Text ....

A main purpose of this book is to explain the concept of valuation of assets. Those of you who study finance further (we hope all of you will) will discover that almost everything in finance is somehow or other related to valuing assets. When you study corporate finance (this course), you will learn some methods to value the assets of a firm and its investment opportunities. You will also study how this method can be used to value the securities that firms issue, for example bonds and stocks. When you study investments, you will concentrate on how to value stocks, bonds, futures, options, and the myriad of investment possibilities that exist in the financial markets. When you study financial institution management, you will spend a considerable amount of time on loan analysis. A loan is nothing but an asset that a bank invests in; it accepts deposits from people (which is equivalent to borrowing money from depositors) and invests them by making loans to its clients. To determine whether to make a loan, the bank will, therefore, have to value that loan. If you study real estate finance, you will value a different category of assets, namely, real estate, including homes, apartment complexes, retail stores, and many others.

Our earlier discussion indicated that the value of an asset is determined by the future cash flows that the asset will generate. To perform the actual valuation we will, therefore, need to know two things: how to determine cash flows and, once we have determined these cash flows, how to value them. Both of these aspects are vitally important. Accordingly, this book is divided into two major sections. The first section (chapters 2–5) focuses on the importance, determination, and management of cash flows, particularly the past and potential future cash flows indicated by a firm's financial statements. The second section (chapters 6–11) concentrates on the principles, process, and applications of valuation in corporate finance.

Questions

1. If within 5 years of receiving your degree you were earning $20,000 per month ($240,000 per year), would you consider yourself to be successful? If your monthly expenses were $25,000 per month and creditors were constantly calling you for payment and threatening repossession of your assets, would you still consider yourself to be successful? In what ways is this example analogous to corporate financial management?

2. In the example concerning Bennie's Auto Parts and Service Center in the beginning of this chapter, assume that Bennie could save, on average, $850 per month with better management of his accounts receivable, $1,200 per month with better inventory management, and $750 per month in better cash management (specifically, saved bounced check fees). These savings total $2,800 per month. The time required to effect this better management would be approximately 20 hours per week. Bennie does not have this amount of time to give to proper financial management. What is the obvious solution?

3. As a follow-up to question 2, what are some of the major job responsibilities or functions of a financial manager?

4. List the three main areas (that is, fields) of finance. Briefly describe each area. How are these areas related?

5. In what major ways does a corporation differ from a sole proprietorship or a partnership? Upon which form of business organization is this book based? Do the principles of financial management described in this book apply to the other forms of business organization?

6. What should be the main goal of a financial manager?

7. Profit maximization is not the same as shareholder value (that is, stock price) maximization. How is it possible that profit maximization might not lead to stock price maximization?

8. According to the text, maximizing shareholder wealth, maximizing stock price per share, and maximizing the value of the firm's assets are one and the same. That is, if a manager maximizes the value of the firm's assets, that manager will also be maximizing shareholder wealth and the price per share of the company's common stock. Explain this relationship.

9. What is the difference between book value and market value? How would you feel about owning stock in a firm whose market value was less than its book value? Could such a relationship exist? If so, what would it indicate?

10. Describe the similarities and differences between physical assets and financial assets. Why are financial assets risky? Why would anyone purchase a financial asset?

11. Given your accounting background, are there any accounting procedures or peculiarities that could make it difficult to compare the performance of one firm to another over time? What specific procedures come to mind? Is it possible to "massage" accounting information, that is, to legally 'window dress' financial statements that are distributed to shareholders? Why might a firm engage in such a practice? What would be the consequence of being caught engaging in outright financial statement fraud? (Note: If you don't know answers to any of these questions, you will know after reading chapters 2 and 3).

12. Does the goal of stockholder wealth maximization necessarily imply that firms will not be socially responsible (that is, responsible for the welfare of their employees, customers, the environment, or the community in which they operate)?

13. Assume that a firm is deciding whether or not to undertake some action that will increase the firm's stock price but hurt the environment (that is, be socially irresponsible). How might government regulations affect the firm's decision?

14. Assume that you own $15,000 worth of stock in a company whose stock is widely held and actively traded on the NYSE. Is it necessary for you to actively monitor the manager's performance (that is, to make sure that the managers of the firm are doing their best to maximize the value of your stock)? Why or why not? Now consider a bank that has made a large loan to this company. Is it necessary for the bank to actively monitor the manager's performance? Why or why not?

Chapter 2

Accounting Review: Income Statements and Balance Sheets

After studying Chapter 2, you should be able to:

◆ Construct a basic income statement.

◆ Identify and define each item on a basic income statement.

◆ Construct a basic balance sheet.

◆ Identify and define each item on a basic balance sheet.

◆ Describe the difference between accounting data and cash.

◆ Explain the importance of accounting to a business.

◆ Identify the major ways in which a firm may legally manipulate its financial data.

2.1 Chapter Overview ....

At most schools, accounting is a prerequisite for the introductory finance course. Thus, you have probably recently taken an accounting course (or perhaps even two) and you might be tempted to skip this chapter. **DON'T!!!**

As finance professors, it has been our experience that students exiting basic accounting courses (though often well versed in accounting) do not have an adequate understanding of the structure and construction of, and basic relationships between, company income statements and balance sheets. Without this understanding, it is impossible to master cash flow and financial statement analysis—topics which make up the next three chapters of this book. Thus, even if you think your accounting background is strong, we still suggest that you read this chapter. And, if you find yourself struggling excessively through the remaining chapters of this section of the book, we recommend that you re-read this chapter—several times if necessary!

In this chapter, we outline the structure and composition of the two main financial statements used by businesses: the income statement and the balance sheet. Specifically, we present a basic description of the most common account items found on financial statements. Keep in mind that the descriptions presented in this chapter are from the point of view of a financial manager as opposed to an accountant. A financial manager is not particularly interested in how accounts are kept or recorded (for example, T-accounts). A financial manager must, however, intuitively understand the nature of financial statement accounts to achieve effective financial analysis and management.

2.2 The Income Statement *Cumulative statement* ....

The income statement, also called an earnings statement or a profit and loss statement, is an accounting statement that matches a company's revenues with its expenses over a period of time, usually a quarter or a year. The components of the income statement involve a company's recognition of income and the expenses related to earning this income. Revenue minus expenses results in a profit or loss.

Rev - Exp - Taxes = Income

The income statement is a flow measure statement, meaning that each value on an income statement represents the cumulative amount of that item through the given accounting period. Thus, the revenue on a first quarter income statement equals the cumulated amount of all sales during the first three months of the firm's fiscal year. The revenue on the second quarter income statement equals the cumulated amount of all sales during the second three months of the firm's fiscal year. The same applies to expenses, and therefore to profits.

Consider the following monthly data for Bixel, Inc. for January through June:

Month	Sales	Expenses
January	$20,000	$15,000
February	$30,000	$20,000
March	$40,000	$30,000
April	$30,000	$20,000
May	$50,000	$40,000
June	$20,000	$15,000

Problem 2.1a   Assuming that the first quarter of the year includes the months of January, February, and March, what would Bixel, Inc. report as revenue on its first quarter income statement? What would Bixel, Inc. report as expenses on its first quarter income statement? What would Bixel, Inc. report as profit (or loss) on its first quarter income statement?

Rev.
1st 20,000 + 30,000 + 40,000 = $90,000

Exp
1st 15,000 + 20,000 + 30,000
$65,000

Answer: $90,000; $65,000; $25,000.

Profit = Rev - Exp.
$P = 90,000 - 65,000$
$P = $25,000$

Problem 2.1b   Assuming that the second quarter includes the months of April, May, and June, what would Bixel, Inc. report as revenue on its second quarter income statement? What would Bixel, Inc. report as expenses on its second quarter income statement? What would Bixel, Inc. report as profit (loss) on its second quarter income statement?

$$2^{nd} \quad \underline{Rev.} \qquad\qquad\qquad \underline{Exp}$$
$$30{,}000 + 50{,}000 + 20{,}000 \qquad 20{,}000 + 40{,}000 + 15{,}000$$
$$= \$100{,}000 \qquad\qquad\qquad = 75{,}000$$
$$P = 100{,}000 - 75{,}000 = \$25{,}000 \ Profit$$

Answer: $100,000; $75,000; $25,000.

Problem 2.1c   What would Bixel, Inc. report as profit (loss) on its income statement covering the period January through June?

$$190{,}000 - 140{,}000$$
$$= 50{,}000 \ Profit$$

Answer: $50,000.

Realize that profit on an income statement seldom corresponds with a company's actual cash flow. In fact, although all companies seek to maximize their cash flow (because cash is necessary to pay bills, salaries, loans, dividends, and so on), not all companies attempt to maximize reported earnings. In fact, many companies actually try to minimize reported earnings in an attempt to reduce taxes.

The reason why income and cash flow seldom match is that most companies elect to prepare their income statements (and thereby their balance sheets) using accrual accounting as opposed to cash accounting. Accrual accounting recognizes revenues as earned when sales are transacted, regardless of when the company actually receives payment. Likewise, expenses are recognized when they are incurred rather than when the actual payment is made. In contrast, cash accounting recognizes revenues as earned only when payment is received and recognizes expenses as costs only when cash is actually paid out. As we will see in chapter four, one part of the statement of cash flows (specifically, cash flows from operating activities) represents the conversion of an accrual accounting income statement into a cash accounting income statement.

The basic structure of a multi-step income statement is outlined in Table 2.1. The term multi-step means that four profit measures are designated on the statement: *gross profit, operating profit* (sometimes referred to as operating income, Earnings before Interest and Taxes, or EBIT), *profit before taxes* (sometimes referred to as Earnings before Taxes or EBT), and *net income* (also referred to simply as earnings). These profit measures will be discussed in greater detail in chapter 5.

Table 2.1

Income Statement
Company Name
For the *Time Period* **Ending** *Date*

Net sales
— Cost of goods sold

Gross profit
— Operating expenses

Operating profit
— Interest expense

Profit before taxes
— Taxes

Net income

Note that these are not the only accounts that may appear on an income statement. Some income statements might use slightly different terminology. Some companies offer more detail on their statements than others. Certain expense items that are important for one company might be minor or nonexistent for another company. Nonetheless, these are the major items and delineations that appear on most standard income statements, and this is the income statement structure that we will use throughout the remainder of this section of the book.

Net Sales – Sales revenue is recorded when a product is shipped, or more precisely, when ownership of the product (or service) is transferred from the seller to the buyer. Whereas identifying this point in time is relatively easy for merchandise sold at a retail store, it is often more complicated to pinpoint the exact transfer time of services. For example, a health club membership provides membership services over a period of time. When is revenue recognized? The law allows the income recognition to take place as soon as the member signs a contract. Although this is not exactly correct in terms of the definition, it is nonetheless allowed and used.

Sales are Net Sales

In general, companies prefer to record revenue as soon as possible. Accurate reporting, however, must note that some of this revenue might never actually be collected. Often, people sign a service contract (for example, a health club membership) and then cancel without ever paying any cash. Companies and individuals sometimes purchase products on credit but do not pay when their bill arrives. Consumer rights legislation, lemon laws, money-back guarantees, trial periods, credit card company stop-payment return policies, defaults, and so on, mean that not all sales will result in full payment.

To account for this fact and possibility, firms calculate net sales as follows:

Net sales = Gross sales – (Returns and allowances).

Some firms also offer sales discounts for large volume purchases. In such cases, these are also netted out of gross sales. Often returns and allowance numbers are estimates. If actual returns turn out to be less than estimated returns, a credit is made to net sales during the next accounting period. If, however, actual returns turn out to be greater than estimated returns, the allowance account should be increased during the next accounting period to reflect this fact.

Problem 2.2   In 2006, Tanner, Inc. had gross sales of $1,253,400. The company's management reported a Returns and Allowances estimate of $53,400 in 2006. What did Tanner, Inc. report as Net sales in 2006?

Gross Sale 1,253,400
R & A   –   53,400
Net Sales   1,200,000

Answer: $1,200,000.

Cost of Goods Sold – Whenever a product is manufactured or sold, certain direct costs are incurred. These costs are designated on the income statement as cost of goods sold, or COGS. For a retail company, direct costs are simply the cost of materials purchased for resale. For a manufacturing company, direct costs can also include labor costs, manufacturing overhead, and depreciation expenses associated with production. Service companies incur few direct costs, so their income statements usually do not include cost of goods sold. For uniformity and simplicity, unless otherwise specifically noted, we will assume throughout this section of the text that all firms are retailers, or at least that COGS is equal to materials purchased for resale.

Whenever an item is sold, that item must be allocated a certain cost, that is, a cost of goods sold. If a retail company sells twenty-five shirts in a given accounting period (assume one day), each of the twenty-five shirts must be assigned a cost. If the retail company purchased the twenty-five shirts from a manufacturer for $10 per shirt, cost of goods sold would be $250. Assume, however, that the retail company actually purchased forty-five shirts from the manufacturer during the accounting period in batches of twenty shirts at $8 per shirt, fifteen shirts at $10 per shirt and ten shirts at $14 per shirt. Thus, the retailer purchased $450 worth of shirts from the manufacturer (at an average cost of $10 per shirt). If the retailer only sells twenty-five shirts during the accounting period, he must assign a cost to these twenty-five shirts as cost of goods sold and record the remaining amount as inventory. If the retailer chooses to assign the average purchase cost to each shirt, cost of goods sold will be $250 and ending inventory will be $200.

In general,

Cost of goods sold = Beginning inventory + Materials purchases − Ending inventory.

Thus,

$$\text{Cost of goods sold} = \$0 + \$450 - \$200$$
$$= \$250.$$

Firms can choose between three methods of inventory valuation: FIFO, LIFO, and Average Cost. Each method can result in a different estimate of COGS for the accounting period in question. We showed the cost estimate for the average cost method above. Refer back to your accounting text to compute answers to the following problems if necessary.

Problem 2.3a Compute COGS assuming that the T-shirt retailer in the example above uses the FIFO method of inventory valuation.

20 @ $8 = 160
5 @ $10 = 50
$210

Answer: $210 (from 20 shirts valued at $8 per shirt + 5 shirts valued at $10 per shirt).

Problem 2.3b Compute COGS assuming that the T-shirt retailer in the example above uses the LIFO method of inventory valuation.

10 @ $14 = 140
15 @ $10 = 150
$290

Answer: $290 (from 10 shirts valued at $14 per shirt + 15 shirts valued at $10 per shirt).

We are not particularly interested in the virtues or flaws of each different inventory valuation technique. Just note that different chosen methods can result in different COGS calculations and therefore different gross profit measures.

Operating Expenses – Operating expenses are business-related expenses other than cost of goods sold that a company incurs in the normal course of business. These include items such as management salaries, advertising expenditures, repairs and maintenance costs, research and development expenditures, lease payments, and general and administrative expenses. This latter category includes everything from salaries of office staff to paper clips. As mentioned above, for a manufacturer, depreciation expense is considered as a cost of goods sold; for a retailer, depreciation is included in operating expenses. Because we are limiting our focus to retail companies only, depreciation will be noted throughout the text as an operating expense— often listed separately on the income statement.

Interest Expense – Interest expense is the cost to the firm of borrowing money. It depends on the overall level of firm indebtedness and the interest rate associated with this debt. Interest expense is generally a small fraction of total firm expenses, however, this expense as a percent of revenue can fluctuate dramatically with changes in the firm's borrowing requirements or with the general level of interest rates in the economy.

Deprec. is not a cash expense
— It adds to cash flow by lowering taxes.

Taxes – Income taxes are a necessary part of business for all profitable for-profit firms. Earned income can be taxed at the federal, state, or local levels, and the provision for income taxes can be calculated using published tax tables from the respective government agencies. Because taxes are paid on an estimated basis throughout the year (with the minimum estimated tax being equal to what was owed in the prior year) and taxes owed are calculated at the end of the year based on the firm's actual profit before taxes, reported taxes and actual cash taxes paid will often differ. This difference is reported on the balance sheet under the deferred tax account.

Net Income – Net income (also called net profit or earnings) is the "bottom line" of the income statement. It represents the base profit earned by a firm in a given accounting period. Net income divided by the number of common shares outstanding is referred to as earnings per share, or EPS. This value represents the profit earned for each share of stock. The current market price of the stock divided by EPS is called a P/E ratio. Analysts often consider EPS and P/E ratios to be important indicators of a firm's current and potential future performance. These measures and their significance will be explained in greater detail later in the book.

Problem 2.4a In 2006, Ruppert, Inc. (a hardware retail company) sold 10,000 units of its product at an average price of $400 per unit. The company reported estimated Returns and allowances in 2006 of $200,000. Ruppert actually purchased 11,000 units of its product from its manufacturer in 2006 at an average cost of $300 per unit. Ruppert began 2006 with 900 units of its product in inventory (carried at an average cost of $300 per unit). Operating expenses (excluding depreciation) for Ruppert, Inc. in 2006 were $400,000 and depreciation expense was $100,000. Ruppert had $2,000,000 in debt outstanding throughout all of 2006. This debt carried an average interest rate of 10 percent. Finally, Ruppert's tax rate was 40 percent. Ruppert's fiscal year runs from January 1 through December 31. Given this information, construct Ruppert's 2006 multi-step income statement.

Answer:

Income Statement
Ruppert, Incorporated
For the 12-Month Period Ending December 31, 2006

Net sales	$3,800,000
Cost of goods sold	3,000,000
Gross profit	**800,000**
Operating expenses (excl. depreciation)	400,000
Depreciation expense	100,000
Operating income	**300,000**
Interest expense	200,000
EBT	**100,000**
Taxes	40,000
Net income	**60,000**

Notes: Net sales = Gross sales − Returns and allowances = (10,000) ($400) − 200,000.
Cost of goods sold = # units sold × Cost per unit = (10,000) ($300).
Interest expense = (Debt outstanding) (Average interest rate) = ($2,000,000) (.10).
Taxes = (EBT) (Tax rate) = ($100,000) (.40).

Problem 2.4b What was Ruppert's 2006 ending inventory balance (in both units and in dollars)?

$$\begin{array}{l} \text{Beg } 270{,}000 \ (900 \text{ units}) \\ + \text{ Purch. } 300{,}000 \ (1000 \text{ units}) \\ \hline 570{,}000 \ @ \ 1900 \text{ units} \end{array}$$

Answer: 1,900 units and $570,000.

Problem 2.4c Assuming that Ruppert had 150,000 shares of common stock outstanding in 2006, compute Ruppert's earnings per share (EPS).

$$EPS = \frac{NI}{\#\text{ outstand's}} \quad = \quad \frac{60{,}000}{150{,}000} = .40/share$$

Answer: $0.40, or 40 cents, per share.

Problem 2.4d Assuming that Ruppert had 150,000 shares of common stock outstanding in 2006 and assuming that Ruppert stock has a P/E ratio of 18, compute the market price per share of Ruppert's common stock.

$$18 = \frac{.40}{P} \qquad\qquad P = \$7.20$$
$$P = .40(18)$$

Answer: $7.20.

2.2.1 Summary

A firm's income statement indicates a great deal about the health of a company. Analysis of this statement, in particular analysis of trends over time, provides a firm's managers, creditors, and stockholders with important insights into the future potential of the company. Good analysis will also highlight areas where changes need to be considered.

Hopefully, you now understand the basic structure and composition of an income statement. This understanding is essential before any type of meaningful financial analysis or management can occur. To verify the former, try to complete the following problem without looking back over this section of the book. Be sure that you can properly define, identify, and classify each item on this company's income statement. If you can do so, then you are ready to go on. If not, be sure that you carefully reread this section of the book.

Problem 2.5 Prepare a multi-step income statement for the Appully Company (a clothing retailer) for the year ending December 31, 2006, given the information below:

Advertising expenditures	68,000
Beginning inventory	256,000
Depreciation	78,000
Ending inventory	248,000
Gross Sales	3,210,000
Interest expense	64,000
Lease payments	52,000
Management salaries	240,000
Materials purchases	2,425,000
R&D expenditures	35,000
Repair and maintenance costs	22,000
Returns and allowances	48,000
Taxes	51,000

Answer:

Income Statement
The Appully Company
For the 12-Month Period Ending December 31, 2006

Net sales	3,162,000
Cost of goods sold	2,433,000
Gross profit	**729,000**
Operating expenses (excluding depreciation)	417,000
Depreciation	78,000
Operating profit	**234,000**
Interest expense	64,000
EBT	**170,000**
Taxes	51,000
Net income	**119,000**

2.3 The Balance Sheet ....

The balance sheet is a summary statement of what a company owns (or is owed) and what a company owes (or what others own) at a specific time. It categorizes all of a company's resources as assets, liabilities, and owner's equity.

The basic structure of a balance sheet is shown in Table 2.2. Note, as with the income statement, that these are not the only accounts that may appear on a balance sheet. Some balance sheets might use slightly different terminology. Some companies offer more detail on their statements than others. Certain accounts that are important for one company might be minor or nonexistent for another company. Nonetheless, these are the major items and delineations that appear on most standard balance sheets, and this is the balance sheet structure that we will use throughout the remainder of this section of the book.

Table 2.2

Balance Sheet
Company Name
For the *Time Period* Ending *Date*

ASSETS	LIABILITIES
Cash	Notes payable
Net accounts receivable	Accounts payable
Inventories	Accrued expenses
Total current assets	Current portion of L. T. debt
Gross fixed assets	**Total current liabilities**
(Less accumulated depreciation)	Long-term (L.T.) debt*
Net fixed assets	**Total liabilities**
Total assets	Preferred stock
	Common stock
	Retained earnings
	Total liabilities and equity

*excluding current portion

The basic balance sheet identity is:

Total Assets = Total Liabilities + Shareholders' Equity.

It is very important to note that a balance sheet is a stock measure statement, meaning that each value on a balance sheet is the value of that account on the specific date associated with the balance sheet. The value of the account (particularly liquid asset and liability accounts) at a later date might differ substantially from that reported on the balance sheet.

Consider the following monthly data for Bixel, Inc. for January through June:

Month	Ending Accounts Receivable	Ending Inventory
January	$2,000	$ 5,000
February	$3,000	$ 8,000
March	$4,000	$10,000
April	$3,000	$16,000
May	$5,000	$12,000
June	$2,000	$ 9,000

Problem 2.6a   What would Bixel, Inc. report as Accounts receivable on its first quarter balance sheet (the balance sheet for the three-month period ending on the last day of March)? What would Bixel, Inc. report as Inventory on its first quarter balance sheet?

$$\frac{Acct\ Rec'v}{1^{st}\ \$4,000} \qquad \frac{Inv.}{\$10,000}$$

Answer: $4,000; $10,000.

Problem 2.6b   What would Bixel, Inc. report as Accounts receivable on its second quarter balance sheet (the balance sheet for the three-month period ending on that last day of June)? What would Bixel, Inc. report as Inventory on its second quarter balance sheet?

$$\frac{AR}{\$2,000}\ \frac{Inv.}{\$9,000}$$

Answer: $2,000; $9,000.

2.3.1 Asset Accounts

Cash – Items on the balance sheet are listed in order of liquidity, and the most liquid asset account is cash. Companies hold cash for various reasons and in various forms, some of which are restricted for special purposes. Cash is most frequently represented by demand deposits at banks that are available for use in a company's operations via checks or in temporary interest-bearing investments.

Note that the availability of reported cash can be restricted if interest-bearing deposits are pledged against debt. Likewise, compensating balances, which may be required for support of bank credit, might also be unavailable for operations. If a company has declared a dividend to be paid on January 10, 2006, and on December 31, 2005 reports cash on its balance sheet, some of the reported cash has actually already been spent. If a company has foreign bank accounts, these accounts must be translated into dollars at the prevailing exchange rate on the balance sheet statement date. Exchange rate fluctuations can substantially alter the value of the account. In summary, although cash is the most liquid asset on the balance sheet, it is not *necessarily* true that a company with a large cash balance can pay its bills as they come due.

Some companies temporarily invest excess cash in **marketable securities** such as certificates of deposits (CDs), Treasury bills, notes, and bonds, other U.S. government securities, bankers' acceptances, or high-grade corporate commercial paper. These temporary investments can earn interest income until the cash is needed in the business. Appropriate marketable securities are highly liquid and maintain a stable market value. For all practical purposes, marketable securities are essentially equivalent to cash and, in fact, are often included in cash on the balance sheet as opposed to being listed separately.

Net Accounts Receivable – When a company sells its products or services on credit, it is shown on the balance sheet as an accounts receivable. Credit sales often stipulate payment terms that allow the purchaser to pay within a specified time, and may offer a discount as an incentive for early payment. Accounts receivable remain on the balance sheet until they are collected.

Some amount of accounts receivable will never be collected and, therefore, constitute a bad debt, or loss. A company prepares for this by calculating the percentage of possible bad debt (from prior actual experience) and creating a corresponding reserve that is deducted from its gross accounts receivable. This reserve is often referred to as an allowance for doubtful accounts. Thus,

Net accounts receivable = Gross accounts receivable − allowance for doubtful accounts.

Expensing for bad debts on the income statement as an operating expense can regularly increase the allowance account. This way, when an account is determined to be uncollectible, it is charged against the allowance for doubtful accounts instead of directly to the income statement. This in turn insulates the income statement from a sudden loss resulting solely from a poor credit decision.

Problem 2.7a   Boswell, Inc. is a temporary help service company. All of the company's services are sold on credit (most customers pay in approximately sixty days). Due to the economy and a lenient credit policy, Boswell's bad debt (that is, accounts that are never collected) is relatively large and highly variable from year to year. Boswell had annual gross sales, gross accounts receivable, and actual bad debt amounts as follows for the years ending December 31, 2002 through 2006:

Year	Gross Sales	Gross Accounts Receivable	Actual Bad Debt
2002	$1,000,000	$167,000	$ 50,000
2003	$2,000,000	$333,000	$150,000
2004	$3,000,000	$500,000	$225,000
2005	$4,000,000	$667,000	$ 75,000
2006	$5,000,000	$833,000	$250,000

Assume that for financial statement reporting purposes, Boswell estimates an allowance for doubtful accounts of 5 percent of annual sales. Accordingly, what did Boswell report as Net sales and Net accounts receivable on its 2002 through 2006 income statements and balance sheets?

Answer:

Year	Allowance for Doubtful Accounts	Reported Net Sales	Reported Net Accounts Receivable
2002	$ 50,000	$ 950,000	$117,000
2003	$100,000	$1,900,000	$233,000
2004	$150,000	$2,850,000	$350,000
2005	$200,000	$3,800,000	$467,000
2006	$250,000	$4,750,000	$583,000

Problem 2.7b   Instead assume that Boswell did not estimate an allowance for doubtful accounts but merely subtracted actual bad debt from gross sales and gross accounts receivable to determine net sales and net accounts receivable. (Ignore the potential timing and identification of the bad accounts problem—this example is merely presented for illustration purposes.) Under these circumstances, what did Boswell report as Net sales and Net accounts receivable on its 2002 through 2006 income statements and balance sheets?

Answer:

Year	Actual Bad Debt	Reported Net Sales	Reported Net Accounts Receivable
2002	$ 50,000	$ 950,000	$117,000
2003	$150,000	$1,850,000	$183,000
2004	$225,000	$2,775,000	$275,000
2005	$ 75,000	$3,925,000	$592,000
2006	$250,000	$4,750,000	$583,000

If you compare the answers to problem 2.7a and 2.7b, you should notice that reported net sales and reported net accounts receivable are less volatile through the five-year period when Boswell uses an estimated allowance for doubtful accounts (that is, 5 percent of annual sales) as opposed to merely reporting sales and accounts receivable net of actual bad debt. That is, use of the allowance account allows a firm to "smooth" out these numbers. Additional information concerning the use (and abuse) of allowance accounts is provided in chapter 4.

Inventories – There are three forms of inventories: raw materials, work in process, and finished goods. For a retailer, finished goods constitute the bulk of all inventories. A manufacturer possesses all three forms of inventory, and it is very important to monitor the distribution between the three inventory levels over time. As noted above, inventory can be valued using either the FIFO, LIFO, or average cost valuation method. Just as different inventory valuation methods can produce different cost of goods sold values, they can also produce different inventory values on the balance sheet.

Total Current Assets – The sum of the items listed above constitutes total current assets. A current asset is, in general, an account that is expected to be converted into cash in less than one year. Note that this definition is somewhat arbitrary and not necessarily applicable to all firms and to all current asset accounts.

Gross Fixed Assets, Accumulated Depreciation and Net Fixed Assets – Fixed assets include equipment, buildings, vehicles, tools, computers, office equipment, leasehold improvements, furniture—in general, any items of a fairly permanent nature that are required for the normal conduct of a business. Accounting standards dictate that balance sheets report the value of fixed assets at book value. Book value is defined as the original historical cost (the purchase price paid by the company) minus allowable depreciation to date.

All fixed assets, with the exception of land, are assumed to lose their economic value over time. When it is purchased, a fixed asset is initially valued at cost. Each year thereafter it is depreciated. (As such, depreciation merely reflects the fact that most fixed assets wear out and must eventually be replaced.) The asset is expensed on the income statement and valued at a progressively lower value (that is, book value) on the balance sheet. In the end, the asset is considered to be either without value or to have reached a salvage value, below which it cannot be reduced any further.

There are two primary methods for figuring annual depreciation: the straight-line method and the accelerated cost recovery system method. Most firms choose to use the straight-line method for reporting purposes (because it tends to smooth earnings through time) and the accelerated method for tax purposes. For simplicity, we will assume the use of only straight-line depreciation throughout the remainder of this book.

By law, a firm needs only to report Net fixed assets on its balance sheet. However, some companies offer additional detail on the fixed asset portion of their balance sheets. Specifically, they include gross fixed assets and accumulated depreciation along with net fixed assets. (If these additional accounts are not specifically listed on the balance sheet, they should appear in a footnote to the statement.) The relationship between these three accounts is illustrated below using the fixed asset section of the Robert Dunnick Company Balance Sheet:

Fixed Asset Portion of Balance Sheet
The Robert Dunnick Company
For the Years Ending December 31, 2004, 2005, and 2006
(all figures in thousands of dollars)

	2004	2005	2006
Gross fixed assets	0	120,000	180,000
Less Accumulated Depreciation	0	10,000	25,000
Net fixed assets	0	110,000	155,000

The Dunnick Company began operations on January 1, 2005—thus, the balance sheet for December 31, 2004 lists $0 fixed assets. In 2005, the company purchased fixed assets (plant and equipment) for $120,000,000, depreciated on a straight-line basis over ten years to a $20,000,000 salvage value (that is, annual depreciation of $10,000,000). The $10,000,000 in depreciation for 2005 is listed on the income statement and added to the accumulated depreciation account on the balance sheet ($0 + $10,000,000).

In 2006, the company purchased another $60,000,000 of fixed assets, causing the gross fixed asset account to grow from $120,000,000 to $180,000,000. Assuming that the new assets are being depreciated on a straight-line basis over ten years to a $10,000,000 salvage value, or at $5,000,000 per year, the company will list depreciation of $15,000,000 on its income statement ($10,000,000 for the assets purchased in 2005 and $5,000,000 for the new assets purchased in 2006). The accumulated depreciation account grows to $10,000,000 + $15,000,000 = $25,000,000 and net fixed assets equals gross fixed assets less accumulated depreciation = $180,000,000 − $25,000,000 = $155,000,000.

Note that if all that the company listed on its balance sheet was net fixed assets, the change in gross fixed assets can be determined by adding depreciation for the year to the change in net fixed assets. Thus, for 2006, the cash spent on new plant and equipment equals depreciation for the year as listed on the income statement of $15,000,000 plus the change in net fixed assets of $45,000,000 ($155,000,000 − $110,000,000). The resulting amount, $15,000,000 + $45,000,000 = $60,000,000 represents the actual cash outflow that occurred in 2006 for fixed assets.

Problem 2.8a   Accumulated depreciation on the Bentley, Incorporated 2005 Balance sheet was $386,000. Accumulated depreciation on the Bentley, Incorporated 2006 Balance sheet was $454,000. Bentley did not sell any existing fixed assets in 2006. What did Bentley report as depreciation expense on its 2006 Income statement?

$$454,000$$
$$- \ 386,000$$
$$\$68,000$$

Answer: $68,000.

Problem 2.8b Assume that Bentley, Incorporated reported gross fixed assets of $3,256,000 on its 2006 balance sheet, assume that Bentley did not buy or sell any fixed assets in 2007, and assume that depreciation expense reported on Bentley's 2007 income statement was $70,000. What did Bentley report as Net fixed assets on its 2007 balance sheet? What did Bentley report as Accumulated depreciation on its 2007 balance sheet? What did Bentley report as Net fixed assets on its 2007 balance sheet?

Answer: $2,802,000; $524,000; $2,732,000.

Total Assets – The sum of all current and long-term assets equals total assets. These are the items that a firm uses to produce revenue. Efficiency dictates that firms generate as much revenue as possible using as few total assets as necessary. Thus, many efficiency statistics and measures focus on the relationship between assets and sales. This is true because assets are not free. Every item on the left-hand side of the balance sheet must be financed with items on the right-hand side of the balance sheet. For example, when a firm sells a product on credit (creates an accounts receivable), the purchase of that product by the firm must be financed in some way. If it is financed with a bank loan, the cost of that bank loan is interest and the higher the interest expense, the lower the firm's net income or profit. To maximize profit, firms should try to finance assets with the lowest cost funds available. That is, for profitability (and other) reasons, not only is it important for a firm's financial managers to focus on assets, but they also must focus on the structure and composition of liabilities and net worth.

2.3.2 Liability Accounts

Notes Payable – Notes payable frequently represent the short-term borrowing of a company from a bank for the seasonal financing of current assets, in particular, accounts receivable and inventory. For example, a retail company may use a short-term bank loan (that is, notes payable) to finance a buildup of inventory just before the Christmas selling season. As the company sells its products, it creates accounts receivable (assuming sales on store credit). When these accounts are collected, the company uses the proceeds to pay off the short-term loan. Often notes payable is a "line of credit" between the company and its bank. The company can borrow against the line of credit whenever funds are needed without having to apply for a new loan each seasonal period.

The time period between the purchase of inventory and the collection of cash to be used to pay down the loan might be only a few weeks, or it might be several months. The time period, and thus the term of the loan, depends on many factors, such as how long it takes to sell items out of inventory, the company's collection policies, credit terms with suppliers, and so on. This time period is sometimes referred to as the cash conversion cycle. Specifically, the cash conversion cycle is the average number of days between the outflow of cash to purchase or produce products for sale and the collection of cash from the sale of those products.

The longer the cash conversion cycle, the longer that notes payable will be carried as a positive amount on the balance sheet, and therefore the greater the annual interest cost to the company. Thus, all else constant, reducing the cash conversion cycle can increase a company's net income. For this reason, many firms carefully monitor their cash conversion cycle.

For seasonal companies, short-term bank debt (notes payable) obviously fluctuates throughout the year. Depending on when in the cash conversion cycle a company's fiscal year-end falls, the company may report a large or zero notes payable year-end balance. Because a company's balance sheet tends to look most favorable when inventory, accounts receivable, and notes payable are at their minimal levels, most companies choose their fiscal year-ends to correspond with this time. That is why many retail firms choose March 31 as a fiscal year-end as opposed to December 31.

Accounts Payable – Accounts payable are the "flip side" of accounts receivable. Whereas accounts receivable represent sales made by the company to customers on credit, trade accounts payable represent purchases (usually for inventory) made by the company from suppliers on credit. Thus, accounts payable owed by the purchasing company are shown as accounts receivable on the supplier's balance sheet.

Accounts payable are, in general, a source of "interest free" financing for a company in the sense that if the company pays its accounts in a timely manner, no interest is charged and financing for additional purchases always remains available. If, however, the company does not pay its suppliers when payment is due, its suppliers may discontinue the extension of credit for future purchases. Then the company will have to find alternative financing sources (for example, notes payable) to purchase inventory. An analysis of trade credit terms and the relative cost of alternative financing sources will be discussed in chapter 5.

Accrued Expenses – Accruals represent specific direct and operating costs that a company has expensed on its income statement which in fact have yet to be paid at the close of the reporting period. These expenses are usually paid at regular intervals and include items such as utilities, rent, wages and salaries, and taxes. For example, if wages are paid every two weeks and the firm's balance sheet is prepared in the middle of the pay period, wages owed as of that date would be reported as an accrual.

Current Portion of Long-Term Debt – Sometimes firms borrow long-term money on an installment basis. That is, the firm makes periodic payments over the life of the loan that include principal reduction in addition to interest. The current portion of long-term debt, sometimes called current maturities of long-term debt, represents the principal portion of these installment payments that is due over the next twelve months. Note that the sum of current portion of long-term debt and long-term debt is the total long-term debt that a firm has outstanding at any time. Designating some debt as current is merely a transfer process.

Problem 2.9a   On June 1, 2006, Brooks, Incorporated borrowed $5,000,000 from the bank. This loan has a term of ten years. The loan represents the only debt that the company has outstanding. Brooks is required to make a $500,000 principal payment on the loan every year for the next ten years, with the first payment due on June 1, 2007. An interest payment of 8 percent of the principal balance that was outstanding for the prior twelve-month period is also due with each principal payment. How should Brooks classify this loan on its December 31, 2006 balance sheet? What would Brooks list as interest expense on its 2006 income statement?

Answer:

Current portion of long-term debt	$ 500,000*
Long-term debt	$4,500,000

Problem 2.9b   How would Brooks classify this loan on its December 31, 2007 balance sheet? What would Brooks list as interest expense on its 2007 income statement?

Answer:

Current portion of long-term debt	$ 500,000
Long-term debt	$4,000,000

Interest expense on 2007 income statement = ($4,500,000) (.08) = $360,000.

* Note that as of December 31, 2006, a payment of $500,000 is due sometime during the following twelve months (specifically, on June 1, 2007). Interest expense on 2006 income statement = ($5,000,000) (.08) = $400,000.

Total Current Liabilities – The sum of the items listed above constitutes total current liabilities. Similar to a current asset, a current liability is, in general, a liability that is expected to be paid off in less than one year. As with current assets, this definition is somewhat arbitrary and not necessarily applicable to all firms and to all current liability accounts. A company normally pays off its current liabilities as current assets are converted into cash.

Long-Term Debt – Long-term debt represents liabilities with maturities in excess of one year. It is usually used to finance long-term assets such as land, buildings, and equipment. Occasionally long-term debt is used to finance "permanent" current assets. These are the base level of inventory and accounts receivable maintained by a firm in a normal (non-peak) season.

For example, a greeting card retailer maintains a base level of birthday, get well, and friendship cards throughout the year. Temporary current assets fluctuate above this permanent level during peak seasons or during pre-seasonal buildups. For a greeting card retailer, Valentine's Day cards in the month of February, Mother's Day cards in the month of May and Thanksgiving Day cards in November represent temporary current assets. Temporary current assets are generally financed with notes payable via the company's line of credit with its bank.

Preferred Stock – Preferred stock is a hybrid security that includes elements of both debt and equity. It promises a fixed periodic payment similar to debt. However, if this payment must be skipped due to insufficient earnings, preferred stockholders have no recourse, similar to equity. Preferred stock is usually cumulative, meaning that skipped payments accrue and must be paid when earnings allow. Finally, preferred stock often does not include voting rights.

Only a small number of companies actually issue preferred stock and most of those that do are regulated companies. For this reason, and for general simplicity, we will ignore this account throughout the remainder of this section of the book.

Common Stock – On many balance sheets, common stock is divided into two components: common stock at par value and additional paid-in capital (or, capital surplus). The first component can be used to determine the number of shares currently outstanding. The second component represents the additional money (over and above par value) generated when the company actually sold the stock.

Consider the following example:

Equity Section of Balance Sheet
The Robert Dunnick Company
For the Years Ending December 31, 2005 and 2006

Common stock ($0.50 par value)	$10,000,000	$12,000,000
Additional paid-in capital	44,000,000	51,000,000
Retained earnings	32,000,000	34,000,000
Total shareholders' equity	**$86,000,000**	**$97,000,000**

The Robert Dunnick Company's common stock has a par value of $0.50 per share. Common stock par value is an arbitrary value that is established when a company authorizes shares to be issued. The $10,000,000 amount of common stock in 2005 at $0.50 per share implies that the Dunnick Company has $10,000,000/$0.50 = 20,000,000 shares of stock outstanding as of December 31, 2005. The total amount of money raised by the Dunnick Company from the sale of all of its stock (net any repurchases) from the start of the company through December 31, 2005 has been:

$$\text{Common stock at par} + \text{Additional paid-in capital} = \$10,000,000 + \$44,000,000$$
$$= \$54,000,000.$$

This amount represents an average value of $2.70 per share. If in fact all 20,000,000 shares had been issued on the same day, the sale price per share would have been $2.70.

Problem 2.10a   How many new shares of stock did Dunnick Company sell in 2006?

$$\frac{2,000,000}{.50} = 4,000,000$$

Answer: ($12,000,000 − $10,000,000)/($0.50) = 4,000,000 shares.

Problem 2.10b   Assuming that all of these new shares sold on the same day at the same price, what was the price per share at which these new shares sold?

$$(12,000,000 - 10,000,000) + (51,000,000 - 44,000,000) =$$
$$9,000,000 / 4,000,000 = \$2.25$$

Answer: $2.25 per share. The total amount of money raised from selling new shares = ($51,000,000 − $44,000,000) + ($12,000,000 − $10,000,000) = $9,000,000. Divide this by the number of new shares sold to get the price per share.

Retained Earnings – Retained earnings represent the cumulative total of all net income that has been reinvested into the company. Many companies retain some of their annual profit to fund the expansion (replacement) of assets to reduce their reliance on outside capital markets. The annual addition to retained earnings is equal to:

Net income – Dividends paid.

Retained earnings on the balance sheet are equal to the prior year's retained earnings balance plus this year's *addition* to retained earnings.

For the Robert Dunnick Company example above, assume that the company's net income for the year ending December 31, 2005 was $12,000,000 and that common stock dividends paid were $3,000,000. Thus, the addition to retained earnings was:

$12,000,000 − $3,000,000 = $9,000,000.

This implies that Retained earnings on the balance sheet for the year ending December 31, 2004 must have been:

$32,000,000 − $9,000,000 = $23,000,000.

Problem 2.11a   If the Dunnick Company reported net income of $6,800,000 in 2006, what did the company pay out as total dividends in 2006?

$$6,800,000 - 2,000,000 = 4,800,000$$

Answer: $4,800,000.

Problem 2.11b   What was the dividend payment per share? (Assume that dividends are paid in a lump sum at fiscal year end.)

$$\frac{4,800,000}{23,000,000} = .20/Share$$

Answer: $0.20 per share.

A common error concerning retained earnings is the notion that the amount listed on the balance sheet for a given year (for example, $32,000,000 for the Dunnick Company as of December 31, 2005) can be used by the firm to cover future losses or to pay off debt. That is, that retained earnings is similar to cash. This is not the case. Retained earnings is money that has been used over the years to purchase assets. Retained earnings cannot be "re-spent" unless a firm wants to liquidate assets previously purchased.

The sum of common stock at par value, additional paid-in capital, and retained earnings is called a company's net worth, owners' equity, or shareholders' equity. It can also be called the book value of the firm's equity. Thus, the book value of Robert Dunnick Company's equity as of December 31, 2005 is $86,000,000. If Dunnick's stock traded on that day in the stock market at a price per share of $6.00, then the market value of Dunnick's equity would be:

20,000,000 shares × $6.00 per share = $120,000,000.

Problem 2.12a   What was Dunnick Company's net worth as of December 31, 2006?

$$\overset{2005}{86,000,000} + 11,000,000 = 97,000,000 \quad or$$
$$(97,000,000 - 86,000,000) + 86,000,000 = 97,000,000$$

Answer: $97,000,000 (remember, net worth, owner's equity, shareholders' equity, and book value of equity are merely different terms for the same concept).

Problem 2.12b   If the **market value** of Dunnick's equity on December 31, 2006 was $152,400,000, what was the market price per share that Dunnick's stock was trading for on that day?

Answer: $6.35.

Note that the market value of equity calculated in this manner already includes retained earnings. Why? Assume that you own 10 percent of a company's stock. If your firm retains money in any given year, it will usually use this money to purchase additional assets, causing the asset value of your firm to grow. You will now own 10 percent of a larger company, and this will be reflected as an increase in the firm's stock price. Thus, the current stock price of any firm reflects, in addition to other things, all accumulated retained earnings.

Problem 2.13   Over its three-year history, the Bunker Company has issued common stock on three separate occasions. The company issued 250,000 shares of stock on March 10, 2004 at an issue price of $6.50 per share. Another 400,000 shares were issued on July 18, 2005 at $8.75 per share. Finally, an additional 350,000 shares were issued on October 24, 2006 at $12.25 per share. All common stock is recorded on the company's balance sheet at a par value of $2.00 per share. Bunker's fiscal year runs from January 1 through December 31, and the firm reported net income of $2,420,000 on its 2004 income statement, $3,680,000 on its 2005 income statement, and $4,840,000 on its 2006 income statement. Bunker paid dividends of $420,000 in 2004, $680,000 in 2005, and $840,000 in 2006. Using this information, fill in the table on the next page.

The Bunker Company
Equity Section of Balance Sheet
For the Years Ending December 31, 2004, 2005, and 2006

	2004	2005	2006
Common stock ($2.00 par value)	_____	_____	_____
Additional paid-in capital	_____	_____	_____
Retained earnings	_____	_____	_____
Total shareholders' equity	_____	_____	_____

Answer:

	2004	2005	2006
Common stock ($2.00 par value)	$ 500,000	$ 1,300,000	$ 2,000,000
Additional paid-in capital	1,125,000	3,825,000	7,412,500
Retained earnings	2,000,000	5,000,000	9,000,000
Total shareholders' equity	**$3,625,000**	**$10,125,000**	**$18,412,500**

Total Liabilities and Equity – As you should well recall from your introductory accounting course, the basic balance sheet identity equation is:

$$\text{Total Assets} = \text{Total Liabilities and Equity.}$$

The identity is often written in simple letter terms as:

$$A = D + E,$$

where A = total assets, D = total liabilities (that is, current liabilities + long term debt), and E = total shareholder equity.

2.3.3 Summary

The fact that the items on the right hand side of the balance sheet show how the items on the left hand side of the balance sheet have been purchased, or more precisely, how they have been financed, means that balance sheets can tell a great deal about a company's past and can reveal certain information concerning its future. This fact also applies to income statements. That is why financial managers, analysts, creditors, and stockholders carefully investigate financial statements.

Hopefully, you now understand the basic structure and composition of a balance sheet. As stated earlier concerning the income statement, this understanding is essential before any type of meaningful financial analysis or management can occur. To verify the former, try to complete the following problem without looking back over this section of the book. Be sure that you can properly define, identify, and classify each item on this company's balance sheet. If you can do so, then you are ready to go on. If not, be sure that you carefully reread this section of the book.

Problem 2.14   Using the following (scrambled) accounts, prepare a balance sheet for Bhatti, Incorporated (a retail company) for the year ending December 31, 2006 (assume that these are the only balance sheet accounts):

Accounts payable	39,000
Accrued expenses	8,000
Accumulated depreciation	51,000
Additional paid-in capital	86,000
Allowance for doubtful accounts	2,000
Cash	23,000
Common stock ($0.20 par)	45,000
Current portion of L.T. debt	6,000
Gross accounts receivable	40,000
Gross fixed assets	486,000
Inventories	54,000
Long-term debt	210,000
Net accounts receivable	38,000
Net fixed assets	435,000
Retained earnings	138,000
Short-term bank loan (notes payable)	18,000

Answer:

Balance Sheet
Bhatti, Incorporated
For the 12-Month Period Ending December 31, 2006

Cash	23,000
Gross accounts receivable	40,000
Allowance for doubtful accounts	(2,000)
Net accounts receivable	38,000
Inventories	54,000
Current assets	**115,000**
Gross fixed assets	486,000
Accumulated depreciation	(51,000)
Net fixed assets	435,000
Total assets	**550,000**
Short-term bank loan (Notes payable)	18,000
Accounts payable	39,000
Accrued expenses	8,000
Current portion of L.T. debt	6,000
Current liabilities	**71,000**
Long-term debt	210,000
Total liabilities	**281,000**
Common stock ($0.20 par)	45,000
Additional paid-in capital	86,000
Retained earnings	138,000
Total liabilities and equity	**550,000**

2.4 The Importance of Accounting for Business Operations ....

Accounting, in its most fundamental sense, is merely a system of record keeping. Income statements and balance sheets are the formalized documents used to summarize and report accounting data. Firms engage in real and monetary activities. These must be recorded and reported to tax authorities, creditors, equity holders, and the firm's managers. The following story is offered as an example of how financial statements can be used to summarize the operations of small firms and large. It also demonstrates that financial statements can be constructed for any time period—a day, a week, a quarter, a year, or any other period.

West Elementary School holds an interesting fundraising event every September. The students at the school must 'earn' all money that is given. They can cut grass, wash cars, clean, or do whatever else they can think of to earn money to give. Donations or contributions from adults are not allowed. Additionally, all money that is given to the school must be earned on a single day, specifically, the second Saturday in September. Money raised from the event is used to purchase books for the library, buy classroom supplies, and fund field trips.

The school also provides a unique incentive for teachers who "push" their students to earn as much money as possible. The teacher whose homeroom class gives the greatest amount of money wins (via a generous donation from a parent who runs a travel agency) a one-week, all-expense-paid family vacation to Disney World. Most teachers spend the week before the fundraiser discussing with their class clever ways to earn money.

On the Saturday morning of the fundraising event, while eating breakfast, Nika, an energetic and enterprising third grader, and her dad, a college finance professor, were discussing the idea that Nika had come up with for raising money. She had decided that she was going to work together with her best friend, Chelsea, to earn money. Because their teacher, Ms. Marz, had told the class that it was important to set a high amount as a goal (though Nika could not recall the exact reason why Ms. Marz had told them that setting a high goal was good) and because Nika and Chelsea wanted to do what their parents always told them to do—be the "best"—they had set the highest goal in the class of wanting to earn and give $250 each.

"Dad," said Nika, "how about if Chelsea and me feed the dog, clean my room and empty all of the trash cans in the house and you give me $250? Then we will go to Chelsea's house, do the same and we will have our money!"

After nearly choking on the muffin he was eating, Nika's dad managed to say: "No way!!! And for two reasons. First, $250 is more than I would give you for doing those things for an entire year, much less than for one day. Second, those are chores that you are supposed to do already for your weekly allowance. Why would I pay you something extra to do something you are already paid to do?"

Fighting back tears, Nika replied: "Me and Chelsea have been talking about this for a whole week and this is the only plan we could come up with. Ms. Marz will be upset with us if we don't reach our goal. What can we do to make that much money?"

"You mean, Chelsea and I."

"What?" said Nika.

"Chelsea and I, not me and Chelsea."

"Dad, why do you always do that?" gasped Nika. "Okay. How can Chelsea and I make that much money?"

"Why don't we think of some kind of business that you and Chelsea could do for a day? I'll help you get started."

After much discussion, Nika and her dad decided that the best business for a third grader to operate was a lemonade stand. The day was perfect for selling lemonade—it was hot, and given the rain earlier in the week, most of the people in the neighborhood would be cutting grass and working in their yards. Moreover, their house was near a trail where many people in the area ran, and an ice-cold glass of fresh-squeezed lemonade would surely be a hit with these people.

After a phone call to Chelsea and her dad, they also got excited about the idea. Thus began Nika and Chelsea's venture into the world of business and corporate finance. Surely, thought each of their dads, this will be a lesson my daughter will never forget!

First, the girls made up a plan. They felt sure that they would be able to sell 500 cups of lemonade during the day. Each cup would require one lemon, two cubes of sugar, some water, and ice. Nika's dad loaned the girls $250 (interest free) to start their business.

With the money, they bought 500 lemons at $0.30 per lemon, 500 plastic cups for $25.00 (five cents per cup), 1,000 sugar cubes at $0.05 per cube, 10 bags of ice for $10, a poster board and magic marker to make a sign for $5.00, a table and two chairs at a local garage sale for $7.00, and a small box in which to keep their money for $3.00.

Nika's dad agreed to loan the girls a lemon squeezer for $8 per day, two ice chests, measuring cups, and mixing spoons for $3 per day and water from the hose for $2 per day (in business, there is no such thing as a free lunch). Nika negotiated terms of "net five" on these items, meaning that these costs (that is, rent for lemon squeezer, ice chests, measuring cups, and mixing spoons, and use of water from the hose) had to be paid within five days of when they were incurred.

The girls priced their lemonade at $1.00 per cup and sold 460 cups during the day. All sales were for cash, except for four cups of lemonade that they sold to Nika's dad while he was cutting the grass and six cups that they sold to Nika's mom for that evening's dinner. Neither Nika's mom nor dad had cash with them when they bought the lemonade, so Nika agreed to sell them the lemonade on credit with credit terms of net two days. At the end of the day they had forty lemons, forty plastic cups, and eighty cubes of sugar left. All of the ice melted.

Chelsea ate dinner that night at Nika's house. After dinner, Nika's dad explained to them the importance of officially recording the day's activities. The current state and operating history of any business, her dad explained, are best summarized with an income statement and a balance sheet. To track actual cash flow, he continued, it is best to use a statement of cash flows, which nets all cash outflows against cash inflows for a given time period. Accordingly, Chelsea, Nika, and Nika's dad sat down at the computer to create a set of financial statements for the lemonade business. The statements they created, together with explanations for each item/account are shown in Table 2.3.

Problem 2.15   Before looking at Table 2.3, try to create an income statement for the lemonade stand business (using accrual accounting) on your own in the space below.

Problem 2.16   Before looking at Table 2.3, try to create a balance sheet for the lemonade stand business (using accrual accounting) on your own in the space below.

Table 2.3

Income Statement
Nika and Chelsea's Lemonade Stand
for the First Day of Operations

Sales revenue	$460	460 cups sold @ $1.00 per cup
Cost of goods sold	217	460 lemons @ $0.30 per lemon + 920 sugar cubes @ $0.05 per cube + 460 plastic cups @ $0.05 per cup + all of the ice (i.e., $10)
Gross profit	243	
Operating expenses	13	rent for lemon squeezer ($8) + rent for ice chests, measuring cups and spoons ($3) + water ($2)
Operating profit	230	
Interest expense	0	loan from dad interest free
Net income	**$230**	

Balance Sheet
Nika and Chelsea's Lemonade Stand
for the Day Ending the First Day of Operations

Cash	$450	plug figure necessary to balance total assets and total liabilities (also see Table 2.4)
Accounts receivable	10	10 glasses to mom and dad @ $1.00 per glass
Inventories	18	40 lemons @ $0.30 per lemon + 80 cubes of sugar @ $0.05 per cube + 40 cups @ $0.05 per cup
Fixed assets	15	poster board and magic marker @ $5.00 + table and chair @ $7.00 + money box @ $3.00
Total assets	**$493**	
Accounts payable	$ 13	see operating expenses negotiated at net 5 days
Loan	250	from dad to start business
Retained earnings	230	net income for first day of operations
Total Claims	**$493**	

As seen in Table 2.3, Nika and Chelsea's lemonade stand produced net income of $230 on total sales revenue of $460. Unfortunately, some of this revenue was not actually collected (the $10 in credit sales to mom and dad) during the accounting period—in this case one day. Likewise, some of the expenses in the income statement were not actually paid during the accounting period (specifically, the $8 rent for the lemon squeezer, the $3 rent for the ice chests, measuring cups and mixing spoons and the $2 for water—these items were negotiated at terms of net five days). These two noncash flows are shown on the balance sheet as accounts receivable and accounts payable. This illustrates a fundamental relationship between income statements and balance sheets: most current asset and current liability accounts on company balance sheets represent cash inflows or cash outflows, which are reported on the income statement but which, in reality, have yet to occur.

Problem 2.17 The income statement reports net income of $230. What was the actual cash flow from operations for Nika and Chelsea's Lemonade Stand?

$$\text{Net cash flow from operations} = \text{cash collected} - \text{cash outlays}$$
$$= (\$460 - \$10) - (\$230 - \$13)$$
$$= \$233$$

The entire simplified statement of cash flows, which includes cash outflows for asset purchases and cash flows from and to financing sources, is shown in Table 2.4.

Table 2.4 indicates that Nika and Chelsea should have ended the day with $450 in their moneybox—they began the period with $0 and experienced a net cash flow during the first day of operations of $450. In fact, they did end the day with $450 in their moneybox. And, not surprisingly, this amount corresponds with the plug figure for cash on the balance sheet in Table 2.3. A more detailed description of the statement of cash flows appears in the next chapter.

Table 2.4

Simple Statement of Cash Flows
Nika and Chelsea's Lemonade Stand
For the First Day of Operations

Cash Inflows:	
Cash collected from customers	$450
Loan from dad	$250
Total cash inflows	**$700**
Cash Outflows:	
Purchase of lemons	$150
Purchase of sugar	$50
Purchase of plastic cups	$25
Purchase of ice	$10
Payment for marker, board, table, chairs	
and money box	$15
Total cash outflows	**$250**
NET CASH FLOW	*$450*

Postnote to the Lemonade Stand Story – After completing the financial statements, partly because selling and record keeping was not their idea of fun, Nika and Chelsea concocted a brilliant scheme. They sold the table, chairs and the magic marker to Chelsea's mom for $15. They sold the leftover lemons, sugar cubes, and plastic cups to Nika's mom for $10. And then they went to visit Chelsea's grandparents (who lived two blocks away) and sweet-talked them into giving the girls $25 for the first sign that their grandchild had made for her first venture into the world of business.

Nika and Chelsea then reasoned that one item that they had forgotten to include in the income statement was wages to themselves, for managing and working the lemonade stand all day. They figured that $250 each (the amount of cash that they had in their money box plus the $25 they had just gotten from their moms, plus the $25 that they got from his Chelsea's grandparents) was a suitable wage payment, so they each extracted $250 in cash from the business.

The girls each put their $250 in an envelope to take to school on Monday. They then went to thank Nika's dad for the great lesson he had taught them about business. They told him about how great they felt about reaching their goals, and that they were excited about being able to tell Ms. Marz about how they had made so much money.

Somewhat surprised, Nika's dad said, "All that is fine and good, but it doesn't work that way because $250 of that money is mine. Remember, I loaned you $250 to start your business. I am sorry that you did not make your goal individually, but raising $250 together is still a great accomplishment."

Nika then calmly replied, "Oh, one thing that I forgot to tell you dad is that we decided to declare bankruptcy. As the sole creditor to the business, you are free to repossess all of our remaining assets, which given that we have sold everything else, is our company's accounts receivable—the $4 that you owe us and the $6 that mom owes us. And dad, thanks for the lesson in business. I sure learned a lot."

"Surely," thought Nika's dad, "I have learned a lesson that I will never forget!!!"

The next two chapters in this book are devoted to the interpretation and analysis of financial statements. Hopefully this accounting review has solidified your understanding of the basic structure and construction of income statements and balance sheets. Because, as Nika's dad tried to explain to Nika before his business went bankrupt, to fully appreciate analysis, you must first understand what you are analyzing. Now, if Nika's dad could only figure out how to analyze a third grader.

Assignment 2.1

Name:_____   Date:_____

Solve the following problems in the space provided.

Prepare a multi-step income statement for Freida, Incorporated (a furniture retailer) for the year ending December 31, 2006, given the information below:

Interest expense	17,090
Beginning inventory	63,210
Depreciation expense	12,510
Management salaries	17,950
Advertising expenditures	12,930
Ending inventory	68,390
Gross sales	462,720
Taxes	3,270
Returns and allowances	10,210
Lease payments	39,270
Materials purchases	228,580
R&D expenditures	4,890
Repairs and maintenance costs	2,910

Handwritten:
Beg. 63,210
+Purc. 228,580
Avail 291,790
−COGS 223,400
EB 68,390

a. What is Frieda's gross profit, operating profit, earnings before taxes, and net income?

Handwritten:
Gross Sales 462,720
− R&A 10,210
Net sales 452,510
− COGS 223,400
Gross Profit 229,110
− opert's Exp 77,950
− Deprec. 12,510
operat's profit 138,650

Operat'g Profit 138,650
− Int. Exp 17,090
EBT 121,560
− Taxes 3,270
Net Income 118,290

b. What is Frieda's net profit margin? (Note: Net profit margin is net income divided by net sales. We will discuss this concept in detail in chapter 5.)

Handwritten:
$NPM = \dfrac{NP}{Sales} = \dfrac{118,290}{452,510} = 26.14\%$

c. Assuming that on Frieda's December 31, 2005 Balance Sheet, Accumulated depreciation was $212,820 and that during 2006 Frieda did not sell any fixed assets, what would Frieda's Accumulated depreciation value be on December 31, 2006?

$$\begin{array}{r} \$212,820 \\ +\quad 12,510 \\ \hline \$225,330 \end{array}$$

Assignment 2.2

Name:_____   Date:_____

Solve the following problems in the space provided.

From the following accounts, prepare a balance sheet for the Windcharter Company for the year ending December 31, 2006 (assume that these are the only balance sheet accounts, and use cash as a plug figure to balance the balance sheet):

Gross fixed assets	284,950
Inventories	136,500
Long-term debt (excluding current portion)	134,300
Accrued expenses	11,850
Accumulated depreciation	82,310
Short-term bank loan (notes payable)	32,570
Preferred stock	8,000
Retained earnings	89,280
Current portion of L.T. debt	4,080
Net accounts receivable	105,770
Additional paid-in capital	71,600
Accounts payable	50,830
Common stock ($0.20 par)	60,000
Cash	??

a. What are Windcharter's Current assets, Current liabilities, Total liabilities, Net fixed assets, and net worth?

[Handwritten work:]

CA   Cash   17,600
         AR   105,770
Total CA Inv   136,500
                    259,870
    LA   GFA 284,950
         less acc. 82,310
         Deprec.
         NFA   202,640

CL   NP   32,570
         AP   50,830
         Aaru.   11,850
         Curren L-T 4,080
      Total CL   99,330
      LL
         L-T debt   134,300
      Total LL   233,630

Equity
   PS   8000
   CS   60000
   Add'l 71600
   RE   89,280
              228,880

Total Lib & Eq.
              462,510

b. Assuming that Windcharter's net income for 2006 was $25,400 and Retained earnings reported on the 2005 annual balance sheet was $79,880, what was Windcharter's dividend payment per share in 2006?

c. If Windcharter's Net fixed assets on its 2005 balance sheet was $184,660 and depreciation on Windcharter's 2006 income statement is $10,260, what amount of cash did Windcharter spend on fixed assets in 2006?

2005

NFA
184,660
202,640
387,300

2006
10,260 Deprec.
82,310
92,570 Total Deprec.

Assignment 2.3

Name:_____   Date:_____

Solve the following problems in the space provided.

1. In 2005, Jackson Incorporated had gross sales of $4,269,200. For 2005, management estimated that returns and allowances would be 5 percent of gross sales. What did Jackson report as net sales on its 2005 income statement?

    Gross Sales   4,269,200
    − R&A (.05×↗)   213,460
    Net Sales   4,055,740

    a. In 2006, Jackson Incorporated had gross sales of $4,183,820. For 2006, management estimated that returns and allowances would be 2 percent of gross sales. What did Jackson report as net sales on its 2006 income statement?

    Gross Sales   4,183,820
    − R&A (.02×↗)   883,676.4
    Net Sales   4,100,143.6

    b. Assuming that Jackson only reports net sales on its income statement (a muddled discussion concerning gross sales and estimated allowances is buried in the firm's footnotes), what do you find curious about your answers to the above two questions?

2. The inventory accounts for Billings, Incorporated for the years ending December 31, 2004, 2005, and 2006 are shown in the table below (all figures are in dollars):

	2004	**2005**	**2006**
Inventories	250,200	272,300	260,100

Billings purchased $196,400 of materials in 2005 and $206,300 of materials in 2006.

a. What did Billings report as cost of goods sold on its income statement in 2005?

$$\begin{array}{r} \text{Beg.} \quad 250,200 \\ + \quad\quad\quad 196,400 \\ \hline - \quad\quad\quad 446,600 \end{array}$$

$$\begin{array}{r} 446,600 \\ - \quad 174,300 \quad COGS \\ \hline 272,300 \end{array}$$

b. What did Billings report as cost of goods sold on its income statement in 2006?

$$\begin{array}{r} \text{Beg.} \quad 272,300 \\ + \quad\quad\quad 206,300 \\ \hline 478,600 \end{array}$$

$$\begin{array}{r} 478,600 \\ - \quad 218,500 \quad COGS \\ \hline 260,100 \end{array}$$

3. On its December 31, 2005 balance sheet, the Jones Company reported gross fixed assets of $3,200,000 and net fixed assets of $1,920,000. On its December 31, 2006 balance sheet, Jones reported gross fixed assets of $4,620,000 and net fixed assets of $3,080,000. Assuming that the Jones Company did not sell any fixed assets in 2006, what did the company list as depreciation expense on its income statement for 2006?

$$\underline{2005} \qquad\qquad \underline{2006}$$

$$\begin{array}{ll} \text{GFA} & 3,200,000 \\ \text{Depr.} & \underline{1,280,000} \\ \\ \text{NFA} & 1,920,000 \end{array} \qquad \begin{array}{l} 4,620,000 \\ \underline{1,540,000} \\ \\ 3,080,000 \end{array}$$

$$\begin{array}{r} 1,540,000 \\ - \quad 1,280,000 \\ \hline \$260,000 \end{array}$$

Additional Questions and Problems

1. You should be able to define each of the following terms in language that a friend who is not a business major could understand:

   a. Accrual accounting [recognizes rev. as earned w/ sales are transacted, regardless of w/ the company actually receives the pymt.]

   b. Cash accounting [recognize rev. as earned when payment is received & recognizes expenses as costs only w/ cash is actually pd. out.

   c. Stock measure statement

   d. Flow measure statement

   e. Gross revenue

   f. Allowance for doubtful accounts

   g. Cost of goods sold

   h. Gross profit

   i. Operating profit

j. Current assets

k. Current liabilities

l. Marketable securities

m. Accumulated depreciation

n. Depreciation expense

o. Cash conversion cycle

p. Permanent current assets

q. Accrued expenses

r. Par value of common stock

s. Additional paid-in capital or capital surplus

t. Book value of equity

u. Addition to retained earnings

2. Sam's Siding had sales of $100,000 in 2006. The cost of goods sold was $65,000, operating expenses (excluding depreciation) were $10,000, interest expenses were $5,000 and depreciation expense was $10,000. The firm's tax rate is 35 percent.

a. What is earnings before interest and taxes (that is, operating profit)?

$15,000

b. What is net income?

$6,500

Rev. 100,000
−COGS 65,000
GP 35,000
−OE 10,000
25,000
−Depr 10,000
OP 15,000
− 5,000
EBT 10,000
−Tax 3,500
NI 6,500

3. Using the following accounts from the Quest-Mar, Incorporated (a retail clothing store) income statement for the year ending December 31, 2006, answer the questions below (all figures in thousands of dollars):

Research & Development expenditures	$ 50
Cost of goods sold	600
Lease payments	30
Advertising	20
Taxes	35
Repairs and maintenance expenses	40
Management salaries	100
Interest expense	30
Net sales	1,000
Depreciation	60

[handwritten:]
Sales 1,000,000
− 600,000
GP 400,000
− OpExp: 50,000
30,000
20,000
40,000
100,000
160,000
Deprec. 60,000
OP 100,000
− IE 30,000
EBT 70,000
− TAX 35,000
NP 35,000

a. Quest-Mar's gross profit is $___400,000___.

b. Quest-Mar's operating profit is $___100,000___.

c. Quest-Mar's net profit is $___35,000___.

4. In 2005, the Chau Company purchased 180,000 units from its supplier at a cost of $42.50 per unit. Chau sold 192,000 units of its product in 2005 at a price of $58.75 per unit. Chau began 2005 with $1,360,000 in inventory (inventory is carried at a cost of $42.50 per unit). Using this information, compute Chau's gross profit for 2005 and compute the company's 2005 ending inventory balance.

5. In 2006, Canandra's, Inc. (a retail clothing company) sold 250,000 units of its product at an average price of $20 per unit. The company reported estimated Returns and allowances in 2006 of 2 percent of gross revenue. Canandra's actually purchased 240,000 units of its product from its manufacturer in 2006 at an average cost of $12 per unit. Canandra's began 2006 with 20,000 units of its product in inventory (carried at an average cost of $12 per unit). Operating expenses (excluding depreciation) for Canandra's, Inc. in 2006 were $1,000,000 and depreciation expense was $100,000. Canandra's had $10,000,000 in debt outstanding throughout all of 2006. This debt carried an average interest rate of 5 percent. Finally, Canandra's tax rate was forty percent. Canandra's fiscal year runs from January 1 through December 31. Given this information, construct Canandra's 2006 multi-step income statement.

6. Blooming Plants, Incorporated sold 3,200 plants to Freda's Florist Shop for $10 per plant in 2006. These plants cost Blooming Plants $6 to produce. In addition, Blooming spent $4,000 on general selling expenses and administration in 2006. Blooming Plants, Inc. borrowed $20,000 on January 1, 2006 on which it paid 14 percent interest. Both interest and principal were paid on December 31, 2006. Blooming's tax rate is 30 percent. Depreciation for the year was $3,000. Compute Blooming's gross profit, operating profit, Earnings before taxes (EBT) and net income for 2006.

7. Classify each of the following balance sheet items as either an asset, a liability, or equity, and as either current or noncurrent:

[handwritten left margin:]
360,000
656,000
010,000
160,000
850,000

Inventory A / C
Accounts receivable A / C
Long-term debt L / NC
Common stock (par value) E
Plant and equipment A / NC
Cash A / C

Retained earnings E
Accounts payable L / C
Accrued wages and taxes L / C
Notes payable (bank loans) L / C
Marketable securities A / C
Prepaid expenses L / NC

8. Construct a balance sheet for Taylor's Tables given the following data (assume that the items listed below are the only entries on Taylor's balance sheet). What is total shareholders' equity?

[handwritten annotations:]

CA
Cash 100,000
Inv 2,000,000
AR 220,000

LA 1,000,000

TA 3,320,000

CL
AP 170,000

LL 1,700,000

TL 1,870,000

EQ 1,450,000

3,320,000

Total shareholder's
1,450,000 EQUITY

- Cash = $100,000
- Long-term debt = $1,700,000
- Net Property = $1,000,000
- Accounts receivable = $220,000
- Inventory = $2,000,000
- Accounts payable = $170,000
- Total shareholders' equity = ???

9. Using the following accounts from the Quest-Mar, Incorporated balance sheet for the year ending December 31, 2006, answer the questions below (all figures in thousands of dollars)—use cash as a plug figure.

[handwritten annotations:]

CA
Cash 2610
AR 100
Inv 190
Total CA

GFA 900
-Deprec. -788 / -300
Lease
NFA 400

Total Assets 3300

CL
S-T 20
AP 90
Accr. 40
Cur L-T 60
Tot.CL 2100

LL
L-T 600

Equity
CS 400
RE 200
Tot Equt 600
Tot Liab 3300

33

Current portion of L.T. debt	$ 60
Leasehold improvements	300
Accrued expenses	40
Accumulated depreciation	200
Gross fixed assets	900
Accounts payable	90
Inventories	190
Common stock ($1.00 par)	400
Short-term bank loan	20
Net accounts receivable	100
Long-term bank loan	600
Retained earnings	200
Cash	???

a. Quest-Mar's current assets are $___2900___.

b. Quest-Mar's current liabilities are $___2100___.

c. Quest-Mar's total assets are $___3300___.

d. Quest-Mar's total liabilities are $___3300___.

e. Quest-Mar's total stockholders' equity is $___600___.

10. The following long-term asset accounts appeared in the Creech, Inc. balance sheets for the years ending December 31, 2004 and 2005:

	2004	2005	2006
Gross fixed assets	$32,652,400	$44,286,300	10,246,200
Accumulated depreciation	(8,342,200)	(9,124,400)	(943,100)
Net fixed assets	$24,310,200	$35,161,900	9,303,100

a. Assuming that the company did not sell any long-term assets in 2005, what did Creech report as Depreciation expense on its 2005 income statement?

$ 8,342,200

b. If Creech, Inc. purchased $10,246,200 of machinery and equipment in 2006 (and did not sell any long-term assets in 2006), what did Creech report as Gross fixed assets on its 2006 balance sheet?

c. If Creech, Inc. reported Depreciation expense of $943,100 on its January 1 through December 31, 2006 income statement, what did the company report as Net fixed assets on its 2006 balance sheet? (Assume that the event described in question b occurred in 2006.)

$$9,303,100$$

11. The Crump Company borrowed $4,200,000 from a local bank on March 1, 1998. The loan requires the company to repay $280,000 in principal every year (the first principal payment on the loan was due and paid on March 1, 1999). Assuming that this is the only long-term loan that the company has ever made and that all principal payments to date have been made on time, fill in the accounts below from Crump's December 31, 2004 through 2006 balance sheets:

Long-Term Debt Accounts
The Crump Company
For the Years Ending December 31, 2004, 2005 and 2006

	2004	2005	2006
Current portion of long-term debt	280,000	_____	_____
Long-term debt (excl. current portion)	2,520,000	_____	_____

12. Consider the equity portion of the Danborn Company's balance sheet for the fiscal years ending December 31, 2005 and 2006.

Equity Section of Balance Sheet
The Danborn Company
For the Years Ending December 31, 2005 and 2006
(all figures in thousands)

	2005	2006
Common stock ($2 par)	$1,100	$1,250
Capital surplus	7,600	9,200
Retained earnings	2,400	3,200

Danborn reported net income for 2005 of $1,100 and net income for 2006 of $1,500. Given this information, answer the following questions.

a. How many new shares of stock did Danborn issue in 2006?

$$\frac{150,000}{2} = 75,000$$

b. Assuming that all new stock was issued at the same time, at what price per share did the new stock sell? $(1,250 - 1,100) + (9,200 - 7,600) =$
$$150,000 + 1,600,000 = 1,750,000 / 75,000 =$$

c. What was Danborn's dividend per share payout in 2006?

13. The year-end 2005 balance sheet for Brad's Copy, Inc. lists common stock ($1.00 par value) at $5,000,000, capital surplus at $10,000,000 and retained earnings at $45,000,000. On the 2006 year-end balance sheet, retained earnings are listed as $47,000,000. The firm's net income in 2006 was $8,000,000. No stock was issued or repurchased in 2006. What were total dividends paid by the firm in 2006? What were dividends per share paid by the firm in 2006?

14. Cecil's Camper Company has an operating profit of $400,000. Interest expense for the year was $28,000, taxes paid were $111,600, and common stock dividends paid were $80,000. Cecil has 42,400 shares of common stock outstanding.

    a. Calculate the earnings per share and the common dividends per share for Cecil's Camper Company.

    b. What was the increase (decrease) in retained earnings for the year?

    c. If Cecil issues 3,000 additional shares of common stock and uses the proceeds from the sale to pay down the firm's debt, interest expense would be reduced to $12,000, but taxes would increase to $115,100. Using the same information concerning operating income and dividends given above, calculate Cecil's earnings per share and common dividends per share, assuming that the 3,000 shares are issued.

15. The Lunder Company has assets of $200,000, current liabilities of $25,000, and long-term liabilities of $70,000. The firm has 20,000 shares of common stock outstanding.

    a. Compute the firm's book value per share (that is, book value of equity divided by the number of shares of common stock outstanding).

    b. If there is $11,000 in earnings available to common stockholders and Lunder has a P/E ratio of 15 times earnings per share, what is the current price of the stock?

    c. What is the ratio of the current price per share of the stock to the book value per share of the stock? What do you think is the significance of this relationship, specifically for Lunder, and also in general?

16. Condensed (incomplete) balance sheets for Moab Lines, Inc. for 2005 and 2006 are shown below (assume that Moab neither issued nor repurchased any stock in 2005):

Moab Lines, Inc. Balance Sheets
For the Years Ending December 31, 2005 and 2006
(figures in dollars)

	2005	2006
Current assets	60,000	74,000
Net fixed assets	400,000	500,000
Total assets	**460,000**	**574,000**
Current liabilities	20,000	30,000
Long-term debt	300,000	400,000
Owners' equity	???	???
Total liabilities & equity	**460,000**	**574,000**

a. What was owner's equity in 2005? In 2006?

b. Compute Net income for 2006 assuming the Moab paid total dividends of $6,000 in 2006.

c. If Moab purchased $140,000 in new fixed assets in 2006, what must have been depreciation expense on the 2006 income statement?

d. Net working capital is defined as Current assets minus Current liabilities. What was the change in Net working capital between 2005 and 2006?

e. If Moab borrowed $150,000 of new long-term debt in 2006, how much long-term debt must have been repaid in 2006?

17. Condensed (incomplete) balance sheets for 2005 and 2006 and the (incomplete) income statement for 2006 for Eli's Everything Shop are shown below:

Eli's Everything Shop Balance Sheets
For the Years Ending December 31, 2005 and 2006
(figures in dollars)

	2005	2006
Current assets	40,000	62,000
Net fixed assets	200,000	318,000
Total assets	**240,000**	**380,000**
Current liabilities	20,000	38,000
Long-term debt	120,000	232,000
Shareholders' equity	???	???
Total liabilities & equity	**240,000**	**380,000**

Eli's Everything Shop Income Statement
For the Period January 1 to December 31, 2006
(figures in dollars)

Revenue	180,000
Cost of goods sold	104,000
Operating expenses (excluding depreciation)	32,000
Depreciation	10,000
Interest expense	24,000

a. What is shareholder's equity in 2005? In 2006?

b. What is Net working capital (see part d of question 16) in 2005? In 2006?

c. Compute Earnings before taxes in 2006.

d. Assuming that Eli's pays taxes equal to 30 percent of taxable income, compute Taxes for 2006.

e. Assuming that no fixed assets were sold in 2006, compute the total dollar expenditure on the purchase of new fixed assets (that is, the change in gross fixed assets from 2005 to 2006) in 2006.

f. If Eli reduced Notes payable by $4,000 in 2006, what was the increase or decrease in all other current liabilities in 2006?

Chapter 3

The Flow of Funds and the Statement of Cash Flows

After studying Chapter 3, you should be able to:

♦ Understand the basic difference between net profit and net cash flow.

♦ Describe the flow of funds through a business.

♦ Construct a statement of cash flows using the indirect method.

♦ Analyze a statement of cash flows.

♦ Identify, using the statement of cash flows, the major strengths and weaknesses of a company.

3.1 Chapter Overview ....

In this chapter we review the basic construction of the Statement of Cash Flows. There is a good chance that you learned about this statement in your basic accounting course. However, as noted in the beginning of chapter 2, it has been our experience that most students exiting an introductory accounting course do not fully understand the finance implications of financial statements. This is particularly true of the statement of cash flows.

The statement of cash flows is a powerful way to review the financial operations of a business for a given accounting period. It specifically shows where cash has come from (that is, the sources of funds) and where cash has been spent (that is, the uses of funds). Also, because the statement of cash flows is merely another way of presenting data that is already contained on the income statement and balance sheet, knowing how to properly construct this statement will reinforce your current understanding about the relationship between income statements and balance sheets.

Finally, as noted in chapter 1, the market value of a business is a function of the cash flow that the business can generate. All else constant, the greater the cash flow, the greater the value. To achieve the goal of financial management, managers must focus on those activities that generate cash flow.

Unfortunately, cash flow is not necessarily the same as net income. Recall from the lemonade example in chapter 2 that whereas net income was $230, net cash flow was $233. For that particular example, the values differed, but were at least close. In this chapter you will learn that net income and net cash flow can differ by significant amounts. In fact, it is entirely possible for a company to produce positive net income and yet have negative net cash flow. Throughout this chapter, we will stress that the best way to measure the success of a business is to focus on the ability of the business to generate cash.

3.2 Net Profit versus Net Cash Flow ....

Proper financial analysis must begin with an assessment of the cash flow potential of the business. Analyzing and correctly interpreting the flow of funds into and out of a business is not only important to stockholders, creditors, and financial managers, but may also be important to you as a potential employee. Consider the following (fictitious, though typical) new, small enterprise.

In 2005, Derrick Dickerson, a chemical engineer who worked for a major petroleum company in Texas, developed and patented a liquid center, dimpleless (smooth cover) golf ball. Derrick named the ball the SuperB-20. Because of its liquid center, the SuperB-20 flies on average 20 percent farther than a regular golf ball (the SuperB-20 is in many ways similar to a super ball—hence the name SuperB). Thus, a golfer who normally drives the ball 200 yards can add forty yards to a drive using the SuperB-20.

Even more amazing than increased distance, because of its smooth cover, even if the ball is mis-hit and begins to spin, the SuperB-20 will not curve or slice. Therefore, no matter how poorly the golfer hits the ball, the SuperB-20 will almost always fly straight. Although Derrick could not convince the USGA to sanction the SuperB-20 for tournament play, the ball has become an instant success among golf hackers. On average, golfers can cut 10 strokes off their regular score using the SuperB-20.

On January 1, 2006, Derrick invested $400,000 of his own money (his entire nest egg) to begin scale production of the SuperB-20 (before this, Derrick had been producing the golf balls one at a time in his garage and selling them online off his own Web site). He sells the balls in packages of three for $5.00 per package. His production costs are $4.00 per package (assume for simplicity that all costs are variable and ignore taxes). Of this $4.00 cost, $3.00 goes to materials and the remaining $1.00 goes to other miscellaneous expenses (considered, for simplicity, to be included in cost of goods sold).

Derrick maintains a thirty-day supply of balls in inventory at all times, bills his customers thirty days net (for simplicity, assume that there are thirty days in every month of the year), pays all of his bills promptly (as soon as they are received), and every month Derrick reinvests all profit back into the firm. In January, he sold 20,000 packages of balls. To end the month with the desired thirty-day supply of inventory, the company produced 40,000 packages of balls during January. At the end of the month, his balance sheet appeared as follows:

Balance Sheet (January 30, 2006)

Cash	$240,000	Stock	$400,000
Receivables	100,000		
Inventory	80,000	R.E.	20,000
Total	**$420,000**	**Total**	**$420,000**

On the balance sheet, the receivables represent the 20,000 packages of balls sold in January at $5.00 per package (all to be collected in thirty days, that is, in the month of February), the inventory represents a thirty-day supply of balls (20,000 packages, which is equal to January sales) carried on the balance sheet at a cost of $4.00 per package, and retained earnings are equal to January's profit as reported on the income statement:

$$(\$5.00 - \$4.00) \times 20,000 \text{ units} = \$20,000.$$

Cash is a plug figure that balances the balance sheet.

In February, sales increased to 30,000 packages. With a corresponding step-up in production to maintain his thirty-day supply of inventory, Derrick made 40,000 packages of balls at a cost of $160,000. He collected all of his January receivables, reported a profit for February of $30,000, and his balance sheet looked like this:

Balance Sheet (February 30, 2006)

Cash	$180,000	Stock	$400,000
Receivables	150,000		
Inventory	120,000	R.E.	50,000
Total	**$450,000**	**Total**	**$450,000**

Here, the receivables represent the 30,000 packages of balls sold in February at $5.00 per package (all to be collected in thirty days, that is, during March), the inventory represents a thirty-day supply of balls (30,000 packages, which is equal to February sales) carried on the balance sheet at a cost of $4.00 per package, and retained earnings are equal to January's retained earnings plus February's profit as reported on the February income statement (recall that all profit is reinvested back into the firm):

$$\$20,000 + [(\$5.00 - \$4.00) \times 30,000 \text{ units}] = \$50,000.$$

Again, cash is a plug figure that balances the balance sheet.

In March, sales blossomed to 50,000 packages. Collections continued on time, production (to adhere to Derrick's inventory policy) totaled 70,000 packages, and profit for the month of March was reported as $50,000, giving a three-month profit of $100,000 ($20,000 + $30,000 + $50,000).

Problem 3.1   Use this information to fill in the lines below:

Balance Sheet (March 30, 2006)

Cash	_____	Stock	_____
Receivables	_____		
Inventory	_____	R.E.	_____
Total	_____	**Total**	_____

Answer:

Balance Sheet (March 30, 2006)

Cash	$ 50,000	Stock	$400,000
Receivables	250,000		
Inventory	200,000	R.E.	100,000
Total	**$500,000**	**Total**	**$500,000**

In April, sales jumped another 20,000 units to 70,000 packages. Derrick was so ecstatic that he went out and bought a new Lexus. His customers continued to pay on time. Production for the month expanded to 90,000 packages, and the month's business netted him $70,000 for a profit to date of $170,000. Derrick got in his Lexus and took off for Florida.

A couple of hours after Derrick left town, his accountant (actually, you) constructed the balance sheet for April (see problem 3.2 below). Try to fill in the statement without first looking at the answer (cover the answer with a sheet of paper if necessary). As you fill in the numbers, think about the following questions:

- Is Derrick's golf ball company a bad company?

- Is Derrick a bad financial manager?

Problem 3.2   Fill in the lines below:

Balance Sheet (April 30, 2006)

Cash	_____	Stock	_____
Receivables	_____		
Inventory	_____	R.E.	_____
Total	_____	**Total**	_____

If you filled in all of the numbers correctly (Receivables = $350,000, Inventory = $280,000, Stock = $400,000, and R.E. = $170,000), you should have discovered a most disturbing result. When Derrick arrived at his hotel in Florida he found the following message waiting for him: RETURN HOME IMMEDIATELY (STOP) CHECKING ACCOUNT DEFICIT IS $60,000 (STOP) CHECKS ARE BOUNCING (STOP) SUPPLIERS ARE REFUSING TO SHIP NEXT MONTH'S MATERIALS (STOP) HHHEEELLLPPP!!! (STOP)

What did Derrick do? The same thing that most firms do when they have cash flow crisis—he called his banker to ask for a loan. Without immediate cash, Derrick would be unable to purchase the materials needed to produce for the coming month.

Is the golf ball company a bad company? No. It is difficult to imagine how a company that is making a bottom line profit of nearly $1 for every unit sold with no inventory writeoff problems and no bad debt (that is, all credit sales are eventually collected) can be completely flawed. Then, is Derrick a bad manager? No and yes. No, in terms of how he has organized his business. He has well defined production, inventory, and collection policies that remain constant, in terms of their relationship with sales, from month to month. Net income is positive and growing and the assets of his business are healthy and growing. Yes, in terms of his focus on net income as opposed to net cash flow. Good financial managers know that to be successful, their firm must be able to generate positive cash flow.

Why is Derrick's company having cash flow problems? His firm is growing too fast! In a sense, Derrick's firm is "growing broke!"

3.2.1 Cash Is King

This example illustrates one of the most fundamental concepts of financial analysis:

Profits Do Not Equal Cash Flow

Although Derrick earned a profit of $170,000 over the four-month period, the assets of his company (receivables and inventory) increased by $630,000. Asset growth must be funded. In Derrick's case, the initial $400,000 plus all of the $170,000 in profit was insufficient to fund his growth. With his cash now exhausted, Derrick was forced to seek external funds—while he was not in the best of bargaining positions.

Assume that Derrick had offered you a management position with his firm at the end of March. Had you relied solely on the March balance sheet and the quarterly income statement, you might have been tempted to join the apparently successful, rapidly growing company. Through March the company had generated $100,000 in profits, had no debt on its balance sheet, and had $50,000 sitting in its checking account. However, had you taken the job, your April paycheck almost certainly would have bounced!

If Derrick had monitored the company's cash flow, he probably could have corrected his problem before it became a crisis. For example, Derrick could have negotiated with his suppliers for payment terms of net thirty days, as opposed to paying his bills promptly. This would have allowed him to better match his outflows to his inflows. Assuming that such a change had taken place on March 31, the April 30 balance sheet would have looked as follows:

Balance Sheet (April 30, 2006)

Cash	$210,000	Stock	$400,000
Receivables	350,000	Payables	270,000
Inventory	280,000	R.E.	170,000
Total	**$840,000**	**Total**	**$840,000**

Receivables represent the 70,000 packages of balls sold in April at $5.00 per package, the inventory represents a 30 day supply of balls (70,000 packages) carried on the balance sheet at a cost of $4.00 per package, the payables represent the materials purchased in April that were needed to produce the 90,000 packages of balls made in that month at a materials cost of $3.00 per package (this amount will be paid to suppliers in May under the negotiated terms of net 30 days), R.E. is March's retained earnings of $100,000 plus April's profit of $70,000, and cash is a plug figure.

This simple change in payment terms results in a dramatic alteration in Derrick's financial position. At the very least, Derrick could have enjoyed his trip to Florida, and had you taken the management job with Derrick's firm, you would have gotten paid!

Identifying the nature of and solution to cash flow problems constitutes the major objective of financial statement analysis. Unfortunately, as evidenced by the example above, financial statements (prepared via the accrual method of accounting) do not directly reveal a firm's cash flow. Consider Derrick's first quarter balance sheet and income statement (reproduced on the next page).

Balance Sheet
Derrick's Company
For the Quarter Ending March 30, 2006

Cash	$ 50,000	Stock	$400,000
Receivables	250,000		
Inventory	200,000	R.E.	100,000
Total	**$500,000**	**Total**	**$500,000**

Income Statement
Derrick's Company
January 1, 1996 through March 30, 2006

Sales	$500,000
Cost of sales	400,000
Net income	**$100,000**

Without any additional information, Derrick does not appear to have a cash flow problem. If, however, Derrick had reported cash flow for the period as opposed to net income (that is, if Derrick had used the cash method of accounting), we would have discovered the following:

Cash Flow Statement
Derrick's Company
January 1, 1996 through March 30, 2006

Cash collections	$250,000
Cash outlays	600,000
Net cash flow	**($350,000)**

Cash collections represent sales for January and February (March sales have yet to be collected, as evidenced by the March receivables amount of $250,000 on the balance sheet). Cash outlays are for the purchase of materials and the payment of miscellaneous expenditures for all items produced in January, February, and March. Production in these months was 40,000 packages, 40,000 packages, and 70,000 packages, respectively. At $4.00 ($3.00 for materials and $1.00 for miscellaneous expenditures) per package this represents a cash outlay of $600,000.

Obviously, the cash flow statement tells a very different story than the firm's income statement. When analyzing a firm's financial statements, remember that this difference might exist. If, when analyzing a financial statement, you discover a difference between net profit and net cash flow, always remember that:

Profits Are Nice, but Cash Is King.

3.3 The Flow of Funds

Five years ago, Carlos and Juanita Gonzalez started a lawn and garden business in the suburbs. The location, coupled with the Gonzalezes' expertise in landscaping and design, made the company an instant success. Sales doubled in each of the first three years of operations. The number of full-time employees grew from one to fifteen. They had a large base of loyal customers and dependable, high quality suppliers.

Nonetheless, at the end of the third year of operations the Gonzalezes nearly filed for bankruptcy. Fortunately, Carlos and Juanita discovered one of the most fundamental principles of business: managing the flow of funds into, within, and out of an organization is at least as important as managing the organization's operations (that is, production and sales). Now the Gonzalezes' business is not only growing rapidly, but producing large cash flows for the owners (the Gonzalezes) as well.

The Gonzalezes now liken business to a hose. Although a hose might look perfect on the surface, if the spigot that pumps water into the hose is broken, or blockages and holes prevent water from efficiently flowing through the hose, or if the nozzle at the end that allows water to come out of the hose is malfunctioning, the hose is worthless. Similarly, if the flow of funds through a business is not managed properly, even the best of businesses will most likely fail.

An analyst can tell a great deal about the financial capabilities (or perhaps, incompetence) of a firm's managers by tracking the flow of funds through the firm over a period of time. Unfortunately, the accounting statements released by firms do not specifically address the issue of fund flow through time. Recall that the balance sheet is a stock measure, reporting the value of certain asset and liability accounts on a specific date. To perfectly track fund flow, an analyst would need to have access to a firm's checking account statements—something no firm would ever release.

Still, financial statements can provide some clues concerning the flow of funds through a business. By monitoring the changes in the accounts on a firm's balance sheet from one reporting period to the next, an analyst can gain some insight into the types of aggregate fund flow decisions made by the firm's managers. This knowledge can provide valuable clues concerning the future prospects of the firm.

Two statements can be used to analyze balance sheet account changes through time: the Sources and Uses Statement and the Statement of Cash Flows. In this chapter, we explain how both statements are prepared, and offer ways to interpret the information contained in the statement of cash flows. Included is an introduction to the significance of cash flow as an analytical tool in assessing current and future financial performance.

3.4 ◆ Sources and Uses of Funds

Until 1988, all firms were required to include a sources and uses statement, sometimes called the statement of changes in financial position, in their annual reports. In 1988, the statement of cash flows replaced this statement. Although the statement of cash flows is considered more relevant for analytical purposes, the two statements are merely different ways of presenting the same data. In this section of this chapter we illustrate the construction of a sources and uses statement. We demonstrate the construction of a statement that firms are no longer required to file because we believe that understanding the construction of a sources and uses statement will make it much easier for you to comprehend the construction of the statement of cash flows. The mechanics and intuition behind each statement are quite similar.

The flow of funds through a firm can be visualized as a continuous process. For every use of funds there must be a corresponding source of funds. In general, the assets of a firm represent the net uses of funds, and the liabilities and net worth of a firm represent the net sources of funds. A Sources and Uses Statement designates changes in balance sheet accounts (with the exception of cash and marketable securities) from one accounting period to another as either a source or a use.

The general rule is:

Sources = Decreases in Assets or Increases in Liabilities or Equity

Uses = Increases in Assets or Decreases in Liabilities or Equity

Any discrepancy between Sources of funds and Uses of funds for the given period explains the change in cash (and marketable securities) for that period.

Creating a Sources and Uses statement involves three simple steps. First, list the *change* in every independent balance sheet account. Second, identify each change as either a source of funds or a use of funds. And third, record all sources in one column and all uses in another column and sum both columns.

Problem 3.3 The balance sheets for Colonial, Inc. for the years ending December 31, 2005 and 2006 are shown in the chart below. On the blank lines provided in the chart, record the change in each independent balance sheet account. Record an increase as a positive number and a decrease as a negative number. (Note that independent balance sheet accounts are all net accounts that, when added together, equal total assets or total liabilities and equity. For example, we know that net fixed assets equals gross fixed assets minus accumulated depreciation. On some balance sheets, all three of these accounts are listed. Because only net fixed assets is added to current assets to derive total assets, list only the change in net fixed assets. In the chart below, you are only provided a blank line for independent balance sheet accounts.)

Balance Sheets
Colonial, Inc.
For the Years Ending December 31, 2005 and 2006
(all figures in dollars)

	2005	2006	Change
Cash	100	200	+100
Accounts receivable	700	900	+200
Inventories	1,300	1,000	−300
Total current assets	**2,100**	**2,100**	
Gross fixed assets	6,800	8,100	
(Accumulated depreciation)	(600)	(800)	
Net fixed assets	6,200	7,300	+1,100
Total assets	**8,300**	**9,400**	
Notes payable	200	400	+200
Accounts payable	900	800	−100
Accruals	100	200	+100
Total current liabilities	**1,200**	**1,400**	
Long-term debt	2,000	1,700	−300
Common stock	1,000	1,350	+350
Capital surplus	1,500	1,950	+450
Retained earnings	2,600	3,000	+400
Total liabilities and equity	**8,300**	**9,400**	

Answer:

Asset accounts

Cash	+100
Accounts receivable	+200
Inventories	−300
Net fixed assets	+1,100

Liability and equity accounts

Notes payable	+200
Accounts payable	−100
Accruals	+100
Long-term debt	−300
Common stock	+350
Capital surplus	+450
Retained earnings	+400

Problem 3.4 Record all of the changes in the independent balance sheet accounts as either sources or uses of funds. Recall that a Source of Funds is a decrease in an asset account or an increase in a liability or equity account. Conversely, a Use of Funds is an increase in an asset account or a decrease in a liability or equity account. Record all dollar changes as absolute values. Omit cash—that is, do not record "cash" as either a source or a use of funds. Finally, sum all sources to compute Total Sources of Funds and sum all uses to find Total Uses of Funds.

Sources of Funds		Uses of Funds	
Balance Sheet Item	Amount	Balance Sheet Item	Amount
Inventories	300	A/R	200
NIP	200	NFA	1100
Accruals	100	AIP	100
CS	350	L-T	300
Capital Surplus	450		
RE	400		
Total Sources of Funds	1,800	Total Uses of Funds	1,700

Answer:

Sources of Funds				Uses of Funds			
(Decrease in)	Inventories		300	(Increase in)	Accounts receivable		200
(Increase in)	Notes payable		200	(Increase in)	Net fixed assets		1,100
(Increase in)	Accruals		100	(Decrease in)	Accounts payable		100
(Increase in)	Common stock		350	(Decrease in)	Long-term debt		300
(Increase in)	Capital surplus		450				
(Increase in)	Retained earnings		400				
Total Sources of Funds			1,800	Total Uses of Funds			1,700

Problem 3.5 Verify that Total Sources of Funds in 2006 minus Total Uses of Funds in 2006 explains (that is, equals) the change in cash for 2006.

$$1800 - 1700 = +100$$

Problem 3.6 Create a Sources and Uses Statement for the Illustration Company for the year 2006 given the financial statements below. (Note that you will need to use only the balance sheet to construct the Sources and Uses statement; we will illustrate some extensions of the statement that use income statement data—and that relate to the statement of cash flows—after this problem).

Balance Sheets
Illustration Company
For the Years Ending December 31, 2005 and 2006

	2005	2006
Cash	10	14
Accounts receivable	30	25
Inventories	50	57
Gross fixed assets	160	190
Less accumulated depreciation	(50)	(70)
Net fixed assets	110	120
Total assets	**200**	**216**

Notes payable	40	29
Accounts payable	20	35
Accruals	28	32
Long-term debt	52	56
Common stock	40	34
Retained earnings	20	30
Total liabilities and equity	**200**	**216**

Income Statement
Illustration Company
For the Year Ending December 31, 2006

Net sales	400
COGS	280
Gross profit	**120**
Operating expenses	40
Depreciation	20
Operating income	**60**
Interest paid	10
Earnings before taxes	**50**
Taxes	20
Net income	**30**

Sources and Uses of Funds Statement
Illustration Company
For the Period December 31, 2005 to December 31, 2006

Sources of Funds		Uses of Funds	
Balance Sheet Item	**Amount**	**Balance Sheet Item**	**Amount**
AR	5	Inv	7
AP	15	CS	6
Accruals	4	NP	11
L-T	4	NFA	10
RE	10		
Total Sources of Funds	38	Total Uses of Funds	34

(*Note:* You may not need all of the lines provided in each column. Leave any extra lines blank).

Answer:

Sources of Funds			Uses of Funds		
(Decrease in)	Accounts receivable	5	(Increase in)	Inventories	7
(Increase in)	Accounts payable	15	(Increase in)	Net fixed assets	10
(Increase in)	Accruals	4	(Decrease in)	Notes payable	11
(Increase in)	Long-term debt	4	(Decrease in)	Common stock	6
(Increase in)	Retained earnings	10			
Total Sources of Funds		38	Total Uses of Funds		34

Total Sources of Funds − Total Uses of Funds = 38 − 34 = +4, which equals the change in cash from 2005 to 2006 (specifically, 14 − 10 = +4), which confirms that our sources and uses statement is correct.

Before we proceed to the Statement of Cash Flows, note a couple of relationships (that we have already reviewed in chapter 2) between the income statement and the balance sheets. First, depreciation as listed on the income statement is equal to the change in accumulated depreciation on the balance sheet. This will always be true as long as the company does not sell any fixed assets during the period (as noted before, we will assume no asset sales throughout the remainder of this section of the book). Second, total dividends paid equals net income minus the change in retained earnings.

Problem 3.7   Verify that depreciation as recorded on the income statement is equal to the change in accumulated depreciation on the balance sheet for the Illustration Company for 2006.

$$20 = 70 - 50$$

Problem 3.8   Compute dividends paid by the Illustration Company in 2006.

$$\text{Dividends paid} = 30 - (30 - 20) = 30 - 10 = 20$$

Thus, we could incorporate income statement data into the Sources and Uses Statement by replacing (the increase in) in retained earnings with net income as a source of funds and dividends paid as a use of funds and by replacing (the increase in) net fixed assets with the change in gross fixed assets as a use of funds and depreciation as recorded on the income statement as a source of funds. We will explore these issues in more detail in the following section.

3.5 The Statement of Cash Flows ····································

As noted in the preceding section, the statement of cash flows replaced the Sources and Uses of Funds statement in 1988. The statement of cash flows provides information about cash inflows and outflows during an accounting period. Because the main focus of the statement of cash flows is on cash as opposed to merely balancing accounting flows, it is generally preferred by those who analyze financial statement data.

There are three sections to the statement of cash flows:

1. Cash flow from operating activities
2. Cash flow from investing activities
3. Cash flow from financing activities

Similar to the Sources and Uses statement, the sum of these three cash flows will equal the change in cash and marketable securities for the period. The statement of cash flows contains all of the same balance sheet accounts as the sources and uses statement together with the income statement relationships mentioned above. All account items are classified as either cash inflows or cash outflows. Most classifications are intuitive. For example, an increase in gross fixed assets, which represents the purchase of a new plant or equipment, is a cash outflow (the company spent money to purchase the new fixed assets). Likewise, an increase in long-term debt, which represents new borrowed funds, is a cash inflow (the company received money from a bank or from other creditors). Some classifications are not as intuitive on the surface, but should become so as you more completely understand the nature of the activity (this is particularly true of operating activities). The main challenge in constructing a statement of cash flows is to determine which account items go in which section of the statement.

3.5.1 Cash Flows from Operating Activities

The first part of the Statement of Cash Flows is the Cash Flow from Operating Activities. Operating activities include all facets of the production and sale of goods and services. Cash flow involves the actual payment of production and operating costs and the collection of revenue. More specifically, the statement of cash flows from operating activities is the **translation of the income statement into a cash flow statement.**

There are actually two methods of calculating cash flows from operating activities: the direct method and the indirect method. As the term implies, the **direct method** directly converts each item on a firm's income statement into a cash inflow or a cash outflow. Then all cash flows are summed to determine the net cash flow from operating activities. Although this method of computing operating cash flow is more logical than the indirect method, it is seldom used in practice. We present its conceptual construction below merely for illustrative purposes.

To directly construct operating cash flow, instead of the accrual income statement from chapter 2,

Income Statement
Company Name
For the *Time Period* **Ending** *Date*

Net sales
− Cost of goods sold
Gross profit

− Operating expenses (excluding depreciation)
− Depreciation
Operating profit

− Interest expense
Profit before taxes

− Taxes
Net income

we want to generate the direct cash flow statement shown below:

Direct Statement of Cash Flows from Operating Activities
Company Name
For the *Time Period* **Ending** *Date*

Cash collected from customers
− Cash paid to suppliers, manufacturing labor, etc.
Gross cash flow

− Cash paid for operating expenses (excluding depreciation)
Operating cash flow

− Cash paid for interest expense
Cash flow before payment of taxes

− Cash paid for taxes
Net cash flow from operating activities

Note that in the cash flow statement there is no cash flow paid to depreciation. Why? To whom would you make out the check and where would you mail it? Also, only those cash flows related to continuing operations are considered. Thus, cash from the gain (or loss) on the sale of an asset is not considered as a cash flow from operations. Finally, note that accrual numbers (from the income statement) can be converted into cash flows (for cash flow from operations) using changes on the balance sheet during the sales accounting period. Recall that revenue reported on an income statement is booked when a sale is made, not when cash is actually collected from the sale. If, however, during an accounting period, there is an increase in accounts receivable, then some of the sales recorded as income have yet to be collected. Likewise, if there is a decrease in accounts receivable, then not only did the firm collect all of the sales reported on the statement, it also collected for sales from a prior period. Thus, to convert revenue into cash collected from customers, the sales revenue on the income statement must be reduced (increased) by the increase (reduction) in accounts receivable.

The **indirect method** begins at the bottom of the income statement (with net income) and then makes all adjustments necessary to convert net income into net cash flow. This method, though somewhat less intuitive, is the most commonly used. The steps necessary to convert net income to cash flow are illustrated in Table 3.1.

There are several items to note in Table 3.1. First, only those asset and liability accounts that are related to the income statement are included in operating activities. The main such accounts are accounts receivable, inventories, accounts payable, and accruals. Each of these is related to some item on the income statement. Specifically, accounts receivable is related to revenue, inventories and accounts payable are related to cost of goods sold, and accruals are related to operating expenses, interest expense, or taxes. Although technically there are other accounts that can relate to income statement data, these are the most common and the only accounts that we will use in this book. Also note that although these are all current asset and current liability accounts, notes payable is **not** included in the statement of cash flows from operations. That is because in this book we assume that notes payable represent only short-term bank loans (which though not always true, is most commonly the case). Because proceeds from a short-term loan do not appear anywhere on a firm's income statement, a change in notes payable is not an operating activity. In fact, it signifies borrowing or the repayment of a loan and is therefore part of the cash flows from financing activities.

Second, recall from the previous section that a decrease in an asset or an increase in a liability is a source of funds and an increase in an asset or a decrease in a liability is a use of funds. For the statement of cash flows from operating activities, a source represents an inflow of cash and a use represents an outflow of cash. Thus,

Decreases in Assets or Increases in Liabilities = CASH INFLOWS

Increases in Assets or Decreases in Liabilities = CASH OUTFLOWS.

Table 3.1

Net income
+ Depreciation
+ Decrease in any asset account related to the income statement (for example, accounts receivable and inventories)
− Increase in any asset account related to the income statement
− Decrease in any liability account related to the income statement (for example, accounts payable and accruals)
+ Increase in any liability account related to the income statement
= **Net cash flow from operating activities**

Note in Table 3.1 that cash inflows are added and cash outflows are subtracted—which makes intuitive sense! Another useful way to picture these relationships is as follows:

DECREASE ASSET	ADD
INCREASE ASSET	SUBTRACT
DECREASE LIABILITY	SUBTRACT
INCREASE LIABILITY	ADD

Finally, the sum of the first two items in Table 3.1, net income plus depreciation, is often referred to as a firm's free cash flow. Depreciation is a non-cash flow expense on the income statement. Thus, by adding depreciation to net income we gain a better picture of the base cash generated by a firm during a given period. Free cash flow, however, might not be the same as cash flow from operating activities. In fact, for some companies, even though free cash flow is positive, cash flow from operations is negative. Though not necessarily a disastrous situation, such a relationship indicates that the growth of some current asset accounts or the pay-down of some current liability accounts is consuming more cash than the firm is internally generating.

3.5.2 Cash Flows from Investing Activities

The second section of the Statement of Cash Flow lists the Cash Flows from Investing Activities. Investing activities include the acquisition or sale of productive assets (specifically, plant and equipment) and financial securities (generally, stock of other companies held for strategic or speculative purposes). Each activity is classified as either an inflow or an outflow as follows:

Inflows

- Sales of long-lived assets such as gross property, plant, and equipment
- Sales of debt or equity securities of other firms (that is, long-term investments)

Outflows

- Acquisitions of long-lived assets such as gross property, plant, and equipment
- Purchases of debt or equity securities of other firms (that is, long-term investments)

Note that Investing Activity essentially refers to changes on the lower left-hand side of the balance sheet—that is, to changes in a firm's long-term asset accounts. Also note that changes in only *gross* property, plant, and equipment are considered. If a firm purchases a new machine during a given accounting period for $1,000,000, the cash outflow to purchase that machine was $1,000,000. Gross property, plant, and equipment represents the original purchase price of long term assets, therefore only the change in this account captures cash outflow. The change in net fixed assets is not cash flow!

3.5.3 Cash Flows from Financing Activities

The final section of the Statement of Cash Flow lists the Cash Flows from Financing Activities. Financing activities include loans from creditors (long-term or short-term), repayment of principal, the sale or repurchase of stock (common or preferred) from the firm's equity holders, and the payment of dividends. Each of these activities is classified as either an inflow or an outflow as follows:

Inflows

- Proceeds from long- and short-term borrowing
- Proceeds from issuing the firm's own equity securities

Outflows

- Repayment of debt principal
- Repurchase of a firm's own shares
- Payment of dividends

Thus, Financing Activity essentially refers to items on the lower right hand side of the balance sheet and the change in short-term bank loans, or notes payable. That is, to any changes in debt (short- or long-term) and payments received from, adjusted by payments made to, preferred and common stockholders.

3.6 Constructing a Statement of Cash Flows: A Simple Example ················

The same income statement and balance sheets for the Illustration Company that you used in problem 3.6 to construct a Sources and Uses of Funds statement are reproduced below. We will use this data to construct a Statement of Cash Flows for 2006.

Balance Sheets
Illustration Company
For the Years Ending December 31, 2005 and 2006

	2005	2006
Cash	10	14
Accounts receivable	30	25
Inventories	50	57
Gross fixed assets	160	190
Less accumulated depreciation	(50)	(70)
Net fixed assets	110	120
Total assets	**200**	**216**
Notes payable	40	29
Accounts payable	20	35
Accruals	28	32
Long-term debt	52	56
Common stock	40	34
Retained earnings	20	30
Total liabilities and equity	**200**	**216**

Income Statement
Illustration Company
For the Year Ending December 31, 2006

Net sales	400
COGS	280
Gross profit	**120**
Operating expenses	40
Depreciation	20
Operating income	**60**
Interest paid	10
Earnings before taxes	**50**
Taxes	20
Net income	**30**

Recall that the Statement of Cash Flows is divided into three parts: Cash Flow from Operating Activities, Cash Flow from Investing Activities, and Cash Flow from Financing Activities. The sum of these three parts should equal the change in cash on the balance sheet between the two time periods in question. Note that for the Illustration Company, the net change in cash for the period 2005 to 2006 was +$4 (that is, $14 − $10). Thus, if properly constructed, the Statement of Cash Flows for this time period should show that the Cash Flow from Operating Activities plus the Cash Flow from Investing Activities plus the Cash Flows from Financing Activities equals this change in cash (that is, positive $4).

To construct the Statement of *Cash Flows from Operating Activities,* begin with Net income, add depreciation, and then make the other adjustments as illustrated in Table 3.1. Thus,

Net income	30
+ Depreciation	20
+ Decrease in accounts receivable	5
− Increase in Inventories	(7)
+ Increase in accounts payable	15
+ Increase in accruals	4
Net cash flow from operating activities	**67**

The Statement of *Cash Flows from Investing Activities* shows the amount of money spent on new plant and equipment during the period in question. Essentially, it is the increase in Gross fixed assets. Thus, for the Illustration Company,

Purchase of gross fixed assets	(30)
Net cash flow from investing activities	**(30)**

Note that the increase in Gross fixed assets represents a cash outflow because the company had to spend money to purchase the new plant and equipment. Therefore, the purchase of gross fixed assets should be listed as a negative value.

Also note that for the Illustration Company, the change in Gross fixed assets is merely equal to the change in Net fixed assets (that is, $120 − $110 = $10) plus depreciation from the income statement (that is, $20) – that is, $10 + $20 = $30. Finally, recall from problem 3.7 that the depreciation expense listed on the 2006 income statement (that is, $20) is equal to the change in accumulated depreciation from the 2005 balance sheet to the 2006 balance sheet (that is, $70 − $50 = $20). These relationships will always hold true if the company does not sell any fixed assets during the period in question. Because many financial statements do not explicitly list Gross fixed assets on the balance sheet or depreciation on the income statement (depreciation expense is often included in reported operating expenses), it is important to remember these relationships when constructing a Statement of Cash Flows.

The Statement of *Cash Flows from Financing Activities* records all money derived from or spent on financial instruments (that is, bank loans, bonds, and stocks). For the Illustration Company,

Decrease in notes payable (bank loan)	(11)
Increase in long-term debt	4
Decrease in common stock	(6)
Payment of dividends	(20)
Net cash flow from financing activities	**(33)**

Note that decreases in financing variables represent cash outflows and increases represent cash inflows. Specifically, a decrease in notes payable represents the repayment of some portion of an outstanding loan balance. A repayment of a loan is cash that must be paid out by the firm. Likewise, an increase in long-term debt represents an additional loan taken out by the company, which means that a creditor or creditors gave money to the firm.

Also, recall from problem 3.7 that the payment of dividends can be derived from the equation:

Dividends paid = Net income − Change in retained earnings

Dividends paid = $30 − ($30 − $20) = $20.

The payment of dividends is a cash outflow, thus it is recorded as negative $20 on the cash flow statement.

Finally, our statements must be correct because the sum of the three statements equals the change in cash for the period in question:

Net change in cash for 2006 = $67 − $30 − $33 = +$4.

Although Illustration Company only reported Net income in 2006 of $30 on its income statement, in fact the firm generated $71 in cash from its continuing operations. This cash was used to purchase fixed assets, pay down debt, pay dividends, and increase the cash balance.

A quick comparison of the Statement of Cash Flows above and the Sources and Uses of Funds that we derived in the preceding section, reveals the following. Both statements contain the same information, only presented in a different manner. Also, the statement of cash flows uses some information from the income statement. Specifically, in the statement of cash flows, the change in retained earnings is replaced by net income minus the payment of dividends. Net income is recorded as an operating activity and minus the payment of dividends is recorded as a financing activity. And, the change in net fixed assets is replaced by the change in gross fixed assets minus depreciation. The change in gross fixed assets is recorded as a negative investing activity and minus depreciation is recorded as a negative (therefore added) in the operating section of the statement.

Problem 3.9   An income statement for the year ending December 31, 2006 and balance sheets for the years ending December 31, 2005 and 2006 for the Elucidation Company are presented below. Use the data in these statements to fill in chart on the following page.

Balance Sheets
Elucidation Company
For the Years Ending December 31, 2005 and 2006

	2005	2006
Cash	30	28
Accounts receivable	60	55
Inventories	80	93
Net fixed assets	160	+30 190 220
Total assets	330	366
Notes payable	50	69
Accounts payable	50	45
Accruals	44	46
Long-term debt	62	60
Common stock	54	50
Retained earnings	70	96
Total liabilities and equity	330	366

Income Statement
Elucidation Company
For the Year Ending December 31, 2006

Net sales	400
COGS	260
Gross profit	**140**
Operating expenses	40
Depreciation	30
Operating income	**90**
Interest paid	20
Earnings before taxes	**70**
Taxes	30
Net income	**40**

Statement of Cash Flows
Elucidation Company
For the Period December 31, 2005 to December 31, 2006

CASH FLOW FROM OPERATING ACTIVITIES

Net income	$40
+ Depreciation	+ 30
AR	+5
Inv.	(−13)
AP	(−5)
Accruals	+2
Net cash flow from operating activities	59

CASH FLOW FROM INVESTING ACTIVITIES

NFA	(60)
Net cash flow from investing activities	(60)

CASH FLOW FROM FINANCING ACTIVITIES

NP	19
S−T debt	(2)
CS	4
RE 40 − 26	(14)
Net cash flow from financing activities	(1)

Net change in cash = $59 - 60 - 1 = (2)$

Answer:

Statement of Cash Flows
Elucidation Company
For the Period December 31, 2005 to December 31, 2006

Net income	40
+ Depreciation	30
+ Decrease in accounts receivable	5
− Increase in Inventories	(13)
− Decrease in accounts payable	(5)
+ Increase in Accruals	2
Net cash flow from operating activities	**59**
Purchase of Gross fixed assets	(60)
Net cash flow from investing activities	**(60)**
Increase in notes payable (bank loan)	19
Repayment of long-term debt	(2)
Repurchase of common stock	(4)
Payment of dividends	(14)
Net cash flow from financing activities	**(1)**

Net change in cash for 2003 = 59 − 60 − 1 = −2, which is correct!

3.7 Analyzing the Statement of Cash Flows

The statement of cash flows is a useful analytical tool. With its focus on cash flow and the division of cash flow into three separate activities, the statement of cash flows provides an analyst or financial manager with a quick glimpse of where cash is coming from and where cash is being spent. Specifically, it can indicate areas of concern. Any unexpected, abnormally large or irreversible negative cash flow (that is, outflow) in the statement can indicate what is sometimes known as a hemorrhaging of cash. Although cash bleeding can continue for some period of time (that is, be covered by loans or additional equity), it must eventually be stopped and reversed (loans or equity must be paid off) or else the firm will be forced into bankruptcy.

Recall the golf ball company example at the beginning of this chapter. On January 1, 2006 (the day the company began operations) the company balance sheet looked as follows:

Balance Sheet (January 1, 2006)

Cash	$400,000	Stock	$400,000
Total	**$400,000**	**Total**	**$400,000**

On April 30, 2006, assuming that the cash balance was reduced to $0 and a bank loan of $60,000 was taken out to pay for bills, the balance sheet would have looked as follows:

Balance Sheet (April 30, 2006)

Cash	$ 0	Bank loan	$ 60,000
Receivables	350,000	Stock	400,000
Inventory	280,000	R.E.	170,000
Total	**$630,000**	**Total**	**$630,000**

Recall that net income for the period was $170,000 and depreciation was $0 (there are no fixed assets). Thus, the statement of cash flows for the period January 1, 2006 to April 30, 2006 would be:

Statement of Cash Flows
Derrick's Company
For the Period January 1, 2006 to April 30, 2006

Net income	170,000
+ Depreciation	0
− Increase in accounts receivable	(350,000)
− Increase in Inventories	(280,000)
Net cash flow from operating activities	**(460,000)**
Purchase of gross fixed assets	0
Net cash flow from investing activities	**0**
Increase in notes payable (bank loan)	60,000
Change in common stock	0
Payment of dividends	0
Net cash flow from financing activities	**60,000**

And the change in cash = (460,000) + 0 + 60,000 = (400,000), which is correct. The initial cash balance of $400,000 was reduced to $0 by April 30, 2006.

For Derrick's Company, the large growth in accounts receivable and inventory relative to free cash flow represents an area of concern. Although an upsurge in these accounts often occurs during the early stages of the life of a company or during periods of rapid sales growth, the gap between these cash outflows and free cash flow must eventually be reduced or the company will need additional bank loans and equity every month. At some point, creditors and stockholders will demand a cash return on their investments, or else they will quit supplying additional funds. If a firm needs additional funding to continue operating but more cannot be found, the firm will be forced to cease operations. Indeed, managing operating cash flow and convincing the financial markets to cover negative operating cash flow when necessary is one of the biggest challenges of financial management.

Analyzing the Statement of Cash Flows is relatively straightforward. Properly constructed the statement should provide answers to the following questions.

1. **What is the relationship between a company's reported net income and its actual net cash flow from operations?** A company with a positive net income, yet negative operating cash flow, is either experiencing severe growth pains (large buildups in accounts receivables or inventories) or is being mismanaged financially (recall Bennie's Auto Parts and Service Center). In such cases, it is usually beneficial to rank the cash inflows and outflows from operations from largest to smallest to identify the factors that are causing the firm's cash drain. Note that for the Illustration Company, Cash Flow from Operating Activities exceeds reported Net Income from the income statement. It even exceeds the firm's free cash flow. These are signs of a healthy cash flow.

2. **In what major long-term assets has the company focused its investments?** Most long-term investing should be for renewal or expansion of plant and equipment. These should produce greater operating efficiencies in the future. Such is the case with the Illustration Company. Sometimes a balance sheet will indicate the purchase of other long-term assets. These could represent the purchase of another company's stock for strategic reasons, such as a joint venture. If a firm's net cash flow from investing is positive, implying the liquidation of assets, an analyst should carefully investigate the reasons for the liquidation(s). It might be a sign of severe financial distress.

3. **Does the company have sufficient cash flow to pay dividends?** By definition, cash dividends can only be paid with cash. In general, cash flow from operations should exceed the payment of dividends, as is the case with Illustration. If dividends exceed cash flow, then either the company has liquidated long-term assets to pay the dividend or the company has issued equity or borrowed to pay the dividend. Neither of these situations is usually healthy.

4. **Has there been any significant change in the company's capital structure?** Capital structure is the relationship between debt and equity. Also important is the relationship between long-term debt financing and short-term debt financing. Rapid run-ups in debt are usually an unfavorable sign. Likewise, substitution of short-term debt for long-term debt might indicate a worsening financial condition. Illustration Company reduced both short-term and long-term debt. This indicates that the firm is using equity to finance its growth. Internal financing of growth is usually, though not necessarily always, a good sign.

In summary, the Statement of Cash Flows is a very valuable analysis tool. It outlines a company's cash flow through a given accounting period. Analysis of a particular statement and comparisons between cash flow statements across different accounting periods can provide useful information to the financial manager attempting to manage a firm efficiently. It can also indicate to an outside analyst the company's strategies and future prospects.

Assignment 3.1

Name:_____ Date:_____

Solve the following problems in the space provided.

Given the following financial statements for Columbia Industries, Inc.:

Balance Sheet
Columbia Industries, Inc.
For the Years Ending December 31, 2005 and 2006

	2005	2006	
Cash	$ 24,000	$ 39,900	~~15,900~~
Accounts receivable	30,000	9,000	+ 21,000
Inventory	62,200	73,100	− 10,900
Total current assets	**116,200**	**122,000**	
Net plant and equipment	285,000	30,000+ 295,000	− 40,000
Total assets	**$401,200**	**$417,000**	
Notes payable	$ 6,000	$ 21,000	+15,000
Accounts payable to suppliers	49,000	37,000	− 12,000
Accruals	16,000	2,000	− 14,000
Total current liabilities	**71,000**	**60,000**	
Long-term debt	150,000	156,000	+ 6,000
Common stock ($2.00 par value)	25,000	30,000	+ 5,000
Capital surplus	90,000	91,000	+1,000
Retained earnings	65,200	80,000	14,800 Addition
Total liabilities and equity	**$401,200**	**$417,000**	to

Income Statement
Columbia Industries, Inc.
For the Year Ending December 31, 2006

Sales	$600,000
Cost of goods sold	390,000
Gross Profit	**$210,000**
General and administrative	70,000
Depreciation	30,000
Operating income	**110,000**
Interest expense	38,000
Earnings before taxes	**72,000**
Taxes	24,000
Net income	**$ 48,000**

1. Construct the Cash Flow from the Operating Activities section of the Statement of Cash Flows.

$$
\begin{array}{ll}
NI & +48,000 \\
Depr & +30,000 \\
& +21,000 \\
& -10,900 \\
& -12,000 \\
& -14,000 \\
\hline
& 62,100
\end{array}
$$

2. Construct the Cash Flow from the Investing Activities section of the Statement of Cash Flows.

$$(40,000)$$

3. Construct the Cash Flow from the Financing Activities section of the Statement of Cash Flows.

$$
\begin{array}{ll}
NP & 15,000 \\
L-T & 6,000 \\
CS & 5,000 \\
DV & 48,000 - (80,000 - 65,200) \\
& 48,000 - 14,800 = (33,200)
\end{array}
$$

$$(7200)$$

Assignment 3.2

Name:_____   Date:_____

Answer the following questions in the space provided.

Given the following financial statements for the Butterfingers Company:

Balance Sheets
Butterfingers Company
For the Years Ending December 31, 2005 and 2006
(dollars in thousands)

	2005	2006
Cash	1,200	1,800
Accounts receivable	2,000	2,500
Inventories	3,600	3,900
Total current assets	**6,800**	**8,200**
Net fixed assets	14,000	14,800
Total assets	**20,800**	**23,000**
Accounts payable	2,500	3,600
Accruals	500	1,000
Total current liabilities	**3,000**	**4,600**
Long-term debt	5,000	5,000
Common stock	10,000	10,000
Retained earnings	2,800	3,400
Total liabilities and equity	**20,800**	**23,000**

Additional Data from 2006 Income Statement

Depreciation	1,600
Net income	1,800

1. Construct the Cash Flow from the Operating Activities section of the Statement of Cash Flows.

NI   1,800,000
Depr   1,600,000
AR   (500,000)
Inv   (300,000)
AP   1,100,000
Accr.   500,000

2. Construct the Cash Flow from the Investing Activities section of the Statement of Cash Flows.

3. Construct the Cash Flow from the Financing Activities section of the Statement of Cash Flows.

Assignment 3.3 ....

Name:_____   Date:_____

Answer the following questions in the space provided.

Given the following information concerning the Coal Equipment Company, answer the questions below:

Balance Sheet
Coal Equipment Company
For the Years Ending December 31, 2005 and 2006

Assets	2005	2006
Cash	$ 24,000	$ 22,200
Accounts receivable	40,000	33,000
Inventory	52,200	83,100
Total current assets	**116,200**	**138,300**
Gross plant and equipment	385,000	425,000
Less accumulated depreciation	(100,000)	(130,000)
Net plant and equipment	285,000	295,000
Total assets	**$401,200**	**$433,300**
Liabilities and stockholders' equity		
Notes payable	16,000	13,000
Accounts payable to suppliers	49,000	57,000
Accruals	6,000	5,000
Total current liabilities	**71,000**	**75,000**
Long-term debt	160,000	175,000
Common stock ($2.50 par value)	25,000	27,000
Capital surplus	80,000	84,000
Retained earnings	65,200	72,300
Total liabilities and equity	**$401,200**	**$433,300**

Income Statement
Coal Equipment Company
For the Year Ending December 31, 2006

Sales	$600,000
Cost of goods sold	460,000
Gross Profit	**140,000**
Operating expenses (including depreciation)	70,000
Operating income	**70,000**
Interest expense	18,000
Earnings before taxes	**52,000**
Taxes	20,000
Net income	**$ 32,000**

1. Construct the Cash Flow from the Operating Activities section of the Statement of Cash Flows.

2. Construct the Cash Flow from the Investing Activities section of the Statement of Cash Flows.

3. Construct the Cash Flow from the Financing Activities section of the Statement of Cash Flows.

Additional ▪▪▪▪▪▪▪▪▪▪▪▪▪▪▪▪▪▪
Questions and
Problems

1. In the Derrick Dickerson example, it was shown that if Derrick could have negotiated with his suppliers for payment terms of net 30 days (as opposed to paying his bills promptly), he could have essentially fixed his cash flow problem. What else could Derrick do to "fix" his cash flow problem?

2. Because cash flow is more important than reported earnings, analysts often look for "evidence" (or the lack of evidence) of cash flow. List several signs that might indicate that a firm is experiencing a cash flow crisis (even though reported net income is positive)? Hint: what are some things that a banker, supplier, employee, or so on, might see or experience?

3. Referring back to the Derrick Dickerson financial statements (see section 3.1.1), assume that Derrick got a loan in April to cover his cash shortfall. Also assume that sales in May, June, and July remained at 7,000 units per month and that all other assumptions in the problem remain the same. Construct Derrick's July balance sheet.

4. If you answered question 3 correctly, you should have discovered that in July, Derrick's company has a positive cash balance. What was the difference between the January through April period and the May through July period that caused the company to go from a cash loser to a cash producer? Why does this happen?

5. Vicker, Inc. recorded the following items on its 2003 through 2006 balance sheets:

	2003	2004	2005	2006
Gross fixed assets	$10,000	$30,000	$70,000	$90,000
Accumulated depreciation	(2,000)	(4,000)	(8,000)	(10,000)
Net fixed assets	8,000	26,000	62,000	80,000

Assuming that Vicker did not sell any fixed assets during this time period, what did Vicker, Inc. report as depreciation expense on its 2004 income statement? On its 2005 income statement? On its 2006 income statement?

6. In the Statement of Cash Flows from Investing Activities, the change in gross fixed assets from one period to the next is considered to be the amount of cash that a company spends on the purchase of new plant and equipment. Referring back to question 5, what did Vicker, Inc. record as the cash outflow for new plant and equipment in 2004? In 2005? In 2006?

7. The purchase of new plant and equipment for a given time period is also equal to the change in net fixed assets during that period plus the corresponding depreciation expense from the income statement covering that period. Referring back to your answer to question 5, what was the

change in net fixed assets plus depreciation expense for the 2003 through 2004 period? For the 2004 through 2005 period? For the 2005 through 2006 period?

8. Construct a Statement of Cash Flows for the ZMZ Company given the following information:

Balance Sheets
ZMZ Company
For the Years Ending December 31, 2005 and 2006

	2005	2006
Cash	$ 4,000	$17,000
Accounts receivable	5,000	9,000
Inventory	10,000	12,000
Net fixed assets	27,000	40,000
Total assets	**$46,000**	**$78,000**
Accounts payable	$ 5,000	$ 3,000
Notes payable	2,000	5,000
Long-term debt	10,000	18,000
Common stock	25,000	40,000
Retained earnings	4,000	12,000
Total liabilities and equity	**$46,000**	**$78,000**

The income statement reflected the following information:

- Net income for the year ending 2006 was $26,000.
- Depreciation on fixed assets for the year was $2,000.
- Dividends paid in 2006 = $18,000

9. Given the following financial data for the Evans Company:

Balance Sheets
Evans Company
For the Years Ending December 31, 2005 and 2006
(dollars in thousands)

	2005	2006
Cash	1,200	1,800
Accounts receivable	2,700	2,200
Inventories	3,600	4,200
Total current assets	**7,500**	**8,200**
Net fixed assets	13,300	14,900
Total assets	**20,800**	**23,100**
Notes payable	800	1,200
Accounts payable	2,500	4,300
Accruals	500	100
Total current liabilities	**3,800**	**5,600**
Long-term debt	4,200	2,900
Common stock	10,000	10,600
Retained earnings	2,800	4,000
Total liabilities and equity	**20,800**	**23,100**

Additional Data from 2006 Income Statement

Depreciation	1,800
Net income	3,200

a. What were the total dividends paid by Evans to its common stockholders in 2006?

b. Assuming that gross fixed assets for Evans as of December 31, 2005 was $20,000 (and assuming that no fixed assets were sold in 2006), what would Evans have listed as gross fixed assets on December 31, 2006 had they included this entry on the balance sheet?

10. Refer to the data given in the previous problem (Evans Company). Construct a Statement of Cash Flows for Evans Company to determine Net Cash Flow from Operating Activities, Net Cash Flow from Investing Activities, and Net Cash Flow from Financing Activities. Verify that the sum of these three parts of the statement equals the change in cash on Evans' balance sheet from 2005 to 2006 (that is, $600).

11. The balance sheets for the Roxton Company for the years ending December 31, 2005 and 2006 are shown below. Roxton had net sales in 2005 of $28,400 and net income in 2005 of $1,850. Roxton had net sales in 2006 of $34,100 and net income in 2006 of $2,100. Using this information, answer the questions below.

Balance Sheets
Roxton Company
For the Years Ending December 31, 2005 and 2006
(dollars in thousands)

	2005	2006
Cash	1,200	1,700
Accounts receivable	3,100	2,300
Inventories	4,000	4,600
Total current assets	**8,300**	**8,600**
Gross fixed assets	26,700	38,900
Less accumulated depreciation	8,200	9,600
Net fixed assets	18,500	29,300
Total assets	**26,800**	**37,900**
Notes payable	1,800	1,200
Accounts payable	2,900	4,300
Wage and tax accruals	900	300
Total current liabilities	**5,600**	**5,800**
Long-term debt	4,200	3,800
Common stock ($0.20 par value)	6,200	10,000
Additional paid-in capital	7,400	13,700
Retained earnings	3,400	4,600
Total liabilities and equity	**26,800**	**37,900**

a. Calculate the Cash flows from operating activities.

b. Calculate the Cash flows from investing activities.

c. Calculate the Cash flows from financing activities.

12. Construct a Statement of Cash Flows for The Mulderton Company given the information below. Analyze your results. (Hint: The change in Long-term Investments is an Investing Activity.)

Balance Sheets
The Mulderton Company
For the Years Ending December 31, 2005 and 2006

	2005	2006
Cash	$ 10,000	$ 20,000
Accounts receivable	140,000	230,000
Inventories	530,000	490,000
Total current assets	**680,000**	**740,000**
Long-term investments	50,000	90,000
Net plant and equipment	800,000	1,000,000
Total assets	**$1,530,000**	**$1,830,000**
Notes payable	$ 120,000	$ 30,000
Accounts payable	310,000	520,000
Accrued expenses	90,000	170,000
Total current liabilities	**520,000**	**720,000**
Long-term debt	680,000	700,000
Common Stock ($1 par value)	100,000	150,000
Paid-in capital	100,000	100,000
Retained earnings	130,000	160,000
Total liabilities and equity	**$1,530,000**	**$1,830,000**

Income Statement
The Mulderton Company
For the Year Ending December 31, 2006

Sales	$2,600,000
Less: Cost of Goods Sold	1,500,000
Gross Profit	**1,100,000**
Less: Operating expenses	700,000
Operating Profit	**400,000**
Less: Depreciation Expense	110,000
Earnings Before Interest and Taxes	**290,000**
Less: Interest Expense	90,000
Earnings Before Taxes	**200,000**
Less: Taxes (40%)	80,000
Net income	**$ 120,000**

13. Given the following financial data for Genera, Inc.:

Balance Sheets
Genera, Inc.
For the Years Ending December 31, 2005 and 2006 (in dollars)

	2005	2006
Cash	3,200	3,000
Accounts receivable	44,500	54,800
Inventories	92,700	90,700
Total current assets	**140,400**	**148,500**
Net fixed assets	145,900	158,600
Total assets	**286,300**	**307,100**
Notes payable	6,400	5,300
Accounts payable	67,500	69,500
Accruals	3,200	2,600
Current portion of Long-term debt	8,300	9,200
Total current liabilities	**85,400**	**86,600**
Long-term debt	85,900	104,300
Common stock	25,600	24,600
Additional paid-in capital	64,200	62,200
Retained earnings	25,200	29,400
Total liabilities and equity	**286,300**	**307,100**

Data from the Genera, Inc. Income Statement for the year ending December 31, 2006:

- Sales (as recorded on year 2006 income statement) = $482,600
- Net income (as recorded on year 2006 income statement) = $19,300
- Depreciation (as recorded on year 2006 income statement) = $10,500

a. What was the *total* amount of long-term debt outstanding for Genera, Inc. in 2005?

b. What was the *total* amount of long-term debt outstanding for Genera, Inc. in 2006?

c. What was the change in *total* long-term debt for Genera, Inc. between December 31, 2005 and December 31, 2006?

14. Refer to the data given in the previous problem (Genera, Inc.). Construct a Statement of Cash Flows for Genera, Inc. to determine Net Cash Flow from Operating Activities, Net Cash Flow from Investing Activities, and Net Cash Flow from Financing Activities. Verify that the sum of these three parts of the statement equals the change in cash on the Genera, Inc. balance sheet from 2005 to 2006 (that is, –$200).

15. JRJ Corporation expects to have sales of $15 million and costs other than depreciation of $12 million. Depreciation is expected to amount to $1 million, and interest expense is expected to total $400,000. Sales revenues will be collected in cash, and costs other than depreciation must be paid for during the year. JRJ's tax rate is 40 percent.

    a. What is JRJ's expected net cash flow from operations?

    b. Suppose Congress changed the tax laws so that JRJ's depreciation expenses doubled. No changes in operations occurred. How much would JRJ save in taxes?

16. The following information is available for Mary's flower shop. Assume that these were the only changes on the balance sheet that occurred during the given accounting period.

Net income	$14,000
Depreciation expense	5,000
Increase in deferred tax liabilities	1,000
Decrease in accounts receivable	4,000
Increase in inventories	18,000
Decrease in accounts payable	10,000
Increase in accrued liabilities	2,000
Increase in gross property and equipment	28,000
Increase in short-term notes payable	38,000
Decrease in long-term bonds payable	8,000
Increase in marketable securities	2,000
Dividends paid	4,000
Change in cash	???

    a. What was the change in cash during this accounting period?

    b. What was the net cash flow from operating activities during this accounting period?

    c. What was the net cash flow from investing activities during this accounting period?

    d. What was the net cash flow from financing activities during this accounting period?

Chapter 4

Financial Statement Analysis

After studying Chapter 4, you should be able to:

◆ Understand the nature and consequences of financial statement fraud.

◆ Explain why and how companies engage in financial statement manipulation.

◆ Explain the objective of financial statement analysis according to who is doing the analysis.

◆ Construct a common size income statement and a common size balance sheet.

◆ Calculate a comprehensive set of financial ratios and use them to evaluate the financial health of a company.

◆ Explain the limitations of ratio analysis.

◆ Link firm performance to creating shareholder value.

4.1 Chapter Overview ....

All public corporations are required to publish three financial statements: an income statement, a balance sheet, and a statement of cash flows. In chapter 2 we reviewed the basic composition of income statements and balance sheets, and in chapter 3 we illustrated the construction of the statement of cash flows and emphasized the importance of cash flow as an indicator of the health of a business. In this chapter, we present the tools and techniques of analyzing financial statements.

Some consider financial statement analysis to be the "boring" part of finance. In fact, properly done, it can be both challenging and exciting. It is our desire that you find this chapter to be the latter as opposed to the former. Indeed, in light of recent corporate scandals involving financial statement fraud and manipulation, the ability to properly analyze a company's financial statements to identify areas of strength and weakness, and possibly even uncover improprieties, is more important than ever.

In this chapter we first discuss ways to analyze the quality of a firm's financial data. Specifically, we illustrate several methods by which a company can manipulate its financial statements, especially its income statement. Such manipulations can make a company's bottom line "look" better than it actually is or make a company's net income over time look less volatile or "smoother" than it actually was. Identifying financial statement manipulation, and more important, uncovering financial statement fraud, is an area of finance called "forensic accounting." Even if you have a solid understanding of accounting, it is unlikely that you have studied or even considered financial statement quality.

Next, we present the common tools used by financial analysts to examine a firm's financial statements. Assuming that the data is of good quality, we show how to identify areas of the business that are functioning properly and areas that require additional attention.

4.2 The Objective of Financial Statement Analysis ....

The main purpose of financial statement analysis is to identify a company's strengths and weaknesses. Specific objectives, however, depend on who is doing the analysis. Three groups are typically interested in the information that financial statements can reveal: creditors, stockholders, and managers.

Creditors are chiefly concerned about the ability of the firm to make interest and principal payments on borrowed funds. A creditor must assess the reason why the firm needs money or how the firm has used borrowed funds in the past. A creditor is also interested in the firm's current capital structure (that is, the ratio of total debt to total assets), and the history of debt service. Identifying the source of cash to be used to repay the loan is extremely important. In particular, the creditor must evaluate cash flow from operating activities to determine if the firm will be able to produce sufficient internal cash flow to pay its debt obligations. Finally, creditors must evaluate the quality of all assets held by the firm to determine their liquidation value in the event of bankruptcy. When a firm goes bankrupt, all assets are sold and the proceeds from the sale are divided among all of the firm's creditors. If the total value of all liquidated assets is less than the claims of all creditors, then some or all creditors will receive less in repayment than what they loaned to the firm.

Stockholders, both current and prospective, are mainly interested in the firm's future prospects. They must estimate the future earnings stream of the firm to determine the value of the company's stock. Stockholders base their investment decisions (that is, buy stock or sell stock) on the relationship between the estimated value of the stock and the current price at which the stock is trading in the stock market. Stockholders are interested in the historical performance record of the company only to the degree that history might help to determine future expectations. Another significant area of interest to stockholders is the relationship between reported earnings and cash flow. Recall from the Derrick Dickerson example, that the wealth of the owners (that is, the stockholders) is a function of cash flow, not net income. Finally, stockholders are concerned about the risk and timing of the firm's future cash flows. The value of immediate, low risk, small cash flows might be greater than the value of distant future, high risk, large cash flows, or vice versa. Specific value can be determined only by estimating risk and timing.

Managers are interested in all of the areas of concern to both creditors and stockholders, because creditors and stockholders provide funds that the firm needs to operate and grow. Companies must be able to attract sufficient and low-cost capital to survive in a competitive environment. Management must also consider the firm's employees, the community in which the firm operates, the environment, government regulators, and the financial press. The company must appear to be friendly and attractive to all of these groups. Finally, managers must identify the strength and weaknesses of the firm's historical operational performance and current financial position, and must estimate the company's future funding needs. Strategic plans must be formulated, communicated, and effectively implemented to accentuate strengths and correct weaknesses.

◆ 4.3 The Issue of Financial Statement Fraud ···

Financial statements are meant to summarize a company's financial operations for a period of time. They should paint an accurate picture of the health of a business, and should provide information concerning the firm's future prospects. Current stockholders rely on financial statements to evaluate firm and management performance, potential stockholders rely on financial statements to determine whether or not to invest in a firm, creditors rely on financial statements to ascertain the risks of lending money to a firm, and the country as a whole relies on financial statements to indicate the general health of the economy. Because so many people rely on financial statements, tremendous financial losses can result if financial statements are not truthful and accurate.

Financial statement fraud occurs when a company distributes financial statements that knowingly contain false information. Unfortunately, the incidence of financial statement fraud in the U.S. is much larger than most realize. According to a recent fraud survey conducted by a major accounting firm, 76 percent of companies admit having experienced fraud during the past year and consider fraud to be a major problem for business today.

Fraud can be very costly to stockholders. For the twenty publicly traded companies investigated in 2002 by the Department of Justice and the Securities and Exchange Commission, total shareholder value declined by nearly $236 billion after the government's investigations were announced or after the company admitted financial mismanagement. In this group, the shareholders of Tyco lost $84.2 billion, the shareholders of Lucent lost $55.5 billion, and the shareholders of WorldCom lost $26.9 billion.

Though interesting, financial fraud is neither glamorous nor amusing. When financial fraud is uncovered, a firm is usually forced to declare bankruptcy. The stock price that was based on the fraudulent information goes to zero, the physical assets upon which creditors made loans are often found to be bogus or of much lower value than stated, retiree pensions that were based on the future performance of the firm become worthless, and, in some cases, tens of thousands of individuals lose their jobs. Financial fraud erodes the public's confidence in the reliability of financial reporting as a means to assess a firm's future prospects. This in turn erodes confidence in financial markets, which impedes economic growth for the entire country.

Fraud occurs when unscrupulous managers, desperate to beat expectations, better the competition, or promote their own egos, decide to lie to achieve their goals. Most fraud begins with a relatively small "fudge" that the managers convince themselves can later be righted or covered over. Often, however, a second, bigger lie is necessary to cover the first lie, and a third to cover the second, and so on until the lie is too big to reverse.

Although financial statement fraud can be perpetrated on the balance sheet, most fraud involves the income statement. Not surprisingly, income statement fraud involves one or more of the following: improper or fictitious revenue recognition, understating cost of goods sold, or improper expense recognition. Consider some of the following examples of income statement fraud committed by publicly traded companies in the recent past. Note that the following examples of fraud investigations are excerpts from public record documents on file in the court records in the judicial district in which the cases were prosecuted.

> *On January 7, 2005, in Columbia, S.C., three former executives of Medical Managers Health Systems, Inc., a subsidiary of WebMD Corporation pleaded guilty to participating in a scheme to fraudulently inflate the reported earnings of Medical Manager between 1997 and 2002, and to obtain kickbacks for themselves in connection with executing the accounting scheme. The fraudulent accounting practices caused Medical Manager to book and record sales revenue before the revenue process was complete in accordance with Generally Accepted Accounting Principles and thereby fraudulently inflating Medical Manager's reported revenue.*

> *On March 1, 2005, in San Diego, Calif., Titan Corporation, a San Diego-based military intelligence and communications company, pleaded guilty to three felony counts, including Foreign Corrupt Practices Act violations, falsifying corporate books and records, and aiding in the filing of a false corporate tax return. Titan funneled $2 million, through an agent in the Republic of Benin, to the election campaign of Benin's then-incumbent President. At the time, Titan was developing a wireless telephone network in the African nation of Benin. Part of Titan's compensation for this project included a management fee worth millions of dollars. By using false invoices to conceal its improper payments in Benin, Titan falsified its books and records and claimed the bribes as deductible business expenses on its corporate tax return.*

> *During the yearlong investigation into WorldCom's accounts, nine billion dollars in discrepancies were found. The SEC levied charges against the corporation's CEO and several executives. Among these, Scott Sullivan (WorldCom's CFO) was indicted on counts of securities fraud, and David Myers (WorldCom's controller) pled guilty to committing securities fraud and falsifying SEC filings. In order to present a successful face to investors when company profits began to wane, former CFO Scott Sullivan led a series of accounting adjustments. Over five financial quarters Sullivan masked $3.8 billion in WorldCom operation costs. Another charge against WorldCom centers on the fact that the corporation's CEO, Bernard Ebbers, took 408 million dollars in personal loans from the corporation's funds.*

> *On October 15, 2003, in Los Angeles, Calif., Sultan Warris Khan, president, CEO, and chairman of the board of directors of NewCom, Inc., pleaded guilty to federal charges related to a scheme to fraudulently inflate the company's revenues. In his guilty plea, Khan admitted that he aided and abetted the making of false statements in quarterly reports that NewCom filed with the U.S. Securities and Exchange Commission. Khan also admitted his part in a scheme with Asif Khan, executive vice president of NewCom, to embezzle more than $1 million from NewCom and launder the proceeds of their fraud through a law firm's client trust account.*

> *Tyco CEO Dennis Kozlowski and CFO Michael Swartz face criminal charges for taking private loans from Tyco in excess of 170 million dollars. The loans, many of which were interest free or fully forgiven, were not revealed to shareholders. Mark Belnick, Tyco's former General Counsel, has also been charged for receiving fourteen million dollars in loans for houses he purchased in New York and Utah.*

The above are examples of blatantly illegal activities (that is, crimes) that at the time they occurred fooled even the firms' auditors. Fortunately, in most cases, the perpetrators of these types of crimes are punished. Nonetheless, many innocent people have suffered and continue to suffer from financial statement fraud.

The issue of financial statement fraud is a timely topic. Several large fraud cases that have resulted in bankruptcy filings for the companies in question have recently been spotlighted, including WorldCom,

Enron, and HealthSouth. Many believe that these and other recent fraud cases have eroded confidence in the financial markets, causing a significant decline in stock market averages and a drag on the economy. In response, the federal government enacted the Sarbanes-Oxley Act in 2002 (*SOX,* for short). The law is named after Senator Paul Sarbanes and Representative Michael G. Oxley.

The Act is designed to regulate the financial reporting landscape for management and finance professionals. Its main purpose is to significantly tighten accountability standards for top officials, board members, auditors, and others involved with financial accounting. *SOX* makes it easier for regulators to hold the top managers of a corporation criminally liable for signing off on a financial statement that knowingly contains false information.

A major victory for SOX, and for corporate ethics and responsibility in general, came on May 25, 2006, when the two former top executives of Enron Corp, Kenneth Lay and Jeffrey Skilling, were convicted on multiple counts of conspiracy and securities fraud. Lay and Skilling were found guilty of lying to investors, creditors, and employees about the health of Enron, and of conspiring to inflate the company's earnings and hide financial losses through a series of complex accounting tricks. Their activities contributed to the collapse of the company's stock, resulting in more than $60 billion in lost market value and over 5,600 lost jobs for individuals and the economy. Lay's total charges carry a maximum penalty in federal (not "country club") prison of 165 years. Skilling's charges carry a maximum penalty of 185 years in prison.

Only time will tell whether tougher penalties will stop financial accounting fraud. The temptation and potential rewards have always been strong. Now, as Enron and other recent cases are showing to managers, this abuse of authority and lack of moral responsibility carries significant consequences, that hopefully many will see are far greater than the consequences of simply telling the truth.

4.4 Earnings Management

Of perhaps greater concern than blatantly illegal financial manipulation, however, is the legal manipulation of financial statements—in particular, of reported earnings. Whereas outright fraud is usually eventually discovered, massaged data is more difficult to uncover. Additionally, many managers seem to believe that the rewards for managing their earnings far exceed the costs.

The first step in the analysis of a company's financial statements must be to consider the quality of the reported numbers. Ascertaining the quality of a firm's reported income and assets is critical in the analysis of financial statements. Generally accepted accounting principles allow management considerable discretion over how and when to report certain events. Consequently, management possesses the ability to legally "manipulate" company statements. Although financial statements should present a fair and accurate picture of the company's historical performance and current condition, this legal manipulation factor can cloud the picture.

Before applying the tools of financial analysis to a firm's financial statements, it is important to know and understand some of the areas of management discretion allowed under GAAP; that is, some of the "legal manipulation" tricks of the trade. It is also important to note that although managers do not have to take liberties when reporting their financial results, the pressure to achieve short-term profit results to please owners often outweighs objectivity.

Why would a firm want to manipulate its reported numbers (in particular, earnings)? Consider the following graph, which compares the earnings per share (EPS) of Company A to the EPS of Company B over a 20-period time span. The average EPS of both companies over this time period is the same (specifically, average EPS = $0.20) but the volatility of Company A's earnings is obviously much higher than the volatility of Company B's earnings. If you were a creditor, to which company would you be more apt to loan money? If you were a stockholder, which company appears to be a less risky, and therefore a more attractive, investment (note that both companies had the same average return of $0.20 per share over this period)? If both of these companies made you an identical job offer, which would you accept?

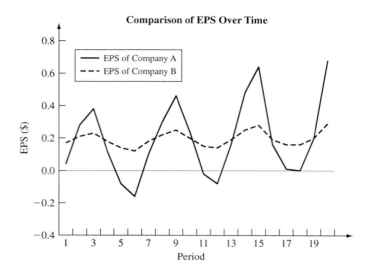

Comparison of EPS Over Time

Our guess is that your answer to all three questions was Company B. The lower level of volatility for the same average return makes Company B appear more attractive to creditors and stockholders, and to potential employees, suppliers, and clients.

The leeway allowed by generally accepted accounting principles to management over how and when to report certain events can actually result in these EPS lines representing the same company. Company A's EPS line can be the actual earnings of the company and Company B's EPS line can be how these earnings are reported to the public. Legal earnings manipulation, often referred to as **earnings management,** allows a company to "smooth" its earnings over time. Peaks are cut down and valleys are raised. The same average earnings are reported over a period of time, but the volatility of these earnings is underreported.

If you managed a company and if this was allowed, would you do it? Recall your answers to the questions above concerning you as a creditor, stockholder, and potential employee. Also, assume that everyone else does this, and that if you don't, you will look even more risky to these groups. Our guess is that you would. We believe that we would, too. And we know that mangers in the real world do. In the following sections of this chapter we will demonstrate some of the most common techniques employed by businesses to make their actual Company A earnings over time look like Company B earnings to the public.

4.4.1 Playing the Résumé Game: An Analogy

Creating a balance sheet and income statement is in some ways analogous to preparing a résumé. Granted, the regulations that govern the presentation of financial data in a set of financial statements is much more stringent than those that govern the presentation of personal information in a resume. Nonetheless, both documents attempt to present the historical achievements of the subject in a condensed format. Additionally, both documents allow the person preparing the statement discretion about the most favorable manner in which to present the data. Consider the following example.

Emily Erickson, a senior at State University, plans to graduate at the end of the current semester. She has just returned to her apartment from a visit to the counseling office, where she was given a set of guidelines for creating an effective résumé. Emily correctly realizes that before she can apply for a job, she needs to have a résumé.

The three major items that concern Emily as she begins to construct her résumé involve her educational achievements, her work experience, and her lack of honors. Emily, an English Literature major, currently has a 2.56 grade-point average. She has only worked at fast-food restaurants on a part-time basis during the summers. And she has never received an academic or athletic award or recognition.

In reviewing her transcript, she realized that in nearly all of the classes that she was forced to take outside of her major to satisfy the University's liberal arts requirements, she got C's. Additionally, her grades in her first three years of college, while she was very active in her sorority, were miserable. Indeed, because she had to repeat many of the courses that she took during that time, it has actually taken her five years to complete her college education. How would you present this information? Emily's Solution: list only her expected graduation date (as opposed to the time period she was in college) and report the grade point average for only the courses taken in her major field of study during the past two years. This allowed her to report a grade-point average of 3.5.

Emily had worked for two summers at a local Louisiana Fried Chicken as a fryer (a cook) and for a summer at Pizza House as a cashier. At Louisiana Fried Chicken, where Emily worked the weekend close-up shift, one of her major responsibilities was to dispose of all unsold chicken at the end of the night. At Pizza House, where she also worked the close-up shift, her major responsibility at closing was to reconcile sales and receipts with the final cash register balance, and to pay out all tips that had been added to credit card purchases and checks.

Emily knew that merely listing fryer and cashier at Louisiana Fried Chicken and Pizza House was not very impressive. How would you jazz up the description of her work experience? Emily's solution: because chicken could technically be considered as inventory at Louisiana Fried Chicken, and because her job at Pizza House involved more or less the management of cash and technically some payroll responsibilities, she input the following lines on her résumé.

Louisiana Fried Chicken, Corporation
—Inventory Control Manager

Pizza House Corporation
—Manager: Cash and Payroll

During the summer of her third year of school, she lived in Paris with her parents, who had been transferred there on a temporary work assignment. While in Paris, Emily learned how to speak and read French and spent most of her time at coffee shops meeting people and reading French magazines. She figured that whereas she technically learned something while she was in France, she could list her experience as a "Literature and Culture Internship in France."

Although Emily had never won any type of official academic award or honor, she was voted in her sorority as the Most Likely to Succeed at getting her parents to buy her a new laptop computer during her second year in college and as the Most Likely to Succeed at getting her parents to buy her a new sports car during her third year in college. In fact, her sorority sisters were correct. On her résumé, under the heading Awards and Honors, Emily recorded the following: Voted by Sorority in 2002 and in 2003 as the Most Likely to Succeed.

Though admittedly exaggerated, the preceding example illustrates the temptations that an individual might face in presenting her personal characteristics and historical achievements as she attempts to get potential employers, via her résumé, to consider her for a job. In many ways, this example parallels the temptations that managers face when they present their historical financial data. Because this data will be analyzed by creditors from whom the firm needs loans, investors from whom the firm needs equity capital, owners evaluating management's performance (and using earnings numbers to determine bonuses paid), the firm's raw materials suppliers, potential employees, and others, many managers believe that the data must "look" good.

4.4.2 Earnings Management: Some Techniques of the Trade

The techniques that financial managers and accountants can use to "dress up" their financial statements are varied and numerous. In fact, assessing financial statement quality is considered by many to be a proverbial can of worms. The following is not meant to serve as a definitive or exhaustive guide to the issue of quality. Rather, it is offered as an introduction to some of the most common techniques that firms use to legally manipulate reported numbers.

Specifically, we will highlight common ways in which a firm can influence its reported net sales, COGS, operating expenses, and non-operating revenues and expenses. This should help to explain how reported income can be "smoothed" over time. It will also hopefully encourage you to consider other ways in which managers can legally "twist, pull and stretch" the truth.

Net Sales—Has the firm used the allowance for doubtful accounts to enhance its reported sales figure?

In accrual accounting, revenue is recognized on the income statement when a product is sold or shipped (as opposed to when cash is collected). Most firms sell their products on credit. When a product is sold on credit, there is a chance that the money for the product will never be collected. To reflect this possibility on the income statement, firms usually report their revenues net of an allowance for doubtful accounts.

The firm's management estimates the allowance for doubtful accounts. Ideally the firm's managers will use its past collection experience relative to its volume of credit sales to estimate this allowance. Unless there has been some change in the firm's credit policy or economic conditions, the relationship between the changes in the allowance for doubtful accounts, accounts receivable, and sales should remain fairly constant through time.

Often, however, this is not the case. Managers can, and do, use the allowance account to smooth out their reported numbers. Specifically, during excessively good sales years, they tend to overestimate the allowance and then they use this "stored up" allowance during lean sales years. Consider the following example.

Over its 25-year history, Boujemaa, Incorporated has generally experienced bad debt equivalent to 5 percent of annual gross sales. 2004 was a relatively normal sales year for Boujemaa and, as shown in the chart below, the company did in fact report an allowance for doubtful accounts of 5 percent of gross sales for that year. This resulted in reported net sales of $9,500,000. If we assume that for each of the years listed in the chart that actual bad debt was 5 percent of gross sales, then the allowance for 2004 was exactly equal to actual bad debt for that year.

Partial Income Statements
Boujemaa, Incorporated
For the Years Ending December 31, 2004, 2005, and 2006

	2004	2005	2006
Gross sales	$10,000,000	$15,000,000	$14,000,000
Allowance for doubtful accounts	(500,000)	(1,350,000)	(100,000)
Net sales	9,500,000	13,650,000	13,900,000

Now assume that gross sales increased dramatically in 2005 and even though the company did not have any reason to believe that there would be any more bad debt (in percentage terms) in 2005 as compared to all other years, Boujemaa's management decided to allocate an allowance of 9 percent of gross sales for 2005. Because only 5 percent of all gross sales did in fact turn out to be "bad," Boujemaa ended up with an "extra" $600,000 in its allowance account.

This "extra" was then used to offset a bad 2006 sales year. Even though gross sales actually declined by $1,000,000 in 2006, the company reported an increase in net sales of $350,000. This completely legal sleight of hand was accomplished by allocating only $100,000 of 2006 gross sales (actually less than 1 percent of gross sales) to the allowance for doubtful accounts, and using the prior year's excess to cover the other 4-plus percent of actual bad debt.

Because companies are required to report only Net sales on their income statements (information concerning the allowance account can be buried in a footnote to the income statement), Boujemaa's decline in gross sales was actually hidden. To the outsider, 2006 looks like another positive sales growth year.

What Boujemaa did in this example is known as income smoothing. An allowance account was overallocated in a good sales year and underallocated in a bad sales year. If the excess allocations equal or exceed the underallocations over time, no real harm is done except that the outsider who looks at only the surface numbers will never know that that sales and net income are much more volatile than they appear.

Cost of Goods Sold—If the firm uses the LIFO method of inventory valuation, did a base LIFO layer reduction occur during the accounting period?

The inventory valuation method that a firm chooses determines how the firm allocates costs to the products that it sells. As you will recall from your accounting course(s), during a period of rising input costs (inflation), FIFO produces a lower cost estimate and therefore a higher earnings value than LIFO. Nonetheless, because LIFO better matches current costs to current revenues, LIFO produces a higher quality earnings value. That is, by costing goods at their current costs, the income statement is more reflective of the current and, in particular, future prospects of the firm. Thus, during periods of inflation, the reported earnings of a firm that uses the LIFO method of inventory valuation should be considered to be of higher quality than the reported earnings of a firm that uses the FIFO method of inventory valuation. Of course, during periods of deflation, the opposite would be true.

Note, however, that there is a tradeoff to choosing the LIFO method. Although LIFO produces a higher quality income statement, LIFO generally results in an undervalued inventory balance on the balance sheet. During periods of rising input costs, LIFO costs items on the balance sheet at distant historical value as opposed to current value.

For a firm that uses LIFO, what is known as a base LIFO layer reduction can occur when a firm's sales for a given period exceed its purchases (or production). Consider the following example. The Hentley Company, a T-shirt retailer, purchased from its supplier 100 T-shirts for $3.00 per unit in January, 100 T-shirts for $4.00 per unit in February, and 100 T-shirts for $5.00 per unit in March. (The monthly cost increases from the manufacturer were due to increases in raw material prices and a phased-in increase in the minimum wage). In the first quarter of the year, Hentley sold 200 T-shirts.

Problem 4.1a   Assuming the LIFO method of inventory valuation, what did Hentley report as COGS for the first quarter?

Answer: $(100 \times \$5.00) + (100 \times \$4.00) = \$900.$

Problem 4.1b   What was Hentley's ending inventory for the first quarter?

Answer: $(100 \times \$3.00) = \$300.$

In the second quarter of the year, Hentley again purchased 100 T-shirts per month in April, May, and June—this time all shirts were purchased at $6.00 per shirt per month, respectively. However, in the second quarter, Hentley sold 375 T-shirts—more shirts than it purchased. Hentley's COGS for the second quarter was:

$$(300 \times \$6.00) + (75 \times \$3.00) = \$2,025.$$

Note that Hentley's COGS includes seventy-five units costed at a value that differs significantly from current cost. These seventy-five units were sold out of Hentley's LIFO layer—that is, out of its inventory. How can a firm use a LIFO layer reduction to enhance its earnings for a given quarter or year? During an off-revenue year or a high-cost year, if the firm's inventory is valued at a cost substantially lower than the current cost of goods, the firm may strategically purchase (or produce) less than it sells. This will result in a base LIFO layer reduction, and thus a lower COGS than otherwise would have occurred had the firm purchased (or produced) an equal or greater amount than it sold.

Discretionary Expense Items—Is the firm attempting to increase reported earnings by reducing discretionary operating expenses to offset a reduction in its gross profit margin or a slowdown in sales?

Some operating expenses, though perhaps necessary, can, at least in terms of timing, be considered to be discretionary spending items. The major such expenditure categories include management salaries, administrative costs, research and development, repairs and maintenance, and marketing and advertising. For example, in response to a period of flat or declining sales, management might decide to quit advertising its product on television. Though this action might improve the firm's current earnings, if the sales problem is due to increased competition, cutting back on advertising today could spell disaster for the future. Likewise, in the face of declining sales, many actions that can enhance short-term profitability (for example, delaying required machinery maintenance, reducing spending on product research and development, laying off managers, cutting back on administrative staff, and so forth) could create long-term inefficiencies that cost much more than they save. Thus, if the analyst focuses merely on the bottom line, the analyst might be seriously misled, particularly with respect to the firm's future prospects.

One way to see if management has engaged in this type of manipulation is to examine the relative relationships between discretionary spending and sales over time. Consider the following partial income statement for the Boller Company:

Income Statement
Boller Company
For the Periods Ending December 31, 2004, 2005 and 2006

	2004	2005	2006
Net sales	$1,000	$2,000	$4,000
COGS	400	1,000	2,400
Gross profit	**600**	**1,000**	**1,600**
Salaries	100	200	400
Advertising	100	170	240
Research & development	100	160	220
Repairs and maintenance	100	130	160
Other operating expenses	100	140	180
Operating profit	**100**	**200**	**400**

Problem 4.2   In the corresponding statement below, compute every item on Boller's Income Statement as a percent of sales (that is, divided by that year's net sales figure):

Common Size Income Statement
Boller Company
For the Periods Ending December 31, 2004, 2005 and 2006

	2004	2005	2006
Net sales	100.0%	100.0%	100.0%
COGS	40.0	50.0	60.0
Gross profit	**60.0%**	**50.0%**	**40.0%**

	2004	2005	2006
Salaries	10%	10%	10%
Advertising	10%		
Research & development	10%		
Repairs and maintenance	10%		
Other operating expenses	10%		
Operating profit	10%	10%	10%

Answer:

	2004	2005	2006
Salaries	10.0%	10.0%	10.0%
Advertising	10.0%	8.5%	6.0%
Research & development	10.0%	8.0%	5.5%
Repairs and maintenance	10.0%	6.5%	4.0%
Other operating expenses	10.0%	7.0%	4.5%
Operating profit	**10.0%**	**10.0%**	**10.0%**

Note that whereas in the dollar figures it appears that both of Boller's profit measures are increasing, as a percent of sales, gross profit is actually decreasing. Boller was earning sixty cents in gross profit for each dollar of sales in 2004, but only forty cents in gross profit on each dollar of sales in 2006. Nonetheless, the operating profit margin was the same for all three years. The reduction in gross profit was effectively eliminated through relative (to sales) reductions in all operating expenses. Although there might be strategic reasons for such relative reductions in discretionary spending, their timing is curious. Is management sacrificing long-term profitability for short-term results?

Non-operating Revenues and Expenses—Does the income statement include gains (losses) on the sales of assets, interest income, or loss recognitions on the write-downs of assets?

When a company sells a long-term asset, the gain or loss (Sale price – Book value) is included on the income statement for that period. Because asset sales do not represent income from continuing operations, they should be subtracted from a firm's reported net income when comparing current earnings to historical earnings or when considering the future operating potential of the firm. A particular problem occurs when a company sells an asset in response to declining sales revenue solely to boost reported earnings. Though the short-term effect might be stable reported earnings, the long-term consequences could be severe.

Interest income usually results from a firm's temporary investments in short-term securities. Because the timing of cash inflows does not always match the timing of cash outflows, firms may build up temporary cash balances. If these cash balances are invested in marketable securities (short-term investments), they will earn interest income. For example, consider a firm that pays dividends on a semi-annual basis. The cash inflows from operations to be used to pay the dividend may occur on a more or less constant monthly basis. Instead of letting the cash merely accrue in its checking account, where it will earn no return, the firm can invest this money in marketable securities. In the sixth month when the dividend is paid, the firm will liquidate its marketable securities. In the meantime, the firm earns interest income, which it must report on its income statement.

If the interest income earned in a given year is excessive as compared to the interest income reported in prior years, the analyst must carefully investigate the reasons for the change. For example, assume that a company raises a large amount of money from a stock sale to purchase new plant and equipment. The sale occurs in January but the equipment is not bought until October. Obviously the interest income earned on the investment of this money from January to October should not be considered as part of the firm's core operating income.

Accounting standards require firms to carry assets on their books at the lower of cost or market value. If the value of an asset falls below its original cost, the asset must be "written-down." An asset write-down on the balance sheet must be matched by a loss recognition of the write-down on the income statement. Because loss recognitions are, hopefully, single occurrence events, they should be added back in to earnings to produce a more meaningful number to compare historically or to use as a measure of future profit potential.

Another problem with write-downs is that the timing of a write-down is, within limits, discretionary. If, in a given quarter, 10 percent of a firm's inventory becomes obsolete, the firm should write off the inventory in that quarter. Or if, in a given quarter, a firm discovers that 20 percent of all of its accounts receivable will never be paid, it should write off the bad debt immediately. Such immediate write-downs would reflect economic reality. However, if the discovery of obsolete inventory or bad debt occurs in a time period when earnings have already been reduced by other economic factors (as will usually be the case), the firm might be tempted to carry the bad inventory or debts on its books until earnings improve. That way the bad accounts can be "buried."

A final interesting method of earnings massage involves the "storing up" of revenue or cost write-offs. If in a given year, sales grow at an excessive rate, a firm may choose to defer some of its revenue recognition into a future accounting period. This is a technique used very effectively by many computer software companies. Recall that, in general, revenue must be recognized when the finished product is shipped. Computer software is an odd final product. Most software comes with a free (usually two-year) update clause— if an update occurs within two years of purchase, the vendor will provide the update for free. The accounting standards for software revenue recognition are very fuzzy. Basically, a firm can recognize revenue any time it wants during the two-year time period. In this way, computer software companies are able to "move" revenue through time to correspond with costs.

In a similar manner, a firm can also store up loss recognitions. In an extremely favorable sales year, it is often considered to be a good time to offset some of the excess revenue with loss recognitions, even if the recognitions are much larger than estimated. That way, during a less favorable sales year, the excess loss recognitions can be reclaimed. It is curious to note that in the same year that a major U.S. soft drink company won a $520 million settlement with the IRS, it chose to write off $500 million in expected inventory losses related to its bottling operations. By most analysts' estimates, the write-off was twenty to 30 percent larger than necessary.

In this section of the chapter we have briefly summarized a few of the techniques that companies can use to manage their income statements, especially their reported earnings. Companies engage in earnings management as a means to reduce the perceived volatility of their operations. Less volatility generally implies less risk.

Creditors, stockholders, and analysts must know how to detect and understand the implications of earnings management to accurately forecast future company performance and financial trends. The decisions that these individuals make are highly dependent on their assessments of company risk. Underestimating the true risk of a business can lead to poor investments and large monetary losses.

Although the list of techniques presented here represents only a few of the many ways that firms can manage their financial data, these are some of the more commonly used and easily identified techniques. It is our desire that this overview has at least increased your awareness of earnings management. Perhaps it will even encourage some of you to explore the field of forensic accounting in greater detail.

4.5 Tools of Financial Statement Analysis

Once the quality of a firm's financial statements has been ascertained, the numbers need to be analyzed. This involves simplifying and categorizing the data so that comparisons can be made during different time periods and between different companies. The tools most commonly used to do comparative analysis are: *common size financial statements* and *ratios.* The basic purpose of these tools is to convert financial statement data into common denominator formats and then to use all to compare different relationships among the measures, to identify and evaluate a firm's strengths and weaknesses.

Converting data to a common denominator format and using several different common denominator measures to analyze the item(s) being described by the data is not limited to financial statements. Assume, for example, that you own a baseball team. During the off-season you are trying to decide which free agent (J.F. Rook or O.Z. Vett) to sign. Both players will require a $7,000,000 annual salary. Last season, Rook had 142 hits and Vett had 57 hits.

Do these numbers necessarily mean that Rook is a better hitter than Vett? What if last season Rook got his 142 hits in 708 plate appearances and Vett only had 132 plate appearances (Vett was injured for the first half of the season, but is now fully recovered)? Dividing the number of hits by the number of plate appearances shows that Rook averaged 2.01 hits for every ten times at bat (a .201 batting average) and Vett averaged 4.01 hits every ten times at bat (a .401 batting average). Don't batting averages allow a better comparison of the hitters than the raw data alone?

A batting average is merely a common denominator format measure (that is, a ratio). It standardizes the number of hits for each player, allowing a more meaningful comparison. All else equal, because Vett has a higher batting average than Rook, Vett is probably a better hitter than Rook. One measure alone, however, might not be sufficient (that is, all else might not be equal). Would your opinion about which player is a better hitter change if you knew that 50 percent of Rook's hits last year were home runs and that all of Vett's hits were singles? Or that Rook had 142 RBI and Vett had only 21 RBI?

Also, additional factors other than hitting might be equally important. Would your decision about which player to pay $7,000,000 be affected by the fact that Vett has a .996 fielding average (number of errorless plays to number of total plays) and Rook has a .726 fielding average (once when Rook was playing in the outfield, a ball bounced off his head and over the fence for a home run)? Or that Rook is 22 years old and Vett is 36 years old? Or that Rook is a switch hitter (can bat either right-handed or left-handed) and Vett can bat only from the right hand side of the plate? Or that because he is vocal about everything, many considered Rook to be a major PR problem?

We hope that the point is obvious. When analyzing a specific problem, it is important to first standardize units of measurement. Also, one measure alone is seldom sufficient. Finally, qualitative factors may be at least as, or more, important than quantitative factors.

4.5.1 Common Size Financial Statements

To create a *common size statement,* every entry on the statement is divided by a common number. For the income statement, each account is divided by net sales. For the *common size balance sheet,* each item on the balance sheet is divided by total assets. Converting the resulting figures to percentages (multiplying by 100 and adding a percent sign) results in an income statement where every account is listed as a percent of sales and a balance sheet where every account is noted as a percent of total assets.

Viewing several years of percent format financial statements of the same company side by side reveals instant visual information about any trends the company might be experiencing. However, trends in and of themselves do not necessarily indicate strength or weakness. All they really indicate are areas that require further investigation.

Problem 4.3 The inventory and total asset accounts for Ipenama, Inc. are listed below. Compute inventory as a percent of total assets for each year.

	2003	2004	2005	2006
Inventory	$135,600	$175,600	$250,900	$320,800
Total Assets	$1,384,000	$1,626,000	$1,915,000	$2,308,000
Percent	9.8%			

Answer: 9.8%, 10.8%, 13.1%, 13.9%.

Ipenama's inventory accounts relative to total assets are growing every year. Is this bad? Greater relative amounts of inventory might mean more storage, warehousing, shipping or insurance costs. All else constant, these will reduce profitability. In this case, the increase in inventory as a percent of total assets would indicate a weakness. However, if higher inventory levels are generating significantly higher levels of sales, then the additional revenue might more than offset the additional costs, and profitability might be higher. In this case, the increase in inventory as a percent of total assets represents a strength.

Problem 4.4 The upper portion of the income statements of Barista, Inc., a men's retail clothing store, for the years ending December 31, 2003, 2004, 2005, and 2006 are listed in the following table. For each year, compute COGS as a percent of net sales. Then, try to think of answers to the following questions:

- In what ways might the trend in COGS as a percent of sales represent a strength?

- In what ways might the trend in COGS as a percent of sales represent a weakness?

	2003	**2004**	**2005**	**2006**
Net Sales	$12,186,000	$14,538,000	$17,751,000	$22,698,000
COGS	$ 9,627,000	$11,846,000	$14,484,000	$18,499,000
Percent	_____	_____	_____	_____

Answer: 79.0%, 81.4%, 81.6%, 81.5%.

The trend observed is a significant increase in COGS as a percent of sales from 2003 to 2004, and then relative stability thereafter. COGS as a percent of sales represents the direct cost per dollar of revenue of the products that the company sells. Thus for Barista, a retail clothing company, for every $1 of revenue made on selling clothes in 2003, it costs the company about seventy-nine cents to purchase the clothing. Another way to look at this is that, in 2003, Barista was able to "mark up" its clothing by about 21 percent. For the following three years, the "markup" was only about 18.5%.

All else constant, a smaller markup will result in less profitability. Assume that all other costs (operating expenses, depreciation, interest, and taxes), as a percent of sales, were 19 percent for all four years. This would mean that Barista made positive net profit of about 2 percent of sales in 2003, but actually lost money (had negative net profit) in 2004, 2005, and 2006. Perhaps Barista's competitors lowered their prices (that is markups) and the only way for Barista to maintain its market share was to match the price cuts.

On the other hand, the lower "markups" might have contributed to (or caused) the large growth in net sales that occurred in 2004 through 2006 (average annual growth of over 20 percent). If the growth rate in other costs as a percent of net sales was less than the increase in COGS as a percent of sales, then profitability would have increased. This relationship could occur if Barista experienced cost-volume savings. Perhaps increases in same store sales generated higher revenue but unchanged rent, utility, and advertising expenses.

Though there are no definitive answers to the strengths/weaknesses questions. You might have come up with different possibilities or explanations. And yours might be just as right (or just as wrong) as ours. Regardless of what possibility is posited, further investigation is needed to draw meaningful conclusions, but at least the common size constructions told us where to start.

Common size statements, when viewed across time periods, can indicate areas that a manager or analyst needs to monitor or investigate. Financial ratios can often help determine whether the trend indicates an area of strength or weakness. If ratios are not sufficient, either cash flow statements or some of the tools described in chapter 5, specifically, pro forma financial statements, cash budgets, and cost-benefit analysis, can also be applied to the issue.

4.5.2 Financial Ratios

Financial ratios are designed to examine the relationships between key accounts on the balance sheet and the relationships between accounts on the balance sheet and certain values on the income statement. Financial ratio analysis is the comparison of these relationships through time for a given firm (trend analysis) and the comparison of these relationships for one firm to competitors or to average ratios compiled for the industry in which that firm operates (industry comparisons). Financial ratios are generally grouped into five main categories: *liquidity ratios, activity ratios, debt utilization ratios, profitability ratios,* and *combination ratios.*

Ratios within each category are defined in Table 4.1. The nature of the information conveyed by each ratio is discussed below. Note that the ratios listed in Table 4.1 are merely a partial list of all of the possible ratios that could be calculated. In the world of financial ratios there is no definitive set of ratios, nor is there a uniform definition for all ratios.

Table 4.1   List of Key Financial Ratios

A. Liquidity Ratios

1. Current ratio $= \dfrac{\text{Current assets}}{\text{Current liabilities}}$ *Can firm pay bills?? Measure of solvency*

2. Quick ratio $= \dfrac{\text{Current assets} - \text{Inventories}}{\text{Current liabilities}}$

B. Asset Utilization Ratios

1. Average collection period $= \dfrac{\text{Accounts receivable}}{\dfrac{\text{Annual credit sales}}{360}} = \dfrac{\text{Accounts receivable}}{\text{Annual credit sales}} \times 360$

   $\dfrac{AR}{(sales / 360)}$ Are customers paying bills

2. Inventory turnover ratio $= \dfrac{\text{Cost of goods sold}}{\text{Inventories}}$ *How long do they hold on to inventory? - Sometimes calculated as (Sales/Inventory)*

3. Inventory conversion period $= \dfrac{\text{Inventories}}{\text{Cost of goods sold}} \times 360$

4. Total asset turnover ratio $= \dfrac{\text{Sales}}{\text{Total assets}}$ *Indicates level of assets req'd to make sales. -If sales incr, assets w/ need to increase.*

5. Payables period $= \dfrac{\text{Accounts payable}}{\text{Cost of goods sold per day}} = \dfrac{\text{Accounts payable}}{\text{Cost of goods sold}} \times 360$ *How well/quickly is co. pay's their bills*

C. Debt Utilization Ratios

1. Debt ratio $= \dfrac{\text{Total liabilities}}{\text{Total assets}}$ *How much of co's assets w/ bought debt.*

2. Times interest earned (TIE) $= \dfrac{\text{Operating income}}{\text{Interest expense}}$ *Bankruptcy safety net   How many times company earned their interest expense*

Higher # better

Table 4.1 (*Continued*)

D. Profitability Ratios

1. Return on assets (ROA) = $\dfrac{\text{Net income}}{\text{Total assets}}$ *Are assets being used effectively?*

2. Return on equity (ROE) = $\dfrac{\text{Net income}}{\text{Total stockholders' equity}}$ *How owners are doing?*
   No debt? ROA = ROE
   Is debt being used effectively?

3. Gross profit margin = $\dfrac{\text{Gross profit}}{\text{Net sales}}$ *What are they making on their product?*

4. Operating profit margin = $\dfrac{\text{Operating profit}}{\text{Net sales}}$ *Is $ business profitable?*

5. Net profit margin = $\dfrac{\text{Net profit}}{\text{Net sales}}$ *Very common indicator of profitability*

E. Combination Ratios

1. Cash conversion cycle = Inventory conversion period + Average collection period
   − Payables period

2. ROE = $\dfrac{\text{Net income}}{\text{Sales}} \times \dfrac{\text{Sales}}{\text{Total assets}} \times \dfrac{\text{Total assets}}{\text{Equity}}$

This last equation is known as the *Extended DuPont Equation*. It can also be written as:

$$\text{ROE} = \text{ROA} \times \frac{\text{Total assets}}{\text{Equity}}.$$

Liquidity Ratios

Liquidity ratios, or solvency ratios, measure the extent to which a firm can meet its short-term obligations. One of the best-known and most widely used measures of a firm's solvency is the **current ratio.** This ratio attempts to measure the ability of a firm to meet its debt requirements as they come due.

The **quick ratio,** or **acid test ratio,** is similar to the current ratio in two respects—both measure the firm's liquidity, and both have the same denominator. The numerators, however, differ. The numerator in the quick ratio includes only those most liquid assets that can be quickly turned into cash. These are sometimes called "quick assets," that is, all current assets except inventory.

These two ratios attempt to indicate the probability that a firm will become insolvent. Insolvency occurs when a firm has insufficient cash to pay its bills on time. This is often the first step on the way to bankruptcy court. In general, the larger these two ratios, the less the chance there is of a firm becoming insolvent. Note, however, that if a firm's current assets are composed of obsolete inventory or bad debt that has yet to be written off, although these ratios might appear to be healthy, the firm might actually be insolvent.

Activity Ratios

Activity ratios, or turnover ratios, measure different kinds of business activity within the firm. The general idea underlying all turnover type ratios is that unused or inactive assets are nonearning assets, and actions should be taken to either use these assets more effectively or eliminate them. This is the offset to the idea that a big current ratio or quick ratio is good. A current ratio of, say ten, would almost certainly indicate an inefficient use of assets. For this reason, the ratios in this category are also sometimes called efficiency ratios.

The **_average collection period_** (ACP) is used to scrutinize the liquidity of the firm's accounts receivable. This ratio is useful in assessing the speed at which bills are being collected. If the credit customers are all paying their bills on time, the average collection period will be small. If, however, the company is being lax in collecting its accounts or the firm is carrying a lot of bad debt in its accounts receivable balance (that is, they are not writing off bad debt as it occurs), the ACP will be large.

The following example is designed to illustrate the nature and costs of accounts receivable. The Crawford Company sells, on average, $1,000 of merchandise per day. All sales are for credit on terms of net ten. That is, customers are given ten days to pay their bills without penalty. Assume that sales commence today (on Day 1). The pattern of sales and collections is shown below:

Day	Dollar Amount Sold	Dollar Amount Collected
1	$1,000	$ 0
2	$1,000	$ 0
.	.	.
.	.	.
.	.	.
10	$1,000	$ 0
11	$1,000	$1,000
12	$1,000	$1,000

For ten days, Crawford sells merchandise for which it receives no money. On the eleventh day the firm receives payment for the merchandise sold on day one. On the twelfth day Crawford receives payment for the merchandise sold on day two. And so on. Thus, from day eleven on, inflows match outflows and Crawford's average collection period is ten days.

The merchandise sold through the first ten days is not free; it had to be purchased or produced at a cost. Assuming (for simplicity) a cost of $1,000 per unit, Crawford spent $10,000 for this merchandise. Where did this money come from? Probably from a loan! For how long will Crawford have to fund this inflow-outflow mismatch? If sales continue at $1,000 per day and customers continue paying in ten days, the mismatch must be funded forever! Assuming an interest rate of 12 percent per year, allowing customers to pay in ten days will cost Crawford $1,200 per year in interest.

Of course, Crawford could require all of its customers to pay cash immediately. This policy, however, might negatively affect Crawford's sales. Would you shop at a clothing store that did not accept credit cards? If the annual reduction in sales due to a cash sale-only policy exceeds the annual interest cost on the net ten accounts-receivable balance, the firm should sell on credit.

Consider what would happen if Crawford had a lax collection policy and, accordingly, customers took on average twenty-five days to pay their bills. Now the company's accounts receivable balance would be $25,000 and the annual interest expense would be $3,000. Obviously, it is in a firm's best interest to collect its accounts as quickly as possible as long as the enforcement of collection standards does not severely reduce sales. Specifics concerning the optimal amount of credit to extend, credit terms, and collection policy, are strategic decisions that managers make on a cost-benefit basis.

Note that the denominator in the average collection period formula is credit sales per day. To compute a firm's credit sales per day, merely divide annual credit sales by 360 (for simplicity, assume that there are 360 days per year). Note that the ACP should be computed using the firm's credit sales. Unfortunately, this number is seldom reported. Therefore, if the firm's annual credit sales are unavailable, total sales may be used in the denominator instead.

The **_inventory turnover ratio_** is a gauge of how efficiently a firm is employing its inventory. In general, the larger the inventory turnover ratio, the more efficiently a firm is using its inventory. This ratio, however, is very industry-specific. Whereas for a fruit stand, inventory (hopefully) turns over rapidly, furniture and jewelry stores have very long turnover periods.

Note that it is generally preferable to use cost of goods sold in the numerator to calculate the inventory turnover ratio. This is because most firms carry inventory on their books at cost. If, however, cost of goods sold is unavailable, sales may be used in the numerator instead.

The *inventory conversion period* is analogous to the inventory turnover ratio. As opposed to measuring the number of times per year that inventory "turns over," it measures the average length of time (in days) that it takes to convert raw materials into finished goods into sales. That is, the time period that an inventory item is in stock before it is sold.

The *total asset turnover ratio* is used to measure how productive a firm's total assets are at producing final sales. The higher the ratio, the more efficient a firm is at using its total assets. However, similar to the inventory turnover ratio, this ratio varies from industry to industry. The turnover of total assets per year varies from a low value of around once per year for heavy manufacturing industries (for example, steel mills) to over a dozen times a year for advertising agencies that own virtually no tangible assets.

The *payables period,* or accounts payable turnover ratio, measures how promptly a company pays its trade accounts. In essence, this ratio is the liability equivalent of the average collection period. If a firm purchases $1,000 per day with credit terms of net ten, paying all of its accounts in ten days will provide the firm with, effectively, a $10,000 interest-free loan. It might be instructive to think of one firm's accounts payable balance as another firm's accounts receivable balance.

Industry credit terms usually include a discount for early payment. Typical credit terms are 2/10 net thirty, where a firm can take a 2 percent discount on the purchase of materials if it pays the supplier within ten days, otherwise the entire invoice price must be paid in thirty days.

Assume, again, purchases of $1,000 per day or total purchases of $360,000 per year. As shown above, if a firm facing these terms pays in ten days, it receives a $10,000 interest-free "loan" from its supplier. If, however, the firm pays in thirty days, the "loan" from the supplier will be $30,000. The additional $20,000, though, has a cost. The firm will lose the 2 percent discount, which is equal to $7,200 per year. This implies an effective cost on the $20,000 loan of 36 percent per year ($7,200/$20,000).

In general, the effective cost of not taking the discount is given by:

$$\frac{\text{Discount percent}}{\text{Extra days if not take discount}} \times 360$$

$$= \frac{2\%}{(30-10)} \times 360 = 36\%.$$

If the firm can borrow from its bank at less than 36 percent per year, it should pay its supplier in ten days, and if it needs the additional $20,000, should borrow it from the bank. If a firm has a large and growing Days payable ratio, it could indicate that the firm is "borrowing" from its suppliers because it is having difficulty securing funds from other sources (that is, the bank). Obviously, this would not be a good sign.

Problem 4.5a　What is the effective cost of not taking the discount for credit terms of 3/15 net sixty?

$$= 24\%.$$

Problem 4.5b What is the effective cost of not taking the discount for credit terms of 1/5 net forty-five?

$$= 9\%.$$

Note that the higher the discount percent or the smaller the gap between the discount period and the non-discount period (that is, extra days if not taking the discount in the equation above), the larger the effective cost of not taking the discount.

Debt Utilization Ratios

Debt utilization ratios are gauges of the extent to which a firm finances its operations with borrowed money rather than owner's equity. Using debt to finance assets is called leverage. To visualize the benefits and risks of leverage, consider the following example.

Several years ago, Tom Crowler, using $100,000 of his own money (stockholder's equity), opened a deli. Tom's deli produces annual earnings (which, because the firm has no debt and for simplicity we assume no taxes, is equal to operating income) of $20,000.

Two years ago, Tom borrowed $100,000 to open a second deli. This doubled his operating income to $40,000. However, because Tom now had to pay interest on his debt (annual interest rate of 10 percent on a loan of $100,000), his net income only rose to $30,000.

The benefit of using debt to finance his second store was that for no additional personal investment, Tom increased his net annual return from $20,000 to $30,000. This increased his expected return on his $100,000 investment from 20 percent to 30 percent per year. True to one of the most basic premises in finance, however, higher expected return involves higher risk. The risk of borrowing the money to open the second store is that now Tom has to pay $10,000 per year in interest. If Tom cannot pay the interest he will technically default on his loan and perhaps lose his stores. This could occur if in any given year his operating income falls below $5,000 per store.

Now Tom is considering borrowing another $100,000 to open a third deli. This will increase his expected total operating income to $60,000 per year, however because he now will have to pay $20,000 per year in interest (10 percent of $200,000), his expected net income will only rise to $40,000 per year. Nonetheless, his return on his initial investment is now expected to rise to 40 percent per year.

Tom is using leverage to boost his annual return. Using leverage, however, adds risk. With three stores, if in any given year his operating income falls below $6,667 per store ($20,000/3), Tom will default on his loans. Note that the additional borrowing raised the break-even threshold from $5,000 per year to $6,667 per year. Furthermore, note that we assumed that Tom could borrow an additional $100,000 at the same interest rate. This might not be valid. In general, the greater the amounts of debt relative to stockholder equity, the higher the interest rate. If the interest rate on the second loan were indeed higher than 10 percent, the break-even threshold level of operating income per store would be even higher.

Thus, the use of leverage represents a tradeoff between risk and return. The greater the leverage, the greater the expected return, but also the greater the risk (in particular, of default). Debt utilization ratios, which are sometimes also referred to as leverage ratios, attempt to measure the risk inherent in the firm's use of debt financing.

The ***debt ratio*** measures the proportion of all assets that are financed with debt. In general, the higher the debt ratio, the higher the risk of default. Additionally, the higher the debt ratio the more difficult it will be for a firm to obtain additional debt at a reasonable cost when needed. A high debt ratio firm will often find that funds are only available at extremely high interest rates.

Another common debt measure is the ***debt to equity ratio,*** which is calculated as total liabilities divided by stockholders equity. Because:

$$\text{Assets} = \text{Debt} + \text{Equity},$$

given the debt to equity ratio, one can calculate the debt ratio or vice versa. For example, assume that a firm has a debt to equity ratio of .5. If Debt was $50 and Equity was $100, the debt to equity ratio would be $50/100 = .5$. Because Debt + Equity = Assets, this firm would have assets of $150 and the debt ratio (Debt/Assets) would be $50/150 = .33 = 33\%$.

The ***times interest earned (TIE) ratio*** measures how many times the firm's annual operating earnings cover its debt-servicing charges (mainly interest). The larger this ratio, the less likely a firm is to default during a major downturn in sales. Interest expense represents a fixed cost that must be paid regardless of how many units a company produces or sells. With a TIE of 10, a firm's operating earnings would have to fall by more than 90 percent before the firm would be unable to pay its fixed interest expense. In the deli example above, with two stores Tom's TIE was 4 (40,000/10,000). Adding a third store caused the TIE to fall to 3 (60,000/20,000).

Profitability Ratios

The profitability ratios reflect the joint effects of the preceding three sets of ratios: activity, liquidity, and leverage. They compare a firm's earnings with various factors that are necessary to generate the earnings. These ratios can shed light on which aspects of the business are particularly profitable and which are not.

The ***net profit margin*** measures the percent by which (all else equal) the selling price of a firm's products can decline before the firm suffers losses. ***Return on assets*** (ROA) measures the after-tax profitability per dollar invested in total assets. Asset intensive businesses, such as steel mills, usually have low rates of return on their huge investments in assets, whereas service companies generally have high rates of return on their small asset investments. The ***return on equity*** (ROE) measures the overall results of operations from the owner's standpoint. This ratio reflects both the profitability with which total investment or total assets have been employed and how effectively the firm has used leverage. The ***gross profit margin*** and ***operating profit margin*** will be discussed in greater detail later in the chapter.

Note that the difference between a firm's ROA and ROE is attributable solely to a firm's use of borrowed funds. If a firm has no debt, these two ratios will yield identical numerical values.

Combination Ratios

Sometimes ratios are combined to produce other ratios. A trend in the combined ratio can be viewed as a combination of parts, and perhaps a single part can be identified as a strength or weakness. The two most commonly used combination ratios are the cash conversion cycle and the DuPont equation.

The ***cash conversion cycle*** (CCC) equals the length of time (in days) between a firm's actual cash expenditures for the resources used to produce products for sale (or to purchase goods for resale) and the collection of cash receipts from the sale of those products. Thus, the CCC represents the average amount of time that a dollar is tied up in current assets. Effective asset management requires that a firm shorten the cash conversion cycle as much as possible without negatively affecting operations. Consider the following example.

Values for selected accounts from the Income statement and Balance sheet of the SkerMax Company are listed below:

Annual credit sales	$360,000,000
Cost of goods sold	270,000,000
Accounts receivable balance	54,000,000
Inventories	90,000,000
Accounts payable balance	36,000,000

Problem 4.6a   What is SkerMax's average collection period, inventory turnover period, and payables period?

Answer:

Average collection period = 54 days
Inventory conversion period = 120 days
Payables period = 48 days

Problem 4.6b   What is SkerMax's Cash Conversion Cycle?

Answer:

120 + 54 − 48 = 126 days.

The first two periods indicate that there is a gap of, on average, 174 days between the time SkerMax purchases raw materials until it sells a finished good and then collects cash for that good. Assuming that SkerMax purchases approximately the same amount of materials every day, then daily purchases average $270,000,000 divided by 360 = $750,000 per day. SkerMax must finance these purchases in some way. The first 48 days of financing is provided by SkerMax's suppliers (interest free, assuming that credit terms are net 48—see discussion concerning accounts payable above). The remaining 126 days of financing must come from some other source, presumably a bank loan. The average size of this loan will be:

($750,000 per day) × (126 days) = $94,500,000.

If the bank loan interest rate is 10 percent, SkerMax is paying on average $9,450,000 in annual interest to cover the time that its current assets sit idle.

Problem 4.7   If, without negatively affecting operations, management can reduce the average collection period to thirty-five days (perhaps by enforcing a tighter collection policy) and reduce the inventory conversion period to seventy-four days (perhaps by speeding up the production and sales processes), and maintain the same forty-eight-day payables period, what will be annual interest expense? (Assume a bank loan interest rate of 10 percent.)

Answer:

= $4,575,000

thereby increasing the firm's net profit before taxes by $4,875,000.

The *extended DuPont equation* is a combination ratio that defines a firm's ROE as a function of activity, profitability, and leverage. The ROE is a ratio that is closely watched by stockholders and management. If a firm's ROE declines, the extended DuPont equation can be used to identify the specific reason for the decline. The equation is:

$$\text{ROE} = \frac{\text{Net income}}{\text{Sales}} \times \frac{\text{Sales}}{\text{Total assets}} \times \frac{\text{Total assets}}{\text{Equity}}.$$

—ROE is dependent upon Co's profitability, asset utilization & use of leverage

Note that the first component of the equation is the net profit margin and the second component is the total asset turnover ratio. The third component of the equation is called the equity multiplier. It indicates the impact on ROE of a firm's use of leverage. Note that because,

$$\text{Total assets} = \text{Total Liabilities} + \text{Equity},$$

another way to measure the equity multiplier is:

$$\text{Equity multiplier} = \frac{1}{1 - \text{Debt ratio}}.$$

If a firm's debt ratio increases, then (all else constant, including net income) the firm is using less equity to finance its assets and therefore its return on equity will naturally increase.

The DuPont equation shows that if a firm experiences a decrease in its ROE, the decrease can be attributed to either a decrease in the firm's profitability (inefficiencies in the management of the income statement), a decrease in the firm's asset turnover (inefficiencies in the management of the balance sheet), or a change in the firm's capital structure (that is, debt ratio).

4.5.3 Analyzing Financial Ratios

There are two main ways to analyze financial ratios for a given firm: trend analysis and industry comparison analysis. The latter method involves comparing the ratios of one firm to those of a peer group of firms. The notion here is that different industries should possess distinctive financial characteristics. That is, for certain industries, certain values should be expected. For example, one would probably expect that the average asset turnover ratio in the electric utility industry would be lower than the asset turnover ratio in the temp-services industry. In fact, the average asset turnover ratio for utilities is 0.7 and for the temp-services industry is over 5.0. An analyst should attach a caution flag to a ratio for a given firm that deviates substantially from the average of that ratio across all other firms in the industry.

Trend analysis involves the comparison of the same ratio for the same firm over a period of years. Though not always available, it is best to have at least three years of ratio data to identify meaningful trends. Ratios that exhibit trends should be more carefully investigated. Is the trend good or bad? What specific factor is causing the trend? Often, comparing the trends of two or more sets of ratios can identify specific problem areas. Note the obvious trend in the following set of current ratios for the Bakker Company:

	2004	2005	2006
Current ratio	1.5	2.0	2.5

This trend is not necessarily bad, but it is curious. What is causing the current ratio to increase? Let's look at the trend in Bakker's quick ratio:

	2004	2005	2006
Quick ratio	0.8	1.3	1.8

Because the quick ratio is also increasing, the trend in the current ratio is not due to an inventory buildup, so let's look at the trend in the average collection period:

	2004	2005	2006
Average collection period	30	40	50

The trend here seems to indicate that the increase in the current ratio is due to a slower collection period. This, in turn, might indicate a strategic shift in management's policy concerning credit collections (relax credit standards to increase sales) or it may indicate a problem. One possibility is that Bakker is carrying an ever-increasing number of bad debt accounts that are not being written off. If a problem exists, management must formulate a solution or workout. Creditors and stockholders, perhaps via discussions with Bakker's management, must discover the true reason for this trend.

4.5.4 Limitations of Ratios

Whereas financial ratios can reveal important information about a firm, it is very important to understand the limitations of ratio analysis. Ratios are useful in theory, but their value might be limited in practice. This is not to say that ratios are worthless. Ratios can alert analysts and management to positive or negative trends or to policies that deviate from industry standards. They cannot, however, provide definitive answers, nor are they necessarily predictive of future outcomes. Ratios should be viewed merely as screening devices. They indicate areas of potential weakness or strength, revealing items that might need further investigation.

Three specific factors limit the usefulness of financial ratios. First, all financial ratios that rely on balance sheet values are computed using "snapshot in time" data. Balance sheet values are stock measures— they are the values of a firm's assets and liabilities on a specific date (perhaps December 31, 2006). The more liquid the asset or liability, the more that number will deviate from its reported value throughout the rest of the year. A firm that reports $1,000,000 in its checking account on December 31, 2006 might have a negative cash balance two days later after making payroll and paying off suppliers. A retail clothing store that reports a relatively small accounts receivable balance in March (and therefore will have a small computed ACP) would report a much larger balance (and would therefore have a large ACP) in December if most of it Christmas sales were credit sales.

The snapshot nature of balance sheet data also allows firms to "window dress" their statements for reporting purposes. For example, if a firm wants to spruce up its current ratio, all it needs to do is borrow long-term money on December 28 and deposit the money in its checking account. Then at fiscal year end (December 31), it can report a healthy cash balance.

You don't think this happens in the real world? Reportedly, to window-dress its current account ratios, several years ago a firm sold a corporate jet in late December and deposited the cash in its checking account for fiscal year-end. The firm then bought the jet back in early January. This happened three years in a row! And each time the firm paid more for the jet in January than what it sold the jet for in December!

Second, financial ratios are calculated with accounting data, not market values. Accounting data is based on an asset's historical cost. Market values are based on the asset's present value.

Consider, for example, a firm that purchased a piece of land thirty years ago in a major metropolitan area. The purchase price of the land was $300,000. Because land neither appreciates nor depreciates on a balance sheet (that is, it is always carried at cost), the current listed value of this land on the firm's balance sheet is still $300,000. In fact, assume that the land is actually worth (its present value) $3,000,000. Thus, every ratio that involves this firm's total assets (total asset turnover, return on assets) will be inaccurate.

Additionally, as demonstrated earlier in this chapter, accounting data (particularly income statement data) can be legally (and illegally) manipulated. If net income has been inflated and is thus neither indicative of current nor future profitability, then all ratios that involve net income (for example, ROE and ROA) can be misleading.

Also, a large and growing net profit margin does not necessarily indicate positive net cash flow (recall Derrick Dickerson). Creditors and stockholders would much rather see evidence of positive cash flow than positive net income. This is why construction of a Statement of Cash Flows is just as important as computation of a firm's ratios.

The third factor that limits the usefulness of financial ratios is the lack of a standard. Consider, for example, the current ratio. What is a good current ratio value? The standard rule of thumb offered by bankers is 2. This, it is reasoned, allows shrinkage in the value of the current assets by 50 percent before the firm is unable to meet its maturing short-term obligations. Another standard often used is the average current ratio of all firms in the industry. Industry average ratios for nearly every industry and ratio imaginable are computed and published annually by Dun and Bradstreet Information Services (Industry Norms and Key Business Ratios), Robert Morris Associates (Annual Statement Studies), Standard & Poor's Corporation (Rating Handbook and Industry Surveys), and Gale Research, Incorporated (Manufacturing U.S.A. Industry Analyses).

Suppose that a firm's managers find in one of these publications that the average current ratio for a firm in the industry in which they operate is 2, with the lowest current ratio in the industry being 1.5 and the highest ratio being 2.6. If the average is 2, then what would be better than average: a current ratio of 1.8 or a current ratio of 2.2? Hopefully the firm's managers are not striving to merely be average; hopefully, their goal is to be better than average, to be the best!

Now suppose that for the firm described above the managers develop a new production and sales system that, with no negative effect on total sales:

1. allows them to perfectly match cash inflows to outflows, thereby eliminating the need to maintain a cash balance,

2. allows them to sell on a cash basis only, thereby maintaining an accounts receivable balance of zero and,

3. allows them to produce their product on demand, thereby eliminating the need to carry any inventory balance (assume that the product can be materialized out of thin air and requires no raw materials).

This firm would have a current ratio of zero. Is that inefficient? Would bankers not make loans to this firm because its current ratio is below 2? Would you not buy stock in this company? In fact, this is a tremendous firm. The sole purpose of assets is to produce sales. If a firm can reduce its investment in assets and produce the same level of sales, it should do so. Assets must be financed and financing costs money. The fewer assets a firm needs to efficiently produce sales, the lower the financing costs that are associated with assets, and thus the higher the annual net cash flow.

Obviously, one must be very careful when using standards. Deviations from industry standards are merely curious indications of areas that should be investigated further. Additionally, as in the example above, one might find that a deviation indicates something very positive; an innovative, aggressive management.

Considering these three limitations to ratio analysis, we again stress that whereas ratio analysis might be useful for identifying potential problems (or strengths), one must use ratio analysis very carefully.

4.6 Financial Statement Analysis: An Example

We will use the data in the following case study to illustrate the construction and analysis of common size statements and ratios. Although the main focus of the analysis of the data will be from the point of view of a financial manager, items of specific interest to creditors or stockholders will be noted.

Several years ago, Karl Marker founded S-A-S Beers, Incorporated, a microbrewery located near Eugene, Oregon. His product, S-A-S Logger-Beer, was an instant success. Marker, a descendent of a long line of Austrian brewmeisters, moved to Spokane, Washington, from Grospedersdorf, Austria, in 1983. Although his dream was to work as a head brewmaster for an American brewery, he was only able to find work as a truck driver for a Spokane logging company. He drove a logging truck throughout the northwestern United States and Canada for fifteen years, during which time he became well acquainted with American beers and American beer consumption. Marker's thick German accent, talent as a master storyteller and witty personality made him a type of local folk hero throughout the logging community. This plus his vocal, though subtle and humorous, criticisms of American beers caused him to become known among his logging friends as "the SASS-MEISTER."

On a logging run through Oregon in 1997, Marker discovered that the water from a logging river that ran near Eugene had a smooth and unique "hickory" taste. He recognized instantly that it could produce a very fine-tasting beer. In 1998, he leased a bankrupt lumber mill on the river and began to experiment with brewing beer. By 2000, using a secret family recipe, special hops imported from his hometown of Grospedersdorf, and the "hickory water" from the river, he had perfected and patented a special brewing and aging process that produced amazingly smooth tasting, dark ale. Marker named the ale S-A-S Logger-Beer (the letters stand for smooth as silk, though are also related to his nickname; Logger-Beer was chosen because his original target market was loggers, though it is obviously also a spoof on lager beer).

With $1,100,000 of venture capital from family members in Austria and a logging company in British Columbia and a $600,000 ten-year term loan from a local bank, by 2001 Marker had converted the lumberyard into a fully modern brewery. He also purchased an adjoining piece of land on which he constructed a warehouse. Sales, which in 2001 totaled $2,100,000, grew to $5,800,000 in 2002 and to $9,450,000 in 2003. S-A-S Logger-Beer is now sold nationally, and last year was picked by the "Beer of the Month" club as one of its August feature beers. Marker is currently negotiating with a bottling and distribution company in Tokyo to begin selling S-A-S Logger Beer in Japan and, perhaps, throughout Southeast Asia. Although S-A-S Beers, Inc. incurred sizable losses in 2001 and 2002, the company reported its first profit of $300,000 in 2003. As evidenced by the accompanying financial statements in Table 4.2, sales have continued to grow and S-A-S Beers has been profitable in each of the following three years. Dividends of $100,000 and $200,000 were paid in 2004 and 2005, respectively.

S-A-S Logger-Beer is only sold in twelve-ounce bottles, and packaged in six-packs. As the beer has grown in popularity, Marker has increased the wholesale price per six-pack each year. The wholesale price per six-pack was $2.75 in 2004, $3.50 in 2005, and $4.50 in 2006. Unfortunately, increased competition in the microbrewery market makes such large future price increases unlikely, but growth in volume should continue. In fact, Marker estimates that sales in 2007 will grow by approximately 26 percent to a level of $36,000,000. Of greater immediate concern to Marker is recent fluctuations of the U.S. Dollar/Deutsche Mark exchange rate which has made it increasingly difficult to estimate the future cost of hops (expenditures on hops account for approximately 40 percent of the firm's cost of goods sold).

4.6.1 Analysis of Common Size Financial Statements for S-A-S Beers, Inc.

The income statements for 2004, 2005, and 2006 and the common size balance sheets for 2004 through 2006 for S-A-S Beers, Incorporated are shown in Tables 4.3 and 4.4, respectively. Note that in the common size income statements, the profit measures have been renamed (also highlighted in bold) as the **gross profit margin,** the **operating profit margin,** and the **net profit margin.** Pay particular attention to the size and relationship between these profit measures over time. The term margin implies the difference per unit. For example, the gross profit margin refers to the gross profit per unit sold. That is, in 2006, for every dollar in sales revenue, the firm earned a gross profit of 24.2 cents.

The common size income statements for S-A-S Beers reveal interesting trends in the firm's expenses and profit margins. The net profit margin has gradually increased over the three-year period. Generally, this is good. It usually means that either the gross profit margin has increased or the firm's operating expense margin has decreased.

Table 4.2

Income Statements
S-A-S Beers, Incorporated
For the Years Ending December 31, 2004, 2005, and 2006[a]

	2004	2005	2006
Sales revenue, net	15,000	20,500	28,500
Cost of goods sold	10,600	15,000	21,600
Gross profit	4,400	5,500	6,900
Selling & adm. expenses	900	1,300	1,800
Advertising	400	300	200
Repairs and maintenance	200	200	200
R&D expenditures	300	200	100
Lease payments	600	600	600
Depreciation	400	600	700
Operating profit	1,600	2,300	3,300
Interest income	0	0	200
Interest expense	200	400	700
Profit before taxes	1,400	1,900	2,800
Taxes	400	500	800
Net income	1,000	1,400	2,000

Balance Sheets
S-A-S Beers, Incorporated
For the Years Ending December 31, 2004, 2005, and 2006[a]

	2004	2005	2006
Cash	100	100	200
Net accounts receivable	1,000	1,900	3,100
Inventories	1,400	2,900	4,700
Current assets	2,500	4,900	8,000
Land	800	800	900
Buildings and equipment	5,500	6,200	7,100
Less accumulated depreciation	(1,000)	(1,600)	(2,300)
Net fixed assets	5,300	5,400	5,700
Total assets	7,800	10,300	13,700
Bank loan (line of credit)	0	300	1,200
Accounts payable	1,200	1,800	2,300
Accruals	200	300	200
Current portion of L.T. debt	200	200	200
Total current liabilities	1,600	2,600	3,900
Long-term bank loan	4,000	4,200	4,900
Common stock ($0.15 par value)	1,500	1,500	1,500
Retained earnings	700	2,000	3,400
Total liabilities and equity	7,800	10,300	13,700

[a]All figures in thousands of dollars.

Table 4.3

Common Size Income Statements
S-A-S Beers, Incorporated
For the Years Ending December 31, 2004, 2005, and 2006

	2004	2005	2006
Sales revenue, net	100.0%	100.0%	100.0%
Cost of goods sold	70.7%	73.2%	75.8%
Gross profit margin	**29.3%**	**26.8%**	**24.2%**
Selling & adm. expenses	6.0%	6.3%	6.3%
Advertising	2.7%	1.5%	0.7%
Repairs and maintenance	1.3%	1.0%	0.7%
R&D expenditures	2.0%	1.0%	0.4%
Lease payments	4.0%	2.9%	2.1%
Depreciation	2.7%	2.9%	2.5%
Operating profit margin	**10.7%**	**11.2%**	**11.6%**
Interest income	0.0%	0.0%	0.7%
Interest expense	1.3%	2.0%	2.5%
Profit before taxes	**9.3%**	**9.3%**	**9.8%**
Taxes	2.7%	2.4%	2.8%
Net profit margin	**6.7%**	**6.8%**	**7.0%**

Table 4.4

Common Size Balance Sheets
S-A-S Beers, Incorporated
For the Years Ending December 31, 2004, 2005, and 2006

	2004	2005	2006
Cash	1.3%	1.0%	1.5%
Net accounts receivable	12.8%	18.4%	22.6%
Inventories	17.9%	28.2%	34.3%
Total current assets	**32.1%**	**47.6%**	**58.4%**
Land	10.3%	7.8%	6.6%
Buildings and equipment	70.5%	60.2%	51.8%
Less accumulated depreciation	(12.8%)	(15.5%)	(16.8%)
Net fixed assets	67.9%	52.4%	41.6%
Total assets	**100.0%**	**100.0%**	**100.0%**
Bank loan (line of credit)	0.0%	2.9%	8.8%
Accounts payable	15.4%	17.5%	16.8%
Accruals	2.6%	2.9%	1.5%
Current portion of L.T. debt	2.6%	1.9%	1.5%
Total current liabilities	**20.5%**	**25.2%**	**28.5%**
Long-term bank loan	51.3%	40.8%	35.8%
Common stock ($0.15 par value)	19.2%	14.6%	10.9%
Retained earnings	9.0%	19.4%	24.8%
Total liabilities and equity	**100.0%**	**100.0%**	**100.0%**

In the case of S-A-S Beers, however, there has been a serious deterioration in the firm's gross profit margin from 29.3 percent to 24.2 percent—a decline of more than five percentage points! This margin basically measures the sales price per unit minus the variable cost per unit. We know that S-A-S Beers' sales price per unit is increasing, therefore the declining margin implies that costs per unit are rising even faster. Perhaps the firm is experiencing runaway labor costs or is being forced to pay overtime wages to meet its rapidly expanding production schedule. Or, possibly there has been a major run-up in the cost of one or more of the products' inputs (for example, the imported hops). Regardless of the cause, because it represents the core of a firm's business, deterioration in a firm's gross profit margin represents a disturbing trend.

To offset this trend, we can see from the common size income statement, that S-A-S Beers has reduced its relative spending on all operating expenses (see the percent of net sales declines in selling and administrative expenses, advertising, repairs and maintenance, and R&D. These spending categories are often referred to as discretionary accounts in that management has some degree of control over how much to spend (or to cut back) on these items. This strategy might have been proper and strategic, or it might be a stopgap measure.

The deteriorating gross margin (over which the company has minimal control) might have caused the company to become more efficient in its discretionary spending. The company has received a great deal of "free" advertising, and if the product is already successful, less R&D might be required. On the other hand, these relative reductions could be a shortsighted way of maintaining the bottom line. Increased advertising could help the firm to differentiate S-A-S Logger Beer from the competition and thereby allow the company to increase the beer's selling price even faster. Increased spending on R&D could help the firm discover substitutes for high cost inputs to reduce the growth rate in cost of goods sold. Increased spending on repairs and maintenance could improve the efficiency of the production process.

One final interesting issue concerns the appearance of "other income" in 2006. This item "boosted" S-A-S Beers' net income for 2006 by 1.1 percent. More specifically, without "other income," the company's net profit margin in 2006 would have been lower than it was in 2004 and 2005. Analysts would need to know the source of this income and, even more important, whether this was a one-time event or if this is income that will be repeated in the future.

As insiders, the firm's managers should know whether these trends are strategic or stopgap. Of course the managers would want creditors and stockholders to assume the former cause, and might provide little direct information, or perhaps even provide misleading information if the latter cause is the case. Thus, creditors and stockholders must be careful to question what management tells them, and need to look at additional measures to ascertain the possible truth.

The common size balance sheets for S-A-S Beers also reveal a few curious trends. First, between 2004 and 2006, net accounts receivable and inventories increased substantially as a percent of total assets. In 2006, these two current asset accounts made up nearly 57 percent of the firm's total assets. In 2004, they accounted for only 31 percent of total assets. Second, there was a significant increase in the relative size of the bank loan through the period, from no bank debt in 2004, to 2.9 percent of total assets in 2005 to 8.8 percent of total assets in 2006. The relative decrease in long-term debt over the corresponding time period indicates that the firm merely swapped short-term debt for long-term debt. Finally, although inventories nearly doubled in percentage terms from 2004 to 2006, accounts payable changed very little. Because accounts payable are related to the purchase of raw materials that are used to produce inventories, one would expect (ceteris paribus) the relative size of these two accounts to change in tandem. One must wonder if the company's suppliers are squeezing S-A-S Beers for faster payments of its trade accounts, and how S-A-S Beers is financing its inventory.

The S-A-S Beers financial manager should carefully investigate these income statement and balance sheet trends. Ratios and other techniques (if necessary) should be applied and examined to determine if continuation of any trends will negatively affect future performance. If so, a plan should be developed to reverse the adverse trend(s). This plan should then be communicated to creditors and stockholders for them to assess its viability, and to convince them to maintain their faith in the ability of management to continue to operate the firm efficiently.

4.6.2 Analysis of Financial Ratios for S-A-S Beers, Inc.

The financial ratios for S-A-S Beers, Incorporated for 2004 and 2005 are listed in Table 4.5. The cash conversion cycle and the components of the extended DuPont equation for 2004 and 2005 appear at the bottom of the table.

Table 4.5

S-A-S Beers, Incorporated
Comparative Financial Ratios

	2004	2005	2006
Liquidity Ratios			
Current ratio	1.6	1.9	_____
Quick ratio	0.69	0.77	_____
Asset Utilization Ratios			
Average collection period[a]	24.0 days	33.4 days	_____
Inventory turnover ratio	7.6	5.2	_____
Inventory conversion period	47.5 days	69.6 days	_____
Total asset turnover ratio	1.9	2.0	_____
Payables period[b]	40.8 days	43.2 days	_____
Debt Utilization Ratios			
Debt ratio	71.8%	66.0%	_____
Times interest earned	8.0	5.75	_____
Profitability Ratios			
Net profit margin	6.7%	6.8%	_____
Return on assets	12.8%	13.6%	_____
Return on equity	45.55	40.0%	_____

Cash Conversion Cycle

2004:	47.5	+	24.0	−	40.8	=	30.7 days
2005:	_____	+	_____	−	_____	=	_____
2006:	_____	+	_____	−	_____	=	_____

Extended DuPont Equation

	Net profit margin	×	Total asset turnover ratio	×	Equity Multiplier
2004:	6.7%	×	1.9	×	3.55
2005:	_____	×	_____	×	_____
2006:	_____	×	_____	×	_____

[a] Based on total net sales because credit sales unavailable.

[b] Credit terms are 2/10 net 30.

Problem 4.8   Verify that all of the computed ratios for 2004 and 2005 are correct. Then, fill in the last column of Table 4.5 by computing the financial ratios for S-A-S Beers for 2006. Try to do this without referring back to the ratio formulas in Table 4.1 if possible. Most ratios actually make some sense if you think about the term some, or think about what the ratio is trying to measure. For example, return on assets implies the dollar return that is earned on the firm's assets. The most basic measure of dollar return is net income. Thus, ROA = net income divided by total assets. In fact, all "return" ratios are just net income divided by some balance sheet account. Try it out to see how you do first; then compare your attempt to the answers listed below.

Problem 4.9   Fill in the components in Table 4.5 of the Cash Conversion Cycle and the extended DuPont equation for 2005 and 2006. For the latter, multiply the components together to verify that they equal the ROE for 2005 and 2006. Note that due to rounding, the numbers may not match exactly. For example, according to the components of the DuPont equation listed in table 4.5, for 2004, ROE = 6.7% × 1.9 × 3.6 = 45.8%. If instead, all ratios were rounded off to four decimal places, we would have, ROE = 6.667% × 1.923 × 3.545 = 45.5%.

Answer to Problem 4.8: Current ratio = 2.1, quick ratio = 0.85, average collection period = 39.2 days, inventory turnover ratio = 4.6 times, inventory conversion period = 78.3 days, total asset turnover = 2.08 times, days payable ratio = 38.3 days, debt ratio = 64.2 percent, times interest earned = 4.7 times, net profit margin = 7.0 percent, return on assets = 14.6 percent, and ROE = 40.8 percent.

Answer to Problem 4.9: The Cash Conversion cycle for 2005 is 59.8 days and for 2006 is 79.2 days. The extended DuPont equation for 2005 is:

$$ROE = 6.8\% \times 2.0 \times 2.94 = 40.0\%$$

and for 2006 it is:

$$ROE = 7.0\% \times 2.08 \times 2.8 = 40.8\%$$

Trends indicated by Table 4.5 can now be evaluated to perhaps better understand some of the issues raised in our analysis of the common size statements. An increase in the current ratio will generally be due to an increase in accounts receivable, inventory, or both. The increased quick ratio for S-A-S Beers indicates that buildups in both accounts receivable and inventory are at issue. A potential accounts receivable problem is shown by the increase in the average collection period from twenty-four to thirty-nine days. It is taking S-A-S beers longer to collect on its accounts, or the company is carrying bad debt in its accounts receivable balance that it has yet to write off.

Perhaps the firm has expanded its sales base too quickly. As a company expands its sales nationally, and perhaps even internationally, it becomes increasingly more difficult to manage its collections. Assume that a client located ten miles from a firm's operations owes the firm $2,000. If the client's payment is late, one merely needs to drive over to the client's office to demand payment. Now assume that the firm's operations are located on the west coast and the client is located on the east coast, or even worse, in a foreign country.

Obviously, the greater the distance and the smaller the account, the more difficult it will be to actually collect cash on the sale.

The decrease in the inventory turnover ratio from 7.6 times per year to 4.6 times per year, suggests that S-A-S Beers is either building up inventory balances or that it is carrying obsolete inventory on its books. Regardless, slower inventory turnover can be particularly problematic for a beer company. The USDA now requires that beer be date-stamped for freshness. Beer not sold before the expiration date is essentially worthless. Slower turnover increases that chance that some inventory might not be sold before its expiration date.

The credit terms from S-A-S Beers' suppliers are 2/10 net thirty. S-A-S Beers, on average, paid its suppliers (days payable ratio) in forty-one days in 2004, forty-three days in 2005, and thirty-eight days in 2006. Although payment speed improved in 2006, in both years S-A-S Beers forfeited the discount and paid beyond the net period. Passing up the discount implies that S-A-S Beers might be having difficulty getting financing from its bank. Paying late implies that S-A-S Beers is having a cash flow problem. Though suppliers will tolerate late payments for a time period, at some point they will begin to demand prompt payment. If payment of all accounts is not made, suppliers may stop delivering to the firm altogether.

The decrease in S-A-S Beers' TIE coverage ratio from 7.0 to 6.3 to 4.0, in 2004, 2005, and 2006, respectively, is due to large annual increases in interest expense. Because the debt ratio has actually declined, the higher interest payments might be due to higher interest rates on existing debt. This, in turn, could be due solely to economic conditions (interest rates might be rising in general). On the other hand, it could be that creditors are beginning to charge S-A-S Beers higher interest rates on borrowed funds because they perceive that there has been an increase in the company's overall risk level. Note the increase in the Cash Conversion Cycle from thirty-one days in 2004 to over seventy-nine days in 2006. This number represents the average number of days that current assets sit idle. The firm's bank might interpret this change as evidence of managerial inefficiency, resulting in a higher cost of borrowed funds.

The profit measures have shown little change. The DuPont equation shows that the slight increase in ROE is due mainly to the higher net profit margin and less total debt. Recall, however, that net income for 2006 includes "other income" that might or might not be repeated in the future. If this "other income" is removed from net income for 2006, the net profit margin for the year falls to 6.0 percent and ROE falls to 34.7 percent.

Other income is one of the manipulation items that affected income statement quality discussed earlier in the chapter. As you can see, the issue of income statement quality affects all measures of financial analysis. That is why a solid understanding of accounting and manipulation techniques is important to effective financial analysis.

In summary, S-A-S Beers does not appear to be a company on the verge of bankruptcy. Indeed, the company exhibits many signs of strength. There are, however, certain areas that deserve further investigation. These include the firm's receivables, inventory, payment to suppliers, relationship with the bank, and perhaps some quality concerns about net income in 2006. The financial manager of S-A-S Beers must decide whether any of these items need to be addressed specifically. The manager must evaluate the effect of these items on the firm's future ability to generate positive and growing cash flow. Finally, the manager must decide what, if anything, should be communicated to the firm's creditors and stockholders (both current and prospective) about these issues. Creditors and stockholders, on the other hand, must determine what any of these trends or relationships implies about the firm's ability to repay its loans or produce a positive return on investment.

Financial ratio analysis seldom produces definitive answers. Instead, ratio analysis is more like detective work. The detective analyzes the crime scene to obtain clues. Clues are further investigated and collaborative evidence is sought to draw preliminary conclusions. The crime scene data is then further investigated to see if additional evidence, perhaps overlooked in the first round, can be found to either support or refute the preliminary conclusions. This process continues until a justifiable conclusion can be made.

You should now possess a healthy concern for the quality of financial statement and understand how to apply the basic tools and techniques of financial analysis to ascertain the strengths and weaknesses of a company. You should also have some understanding of how to apply and evaluate these tools and techniques from three different viewpoints—specifically, as a creditor, as a stockholder, and as a financial manager. As such, you are equipped to enter the world of financial detective work. We know that you will find the task to be challenging. We hope you also find it to be interesting as much as rewarding.

Assignment 4.1 ··········

Name:_____   Date:_____

Answer the following questions in the space provided.

1. Income statements of Labal Company for 2005 and 2006 are as follows:

Income Statements
Labal Company
For the Years Ending September 30, 2005 and 2006

	2005	2006
Net sales	$1,900	$2,200
Cost of goods sold	1,196	1,410
Gross profit	704	790
Operating expenses	514	582
Operating profit	190	208
Income taxes	80	90
Net income	$ 110	$ 118

a. Prepare common size income statements for 2005 and 2006.

	2005	2006
Net sales	100%	100%
Cost of goods sold	63%	64%
Gross profit	37%	36%
Operating expenses	27%	26%
Operating profit	10%	10%
Income taxes	4%	4%
Net income	6%	5%

121

2. Balance sheets for Labal Company for 2005 and 2006 are as follows:

Income Statements
Labal Company
For the Years Ending September 30, 2005 and 2006

	2005	2006
Cash	100	200
Net accounts receivable	1,500	2,200
Inventories	3,000	3,600
Current assets	**4,600**	**6,000**
Net fixed assets	2,100	3,100
Total assets	**6,700**	**9,100**
Bank loan (line of credit)	300	400
Accounts payable	1,600	1,900
Accruals	100	200
Current liabilities	**2,000**	**2,500**
Long term bank loan	1,800	2,900
Common stock ($0.15 par)	300	300
Retained earnings	2,600	3,400
Total liabilities and equity	**6,700**	**9,100**

b. Compute the following ratios for Labal Company (note that you will need some data from the income statement in problem 1 to compute some of the ratios).

	2005	2006
Current ratio	_____	_____
Average collection period	_____	_____
Inventory turnover ratio	_____	_____
Total asset turnover ratio	_____	_____
Payable ratio	_____	_____
Debt ratio	_____	_____
Cash Conversion Cycle	_____	_____
Net profit margin	_____	_____
Return on equity	_____	_____

Assignment 4.2

Name:_____   Date:_____

Answer the following question in the space provided.

1. The Pilson Company's balance sheets and income statements for the years ending March 31, 2005 and 2006 are shown below (all figures in thousands of dollars):

	2005	2006
Current assets	$2,000	$3,000
Net fixed assets	4,000	7,000
Total assets	**6,000**	**10,000**
Current liabilities	$ 500	$1,800
Long-term debt	2,000	2,300
Common stock (.25 par value)	1,500	1,900
Additional paid-in capital	1,000	2,400
Retained earnings	1,000	1,600
Total liabilities and equity	**6,000**	**10,000**
Net sales	$7,000	$9,000
Cost of goods sold	3,000	4,400
Operating expenses	2,000	2,200
Interest expense	500	600
Taxes	100	200
Net income	**1,400**	**1,600**

a. What was the total dollar amount of dividends paid by Pilson in 2006?

b. How many shares of common stock did Pilson have outstanding in 2005?

c. How many shares of common stock did Pilson have outstanding in 2006?

d. What was the per share dividend payment in 2006 (rounded to the nearest cent)?

e. What was Pilson's ROE in 2005?

f. What was Pilson's ROE in 2006?

g. Using the extended DuPont equation, explain the reason(s) for the change (if any) in Pilson's ROE from 2005 to 2006.

Assignment 4.3 ·········

Name:_____ Date:_____

Answer the following questions in the space provided.

1. Complete the balance sheet and sales information in the table that follows for Johnson Company using the following information (all sales are on credit):

Debt ratio $= .60 = \frac{TL}{1,000,000} = 600,000$ 60% *300,000*

Inventory turnover ratio $5 = \frac{1,500,000}{Inv}$ 5.0x

Net profit margin 10% $.10 = NP/2000m = 200,000$

Total asset turnover $2.0 = \frac{S}{1,000} = 2,000,000$ 2.0x

Quick ratio 1.0x

Average collection period $45 = \frac{AR}{5556} = 250,000$ 45 days

Gross profit margin $-25 = \frac{GP}{2000000} = 500,000$ 25%

Return on equity $.50 = \frac{200,000}{E}$ $E = 400,000$ 50%

2,000,000
= 100.5
_____
5,00,000

$1 = \frac{CA - 300,000}{42,000}$
$420,000 = CA - 300,000$
$720,000 = CA$

Balance Sheet

Cash	170,000	Accounts payable	420,000
Accounts receivable	250,000	Long-term debt	180,000
Inventories	300,000	Common stock	200,000
Fixed assets	380,000	Retained earnings	200,000
Total assets	**$1,000,000**	**Total Claims**	1,000,000

2. Fill in Johnson's net sales and cost of goods sold on the lines below:

Net sales 2,000,000

Cost of goods sold 1,500,000

3. Compute Johnson's Cash Conversion Cycle. $=$ *Inv. conv. pd + Avg Coll. pd − Pybus Pd*

$Inv. pd = \frac{300,000}{1,500,000 / 360} = 72 \ days$

$72 + 45 - 101 = 16 \ CCC$

$Avg. Coll pd = \frac{250,000}{2,000,000 / 360} = 45 \ days$

$Pybus Pd = \frac{420,000}{1,500,000 / 360} = 101 \ days$

125

4. List and compute the component of the Extended DuPont Equation for Johnson. Prove that the DuPont ROE is equal to 50 percent as given in the previous table.

Additional Questions and Problems

1. To which firm would the inventory turnover ratio be more important: a grocery store or an insurance company? Why?

2. In what specific ways would high inflation affect a firm's balance sheet and income statement? How would high levels of inflation affect comparison of the financial ratios of a particular firm over time?

3. Given the other ratios listed, identify the possible specific cause of the trend in the current ratio:

	2004	2005	2006
Current ratio	2.0	1.6	1.4
Inventory turnover	6x	6x	6x
ACP	30	30	30
Payables period	40	50	60

4. Calculate the effective cost of passing up the discount for each of the following credit terms:

   2/10 net 20
   1/15 net 40
   5/20 net 60

5. Assume you are given the following relationships for the In-Fer Company:

Current ratio	2x
Quick ratio	1.5x
Current liabilities	$100,000

   Compute Inventory.

6. Assume you are given the following relationships for the En-Fer Company:

Return on assets	20%
Return on equity	50%

Compute the debt ratio.

7. Assume you are given the following relationships for the An-Fer Company:

Total asset turnover ratio	4x
Debt ratio	20%
Return on equity	10%

Compute the net profit margin.

8. Assume you are given the following relationships for the Un-Fer Company (all sales are credit sales):

Average collection period	20 days
Accounts receivable	$1,000
Net profit margin	5%
Total asset turnover ratio	2x
Debt ratio	75%

Compute the return on equity.

9. Assume you are given the following relationships for the Givens Corporation:

Return on assets (ROA)	12%
Return on equity (ROE)	25%
Total asset turnover	1.5x

Calculate Givens' net profit margin and debt ratio.

10. Last year Popsicles and Confetti, Inc. (P&C) had sales of $10 million, a net income of $1 million, assets of $8 million, a debt ratio of 25 percent and a gross margin of 30 percent. Calculate return on assets (ROA) and return on equity (ROE).

11. The International Imports Company has $1,950,000 in current assets and $800,000 in current liabilities. Its initial inventory level is $700,000 and it will raise funds as commercial paper and use them to increase inventory. If International Imports raises the maximum short-term debt allowable without violating a current ratio of 2 to 1, what will be their new quick ratio?

12. Atlanta Unlimited has a debt ratio of 75 percent. What is Atlanta's equity multiplier?

13. The following data apply to J.S. Billings & Sons (dollars in thousands):

Cash	$200
Average collection period	40 days
Net fixed assets	$600
Net income	$ 60
Quick ratio	2.0x
Sales	$900
Current ratio	3.0x
Return on equity (ROE)	12%

Billings has only current liabilities, long-term debt, and common equity on the right-hand side of its balance sheet and only cash, accounts receivable, inventories, and net fixed assets on the left-hand side of the balance sheet. Find Billings':

a. Accounts receivable balance

b. Current assets

c. Current liabilities

d. ROA

e. Long-term debt

f. Common equity

14. Assume the Firm is 100 percent equity financed. Calculate the ROE, given the following information:Earnings before taxes $1,500

Sales	5,000
Dividend payout ratio	60%
Total asset turnover	2.0x
Applicable tax rate	30%

15. Geometrics Inc. would like to expand to take advantage of new product opportunities. However, the terms of existing bond indentures and term loans with insurance companies restrict total debt to 55 percent of total assets. Currently, the firm has $3 million in total debt and $3 million in equity. It projects $1 million in profits after taxes in the current year, and dividends of $400,000. Compute the increase in total debt that can be raised without a violation and without an equity issue by the end of the coming year (rounded if necessary).

16. Supertronics is planning a new division with its newly developed products and finds that it can operate equally well with either of two different structures. The sales, debt ratio, net fixed assets, current liabilities, and profit margin would all be the same, but there are two alternative current asset plans. These two plans involve only different levels of accounts receivable (AR) and inventory, as follows:

Plan A	Plan B
AR with 18 ACP (days)	AR with 36 ACP (days)
Inventory turnover of 5	Inventory turnover of 10

If sales are projected at $10 million, which plan should produce the higher ROE (that is, which plan requires the least equity investment)?

a. Plan A because of less receivables.

b. Plan B because of lower current assets.

c. Plan A because currents assets are higher.

d. The equity required would be the same, but Plan A has greater liquidity.

e. Cannot be determined without an asset turnover figure.

17. Johnson Corporation sells all of its merchandise on credit. It has a profit margin of 4 percent, ACP (average collection period) of sixty days, accounts receivable of $150,000, $3,000,000 in total assets, and a debt ratio of 0.64. What is Johnson's ROE?

18. The Berby Company had a quick ratio of 1.4, a current ratio of 3.0, an inventory turnover of six times, total current assets of $810,000, and cash and marketable securities of $120,000 in 2006. What were Berby's annual sales and its average collection period for that year?

19. Determine the times-interest earned ratio (TIE) of a firm whose total interest charges are $20,000, whose sales are $2 million, whose tax rate is 40 percent, and whose net profit margin is 6 percent. (Hint: Reconstruct the income statement from the bottom up, and find EBT and EBIT).

20. Find the debt ratio for the ABC Company that will double its current return on equity (ROE) to 10 percent for a projected net profit margin of 14 percent. Currently, ABC has a debt ratio (debt to total assets) of 0.5, a total asset turnover ratio of 0.25 and a net profit margin of 10 percent. Although the company expects that the net profit margin will rise to 14 percent, the total asset turnover ratio will remain the same. The new debt ratio is?

21. The Chicago Company has determined that its return on equity is 15 percent. You have the following information: debt ratio = 0.35 and total asset turnover = 2.8. What is the firm's profit margin?

$ROE = 15\%$

$DR = .35$

$TAT = 2.8$

$A = L + E$

$A = .35 + .65$

$\frac{NI}{E} = .15$

$NPM = NP$

$\frac{NI}{S} = \frac{.15}{1.15}$

22. Convert the following debt to equity ratios into debt to asset ratios and Equity multipliers:

Debt-to-equity ratio	Corresponding debt-to-asset ratio	Corresponding Equity Multiplier
2.5	.714	3.5
1.0	.5	2
0.6	.375	1.6

23. Complete the balance sheet in the table that follows for the MacClemore Company using the following information (if necessary, round figures to the nearest dollar):

Sales	$2,000,000
Net profit margin	7.5%
Gross profit	$400,000
Return on equity	24.0%
Return on assets	15.0%
Inventory turnover ratio	4.0x
Average collection period	40 days
Days payable ratio	20 days
Current ratio	3.8x

Balance Sheet

Accounts receivable	_____	Notes payable	_____
Inventories	_____	Accounts payable	_____
Fixed assets	_____	Long-term debt	_____
Total assets	_____	Equity	_____
		Total liabilities and equity	_____

24. Complete the balance sheet in the table that follows for the OptiPlex Company using the following information (if necessary, round figures to the nearest dollar):

Sales	$4,000
Net profit margin	10.0%
Return on equity	25.0%
Total asset turnover ratio	1.0x
Gross profit margin	30.0%
Average collection period	40 days
Current ratio	3.0x
Dividend payout ratio	65.0%
Quick ratio	1.0x

Note: 90 percent of all sales are credit sales; 10 percent are cash sales. Assume a 360 day year.

Balance Sheet

Accounts receivable	_____	Current liabilities	_____
Inventories	_____	Long-term debt	_____
Fixed assets	_____	Equity	_____
Total assets	_____	**Total liabilities and equity**	_____

Chapter 5

Strategic Financial Management

After studying Chapter 5, you should be able to:

◆ Discuss the importance of efficient working capital management and identify some of the components of setting and changing working capital policies.

◆ Understand the purpose and importance of a monthly cash budget and identify the effects of seasonality on monthly net cash flow.

◆ Explain the need for companies to create pro forma financial statements.

◆ Use the percent of sales method to create a pro forma financial statement.

◆ Identify a spontaneous asset, a spontaneous liability, internally generated funds, and a financing variable.

◆ Compute "outside funds needed" under various assumptions concerning short-term bank loans, long-term debt, and issuance of new common stock.

5.1 Chapter Overview ....

Three issues that occupy much of a financial manager's time and attention are managing working capital, estimating seasonal fund needs, and projecting long-term fund requirements. Working capital management involves the strategic management of current assets and current liabilities, and involves estimating cost/benefit tradeoffs. Estimating seasonal fund needs requires constructing and managing a monthly cash budget. Projecting long-term fund requirements involves the construction of pro forma financial statements.

In this chapter we discuss the principles of working capital management, demonstrate the basic outline of a cash budget, and illustrate the construction and interpretation of pro forma statements. The material presented in this chapter is purposely limited in scope. Entire books and entire courses are devoted to this subject matter. Our goal is to make you aware of these topics and to help you to appreciate the important role of a financial manager in the day-to-day operations of a company.

5.2 Working Capital Management ....

Although managing working capital requires a significant amount of a financial manager's time and energy, it is often considered to be the mundane part of finance. This is because managing working capital requires discipline, effort, and attention to detail that produces few immediate tangible results. Nonetheless, efficient working capital management is essential to the long-term success of any organization. Consider the following illustrative example.

Over her lifetime, Mary Fernandez earned an average salary of $30,000 per year working as a house cleaner. Mary, whose husband died soon after the birth of their fourth child, was an intensely frugal individual. She monitored every single dollar she earned and spent. She never bought anything that wasn't on sale, she never bought anything she didn't need, she seldom bought anything new, she sold everything she no longer needed, she paid all of her bills on time, she developed an excellent credit record, and she put 10 percent of every paycheck she received into a stock mutual fund. By the time she was 55 years old, Mary had bought and paid for a house (she bought the house for $40,000; it recently appraised for $215,000), had witnessed all four of her children graduate from college, and had accumulated over $2,500,000 in her stock market account.

Over his lifetime, Reginald Baxter, a highly successful stockbroker, earned an average annual salary of $300,000 per year. Reginald, who never married or had any children (that he knew of), was the ultimate playboy. He spent money as fast as he could on whatever he wanted, whether he needed it or not. He lived in a fourteen-room mansion, had seven different new cars, and employed a housecleaner, a private chef, a butler and a chauffeur. Reginald was an avid gambler, had more loans outstanding than he could keep track of, paid all of his bills late, and never even considered any type of savings plans other than highly speculative ventures. He always figured that he would begin saving money when he was older. When he was 55 years old, the stock market turned sour, his speculative venture investments became worthless, he lost all of his clients, the bank foreclosed on his house due to excessively late payments, and he was forced to file for personal bankruptcy. He now has absolutely nothing to his name.

The main reason for the difference between the long-term success of Mary and the long-term failure of Reginald is that Mary efficiently managed her personal working capital and Reginald did not. Specifically, Mary managed the day-to-day details of her financial life, which secured her long-term future. Reginald thought that attention to such tedious detail was not worth the required discipline or effort. Even though Reginald had annual income that was ten times greater than Mary's, Mary is now living in luxury and Reginald is broke. (Actually, Reginald's woes did not end with his bankruptcy filing. As his personal financial empire began to crumble, Reginald got involved in an insider-trading scheme that turned out to be a sting operation. He is now serving time in a federal penitentiary.)

Managing the working capital of a company is similar to the personal working capital management example above in that it requires attention to the day-to-day details of the financial operations of the business. For a company, working capital management includes, but is not limited to, the following:

1. Determining minimum cash requirements, maintaining the checking account, and managing the cash balance.

2. Setting credit policy and managing the collection of accounts receivable.

3. Establishing inventory target levels and managing inventory turnover.

4. Establishing and maintaining banking relationships to ensure access to short-term funds due to seasonality and other needs.

5. Negotiating and monitoring trade credit terms and managing supplier relationships.

6. Monitoring and evaluating operating expenses, interest, and taxes, and maintaining efficient payment patterns.

None of the above represents activities that capture newspaper headlines or turn heads. However, as with Mary, they are the activities necessary to build long-term success and wealth.

Recall (or even better, go back and reread) the opening story in Chapter One concerning Bennie's Auto Parts and Service Center. As you can now see, Bennie did a very poor job managing the working capital of his business. Even though he had a sound long-term business plan, a great product, an excellent business reputation and customer service, and tremendous potential, his lack of attention to the daily details of his business resulted in bankruptcy, and even worse, prison. (On the positive side, at least he has interesting companionship—Bennie and Reginald Baxter are cellmates!)

Basically, effective working capital management involves establishing targets and evaluating the cost/benefit tradeoffs of altering these targets. A main focus of working capital management is identifying and estimating the costs and benefits of different policies. Enumerating the details of the cost/benefit tradeoffs of all net working capital accounts and policies can be tedious, and it is definitely beyond the scope of this book. However, the following example should help you to visualize the basic process of evaluating tradeoffs, and should enable you to more fully appreciate the challenge of effectively managing working capital.

Exeter, Inc. manufactures robotic tools that are used by companies in the automobile, aeronautics, and defense industries. Exeter is well established as a leading producer of robotics tools; however, competition in the industry is becoming increasingly stiff. Exeter currently sells all of its products on credit terms of 2/15 net forty, which are the standard credit terms offered by other firms in the industry. All sales are on credit and for these credit terms, 60 percent of all of Exeter's customers take the discount and pay in fifteen days, and all other customers pay in forty days. Exeter has no bad debt and no product returns. Finally, on its income statement, Exeter records sales revenue as all shipments at full price and lists trade credit discounts as an operating expense.

Problem 5.1 If annual sales revenue for the next twelve months is forecasted to be $360,000,000, compute Exeter's Average Collection Period (ACP) and compute Exeter's average Accounts Receivable balance. Assume a 360-day year.

$$ACP = \frac{AR}{Sales/360} = \overline{360,000,000/360}$$

$$ACP = (.60)(15 \text{ days}) + (.40)(40 \text{ days}) = 25 \text{ days}$$

Accounts receivable $= (25)(360,000,000/360) = 25,000,000$

Problem 5.2 Exeter's gross profit margin is estimated to be 30 percent and operating expense (including depreciation but excluding trade credit discounts) are forecasted to be 15 percent of annual sales revenue. Interest expense for the next twelve-month period is forecasted to be $30,000,000 and the company's average tax rate is 30 percent. Given this information, construct Exeter's projected income statement (that is, fill in the chart below) for the next twelve-month period. (Hint: To compute trade credit discounts, recall that all sales are on credit and that 60 percent of all of Exeter's customers take a 2 percent discount.)

Projected Income Statement
Exeter, Incorporated
For the Next 12-Month Period
(all figures in dollars)

Sales revenue	360,000,000
Cost of goods sold	252,000,000
Gross profit	168,000,000
Operating expenses	54,000,000
Trade credit discounts	4,320,000
Operating profit	
Interest expense	30,000,000
Earnings before taxes	
Taxes	
Net income	

Answer:

Projected Income Statement
Exeter, Incorporated
For the Next 12-Month Period
(all figures in dollars)

Sales revenue	360,000,000
Cost of goods sold	252,000,000
Gross profit	**108,000,000**
Operating expenses	54,000,000
Trade credit discounts*	4,320,000
Operating profit	**49,680,000**
Interest expense	30,000,000
Earnings before taxes	**19,680,000**
Taxes	5,904,000
Net income	**13,776,000**

*(360,000,000)(.60)(.02) = 4,320,000.

Exeter is considering changing its credit terms to 3/15 net forty. To evaluate this proposed policy change, Exeter must identify and estimate its costs and benefits. The main benefit of offering a larger discount should be an increase in sales. Trade credit discounts effectively lower the price of the product. In a highly price-competitive industry, lower prices can mean more sales volume. Most of these increased sales will be "stolen" from competitors, but some could be totally new sales to the entire industry.

A second benefit may be that some of Exeter's current customers who are paying in forty days might begin to pay in fifteen days to take advantage of the now more attractive discount. This will increase the percentage of customers who pay in fifteen days and reduce the percentage who pay late. In turn, this mix will reduce the company's Average Collection Period.

Depending on the actual increase in sales, the smaller average collection period might decrease the company's average accounts receivable balance. Because all assets must be financed in some way, a reduction in accounts receivable could allow the company to reduce its notes payable balance (that is, bank loan). Finally, a decrease in the average bank loan could reduce the company's interest expense and thereby increase its net income.

Problem 5.3   Assume the change in credit terms to 3/15 net forty is expected to increase the percentage of customers who take the discount and pay in fifteen days to 80 percent. All other customers are expected to pay in forty days. Compute Exeter's new projected Average Collection Period (ACP).

$$ACP = (.80)(15) + (.20)(40) = 20 \text{ days}$$

Problem 5.4   Also assume that Exeter believes that the change in credit terms will increase the sales revenue forecast over the next twelve-month period by 10 percent to $396,000,000. Compute Exeter's new projected average Accounts Receivable balance.

$$= \$22,000,000$$

That is, the change in credit terms is expected to reduce the projected average Accounts receivable balance from $25,000,000 to $22,000,000.

Problem 5.5   Assume that Exeter's short-term interest rate is 12 percent and suppose that the accounts receivable decrease of $3,000,000 will be matched by a corresponding and equal decrease in the company's short-term bank loan. Compute the reduction in projected annual interest expense due to the $3,000,000 decrease in notes payable.

$$= \$360,000$$

Accordingly (and all else constant), under these new terms, annual interest expense is projected to be $29,640,000 instead of $30,000,000 as assumed in problem 5.3 above.

Problem 5.6   Finally, to visualize the net benefit (or net cost) of this proposed policy change, reconstruct the projected income statement using all of the same assumptions that you used in problem 5.3, except now assume that Sales revenue = $396,000,000, that 80 percent of all of Exeter's customers will take a 3 percent discount, and that annual interest expense is projected to be $29,640,000. Fill in the table below.

Projected Income Statement
Exeter, Incorporated
For the Next 12-Month Period
(all figures in dollars)

Sales revenue	_____
Cost of goods sold	_____
Gross profit	_____
Operating expenses	_____
Trade credit discounts	_____
Operating profit	_____
Interest expense	_____
Earnings before taxes	_____
Taxes	_____
Net income	_____

Answer:

Projected Income Statement
Exeter, Incorporated
For the Next 12-Month Period
(all figures in dollars)

Sales revenue	396,000,000
Cost of goods sold	277,200,000
Gross profit	**118,800,000**
Operating expenses	59,400,000
Trade credit discounts*	9,504,000
Operating profit	**49,896,000**
Interest expense	29,640,000
Earnings before taxes	**20,256,000**
Taxes	6,076,800
Net income	**14,179,200**

*(396,000,000)(.80)(.03) = 9,504,000.

Should Exeter change its credit terms? If all of the assumptions bear out, the policy change will increase projected net income from $13,776,000 to $14,179,200. That is, the firm will be more profitable. Benefits exceed costs, so the answer appears to be "yes."

Are there any other issues that should be considered? Most definitely! First of all, as will be shown in the section three of this chapter, an increase in sales will also necessitate an increase in other current and long-term assets, and in corresponding increases in current liabilities, long-term debt, and equity. All of these factors must be considered before computing the actual change in interest expense. Interest expense might actually even increase when all other factors are considered.

Second, we ignored bad debt and collection costs in this example. In fact, all firms that sell on credit experience some bad debt expenses and must spend money to monitor and collect accounts. If the change in credit terms attracts new customers that are of a different credit quality than existing customers, bad debt and collection costs could either increase or decrease, depending on whether the new customers are of better quality or of lesser quality than existing customers.

Third, we completely ignored any potential response from other firms in the robotics tools industry. What if other firms matched Exeter's higher discount percent to retain their customers? Then, unless the new policy attracted sufficiently higher sales to the entire industry, each firm might end up with the same customers merely benefiting from more generous discount terms. The net result could be little to no change in Exeter's sales revenue, but significantly higher trade credit discount costs.

Fourth, the entire analysis presented above is dependent on estimates and forecasts. What if the numbers are all wrong? Vigilance, prudence, and candor are of premium importance in the efficient management of working capital.

These are merely some of the major issues to consider before actually enacting a new policy. You can probably think of others. As noted above, working capital management can be tedious and time-consuming, and the effort required often goes unnoticed. In fact, many evaluations merely produce an answer *not* to do something; that is, to merely maintain the status quo. Whereas such decisions are seldom, if ever, rewarded in the short run, as illustrated in the examples concerning Mary Fernandez, Reginald Baxter, and Bennie's Auto Parts and Service Center, the time and effort required to efficiently manage a firm's (or an individual's personal) working capital can spell the difference between long-term success and failure, security and uncertainty, or happiness and pain.

5.3 ◆ Cash Budgets ···

Determining funding needs due to seasonality of sales is another extremely important item of interest to a financial manager. Most firms experience some seasonality in their monthly revenue flows. For example, more ice cream sales occur during the summer months than in the winter months. On the other hand, sales of snow ski equipment are obviously most pronounced in the winter months. In fact, all industries whose production or sales are affected by weather experience some effects from seasonality. Holidays also cause demand seasonality. The months leading up to Christmas are the most important months of the year for most firms in the retail sales industry. For many companies that produce or sell toys, up to 80 percent of total annual sales occur between September and December. Indeed, it is actually difficult to find industries that experience no demand seasonality.

Seasonality in sales usually results in cash flow problems. Although revenue (and therefore cash inflow) can be seasonal, most expenses (cash outflows) are basically fixed (or at least not as volatile) from month to month. Managers of snow ski equipment manufacturers are paid the same amount every month, generally regardless of revenue. The same is basically true for rent, insurance, utilities, and most other operating and other expenses.

Consider the following example. Monthly cash inflows (cash sales, collections of accounts receivable, and other income) for Smith Retail are:

January	$100,000
February	$200,000
March	$400,000
April	$500,000
May	$400,000
June	$300,000

Monthly cash outflows (payments for purchases of inventory, payment of operating expenses, payment of interest, and payment of taxes) are:

January	$250,000
February	$270,000
March	$310,000
April	$330,000
May	$310,000
June	$290,000

Problem 5.7   Given these inflows and outflows for Smith Retail, compute monthly net cash flows (cash inflows minus cash outflows) for the months of January through June:

January	(150,000)
February	(70,000)
March	90,000
April	170,000
May	90,000
June	(10,000)

Answer: ($150,000), ($70,000), $90,000, $170,000, $90,000, ($10,000) for January through June, respectively.

Assume that Smith Retail enters the month of January with an excess cash balance (that is, over and above the minimum amount necessary to efficiently operate the business) in its checking account of $40,000. This excess cash can cover some of the negative cash flow in January. However, when this amount is exhausted, the firm will need to borrow money to pay its bills. The Smith Retail financial manager must secure funds, usually from a bank (for example, Notes payable), to cover the negative cash flows in January and February and use the positive cash flows in March, April, and May to repay these funds and to store up excess cash to cover the June shortfall, and for the next period of low monthly cash inflows.

It is a significant challenge to forecast seasonal funds needs many months in advance, and to strategically manage monthly fund needs so as to maximize sales, yet minimize the cost of borrowing funds (interest expense). The tool used to accomplish this task is a monthly cash budget. The Smith Retail example illustrates the basic outline of a cash budget.

Most firms construct rolling cash budgets that project twelve months into the future. Because each month provides new information about the future and because future events are constantly changing, the 12-month projected cash budget must be redone every month. More specific details concerning the construction of a complete cash budget, though interesting and important, are beyond the scope of this book.

5.4 Pro Forma Financial Statements ·····································

Long-term financial forecasting is another central responsibility of a financial manager. Long-term financial planning is essential to ensure that required funds are available for any new facilities, personnel, or working capital needed to support the firm's projected growth in sales. Growth will generally require that funds be obtained from outside the firm through selling additional common stock or by incurring additional debt (short-term or long-term). Because the cost and terms under which funds are obtained have major effects upon the firm's future profitability, required capital to fund growth must be planned for and analyzed carefully. This is the essence of long-term financial forecasting.

Long-term financial planning begins with an estimate of future sales. Any growth in projected sales must be supported with additional assets. For example, a manufacturing company that is currently operating at full capacity will need additional plant and equipment to increase production. A retail company might need to expand the size of its store or add an additional store to meet a projected increase in sales volume.

Additional sales and additional fixed assets will also require additions to working capital. In the case of a retail company that builds a new store to increase sales, unless the new store is stocked with inventory, the new fixed asset (the store) will be worthless, in that it will generate few, if any, new sales. Likewise, if the company currently sells its products on credit, additional sales from the new store will increase the company's uncollected accounts, that is, its accounts receivable balance. Finally, if the new store does not maintain a cash balance in its cash registers to make change for customers, additional sales might be limited. Thus, increases in both current assets (cash, accounts receivable, and inventory) and long-term fixed assets are generally necessary to support a higher level of sales.

Problem 5.8   Lassiter, Inc. has established the following optimal target ratios (this involves efficient working capital management) for cash, accounts receivable, and inventory:

$$\text{Cash} = 2 \text{ percent of sales}$$
$$\text{Average collection period} = 30 \text{ days}$$
$$\text{Inventory turnover ratio} = 5$$

The company projects that sales for the next year will increase by 20 percent, from $10,000,000 to $12,000,000, and the gross profit margin currently is and will remain at 25 percent. Compute projected Cash, Accounts receivable and Inventory for the current $10,000,000 level of sales and then compute projected Cash, Accounts receivable, and Inventory for the forecasted $12,000,000 sales amount. (Assume a 360-day year.)

Answer:
For sales = $10,000,000: Cash = $200,000; Accounts receivable = $833,333; Inventory = $1,500,000.
For sales = $12,000,000: Cash = $240,000; Accounts receivable = $1,000,000; Inventory = $1,800,000.

Problem 5.9   Assume that these are Lassiter's only current assets and that Lassiter's optimal total asset turnover ratio is 2.0. If Lassiter is currently operating at full capacity, compute Lassiter's total assets for the current $10,000,000 sales level and compute projected total assets for the forecasted $12,000,000 sales level. Then, subtract from these amounts projected total current assets to determine current net fixed assets and projected net fixed assets.

Answer:
For sales = $10,000,000: Projected total assets = $5,000,000; Projected net fixed assets = $2,466,667.
For sales = $12,000,000: Projected total assets = $6,000,000; Projected net fixed assets = $2,960,000.

Problem 5.10   Compute the increase in total current assets and the increase in net fixed assets needed to support the 20 percent projected increase in sales.

Answer: Increase in total current assets = $506,667; Increase in net fixed assets = $2,000,000.

Thus, given that a firm is currently operating at its peak efficiency level with respect to assets and sales (the financial manager is efficiently managing the firm's working capital), to increase sales, assets must usually grow. To purchase additional assets, funding (changes on the right hand side of the balance sheet) must be obtained. For example, building a new store requires a large sum of money, which (usually) either comes from debt holders who demand interest payments, or from stockholders who desire a return on their investment (net income). Additions to working capital must also be funded.

Some funding may be spontaneous. For example, wage and tax accruals tend to "spontaneously" increase with sales. Likewise, because most inventory is purchased on credit, accounts payable tend to increase "spontaneously" with the increased inventory needed to support the increase in sales. Other funding may be generated internally. If the firm earns a profit on its sales, this profit can be reinvested—be used to fund some of the increase in assets. If more funds are needed than what are created spontaneously and generated internally, outside financing must be obtained. The firm must either sell additional stock or borrow from creditors, either short-term or long-term.

To determine the amount of money needed from outside sources, financial managers often construct pro forma financial statements. A pro forma statement is merely a projected or forecasted statement. The nature of the relationship between projected sales growth and financing requirements (that is, the process of producing a *pro forma* statement) can be illustrated by the percent of sales method of forecasting financial requirements. Although this is the simplest of several techniques used to create pro forma financial statements, it sufficiently demonstrates the necessary concept.

For the percent of sales method, each balance sheet asset account and each balance sheet spontaneous liability account is assumed to maintain a constant percent of sales relationship. Thus, if sales are $100 and inventories are $20, inventories are 20 percent of sales. If sales increase to $200, inventories will maintain the 20 percent of sales relationship (that is, inventories will need to grow to $40). This constant relationship will be achieved if inventories grow at the same rate as sales. Thus, for the percent of sales method, each balance sheet account and each spontaneous liability account is assumed to grow at the same rate as sales.

Problem 5.11   Compute the percentage growth in forecasted cash, accounts receivable, inventories, and net fixed assets for Lassiter, Inc. that corresponded with the projected 20 percent increase in sales.

Your answer should show that each asset account grew by 20 percent, which was merely the same amount by which sales were projected to grow. Note that the current and projected asset values were based on the assumption that ratio relationships remained constant (that is, ACP = 30 days, Inventory turnover ratio = 5, and so on). Thus, the percent of sales method implies that ratios that illustrate the relationship between sales and various asset (and spontaneous liability) accounts remain constant. As long as the company is currently operating at peak efficiency with respect to assets and sales, it is reasonable to expect continued peak efficiency in operations to imply constant ratio relationships. Thus, using the percent of sales method to construct a pro forma balance sheet is both reasonable and simple. To demonstrate the percent of sales method, consider the following example.

5.5   COFFY'S Coffee Shop: A Simple Example ....

Three years ago Whitney Walker opened a coffee and pastry shop just north of the campus of State University. The shop, named COFFY'S, was an instant success. The coffee was always fresh, the pastry was delicious, and the aroma was pleasant. Students at State University (annual enrollment of 26,000) considered COFFY'S to be a perfect study lounge. Whitney capitalized on this idea by expanding the size of the shop in her second year of operations to a 5,000-square-foot facility. One third of the shop was set up as a traditional coffee shop designed to accommodate conversation. The remainder of the shop resembled a bookless library, complete with study carrels, padded chairs, and carpeting, drapes, and acoustic ceiling tiles to produce a quiet atmosphere perfect for studying. Some of Whitney's most dependable customers were the students enrolled in finance—particularly near exam time. The balance sheet and income statement for COFFY'S for the year ending June 30, 2006, are presented in Table 5.1.

Table 5.1

Income Statement
COFFY'S
For the Year Ending June 30, 2006

Sales	$800,000
Cost of Sales	480,000
Gross profit	**320,000**
Operating expense	220,000
Operating income	**100,000**
Interest expense	30,000
Profit before taxes	**70,000**
Taxes	28,000
Net income	**42,000**

Balance Sheet
COFFY'S
For the Year Ending June 30, 2006

Cash	$10,000	Notes payable	$10,000
Accounts receivable	8,000	Accounts payable	25,000
Inventories	72,000	Accruals	5,000
Current assets	**90,000**	**Current liabilities**	**40,000**
Gross fixed assets	820,000	Long-term bank loan	400,000
Accumulated depreciation	(60,000)	Common stock	200,000
Net fixed assets	760,000	Retained earnings	210,000
Total assets	**850,000**	**Total liabilities and equity**	**850,000**

Problem 5.12   Without looking up the formulas, compute COFFY'S Gross profit margin, Operating profit margin, and Net profit margin for 2006.

Answer: Gross profit margin = 40%, Operating profit margin = 12.5%, Net profit margin = 5.25%.

Problem 5.13   Without looking up the formulas, compute COFFY'S Current ratio, Average collection period (assuming 30 percent of sales are credit sales and 70 percent are cash sales), Inventory turnover ratio, and Debt ratio for 2006.

Answer: Current ratio = 2.25, Average collection period = 12 days, Inventory turnover ratio = 5.67, and Debt ratio = 51.8%.

Problem 5.14   Without looking up the formulas, compute COFFY'S Return on equity, Return on assets, and write out the extended DuPont equation for 2006.

Answer: ROE $= 10.2\%$ and ROA $= 4.9\%$. The extended DuPont equation $= 5.25\% \times .9412 \times 2.073$.

Whitney believes that sales for 2007 will grow by 20 percent (that is, to $960,000). She plans to pay a $20,000 dividend in 2007. Currently all of COFFY'S assets are at optimal efficiency levels. Additionally, there is no excess capacity. Thus, to expand sales by 20 percent, Whitney will need to increase the size of the shop. This need not always be the case. Firms often maintain excess capacity or are able to increase sales without major increases in fixed assets. For example, Whitney could increase sales without increasing the size of the shop by extending the shop's hours or by staying open one additional day per week (assuming she currently is open only five days per week). For this example, however, assume that the shop will need to be enlarged. Finally, Whitney projects that the net profit margin for 2007 will be equal to the net profit margin for 2006.

5.5.1 Determining Total Outside Funds Needed

To generate a 2007 pro forma balance sheet for COFFY'S:

1. Compute the expected net income for 2007. Note that the net profit margin in 2006 was 5.25% (42,000/800,000). Thus, in 2007, net income will be expected to be (960,000)(.0525) = $50,400.

2. Determine the addition to retained earnings. Net income can either be paid out in the form of dividends or retained. Because Whitney plans to pay a $20,000 dividend, the addition to retained earnings for 2007 will be (50,400 – 20,000) = $30,400. Thus, retained earnings for 2007 will be (210,000 + 30,400) = $240,400.

3. Recreate the balance sheet (create a pro forma balance sheet) assuming that all asset accounts and all spontaneous liability accounts increase by the same rate as the growth rate in sales. For simplicity, assume that depreciation grows at the same rate as the increase in gross fixed assets.

4. Leaving all "financing decision variables" (notes payable, long-term debt, and common stock) constant, determine the amount by which Total assets exceed Total liabilities and Equity. This amount is designated as the "*Total Outside Funds Needed.*"

Thus, we have the following:

Pro Forma Balance Sheet
COFFY'S
For the Year Ending June 30, 2007

Cash	$12,000	Notes payable	$10,000*
Accounts receivable	9,600	Accounts payable	30,000
Inventories	86,400	Accruals	6,000
Current assets	**108,000**	**Current liabilities**	**46,000**
Gross fixed assets	984,000	Long-term bank loan	400,000*
Accumulated depreciation	(72,000)	Common stock	200,000*
Net fixed assets	912,000	Retained earnings	240,400
Total assets	**1,020,000**	**Total liabilities and equity**	**886,400**

And, *Total Outside Funds Needed* = \$133,600 (1,020,000 − 886,400). The *'s indicate financing decision variables which are held constant (note that notes payable is not a spontaneous liability account because this is an account which is controlled by the financial manager and is essentially independent of sales). Once the financial manager knows how much additional money is needed, the manager can determine the most optimal method of raising that money.

An alternative method of determining Outside Funds Needed (OFN) involves recognizing that OFN = the change in the total on the left-hand side of the balance sheet minus the change in the total on the right hand side of the balance sheet. More precisely,

**OFN = Change in total assets − (Change in spontaneous liabilities
+ Change in retained earnings).**

In general, for the percent of sales method, the Change in Total Assets is simply equal to $(TA_0)(g)$, where TA_0 is the total asset amount listed on the current balance sheet (for COFFY'S, $TA_0 = \$850,000$) and g is the projected growth rate in sales (for COFFY'S, g = 20%). Similarly, the Change in Spontaneous Liabilities equals $(L_0)(g)$, where L_0 is the sum of all spontaneous liability accounts on the current balance sheet (for COFFY'S, L_0 = Accounts payable + Accruals = \$25,000 + \$5,000 = \$30,000). Finally, the Change in Retained Earnings is the profit expected to be earned on next year's projected sales less any planned dividend payment. Thus, for COFFY'S,

Change in retained earnings = $[S_0 + (g)(S_0)](NPM) − Div_1$

where S_0 is current year sales (for COFFY'S, $S_0 = \$800,000$), $(g)(S_0)$ is the projected increase in sales (for COFFY'S, addition to sales = (.20)(\$800,000) = \$160,000), NPM is the projected net profit margin (for COFFY'S, NPM = 5.25% = .0525) and DIV_1 is the planned dividend payment (for COFFY'S, $DIV_1 = \$20,000$).

Problem 5.15 Using the following equation, which is merely Outside Funds Needed = Change in Total Assets − (Change in Spontaneous Liabilities + Change in Retained earnings), compute OFN:

OFN = $(TA_0)(g) − [(L_0)(g) + [S_0 + (g)(S_0)](NPM) − Div_1]$.

OFN = $(850,000)(.20) − [(30,000)(.20) + [(800,000 + (.20)(800,000)](.0525) − 20,000]$
**   = $170,000 − [6,000 + [960,000](.0525) − 20,000]$**
**   = \$133,600**

5.5.2 Determining Long-Term Outside Funds Needed

In general debt is "cheaper" than equity and short-term debt is "cheaper" than long-term debt. Thus, there might be a tendency to raise all of the needed funds as short-term debt. However, the use of short-term debt might be limited by restrictions that either the firm's management or the firm's current creditors have placed on the current ratio. For example, if the firm is restricted (either internally or externally) to maintain a current ratio of at least 2, current liabilities could be at a maximum CA/CL = \$108,000/2 = \$54,000 and thus notes payable could be $54,000 – Accounts payable – Accruals = $54,000 – $30,000 – $6,000 = $18,000. Thus,

Pro Forma Balance Sheet
COFFY'S
For the Year Ending June 30, 2007
(assuming current ratio restriction of 2 to 1)

Cash	$12,000	Notes payable	$18,000
Accounts receivable	9,600	Accounts payable	30,000
Inventories	86,400	Accruals	6,000
Current assets	**108,000**	**Current liabilities**	**54,000**
Gross fixed assets	984,000	Long-term bank loan	400,000*
Accumulated depreciation	(72,000)	Common stock	200,000*
Net fixed assets	912,000	Retained earnings	240,400
Total assets	**1,020,000**	**Total liabilities and equity**	**894,400**

And, *Long-Term Outside Funds Needed* = $125,600 (1,020,000 – 894,400).

Again, the *'s indicate financing decision variables which are held constant. Note that with Notes payable set equal to $18,000 (an increase of $8,000), the current ratio equals ($108,000/$54,000) = 2. Once the financial manager knows how much additional long-term money is needed, the manager can determine the most optimal method of raising this money.

5.5.3 Determining New Common Stock Funding Needed

Finally, because debt is cheaper than equity, the firm might be tempted to raise all of the long-term funds needed as long-term debt. However, this could be limited by restrictions on the firm's debt ratio. Assuming that the firm must maintain a debt ratio of no more than 50 percent, the maximum amount of debt it can have is $1,020,000/2 = $510,000. Given current liabilities of $54,000, the maximum size of the long-term bank loan would be $510,000 – $54,000 = $456,000. Thus,

Pro Forma Balance Sheet
COFFY'S
For the Year Ending June 30, 2007
(assuming current ratio restriction of 2 to 1
and debt ratio restriction of 50 percent)

Cash	$12,000	Notes payable	$18,000
Accounts receivable	9,600	Accounts payable	30,000
Inventories	86,400	Accruals	6,000
Current assets	**108,000**	**Current liabilities**	**54,000**
Gross fixed assets	984,000	Long-term bank loan	456,000
Accumulated depreciation	(72,000)	Common stock	200,000*
Net fixed assets	912,000	Retained earnings	240,400
Total assets	**1,020,000**	**Total liabilities and equity**	**950,400**

And, *New Common Stock* = $69,600 (1,020,000 – 950,400).

Extensions of the percent of sales pro forma forecasting method (though beyond the scope of this book) are straightforward and easy to visualize. Instead of a simple percent of sales relationship, a firm may assume certain linear relationships between various asset accounts and sales. For example, it may be assumed that the optimal relationship between inventory and sales is given by:

$$\text{Inventory} = \$10,000 + 70 \times \text{Sales}^{(1/2)}$$

Thus, given the Sales forecast of $960,000, the pro forma inventory level would be $78,586. Similar relationships (perhaps generated from historical observation and trends) could be specified for other asset or liability accounts. Once specified and calculated, however, the procedure for determining *funds needed* is identical to that shown above.

5.6 S-A-S Beers Revisited

Problem 5.16   Prepare a pro forma balance sheet for S-A-S Beers, Incorporated, assuming that sales for 2007 will grow at 40 percent, the 2007 net profit margin will be 6 percent, dividends paid in 2007 will be $800, all current assets and net fixed assets will grow as a percent of sales, and spontaneous liabilities (accounts payable and accruals) will grow as a percent of sales. Determine the *Total Outside Funds Needed.* (From income statement: 2006 Sales = $28,500.)

Actual Balance Sheet for 2006 and Pro Forma Balance Sheet for 2007
S-A-S Beers, Incorporated
For Years Ending December 31
(All figures in thousands of dollars)

	2006	2007
Cash	200	280
Net accounts receivable	3,100	4,340
Inventories	4,700	6580
Current assets	**8,000**	11,200
Net fixed assets	5,700	7,980
Total assets	**13,700**	19,180 —
Bank loan (line of credit)	1,200	1,680
Accounts payable	2,300	3,220
Accruals	200	280
Current portion of L.T. Debt	200	200
Current liabilities	**3,900**	5380
Long-term bank loan	4,900	4900
Common stock ($0.15 par)	1,500	1,500
Retained earnings	3,400	4,994
Total liabilities and equity	**13,700**	16,294

$$.06 = \frac{NP}{28,500}$$

$$19,180 - 16,294 = 2886 \ OFN$$

$$S_a + S_a(g)(NPM(or))$$
$$28,500 + (28500 \times .4)(.06(.4) = 4994$$

Answer:

Actual Balance Sheet for 2006 and Pro Forma Balance Sheet for 2007
S-A-S Beers, Incorporated
For the Years Ending December 31
(All figures in thousands of dollars)

	2006	2007
Cash	200	280
Net accounts receivable	3,100	4,340
Inventories	4,700	6,580
Current assets	**8,000**	**11,200**
Net fixed assets	5,700	7,980
Total assets	**13,700**	**19,180**
Bank loan (line of credit)	1,200	1,200
Accounts payable	2,300	3,220
Accruals	200	280
Current portion of L.T. Debt	200	200
Current liabilities	**3,900**	**4,900**
Long-term bank loan	4,900	4,900
Common stock ($0.15 par)	1,500	1,500
Retained earnings	3,400	4,994
Total liabilities and equity	**13,700**	**16,294**

Total Outside Funds Needed = Pro forma Total Assets − Pro forma Total Liabilities and Equity

$$= 19{,}180 - 16{,}294$$
$$= \$2{,}886$$

Thus, given these assumptions, S-A-S Beers would have to raise $2,886,000 in outside financing to support the projected growth rate in sales for 2006. This financing must come from some combination of short-term debt, long-term debt, or new outside equity.

Problem 5.17   Prepare a pro forma balance sheet for S-A-S Beers, Incorporated, assuming that sales for 2007 will grow at 30 percent, the 2007 net profit margin will be 6 percent, dividends paid in 2007 will be $900, all assets will grow as a percent of sales, spontaneous liabilities (accounts payable and accruals) will grow as a percent of sales, and the company's bank requires that the debt ratio be no greater than 60 percent. Determine the *New Common Stock* that needs to be issued. (From income statement: 2006 Sales = $28,500.)

Actual Balance Sheet for 2006 and Pro Forma Balance Sheet for 2007
S-A-S Beers, Incorporated
For the Years Ending December 31
(All figures in thousands of dollars)

	2006	2007
Cash	200	_____
Net accounts receivable	3,100	_____
Inventories	4,700	_____
Current assets	**8,000**	_____
Net fixed assets	5,700	_____
Total assets	**13,700**	_____

	8,800	_____
Total liabilities*	8,800	_____
Common stock ($0.15 par)	1,500	_____
Retained earnings	3,400	_____
Total liabilities and equity	**13,700**	_____

* Note that for 2006, total liabilities = current liabilities + long-term debt = 3,900 + 4,900 = 8,800. The assumption for this problem is that the pro forma debt ratio (that is, total liabilities divided by total assets) = 60 percent, so we include only total liabilities on the actual and pro forma statements.

Answer: Note that the assumption for the growth rate in sales and the amount of dividends to be paid differ from problem 5.16. Different assumptions will generate different pro forma estimates and thus also different funds needed conclusions. If you apply the assumptions for problem 5.16 to this problem (restricting total debt to 60 percent of total assets), you will find that the amount of new common stock needed will be even greater.

Actual Balance Sheet for 2006 and Pro Forma Balance Sheet for 2007
S-A-S Beers, Incorporated
For the Years Ending December 31
(All figures in thousands of dollars)

	2006	2007
Cash	200	280
Net accounts receivable	3,100	4,340
Inventories	4,700	6,580
Current assets	**8,000**	**11,200**
Net fixed assets	5,700	7,980
Total assets	**13,700**	**19,180**
Total liabilities	4,900	10,686
Common stock ($0.15 par)	1,500	1,500
Retained earnings	3,400	4,723
Total liabilities and equity	**13,700**	**16,909**

New Common Stock Needed = Pro forma Total Assets – Pro forma Total Liabilities and Equity

$$= 17,810 - 15,128$$

$$= \$901 \text{ (Assuming debt ratio of exactly 60\%)}$$

It is interesting to note that for Mr. Marker to raise the necessary funds to support a 30 percent growth in sales (with a debt restriction of 60 percent), he will need to issue a very large amount of new stock, which could adversely effect his current majority ownership position. Currently there is $1,500 in outstanding common stock. An additional $901 will increase the amount of outstanding stock by nearly 60 percent. Unless Mr. Marker has a sizable amount of money stashed away that he can use to purchase this new stock, he will almost certainly lose control of his firm. Given that most of his wealth is probably tied up in his own firm, it is unlikely that he has such funds. And, if someone else gains majority control of the firm, that person could even fire Mr. Marker.

Not only is it possible to grow yourself broke (recall the Derrick Dickerson example in cphapter 3), it is also possible to grow yourself out of control of the firm that you founded and built. Whereas such risks can never be completely eliminated, generating, evaluating, and managing pro forma statements will at least minimize these possibilities. Obviously, financial planning is an important business function.

In this chapter we have demonstrated the necessity for sound financial management of a firm's day-to-day operations, for cash budgeting and for long-term planning. As noted in the introduction to this chapter, these are central responsibilities of any financial manager. They are activities that form the basis of strategic financial management, and they are necessary to ensure long-term survival and success.

In the business world, the old adage: "if you don't know where you are going, you will almost certainly never get there," rings loud and clear. Corporate financial managers must plan for the future to be certain that they have the funds (more accurately, the cash) needed to support the growth and strategic plans for their firms. Also, to know where you are going you must often understand where you are coming from. Corporate financial managers must engage in efficient evaluation and management of working capital to formulate future strategies. Without sufficient attention to these matters and details, there is little hope of maximizing shareholder wealth, which, of course, is the goal of corporate financial management.

5.7 Section Summary

As noted in section 8 of chapter 1, this book is divided into two major sections. The first section focuses on the importance, determination and management of cash flows, particularly the past and potential future cash flows indicated by a firm's financial statements. We have almost concluded the first section of the book.

In chapters 2 and 3 we reviewed financial statements and discussed ways to extract cash flow information from income statements and balance sheets. In chapter 4 we discussed financial ratios. Ratios can be used to evaluate past performance (as noted in chapter 4). They can also be used to target or project future events. That is, financial ratios can be used to create pro forma financial statements. In this chapter, we demonstrated how to construct a pro forma balance sheet using the percent of sales method. This method produces essentially the same pro forma statement as would be generated assuming that all ratio relationships remain constant from one year to the next. More robust (and perhaps realistic) pro forma statements can be produced using target or trend implied ratios as predictors.

The following continuation of the S-A-S Beers example is meant to tie together chapters 3, 4, and 5 and to demonstrate how the tools and techniques discussed in these chapters can be used to forecast expected future cash flows. The example is simplified so as to be manageable. In a real world setting, additional and more advanced assumptions would be applied. After you complete the second section of the book, which focuses on how to value cash flows, you will be able to see how company values are determined. You should also be able to appreciate the difficulty of doing this type of work. This fact helps to explain why good financial analysts and managers are so highly valued by companies, and so highly compensated.

Given the analysis of the trends in S-A-S Beers' financial statements and ratios, assume that we forecast the following relationships for the company for the year ending December 31, 2007. Brief reasons for the assumptions appear after each value. Different individuals would probably have different interpretations of the trends, and therefore put forward different assumptions. Determining reasonable assumptions with justified reasoning is a significant task.

- Projected growth rate in sales = 26.3% to $36,000 (this is Mr. Marker's estimate for sales in 2007 as noted in case)

- Projected average collection period = 45 days (continuation of upward trend)

- Projected inventory conversion period = 90 days (continuation of upward trend)

- Projected payables period = 30 days (due to pressure from suppliers, assumed that S-A-S Beers will begin paying suppliers on time—recall terms are 2/10 net 30)

- Projected current ratio = 1.9 (average of current ratio for 2004, 2005 and 2006)

- Projected debt ratio = 60% (continuation of trend)

- Projected depreciation expense = $800 (continuation of trend in income statement)

- Projected gross profit margin = 24% (continuation of upward trend due to assumed continued increases in input costs and increased competition)

- Projected net profit margin = 6% (assumed to be lower than 2006 because other income in not expected to be repeated).

- No change in land; building and equipment assumed to grow by 14% (similar to trend to date); cash to grow as a percent of sales; accruals to grow as a percent of sales; and no change in current portion of long-term.

- Projected dividend payment in 2007 = $600 (same as 2006 dividend payment)

- Common stock will be the "plug" figure. That is, common stock will be whatever amount in needed to make sure the balance sheet balances.

We will now use these forecast assumptions to create a pro forma balance sheet and then use the pro forma statement and other given projections to create a projected statement of cash flows. This projected cash flow statement will indicate the company's internally generated cash flow and external financing needs and sources.

Problem 5.18   Given these assumptions, prepare a pro forma balance sheet for S-A-S Beers, Incorporated, for 2007.

Actual Balance Sheet for 2006 and Pro Forma Balance Sheet for 2007
S-A-S Beers, Incorporated
For the Years Ending December 31
(All figures in thousands of dollars)

	2006	2007
Cash	200	_____
Net accounts receivable	3,100	_____
Inventories	4,700	_____
Current assets	**8,000**	_____
Land	900	_____
Buildings and equipment	7,100	_____
Less accumulated depreciation	(2,300)	_____
Net fixed assets	5,700	_____
Total assets	**13,700**	_____
Bank loan (line of credit)	1,200	_____
Accounts payable	2,300	_____
Accruals	200	_____
Current portion of L.T. Debt	200	_____
Current liabilities	**3,900**	_____
Long-term bank loan	4,900	_____
Common stock ($0.15 par)	1,500	_____
Retained earnings	3,400	_____
Total liabilities and equity	**13,700**	_____

Answer:

Actual Balance Sheet for 2006 and Pro Forma Balance Sheet for 2007
S-A-S Beers, Incorporated
For the Years Ending December 31
(All figures in thousands of dollars)

	2006	2007
Cash	200	253
Net accounts receivable	3,100	4,500
Inventories	4,700	6,840
Current assets	**8,000**	**11,593**
Land	900	900
Buildings and equipment	7,100	8,094
Less accumulated depreciation	(2,300)	(3,100)
Net fixed assets	5,700	5,894
Total assets	**13,700**	**17,487**
Bank loan (line of credit)	1,200	3,369
Accounts payable	2,300	2,280
Accruals	200	253
Current portion of L.T. Debt	200	200
Current liabilities	**3,900**	**6,102**
Long-term bank loan	4,900	4,390
Common stock ($0.15 par)	1,500	2,235
Retained earnings	3,400	4,760
Total liabilities and equity	**13,700**	**17,487**

Problem 5.19   Construct a pro forma (that is, projected) statement of cash flows for S-A-S Beers for 2007.

Answer:

Net income	2,260
+ Depreciation	+ 800
− Increase in accounts receivable	− 1,400
− Increase in inventories	− 2,140
− Decrease in accounts payable	− 20
+ Increase in accruals	+ 53
Net Cash Flow from Operating Activities	**(547)**
Purchase of new fixed assets	− 994
Net Cash Flow from Investing Activities	**(994)**
Increase in bank loan	+2,169
Decrease in long-term debt	− 510
Increase in common stock	+ 735
− Payment of dividends	− 800
Net Cash Flow from Financing Activities	**1,594**

Check: (547) + (994) + 1,594 = 53 = change in cash from 2006 to 2007.

S-A-S Beers is projected to generate negative cash flow from operating activities in 2007. The positive free cash flow (net income + depreciation) of the company is being "eaten up" by the rapid growth in accounts receivable and inventory. In chapter 1 we stated that the fundamental concept of finance (and valuation) is:

The value of an investment is determined by the future cash flows that the investment is expected to generate for the investor.

If this were the only cash flow expected to be generated by S-A-S Beers, the value of the company would be negative. More directly, S-A-S Beers would be a worthless investment!

Fortunately for companies like S-A-S Beers, cash flows are expected to last many, many years. If cash flow in future years is expected to be positive, these can offset a single or even several negative cash flow years and the overall value of the company might be positive. Determining whether future cash flows might be positive requires additional analysis and pro forma statements. Determining the precise value of a stream of cash flows is the main topic soon to be covered in the second section of this book.

Assignment 5.1

Name:_____   Date:_____

Answer the following questions in the space provided.

1. FreshFish, Inc. Inc. expects sales to grow by 50 percent in 2007. The company plans to pay out 40 percent of net income as dividends in 2007, and expects that the Net Profit Margin in 2007 will be the same as it was in 2006. Assuming that all assets and all spontaneous liabilities grow as a percent of sales, construct a pro forma balance sheet for FreshFish (that is, fill in the lines on the sheet below).

Balance Sheet
FreshFish, Inc.
For the Years Ending December 31, 2006 and 2007

	2006	2007
Cash	$ 20,000	_____
Accounts receivable	10,000	_____
Inventory	80,000	_____
Total Current Assets	**$110,000**	_____
Net plant and equipment	$430,000	_____
Total assets	**$540,000**	_____
Notes payable	15,000	_____
Accounts payable to suppliers	50,000	_____
Accruals	5,000	_____
Total current liabilities	**$ 70,000**	_____
Long-term debt	190,000	_____
Common stock ($2.00 par value)	20,000	_____
Capital surplus	150,000	_____
Retained earnings	110,000	_____
Total Liabilities and Equity	**$540,000**	_____

Selected Items from FreshFish, Inc. Income Statements:

Sales (2006) = $900,000
Net income (2006) = $31,500

2. Referring back to the pro forma statement you completed on the previous page, compute the Outside Funds Needed in 2007 to support this projected growth in sales for FreshFish, Inc.

3. Using the equation method, compute the Outside Funds Needed (OFN) for FreshFish, Inc. for 2007.

Assignment 5.2 ....

Name:_____   Date:_____

Answer the following questions in the space provided.

1. In 2006, Tabler, Incorporated reported Total assets of $1,220,000 and spontaneous liabilities of $500,000. Sales for 2006 were $4,000,000 and the current (and projected) net profit margin is 5 percent. Tabler pays out 40 percent of all of its annual profit in dividends (thus, for 2006, Tabler earned $200,000 in profit, paid $80,000 in dividends and added $120,000 to retained earnings). For each of the possible 2007 growth rates listed below, calculate the Total *Outside Funds Needed* (OFN). Note that a negative OFN figure merely implies that Tabler is able to more than fund the projected growth internally—in fact, that the firm will have excess internal funds that can be used to pay down debt, buy back stock, and so on.

a. g = 0%

b. g = 10%

c. g = 20%

d. g = 30%

e. g = 40%

f. g = 50%

2. The growth rate that results in OFN = 0 is called a firm's sustainable growth rate. This is the rate of growth that a firm can afford to finance internally—that is, without any outside financing. What is Tabler's sustainable growth rate?

Assuming that Tabler is unable to raise any outside funds (additional short-term debt, long-term debt or common stock), what would happen if Tabler attempted to grow sales at a rate above its sustainable growth rate?

Assignment 5.3

Name:_____   Date:_____

Answer the following questions in the space provided.

1. The balance sheet for the Tim-Tow Company for 2006 is shown below. Sales in 2006 were $90,000 and the firm's net profit margin was (and is projected to continue to be in the future) 5 percent.

Balance Sheet
The Tim-Tow Company
For the Year Ending Dec. 31, 2006

Cash	$ 10,000	Current liabilities	$ 60,000
Accounts receivable	20,000	Long-term debt	50,000
Inventory	50,000	Common stock ($2 par value)	60,000
Net plant and equipment	120,000	Retained earnings	30,000
Total assets	**$200,000**	**Total liabilities and equity**	**$200,000**

a. What were earnings per share for Tim-Tow in 2006?

b. Retained earnings reported on Tim-Tow's December 31, 2005 balance sheet were $28,200. Given this information, what was Tim-Tow's 2006 dividend payout ratio?

b. Given that Tim-Tow expects sales to grow in 2007 by 40 percent, that the company plans to pay a dividend in 2007 of $4,000, and that all assets are currently being fully used, compute the *Outside Funds Needed* to support this projected growth in sales.

2. New World Enterprises' 2006 financial statements are shown below:

2006 Income Statement for New World Enterprises

Sales	$300,000
Operating costs (70%)	210,000
Fixed costs	60,000
EBIT	**30,000**
Interest	10,000
EBT	**20,000**
Taxes (40%)	8,000
Net Income	**12,000**
Dividends	6,000
Addition to retained earnings	**6,000**

2006 Balance Sheet for New World Enterprises

Current assets	$100,000	Notes payable	$ 20,000
Net fixed assets	50,000	Accounts payable	20,000
		Accrued expenses	10,000
		Long-term debt	50,000
		Common equity	50,000
Total assets	**$150,000**	**Total**	**$150,000**

Next year you, the owner of this firm, expect sales to increase by 10 percent and you expect that operating expenses will be 70 percent of sales, fixed costs will remain at $60,000, interest will remain at $10,000, the tax rate will be 40 percent, and the dividend payment will be $9,000. Given these expectations, and assuming that all assets and spontaneous liabilities will increase as a percent of sales, calculate next year's additional outside funds needed (OFN). (Note: You will have to make the income statement pro forma to determine the addition to retained earnings.)

Additional Questions and Problems

1. Given the definition of a sustainable growth rate (see question 2 of assignment 5.2), what are two actions that management of a firm can take to increase their company's sustainable growth rate?

2. Harrelson Hydraulics sells drydock boatlift systems. Harrelson's sales are highly seasonal. All sales are on credit with terms of net thirty days, and Harrelson has no bad debt (that is, cash from all sales is collected exactly thirty days after the actual sale occurs). Sales for April through September are expected to be as follows:

April Sales	$100,000
May Sales	$300,000
June Sales	$500,000
July Sales	$900,000
August Sales	$500,000
September Sales	$200,000

Harrelson's monthly expenses are expected to be perfectly constant, equal to $350,000 per month. All expenses are paid immediately. Assume that sales and expenses are evenly distributed through each month and that there are thirty days in every month (thus, if monthly sales/expenses equal $3,000, then sales/expenses equal $100 per day). At the current time, (that is on March 30), Harrelson has $350,000 in its checking account, the checking account balance can never go below $50,000, there is currently no short-term bank loan outstanding, and the company's current account receivables balance is $75,000 (which, given the thirty-day collection period, was March sales).

a. Compute Harrelson's projected monthly net cash flow for April, May, June, July, August, and September.

b. Compute Harrelson's projected end-of-month cash balance and short-term bank loan balance for April, May, June, July, August, and September. (To find these values, assume that negative monthly net cash flows will be covered with cash that is in the checking account as long as the cash account is greater than $75,000 and will be covered by additions to the short-term bank loan if cash is equal to $75,000. Also assume that positive monthly net cash flows will be used

161

to pay down the short-term bank loan as long as it is greater than $0 and will be deposited into the checking account if short-term bank loans equal $0.)

c. If the sales and collection period assumptions hold true, what will be Harrelson's account receivables balance on April 30, May 30, June 30, July 30, August 30, and September 30 (recall that we are assuming there are exactly thirty days in every month).

3. Sarah's Sofas, Inc. sells, on average, thirty sofas per month. At the beginning of each month, Sarah's purchases thirty new sofas from the manufacturer to place on the showroom floor (Sarah's also keeps ten extra sofas in the back storeroom at all times). When the total number of sofas in inventory is equal to ten, Sarah's orders thirty additional new sofas from the manufacturer. This order usually occurs near the end of each month. Thus, the maximum inventory held by Sarah's Sofas, Inc. is forty sofas and the average inventory at any point in time is twenty-five sofas.

Sarah's is considering changing the way they order sofas from once per month to three times per month. That is, Sarah's will order ten sofas at the beginning of each month, another ten sofas near the tenth of each month, and another ten sofas near the twentieth of each month (the company will still keep the ten extra sofas in the back storeroom at all times). Thus, the maximum inventory held by Sarah's Sofas, Inc. will be twenty sofas and the average inventory at any point in time will be fifteen sofas. Sarah's believes that this change in policy will have no effect on annual sales.

Sarah's estimates that this new inventory ordering policy will have two benefits. First, this policy change will lower average inventory, which will allow Sarah's to reduce its average short-term loan balance. Each sofa has a cost of $500 and Sarah's interest rate on short-term debt is 10 percent. Second, Sarah's plans to reduce the size of its showroom to one-third of the current size, because the maximum number of sofas on the showroom floor at any point in time will be ten sofas, as opposed to thirty sofas under the current policy. Because Sarah's rents space for its showroom, the company estimates that this reduction in showroom space will save the company $5,000 in rent annually.

The cost of this policy change will be that Sarah's will need to pay additional fees for ordering and shipping inventory. Ordering and shipping costs are $250 per order. If these are the only costs and benefits of this policy, compute the costs and benefits and determine the net benefit or net cost. Should Sarah's adopt this new inventory order policy?

4. Rework the pro forma statement for COFFY'S assuming a 40 percent growth rate, a projected net profit margin of 5 percent, and a planned dividend payment of $40,000. Determine the *Total Outside Funds Needed.*

5. Rework the pro forma statement for COFFY'S assuming a 40 percent growth rate, a projected net profit margin of 5 percent, a planned dividend payment of $40,000, and a desired pro forma current ratio of 2.5. Determine the *Long-Term Outside Funds Needed.*

6. Rework the pro forma statement for COFFYS assuming a 40 percent growth rate, a projected net profit margin of 5 percent, a planned dividend payment of $40,000, a desired pro forma current ratio of 2.0 *and* a debt ratio of 40 percent. Determine the additional amount of money that COFFY'S must raise by selling new common stock.

7. Given the following information for Dune Inc.:

Balance Sheet
Dune, Inc.
As of December 31, 2006

Cash	20,000	Notes payable	250,000
Accounts receivable	200,000	Accounts payable	200,000
Inventories	300,000	Other current liabilities	50,000
Other current assets	50,000	**Total current liabilities**	**500,000**
Total current assets	**570,000**	Long-term debt	200,000
Net fixed assets	650,000	Common stock ($.50 par value)	50,000
Other long-term assets	30,000	Capital surplus	200,000
Total assets	**1,250,000**	Retained earnings	300,000
		Total liabilities and equity	**1,250,000**

Additional Information for Dune, Inc.

Sales in 2006	1,000,000
Projected sales growth in 2007	15%
Projected net profit margin in 2007	6%
Projected dividends in 2007	20,000

a. Use the percentage of sales method to create a pro forma 2007 balance sheet for Dune Inc. Based on the pro forma balance sheet what is the projected Total Outside Funds Needed for Dune, Inc. in 2007?

b. Assuming that Dune, Inc. plans wants its debt ratio to be 60 percent in 2007, modify the pro forma balance sheet you created in part a of this question to determine the amount of New Common Stock that Dune must issue to balance its projected balance sheet?

8. Given the financial statements and the bullet points below, use the percentage of sales method to create a pro forma 2007 balance sheet for Seebrock Company. Based on the pro forma balance sheet, what is the projected Total Outside Funds Needed for Seebrock in 2007?

- Seebrock expects sales to grow in 2007 by 40 percent
- Seebrock expects the net profit margin in 2007 to be the same as it was in 2006
- Seebrock plans to pay a dividend in 2007 of $24,000

Balance Sheet
Seebrock Company
For the Years Ending December 31, 2005 and 2006

	2005	2006
Cash	$ 24,000	$ 22,000
Accounts receivable	41,000	33,000
Inventory	51,000	83,000
Total current assets	**$116,000**	**$138,000**
Net plant and equipment	$284,000	$295,000
Total assets	**$400,000**	**$433,000**
Notes payable	16,000	13,000
Accounts payable to suppliers	48,000	57,000
Accruals	7,000	5,000
Total current liabilities	**71,000**	**75,000**
Long-term debt	160,000	175,000
Common stock ($2.50 par value)	25,000	27,000
Capital surplus	80,000	84,000
Retained earnings	64,000	72,000
Total liabilities and equity	**$400,000**	**$433,000**

Income Statement
Seebrock Company
For the Year Ending December 31, 2006

Sales	$600,000
Cost of goods sold	450,000
Gross Profit	**$150,000**
General and administrative	40,000
Depreciation	30,000
Operating income	**80,000**
Interest expense	18,000
Earnings before taxes	**62,000**
Taxes	32,000
Net income	**$ 30,000**

9. The following financial statement belong to Stackelberg Industries, Incorporated.

Balance Sheet
Stackelberg Industries, Inc.
For the Years Ending December 31, 2005 and 2006
(in millions)

Assets	2005	2006
Cash	$ 24,000	$ 39,900
Accounts receivable	40,000	29,000
Inventory	52,200	53,100
Total current assets	**116,200**	**122,000**
Net plant and equipment	285,000	295,000
Total assets	**$401,200**	**$417,000**
Liabilities and stockholders' equity		
Notes payable	16,000	18,000
Accounts payable to suppliers	49,000	37,000
Accruals	6,000	5,000
Total current liabilities	**71,000**	**60,000**
Long-term debt	160,000	166,000
Common stock ($2.00 par value)	25,000	30,000
Capital surplus	80,000	91,000
Retained earnings	65,200	70,000
Total liabilities and equity	**$401,200**	**$417,000**

Income Statement
Stackelberg Industries, Inc.
For the Year Ending December 31, 2006

Sales	$500,000
Cost of goods sold	360,000
Gross Profit	**140,000**
General and administrative	40,000
Depreciation	30,000
Operating income	**70,000**
Interest expense	18,000
Earnings before taxes	**52,000**
Taxes	20,000
Net income	**$ 32,000**

Stackelberg Industries Inc. expects sales to grow by 30 percent in 2007. The company plans to pay out $39,000 in dividends in 2007, and expects that the Net Profit Margin in 2007 will be 6 percent. Compute the Outside Funds Needed in 2007 to support this projected growth in sales (see the balance sheet and income statement above).

10. The following balance sheets and income statement data belong to the Health Valley Company.

Balance Sheet
Health Valley Company
For the Years Ending December 31, 2005 and 2006

	2005	2006
Cash	$ 20,000	$ 12,000
Accounts receivable	40,000	48,000
Inventory	60,000	50,000
Total current assets	**$120,000**	**$110,000**
Gross fixed assets	$400,000	$450,000
(Accumulated depreciation)	(120,000)	(150,000)
Net fixed assets	$280,000	$300,000
Total assets	**$400,000**	**$410,000**
Notes payable	5,000	10,000
Accounts payable to suppliers	25,000	30,000
Accruals	10,000	5,000
Total current liabilities	**40,000**	**45,000**
Long-term debt	100,000	140,000
Common stock ($2.00 par value)	60,000	45,000
Capital surplus	50,000	30,000
Retained earnings	150,000	150,000
Total liabilities and equity	**$400,000**	**$410,000**

Health Valley Company Income Statement Data:

2005 Net income = $15,000
2006 Net income = $18,000
2006 Sales = $300,000

a. Assuming that Health Valley projects that sales in 2007 will be $420,000, the net profit margin in 2007 will be the same as it was in 2006, and that all 2007 net income will be paid out in dividends (that is, the dividend payout ratio will be 100 percent), use the OFN formula to compute Outside Funds Needed, assuming that all assets and all spontaneous liabilities will grow as a percent of sales.

b. Now assume that Health Valley plans to pay out 50 percent of its earnings as dividends in 2007. Using the OFN formula, compute Outside Funds Needed.

c. Finally, assume that Health Valley plans to pay out all of its earnings as dividends in 2007. Using the OFN formula, compute Outside Funds Needed.

11. The following information is available for the Sharkton Company:

Balance Sheet for 2006

Cash	$ 400,000
Accounts receivable	900,000
Inventory	1,200,000
Net property and plant	2,500,000
Total assets	**$5,000,000**
Accounts payable	$ 800,000
Long-term debt	1,500,000
Common stock	1,800,000
Retained earnings	900,000
Total liabilities and net worth	**$5,000,000**

Additional Information:

Projected sales for 2007 = $10,000,000
The dividend payout ratio is 40 percent
Sales for 2006 = $8,000,000
Net profit margin = 4 percent

a. Compute the expected additional debt and/or common stock needed by Sharkton in 2007 to support this increase in sales. Assume that the plant is operating at full capacity.

b. Compute the expected additional common stock needed by Sharkton in 2007 to support this increase in sales assuming that the firm's debt ratio for 2007 will be 60 percent. Assume that the plant is operation at full capacity.

12. The following balance sheet belongs to the Punkerton Corporation:

Balance Sheet
The Punkerton Corporation
For the Year Ending December 31, 2006

Cash	$ 100,000
Accounts receivable	500,000
Inventory	3,800,000
Net property and plant	5,400,000
Total assets	**$9,800,000**
Accounts payable	$ 300,000
Long-term debt	4,500,000
Common stock	2,800,000
Retained earnings	2,200,000
Total liabilities and net worth	**$9,800,000**

Additional Information:

Projected sales for 2007 = $28,000,000
The dividend payout ratio is 80 percent
Sales for 2006 = $22,400,000
Net profit margin = 2.5 percent

a. Compute the *Total Outside Funds Needed* by Punkerton in 2007 to support this increase in sales assuming that the plant is operating at full capacity.

b. Compute the *Total Outside Funds Needed* by Punkerton in 2007 to support this increase in sales assuming that the plant is not operating at full capacity and so no additional Net Property and Plant will be needed to support the increase in sales.

Chapter 6

Time Value of Money: The Basic Concepts

After studying Chapter 6, you should be able to:

♦ Explain the mechanics of compounding: how money grows over time when it is invested.

♦ Understand the difference between a nominal interest rate and a real interest rate.

♦ Mathematically define and be able to describe each of the variables of the single period present value and future value equations that underlie the time value of money.

♦ Compute the present value of a lump sum of money to be received one year from today.

♦ Compute the single period future value of a lump sum of money.

♦ Compute the present value and future value of a two-year cash flow.

6.1 Chapter Overview ....

The notion that money has a time value is one of the most important concepts in valuation and, consequently, in finance. It is a fairly simple concept and is best illustrated as the answer to the following question. If we gave you a choice between receiving $100 today versus receiving $100 one year from now, which alternative would you choose? We are sure that your answer will be: $100 today.

Let us spend a few minutes analyzing the reason you chose to receive the $100 today. Was it because you could invest the money received today in a bank or shares or some investment opportunity and hope to have more than $100 at the end of the year? Clearly, if there are such investment opportunities available, it makes perfect sense to choose to receive the money today. Now suppose that you are living in an environment where there are absolutely no investment opportunities and the only use of money is for spending it to buy things, that is, for consumption. In such an environment, would you still choose to receive the $100 today rather than one year later? Again, intuitively, you would still choose to receive the money earlier. The reason for this is that if you receive the money today, you could use it for consumption. For rational persons, consumption always brings in some benefits, or, if you prefer, utility. If the amount were to be received one year later, you would have to postpone your ability to consume by one year. Rational people prefer to consume today rather than later. Thus, even in an environment with no investment opportunities, money has time value.

A practical implication of the concept of time value of money is that you cannot add sums of money that are received at different points in time. It would be equivalent to the proverbial adding of apples and oranges. For example, if an investment generates $100 at the end of one year and another $100 at the end of two years, one cannot say that the investment yields a total of $200.

The most important implication of the concept of time value of money is the clear distinction between the amount of the money to be received in the future and its value today. The fact that you prefer to receive $100 today over receiving $100 one year from now implies that you place a lower value on the amount that is received at the later date. Recall that finance is all about valuing assets, and assets have value because they generate cash flows. These cash flows, however, occur at different times in the future. Therefore, to compute the value of an asset or its price today, we have to be able to determine a method for assigning a value (at the current time) to cash flows that occur in the future. This chapter is intended to provide the basics of computing values of cash flows at a point in time that is different from the point in time at which the cash flows actually occur.

6.2 Interest Rates and the Inflation Adjustment ....

Recall that money has time value because rational persons prefer to consume sooner than later. Now suppose that a friend of yours asks you for a one-year loan of $100. If the friend offered to return to you $100 at the end of the year, you would probably not be happy with the arrangement because you know that the value of the $100 that you are giving up today is greater than the $100 that you will receive after one year. Therefore, you would require the borrower to return the $100 and some extra amount at the end of the year. The extra amount is the interest that you would charge.

How is the interest determined? Let us again consider the strange environment where there are no investment opportunities, that is, money is used only for consumption. Suppose that with the $100 that you have you can buy twenty meals (burger, fries, and a soda). By loaning this amount, you are giving up your ability to purchase these twenty meals and you require compensation for postponing your consumption. You believe that the borrower should compensate you by returning an amount that will enable you to buy two additional meals, that is, twenty-two meals, at the end of the year. How does this translate into an interest rate?

1. **What is the price of one meal?** Because you can buy twenty meals with $100, the price is:

$$\frac{\$100}{20} = \$5 \text{ per meal.}$$

2. **Because you require the ability to purchase twenty-two meals at the end of one year, how much would you require?** You would require:

$$22 \times \$5 = \$110.$$

3. **What is the dollar amount of the interest on this loan?**

$$\$110 - \$100 = \$10$$

4. **What is the interest in percentage terms?** You can do this two ways:

$$\frac{\$10}{\$100} = 0.10 \text{ or 10 percent, or } \frac{\$110 - \$100}{\$100} - 1 = 0.10 \text{ or 10 percent.}$$

real rate of interest

Problem 6.1 You require $1,700 to buy a computer and the bank is offering a loan at an interest rate of 14 percent. If you plan to repay the loan after one year, how much will you have to pay the bank?

$$\frac{x - 1700}{1700} = .14$$
$$x - 1700 = 238$$
$$x = 1938$$

Answer: $1,938.

Problem 6.2 You loan your friend $300 and he promises to give you $340 at the end of one year. What is the interest rate that you are charging your friend?

$$\frac{340 - 300}{300} = \frac{40}{300} = 13.33\%$$

Answer: 13.3333 percent.

Problem 6.3 You have to choose between the following two investment opportunities: (a) invest $1,200 today to obtain $1,412 at the end of one year or (b) invest $1,200 at 12 percent for one year. Which one would you choose? Make sure you obtain both the given answers.

a) $$\frac{1412 - 1200}{1200} = \frac{212}{1200} = 17.67\%$$

b) $$\frac{x - 1200}{1200} = .12$$
$$x - 1200 = 144$$
$$x = 1344$$

Choose a b/c higher interest return

Answer: You should choose alternative (a), because the first alternative represents a return of 17.667 percent. Also, note that the second alternative is only worth $1,344 at the end of one year.

Now let us add a small wrinkle to our environment; let there be inflation. What is inflation? It is a general rise in prices. Let us suppose that the inflation in the environment is at a rate of 5 percent. How does this change the above? You still require that your friend return you an amount that will enable you to purchase twenty-two meals. However, because of inflation, the price of a meal at the end of the year will be higher by 5 percent, the rate of inflation. The price after one year will be:

$$\$5 \times 1.05 = \$5.25 \text{ per meal.}$$

nominal rate of interest + real rate of interest

Therefore, to buy twenty-two meals, you will require:

$$22 \times \$5.25 = \$115.50.$$

The interest that you will now require is $115.50 - $100 = $15.50. In percentage terms, this amounts to:

$$\frac{\$15.50}{100} = 0.155 \text{ or } 15.50 \text{ percent.}$$

Notice that because of the inflation of 5 percent, the interest rate that you require has increased from the 10 percent when there was no inflation, to 15.50 percent.

In this 15.50 percent, the return for postponing consumption is 10 percent and the remaining 5.50 percent is the adjustment for inflation. The return for postponing consumption is known as the **real rate of interest** and the inflation-adjusted return is known as the **nominal rate of interest.** In a world where there is no inflation, the real and the nominal rates are equal. However, we live in an economy where inflation is forever expected and hence the two rates are different. If you went to a bank to finance a new car and the bank quoted an interest rate of 9 percent, is the bank quoting the real or the nominal rate? All quoted rates are always nominal. In fact, the real rate is never observed, all the rates that you observe at banks or in the financial press are nominal rates.

What is the relation between real and nominal rates? Recall that in our earlier calculations for determining the 15.50 percent rate, we first computed the amount that the borrower would need to repay to enable you to buy twenty-two meals and then adjusted the price of the meal for inflation. In other words, we made the following computation:

$$[20 \times (1.10)] \times [\$5 \times (1.05)] = 22 \times \$5.25 = \$115.50.$$

In the equation above, the terms in the first brackets imply that you require a 10 percent increase in your consumption ability, from twenty to twenty-two. The terms in the second set of brackets make the adjustment for the price increase over one year assuming an inflation rate of 5 percent.

In general, if we let '$r_{nominal}$' represent the nominal rate, 'r_{real}' the real rate, and 'i' the rate of inflation, then

$$(1 + r_{nominal}) = (1 + r_{real}) \times (1 + i), \quad \text{or, rearranging}$$
$$r_{nominal} = r_{real} + i + (r_{real} \times i).$$

If the real interest rate and the inflation rate are fairly small, one can say that the nominal rate is approximately the sum of the real rate and the rate of inflation. In our example, this approximate relationship would yield a nominal rate of 15 percent. The additional 0.50 percent is simply the value of the third term in the above equation.

Problem 6.4 In a world without inflation, you require a return of 8 percent. If the inflation were 4 percent, what rate of return would you require?

$r_{real} = .08\% + .04 + (.08 \times .04)$
$r_{real} = .12\% + .32$
$r_{real} = 12.32\%$

Answer: 12.32 percent.

Problem 6.5 If the interest rate in the financial markets on U.S. Treasury bills is 8 percent and the expected inflation rate is 5 percent, what is the real rate of interest?

$r_{real} = \frac{1.05}{1.08} = 2.8571\%$

Answer: 2.857 percent.

In later chapters, the distinction between real and nominal rates will become important. For the time being, however, let us not worry about this distinction and assume that there is no inflation.

6.3 Present and Future Values: Single Period ....

Suppose that for giving up the ability to consume 100 units of a good today, you need to receive 110 units of the good at the end of the year. This implies that the minimum rate of return that you require is 10 percent. Another way to think about this is that if some investment offered you a return of less than 10 percent, you would not invest; you would prefer to consume today. On the other hand, if an investment promised a return of greater than 10 percent, you would prefer to forgo consumption today and make the investment. Thus, 10 percent is the minimum return that you require for foregoing consumption. The minimum interest rate that is required to decide to forgo current consumption is called the ***required rate of return.***

Suppose that your required rate of return is 10 percent, and we gave you a choice between receiving $100 today versus $120 one year from today. Which would you choose? Clearly the alternative of receiving $120 after one year. By waiting for one year, you obtain 20 percent more money and your required rate of return is only 10 percent. Hence, you prefer to wait. You can think of the 20 percent as the return from waiting. On the other hand, if the choice were $100 today versus $105 after one year, you would prefer the $100 today. Now, suppose the choice is $100 today or $110 at the end of the year, what would you choose if your required rate of return is 10 percent? In this case, the answer is not immediately obvious. Because your required rate is 10 percent, you have no clear preference for either one of the alternatives.

In other words, if your required rate of return is 10 percent, you are ***indifferent*** between receiving $100 today and receiving $110 after one year. Viewed another way, the "value" that you put on receiving $110 after one year is the same as the "value" you put on receiving $100 today. This is the same as either one of the following statements.

If your required rate of return is 10 percent, the <u>present value</u> of a cash flow of $110 at the end of the year is $100

or

If your required rate of return is 10 percent, the <u>future value</u> of a cash flow of $100 today is $110 at the end of the year.

Let PV denote the present value, let FV denote the future value, and let r be the required rate of return. Then, when the time horizon is one year (or period), the relationship between PV and FV is:

$$PV = \frac{1}{1 + r} \times FV,$$

or, equivalently

$$FV = (1 + r) \times PV.$$

Note that the above relationships apply only when the time horizon is one year. We shall look at a longer horizon soon.

Note that r is, for all practical purposes, always positive, that is, greater than zero. This just means that interest rates are positive. Although in theory it is possible for an interest rate to be less than zero (this can occur if the inflation rate is expected to be negative), in practice negative interest rates do not occur. A negative interest rate would imply that someone would pay you to borrow money from them! If you think this is a good idea, then I would like to refinance my house with you being the lender. In our economy and throughout this section of the book we will ALWAYS assume positive interest rates.

Given that interest rates are assumed to be greater than zero, the following observations can be made.

   a. PV is always less than FV.

   b. $\dfrac{1}{1+r}$ is always less than one.

   c. $(1 + r)$ is always greater than one.

   d. $\dfrac{1}{1+r}$, which is always less than one, can be thought of as the weight (or importance) that one puts on a cash flow that occurs after one year. Since it is always less than one, we can say that we put a lower weight on the cash flow that occurs later.

Converting future cash flows into their present values is called **_discounting,_** and converting current cash flows into their future values is called **_compounding._** The rate of return that is used in these processes, the required rate of return, is also called the **_discount rate._** The relationship between present value and the interest or discount rate is graphically depicted in Figure 6.1. Notice that as the discount rate increases, the present value decreases. In fact, the decrease is not linear, that is, the graph is not a straight line.

Problem 6.6   What is the present value of $16,000 to be received at the end of one year if the discount rate is 10 percent?

$$PV = \frac{1}{1+.10} \times 16,000 = \frac{1}{1.10} \times 16000 = 14,545.45$$

Answer: $14,545.45.

Problem 6.7   What is the future value of $11,138 after one year if the discount rate is 11 percent?

$$FV = (1+.11) \times 11,138 = 1.11 \times 11,138 = 12,363.18$$

Answer: $12,363.18.

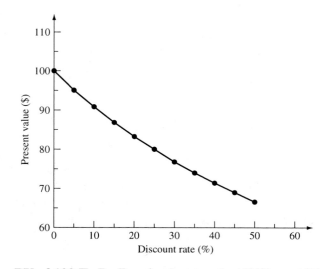

Figure 6.1   PV of 100 To Be Received at t = 1 at Different Discount Rates

Problem 6.8   If the bank promises to give you $28,400 after one year if you deposit $27,000 today, what is the interest rate that the bank is giving you?

$$\frac{28{,}400}{27{,}000} - 1 = 5.1852$$

Answer: 5.185 percent.

Problem 6.9   You make two investments. The first investment will give you $4,800 after one year and the second investment will give you $23,600 after one year. If your required rate of return is 10 percent, what is the current value of your investments?

$$FV = PV \times (1 + r)$$

$$= \frac{4800}{1.1} + \frac{23600}{1.1} = 25{,}818.1818$$

Answer: $25,818.18.

The last problem may have been a little trickier than the earlier ones. There are two ways to look at this problem. In either case, you know that the current value is the present value of future cash flows, therefore you have to find present values. One way to do this is to sum all the cash flows that you are going to obtain at the end of the year and then find the present value of the sum. Note that you are not summing apples and oranges; the addition is justified because you are adding cash flows that occur at the same time, that is, at the end of the year. In this case, the sum of the cash flows at the end of the year is:

$$\$4{,}800 + \$23{,}600 = \$28{,}400.$$

The present value of this cash flow is:

$$\frac{\$28{,}400}{1.1} = \$25{,}818.18.$$

Alternatively, you could have found the present values of the two cash flows separately and added the present values. Again the addition is justified, because you are adding values at the same point in time, now. In this case, the present value of the first investment is:

$$\frac{\$4{,}800}{1.1} = \$4{,}363.64,$$

and the present value of the second investment is:

$$\frac{\$23{,}600}{1.1} = \$21{,}454.55.$$

The sum of the two present values is $25,818.19. Either method has to give you the same answer except for a small rounding error.

The last problem and the second method of solving it illustrate an important concept in finance. This concept is called **value additivity.** According to this principle, you can add values. An application of this is in valuing a firm. Note that a firm consists of several assets, each of which generates future cash flows. The value of the firm is simply the sum of the values of each of the assets. In other words, to find the value of the firm, you would find the present value of the future cash flows of each of the assets, and then sum all the assets' present values.

For the following questions, circle the one correct answer (there is always one). We strongly suggest that you not use a financial calculator to find these answers. Merely use what you have learned in this chapter to this point. Calculator applications will be used in the following chapter. The current chapter is designed to demonstrate the intuition behind time value of money. Merely plugging numbers into a calculator without understanding why you are doing what you are doing is unproductive and, more often than not, produces the wrong answer. You need to understand if and why answers that you derive make sense.

Problem 6.10   If the discount rate is 12.5 percent, the present value of $16,389 obtained at the end of one year is:

    a. $16,394

    b. $14,568

    c. $18,437.63

Which answer did you circle? Even without calculations, you know that the answer has to be $14,568 because the other two numbers cannot be present values as they are both greater than $16,389.

Problem 6.11   A bank has promised to give you $11,438 after one year if you deposit $11,000 today. What is the interest rate that the bank is offering you?

    a. 3.98 percent

    b. zero percent

    c. −4 percent.

Again, without calculations, you know that zero and negative 4 percent cannot be right since the future value is greater than the present value. Therefore, the correct answer must be 3.98 percent.

These are the basic concepts in the time value of money. The material in the rest of this chapter and the next chapter is identical in concept, but is more complicated, because we will consider two time periods and two cash flows in the remainder of this chapter and multiple time periods in the next chapter.

6.4   Present and Future Values: Two Periods ....

In this section, we will analyze the concept of the time value of money when the number of periods is two as opposed to the one-year cases above. You will find that the concepts of present and future values remain the same, only the calculations become a little more tedious.

Suppose you deposit $100 in a bank and the bank pays an interest of 5 percent per year on this account and the interest is compounded annually. How much money will you have in your account at the end of two years? Before solving this problem, let us discuss a couple of things. First, unless otherwise stated, the interest rate, or the discount rate, is always for one year. Sometimes 5 percent per year will be written as 5 percent p. a., where p. a. stands for per annum, which is the same as per year. Next, it is important to note the frequency of the compounding because it affects the interest that you earn. In this example, it is stated that the interest will be compounded annually, that is, the frequency of compounding is one per year. In the following chapter we will demonstrate the effect that increasing this frequency has on future and present values. Throughout this book, unless otherwise specifically stated, assume that the frequency of compounding is one time per year.

Now let us solve the problem. To do this, let us introduce the concept of a time line. This may seem a little redundant at this stage but will prove invaluable as the problems become more complicated. A time line is simply a pictorial representation of the occurrence of cash flows over time. As a rule, we will denote money that leaves your pocket with a "minus" sign, and the money that enters your pocket with a "positive" or "no" sign. Thus, if you deposit money in the account, this represents money leaving your pocket; the cash flow will have a minus sign preceding it.

One of the most important issues in working a time value of money problem is to make sure that the exact time periods for the cash flows are clearly understood. For this reason, standard definitions have been developed in finance classes for time. We denote "time" with the letter t. Today is defined as t = 0; today is also often referred to as the "**end** of year (or period) 0." One year (or period) from today is defined as t = 1; this is also known as the "**end** of year (or period) 1." Thus, fourteen years from today would be t = 14, or the "**end** of year 14."

In the next chapter we will discuss cash flows that occur at the **beginning** of a year or time period, as opposed to at the end of a time period. If the end of year 1 is exactly one year from today, then the beginning of year 1 is actually the end of year 0—that is, today. Likewise, the beginning of year 2 is actually the end of year 1. And so on.

This may be easier to picture if you think in terms of dates. Assume that today is June 1, 2006. Then, June 1, 2007 will be exactly 1 year from today or, the end of year 1. Because the beginning of year 1 will be 365 days earlier (we ignore leap years in TVM problems), the beginning of year 1 is actually today (that is, June 1, 2006).

So, for the problem at hand, we will denote t = 0 as today or now, t = 1 as the end of the first period (or year), and t = 2 as the end of the second period or year. The time line for our problem is drawn below.

We can divide this problem into two single period problems as follows. First, based on what we did in the previous section, we know that the amount we will have in the account at the end of the first year is:

$$\$100 \times 1.05 = \$105.$$

We can now consider the second year as another single period case in which we deposit $105 into the account that pays an interest rate of 5 percent. Thus, at the end of the second year, we will have the following amount in the account.

$$\$105 \times 1.05 = \$110.25$$

And that is the answer to the problem. However, doing every problem as a series of single period problems becomes tedious, so let us find a more direct route. We multiplied $100 by 1.05 to obtain the amount in the account at the end of the first period and we again multiplied the amount in the account at t = 1 obtained thus ($105) by 1.05, to account for the interest earned in the second year. We can do all this in one step as follows:

$$\$100 \times (1.05) \times (1.05) = \$110.25.$$

Or, equivalently,

$$\$100 \times (1.05)^2 = \$110.25.$$

Note that the power term denotes the number of periods that the amount earns interest, which, in this problem, is two. Also note that the interest earned in the first year ($5) earns interest in the second year. How much will this be? $5 \times 0.05 = \$0.25$. Thus, the interest amount of $10.25 comprises $10 on the $100 dollars that we deposited and $0.25, the interest earned in the second year on the interest earned in the first year. In general, therefore, when the number of periods is two,

$$FV = (1 + r)^2 \times PV.$$

Similarly, by rearranging the terms in the above equation, we obtain the following expression for computing the present value when the number of periods is two.

$$PV = \frac{1}{(1+r)^2} \times FV$$

Note that the observations made after presenting the PV and FV relations for the single period case in the previous section also apply here.

Now solve the following simple problems in the space provided and see if you obtain the given answers. Make sure that you fill in the correct numbers on the time line.

Problem 6.12　You plan to loan $11,000 to your friend at an interest rate of 8 percent per year compounded annually. The loan is to be repaid in two years. How much will your friend pay you at $t = 2$?

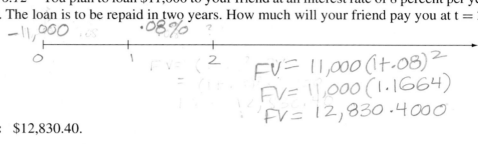

Answer: $12,830.40.

Problem 6.13　You are offered the chance to buy into an investment that promises to pay you $28,650 at the end of two years. If your required rate of return is 12 percent, what is the maximum amount that you would pay for this investment? (Don't forget to draw the time line.)

Answer: $22,839.60.

Problem 6.14　You are offered an investment opportunity that requires you to pay $31,500 today and promises to give you $39,700 at the end of two years. What is the return on this investment?

Answer: 12.26 percent.

The last problem might be a little tricky. In this problem you are given the present and the future values and are required to find the return r. We use the formula:

$$FV = (1+r)^2 \times PV.$$

Here FV is $39,700 and PV is $31,500 and we have to solve for r. Substituting the values for PV and FV, we have:

$$\$39,700 = (1+r)^2 \times \$31,500.$$

Therefore,

$$(1+r)^2 = \frac{\$39,700}{\$31,500} = 1.2603.$$

Then

$$1 + r = \sqrt{1.2603}$$

$$= 1.1226.$$

Thus,

$$r = 1.1226 - 1 = 0.1226 \text{ or } 12.26 \text{ percent.}$$

Now let us look at the case when cash flows occur not just at the end of one of the periods but at the end of both periods. Suppose that you have the opportunity to invest in a venture that offers $12,000 at the end of the first year and $16,350 at the end of the second year. What is the maximum price that you would pay for this investment if your required rate of return is 12 percent?

To solve this problem, we have to find the present value for a cash flow that occurs at $t = 1$ and one that occurs at $t = 2$. Then we will use the concept of value additivity and sum the present values (that is at $t = 0$) of both these cash flows to obtain the maximum price that we will be willing to pay. Here is how it goes. The time line is

$$PV = \frac{\$12,000}{1.12} + \frac{\$16,350}{(1.12)^2}$$

$$= \$10,714.29 + \$13,034.12$$

$$= \$23,748.41$$

Now solve the following problems in the space provided and try to obtain the given answer. Remember to draw the time line.

Problem 6.15   You deposit $5,000 in a bank account today. You make another deposit of $4,000 into the account at the end of the first year. If the bank pays interest at 6 percent compounded annually, how much will you have in your account at the end of two years, that is, at $t = 2$?

$$5000 + 4000 = 8,773 \times (1.06)^2 = 9,858$$

$$\frac{}{1.06}$$

Answer: $9,858.

Problem 6.16   You are planning to spend a summer in Europe one year from now. You expect that the trip will cost you $15,000. Two years from now, you want to spend the summer in Asia and you expect this trip to cost you $19,000. How much should you deposit in your bank account today so that you can make both these trips? Your bank pays you interest at 8 percent per year.

$$PV = \frac{15,000}{1.08} + \frac{19,000}{(1.08)^2}$$

$$PV = 30,178.33$$

Answer: $30,178.33.

Solving the last problem requires the same method as before—find the present value of the two cash flows, $15,000 occurring at t = 1 and $19,000 occurring at t = 2 and then sum the present values. That is,

$$PV = \frac{\$15,000}{1.08} + \frac{\$19,000}{(1.08)^2} = \$30,178.33.$$

It is, however, interesting to trace your account balance over time in this problem. You have deposited $30,178.33 into the account at t = 0. At t = 1, just before you make the withdrawal of $15,000, the account will have in it:

$$\$30,178.33 \times 1.08 = \$32,592.60.$$

After you make the withdrawal of $15,000 for your European binge, you will have left in the account an amount of:

$$\$32,592.60 - \$15,000 = \$17,592.60.$$

This amount is left in the account at t = 1 just after the withdrawal of $15,000. At t = 2, just before your withdrawal for the Asia trip, the account balance will have become:

$$\$17,592.60 \times 1.08 = \$19,000,$$

which, not surprisingly, is exactly the amount you need for the summer in Asia.

Finally, let us consider two assets A and B. The discount rate is 10 percent and the cash flows from these assets are as follows:

	t = 1	t = 2
Asset A	$100	$200
Asset B	$200	$100

Which of these assets will have the higher present value? Can you answer that without performing any calculations? You can. It has to be asset B because this asset generates the higher cash flows sooner. Let us see if it is indeed the case.

$$PV_A = \frac{100}{1.1} + \frac{200}{(1.1)^2} = \$256.20$$

$$PV_B = \frac{200}{1.1} + \frac{100}{(1.1)^2} = \$264.46$$

Now suppose that there is another asset C that generates $300 at the end of each of the next two years. What would be its present value?

$$PV_C = \frac{300}{1.1} + \frac{300}{(1.1)^2} = \$520.66$$

Notice that the sum of the present values of assets A and B is $256.20 + $264.46 = $520.66 which is exactly the same as the present value of asset C. Why is this the case? Look at the cash flows from the three assets.

	t = 1	t = 2
Asset A	$100	$200
Asset B	$200	$100
Asset C	$300	$300

Notice that the cash flows from asset C represent the exact sum of the cash flows from A and B in each of the two periods. Therefore, recalling the principle of value additivity discussed earlier, it must be the case that $PV_A + PV_B = PV_C$.

6.5 Chapter Summary and Looking Forward ....

In this chapter we introduced the basic math of time value of money for one and two periods. We demonstrated how to use the fundamental time value of money equation:

$$FV = (1 + r) \times PV \quad ; \quad PV = \frac{FV}{1+r}$$

to solve for the future value one year from today of an immediate cash flow, and the present value of a cash flow to be received one year from today. We also showed how to find the discount rate, or required rate of return, that equates future value and present value.

$$r = \frac{FV}{PV} - 1$$

Next we showed how to use a simple extension of the basic time value of money equation:

$$FV_2 = (1 + r)^2 \times PV$$

to solve the same variables for cash flows that are two years apart. Lastly, we proved that the principle of value additivity applies to both individual and yearly cash flows, and also to the present values of those cash flows.

In the following chapter we will merely extend the time value of money equation to multiple years and to other than yearly (for example, monthly) cash flows. Because multiple year calculations can be tedious and complex, we will show how to use a financial calculator to assist in computing values. Never forget, however, that the simple math and ideas presented in this chapter are the foundations that underlie all time value of money calculations. This will be true no matter how complex the problems might appear or what aids (calculator, spreadsheet, and so on) they might require to determine a solution.

Assignment 6.1

Name:_____   Date:_____

Solve the following problems in the space provided.

1. Your neighbor is asking you to invest in a venture that will double your money in one year (you know what to do about such fantastic promises). How much return (in percentage terms) is he promising you?

$$FV = PV \times (1+r)$$
$$FV = 2$$
$$PV = 1$$
$$2 = 1 \times (1+r)$$
$$1 = r$$

$$PV = 1 \qquad 2 = 1 \times (1+r)$$
$$FV = 2 \qquad 2 = 1+r$$
$$1/y = \qquad 100\% = r$$

2. You have just deposited X dollars in your bank account that pays interest of 4.39 percent p.a. You discover that at the end of one year you have $7,397 in the account. What was X, that is, the amount of money that you deposited today?

$$PV = ?$$
$$1/y = 4.39$$
$$FV = 7,397$$

$$PV = \frac{1}{1+4.39} \times 7,397$$
$$PV = \frac{1}{5.39} \times 7,397$$
$$PV = \$7,085.93$$

$$4.39\%$$
$$\overset{0}{\vdash}\rule{3cm}{0.4pt}\overset{1}{7397}$$

3. You are going to retire after exactly one year and you plan to take a world cruise after retirement for which you will require $13,000. What is the least amount that you must set aside today at an interest rate of 8 percent p.a. so that you can take the cruise?

$$\overset{?}{\vdash}\overset{8\%}{\rule{3cm}{0.4pt}}\overset{}{\dashv}_{13,000}$$

$$PV = ?$$
$$FV = 13,000$$
$$1/y = 8\%$$

$$PV = \frac{1}{1+.08} \times 13,000$$
$$PV = \$12,037.04$$
$$Deposit$$

4. Assume that you need to have exactly $25,000 in your savings account exactly one year from today. Suppose that you expect to receive $4,500 exactly one year from today from your company as a bonus, and that you plan to deposit this entire amount into your savings account. What amount do you need to deposit into the account today to reach your goal, assuming that your account pays interest of 7.5 percent p.a.?

$$25,000$$
$$-4,500$$
$$\overline{20,500}$$

$PV = ?$
$FV = 29,500$
$I/Y = 7.5\%$

$$PV = \frac{1}{1+.075} \times 20,500$$

$$PV = \text{~~~~~~~~~~}$$

$$19,069.77$$

$$4,500$$
$$25,000$$

$$PV = \frac{20,500}{1.075}$$
$$PV = 19,069.7674$$

5. Suppose that your required rate of return is 12 percent p.a. and that you are offered an investment into an asset that will yield $14,739 at the end of one year. What is the maximum price that you would be willing to pay for this asset?

12% $14,739$

$$PV = \frac{14,739}{1.12}$$
$$PV = 13,159.8214$$

$I/Y = 12\%$ $PV = ?$

$FV = 14,739$

$$PV = \frac{1}{1+12\%} \times 14,739$$

$$PV = 13,159.82$$

Assignment 6.2

Name:_____ Date:_____

Solve the following problems in the space provided.

1. You neighbor (from Assignment 1) comes back to you (after you spurned him the first time) with another investment opportunity. He claims that you will be able to double your money in two years. What is the annual rate of return that this investment promises?

$$2 = 1 \times (1+r)^2$$
$$\sqrt{2} = \sqrt{1+r^2}$$
$$1.4142 = 1 + r$$
$$-1$$
$$.4142 = r$$

2. You want to withdraw $3,200 from your account at the end of one year and $7,300 at the end of the second year. How much should you deposit in your account today so that you can make these withdrawals? Your account pays 6 percent p.a.

6% $PV = \dfrac{3,200}{1.06} + \dfrac{7,300}{(1.06)^2} = \$9,515.84$

3200   7300

$PV = \dfrac{3,200}{(1.06)^1} + \dfrac{7,300}{(1.06)^2} = 9,515.8419$

3. You deposit $7,448 in your account today. You make another deposit at t = 1 of $2,476. How much will be there in your account at the end of year 1 if the interest rate is 7 percent p.a.?

7%

−7,448   2,476

$7448(1.07) = 7969.36$
$\qquad\qquad +2476$
$\qquad\quad \overline{10,445.36}$

$PV = \begin{array}{r} 7,448 \\ +2,476 \\ \hline 9,924.^{00} \end{array}$ 1/y = 7%

$FV = (1+.07) \times 9,924$

$FV = 10,618.68$

185

4. You deposit $7,448 in your account today. You make another deposit at t = 1 of $2,476. How much will be there in your account at the end of year 2 if the interest rate is 7 percent p.a.?

$$FV = (1.07)^2 \times 9924$$

$$FV = 11,361.99$$

7%

7448   2476   ?

├────┼────┤
O   1   2

10,445.36

10,445.36 × 1.01
────────────
1.01²

$$.7448 + \frac{2476}{1.07} = 9,762.0187 \times 1.07^2$$

$$= 11,176.5352$$

5. You must have $15,000 in your account exactly two years from today. Assuming an interest rate of 12 percent p.a., what equal annual amount must you deposit today and at the end of year 1 to reach your goal?

12%

15,000

├────┼────┤ 15,000
O   1   2

15,000

$$PV = \frac{{}_0^? X}{1.12} + \frac{15,000}{(1.12)^2}$$

$$\frac{1.12\ PV}{1.12} = \frac{13,392.8571}{1.12}$$

$$\boxed{PV = 11,957.91}$$

$$PV = \frac{1}{(1.12)^2} \times 15,000$$

$$\boxed{PV = 11,957.91}$$

$$FV = PV \times (1+r)$$

$$15000 = (1.12)^2\ PV + PV\ 1.12$$

$$15,000 = 12.544\ PV + 1.12\ PV$$

$$15,000 = 2.3744\ PV$$

$$PV = 6,317.3854$$

Assignment 6.3

Name:_____   Date:_____

Solve the following problems in the space provided.

1. Your account pays interest at 4 percent p.a. You deposit $8,000 in it today. You must have exactly $4,000 in the account at the end of two years. What should you do at the end of the first year to ensure this?

$$FV = PV \times (1+r)^2$$
$$4000 = 8,000(1.04)^2 + Deposit\ (1.04)^1$$
$$4000 = 8652.80 + Deposit\ (1.04)^1$$
$$-4652.80 / 1.04 = 4,473.8462$$

2. You come across an investment opportunity that requires you to invest $10,000 today and will yield you $6,500 at the end of the first year and $5,000 at the end of the second year. If your required rate of return is 12 percent p.a., would you make this investment?

$$PV = 10,000 + 6,500$$
$$PV = \frac{\$6,500}{1.12} + \frac{5,000}{(1.12)^2}$$

$$\$8,478.04$$
$$PV = 9,789.54 \quad \text{Do not make investment}$$

3. You invest $500 in an account today. You make no additional deposits into the account. One year from today there is $538 in the account. What is the nominal interest rate that you earned on your money?

$$PV = 500$$
$$FV = 538$$
$$yy = 2$$

$$\frac{538}{500} = 500 \times (1+r)$$

$$1.076 = \frac{1+r}{-1}$$
$$\frac{-1}{7.6 = r}$$

187

4. If the real interest rate is 8 percent and the inflation rate is 4 percent, what is the nominal interest rate?

$$r_{nominal} = r_{real} + i + (r_{real} \times i)$$
$$= .08 + .04 + (.08 \times .04)$$
$$= 12.32\%$$

5. If the nominal interest rate is 12.2 percent and that inflation rate is 3.6 percent, what is the real interest rate?

$$1 + r_{nominal} = (1 + real) \times (1 + i)$$
$$\frac{1.122}{1.036} = (1 + real)(1.036)$$
$$r_{real} = 8.3011\%$$

6. If the nominal interest rate is 8.6 percent and the real rate is 4.7 percent, what is the inflation rate?

$$1 + r_{nominal} = (1 + real) \times (1 + i)$$
$$\frac{1.086}{1.047} = (1.047)(1 + i) \frac{1}{1.047}$$
$$i = 3.7249\%$$

Additional Questions and Problems

1. If the real interest rate is 4 percent and the inflation rate is 6 percent, what is the nominal interest rate?
   $$\text{nominal} = 1.04 \times 1.06 - 1 = 11.0240 \% - 1 = 10.24\%$$

2. If the real interest rate is 1.8 percent and the inflation rate is 6.2 percent, what is the nominal interest rate?
   $$\text{nominal} = 1.018 \times 1.062 = 10.8112 - 1 = 8.112\%$$

3. If the nominal interest rate is 10 percent and that inflation rate is 4 percent, what is the real interest rate?
   $$\frac{1.10}{1.04} = (1 + \text{real})(1.04) = 5.7692\%$$

4. If the nominal interest rate is 14.4 percent and that inflation rate is 8.8 percent, what is the real interest rate?
   $$1.144 = (1 + \text{real})1.088 = 5.1471\%$$

5. If the nominal interest rate is 6 percent and the real rate is 4 percent, what is the inflation rate?
   $$1.06 = 1.04 (1 + i) = 1.9231\%$$

6. If the nominal interest rate is 18.4 percent and the real rate is 7.6 percent, what is the inflation rate?
   $$1.184 = 1.076 \; IR = 10.0372\%$$

7. Assume that you deposit $1,200 into an account today. If the account pays interest of 7.9 percent p.a., how much will you have in your account exactly one year from today?

8. Assume that you deposit $3,500 into an account today. If the account pays interest of 8.35 percent p.a., how much will you have in your account exactly two years from today?

9. Assume that you deposit $225 into an account exactly one year from today. If the account pays interest of 5.6 percent p.a., how much will you have in your account exactly two years from today?

10. Assume that you deposit $2,400 into an account today and that you deposit another $2,400 into the same account exactly one year from today. If the account pays interest of 4.88 percent p.a., how much will you have in your account exactly one year from today?

11. Assume that you deposit $318 into an account today and that you deposit another $552 into the same account exactly one year from today. If the account pays interest of 8.18 percent p.a., how much will you have in your account exactly two years from today?

12. Assume that you deposit $750 into an account exactly one year from today and that you deposit another $875 into the same account exactly two years from today. If the account pays interest of 9.5 percent p.a., how much will you have in your account exactly two years from today?

13. If you want to have exactly $4,000 in your account at $t = 1$, how much must you deposit into that account at $t = 0$ if the account pays interest of 6.6 percent p.a.?

189

14. If you want to have exactly $675 in your account at t = 2, how much must you deposit into that account at t = 0 if the account pays interest of 4.95 percent p.a.?

15. Your required rate of return is 11 percent p.a. and you have access to two investment opportunities. The first one costs $13,631 today and yields $15,200 at the end of the year. The second one costs $3,211 today and will yield $3,600 at the end of one year. Which, if any, investment or investments would you choose?

16. Your required rate of return is 14 percent p.a. and you have access to two investment opportunities. The first one requires you to invest $38,439 today and will yield $42,346 at the end of the first year. The second one costs you $41,489 today and will yield you $23,100 at the end of each of the next two years. Which, if any, investment or investments would you choose?

17. Choose the one answer that can be correct *without using a calculator.* Your required rate of return is 10 percent.

    a. The present value of $432 to be received at t = 1 is $432.

    b. The t = 1 value of a t = 0 cash flow of $7,811 is $7,770.

    c. You would pay $6,600 today for an asset that yields $2,300 at the end of each of the next two years.

    d. You would pay $6,600 today for an asset that yields $3,905.21 at the end of each of the next two years.

18. You require making the following withdrawals from your account—$35,000 at the end of the first year and $47,000 at the end of the second year. If the interest rate is 10 percent p.a., what is the least amount that you would need to deposit into the account today so that you can make these withdrawals? Check your answer by tracing the amounts in your account over time as we did in the chapter.

19. You deposit $12,000 today in an account that pays 14 percent p.a. interest. You plan to withdraw $12,000 from this account at the end of the first year. How much will be left in your account:

    a. at the end of the first year after the withdrawal?

    b. at the end of the second year?

20. Your required rate of return is 13 percent p.a. A two-year investment requires you to pay $10,000 today and will yield $7,000 at the end of the first year and an amount $X at the end of the second year. What is the least amount that X should be for you to make this investment?

21. You deposited $3,500 in the bank two years ago, and the account now has $4,100 in it today. What has been the "p.a." interest rate on this account?

22. A magazine subscription offer states that you can purchase a one-year subscription for $48 today and a two-year subscription for $70 today. Assuming that there will be no price changes in the future, which subscription would you choose if your required rate of return is 10 percent p.a.?

23. You have two monthly car payments of $400 each left on your car. If the interest rate is 0.75 percent per month, how much would you be required to pay the lender if you wanted to pay off the loan today?

24. A car dealer offers you the following two payment choices on a car that you would like to buy. The price of the car is $20,000. (a) Pay the entire amount today and receive a discount of $2,850. (b) Pay $20,000 at the end of two years. Which alternative would you choose if the interest rate is 8 percent p.a.?

Chapter **7**

Time Value of Money: Advanced Topics

After studying Chapter 7, you should be able to:

♦ Mathematically define and be able to describe each of the variables of the multi-period Present Value and Future Value equations that underlie the time value of money.

♦ Differentiate between an ordinary annuity and an annuity due.

♦ Determine the future or present value of a sum when there are non-annual compounding periods.

♦ Calculate the annual percentage yield or effective annual rate of interest and then explain how it differs from the nominal or stated interest rate.

♦ Use a financial calculator to solve time value of money problems.

7.1 Chapter Overview ....

In this chapter, there are really no new concepts from those presented in the earlier one. However, the computations for computing present and future values, and so on, will become more complex. In fact, the time line representation that was introduced in the previous chapter (and had seemed so redundant then) will prove invaluable in solving the more complex problems in this chapter. The computational methods necessary for solving time value problems with multiple cash flows in multiple periods are conceptually very similar to those with just one or two time periods. But computationally, they are much more complex. Therefore, we will resort to the use of financial calculators in solving these problems.

7.2 The Basic Approach ....

Let us take the simplest case when there is one cash flow of $100 occurring at $t = 4$. What would be the present value of this cash flow if the discount rate r is 10 percent p.a.? Based on what we have done in the previous chapter, you would divide this problem into two two-period problems. First, you could find the value of this cash flow at $t = 2$ and then discount the value thus obtained to that at $t = 0$. In other words, the value at $t = 2$ would be:

$$\frac{100}{(1.1)^2} = \$82.64.$$

Then the value at $t = 0$ would be:

$$\frac{82.64}{(1.1)^2} = \$68.30.$$

A more direct way of doing this would be to compute the present value as below:

$$PV = \frac{100}{(1.1)^4} = \$68.30.$$

Similarly, the value of $100 deposited in a bank today at the 10 percent at $t = 4$ would be:

$$FV = 100\,(1.1)^4 = \$146.41.$$

The general expression for present value of a single cash flow C_n occurring at $t = n$ is therefore given by

$$PV = \frac{C_n}{(1+r)^n},$$

and for the future, $t = n$, value of a $t = 0$ cash flow, C_0, is given by

$$FV_n = C_0\,(1+r)^n.$$

Figure 7.1 graphically depicts the relationship between the present value of a future cash flow and n the number of years after which that cash flow occurs. Notice that the later the cash flow occurs, the lower is the present value. Additionally, the relationship between PV and n is not a straight line.

Consider an asset that generates cash flows for two years with $\$C_1$ at the end of the first year and $\$C_2$ at the end of the second year. Then, denoting the required rate of return by r, the present value of the asset is given by

$$PV = \frac{C_1}{1+r} + \frac{C_2}{(1+r)^2}.$$

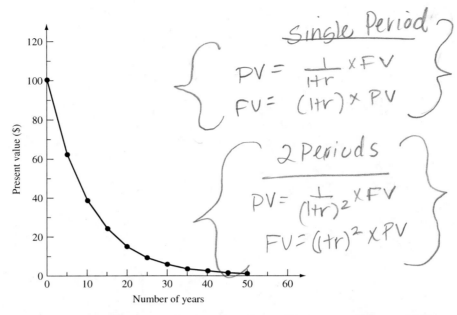

Figure 7.1 **Relation between Present Value and Number of Years (Discount Rate = 10%)**

Now suppose that, instead of the asset generating cash flows for only two years, it generates them for four years, then the method shown above can be logically extended to the following. In addition to C_1 and C_2, let C_3 and C_4 denote the cash flows at the end of years three and four, respectively (we have dropped the "$" sign for notational convenience). Then, the present value of the asset is given by

$$PV = \frac{C_1}{1 + r} + \frac{C_2}{(1 + r)^2} + \frac{C_3}{(1 + r)^3} + \frac{C_4}{(1 + r)^4}.$$

In the above, note that the cash flow in the third year, C_3, is discounted by $(1 + r)^3$ and the fourth one by $(1 + r)^4$. In general, the number in the power term for $(1 + r)$ equals the number of time periods from $t = 0$. The future value of these cash flows, that is, at the end of the fourth year, is given by

$$FV = C_1(1 + r)^3 + C_2(1 + r)^2 + C_3(1 + r)^1 + C_4(1 + r)^0.$$

In the above expression for the future value, it might appear strange that the cash flow at the end of the first year is multiplied by $(1 + r)^3$ rather than by $(1 + r)^4$. To see why this is so, let us draw the time line.

$$
\begin{array}{ccccc}
& C_1 & C_2 & C_3 & C_4 \\
\vdash & + & + & + & + \\
t = 0 & t = 1 & t = 2 & t = 3 & t = 4
\end{array}
$$

Recall that we have to find the future value as of the end of the fourth year, that is, at $t = 4$. Count the number of periods that cash flow C_1 needs to be compounded to be at $t = 4$. It is three times and not four. Therefore, in the future value equation given above, the cash flow at the end of the first year is multiplied by $(1 + r)^3$ *and not* by $(1 + r)^4$. However, if there were a cash flow at $t = 0$, say C_0, then its future value at $t = 4$ would be $C_0(1 + r)^4$. Another point to note is that the cash flow C_4 occurs at $t = 4$, the very point in time at which we want to determine the value. What is the value of C_4 at $t = 4$? It is simply C_4. Therefore, the cash flow C_4 is multiplied by $(1 + r)^0$, and we know that anything to the power of zero equals one.

Let us look at the general case where the number of time periods is n and the cash flows occur at the end of each time period are denoted by C_t, where $t = 1, 2, 3, \ldots, n$. The general present valuation equation, therefore, is given by

$$PV = \frac{C_1}{1 + r} + \frac{C_2}{(1 + r)^2} + \ldots + \frac{C_4}{(1 + r)^n}.$$

Another way of expressing this is:

$$PV = \sum_{t=1}^{n} \frac{C_t}{(1+r)^t}, \ t = 1, 2, \ldots, n.$$

The expression for future value at time $t = n$ is given by

$$FV_n = \sum_{t=1}^{n} C_t(1+r)^{n-t}, \ t = 1, 2, \ldots, n.$$

Some observations from these expressions are immediately apparent. They are very similar to the ones we made in the one- and two-period cases in the previous chapter. These observations are, when r is greater than zero:

a. PV is always less than FV.

b. $\frac{1}{(1+r)^n}$ is always less than one, and

$$\frac{1}{(1+r)} > \frac{1}{(1+r)^2} > \frac{1}{(1+r)^3} > \ldots > \frac{1}{(1+r)^n}.$$

c. $(1+r)^n$ is always greater than one, and

$$(1+r) < (1+r)^2 < (1+r)^3 < \ldots < < (1+r)^n.$$

d. Because $\frac{1}{(1+r)^n}$ is always less than one, we can say that we put a lower weight on the cash flow that occurs later. Additionally, because

$$\frac{1}{(1+r)} > \frac{1}{(1+r)^2} > \frac{1}{(1+r)^3} > \ldots > \frac{1}{(1+r)^n},$$

we can also say that the further out a cash flow occurs, the lower is the weight that we assign to it.

Although the above observations are important and you should know them, understand them, and remember them well, you do not really need to memorize all the equations unless you want to do long time-value problems in the most tedious manner possible. You could if you wanted to. However, in the remaining part of this chapter, we will consider several short cuts, one of the major ones being the use of a financial calculator. The purpose of introducing these equations was to convey that what we will study in this chapter is conceptually very similar to that in the previous chapter.

Now try the following problems. These require you to circle the correct answer and do not require any calculations. You should be able to do them using the concepts that we have covered so far.

Problem 7.1 Suppose that an asset generates cash flows of $100, $200, and $300 at the end of years one, two, and three, respectively. If the discount rate is zero, of the following answers which is the only one that can be correct?

a. The PV = $600 and FV at $t = 3$ (FV$_3$) equals $600.

b. PV < $600, FV$_3$ > $600.

c. PV = $481.59, FV$_3$ = $641.00.

Because the discount rate is zero, the present value and the future value is simply the sum of the cash flows. Therefore, answer (a) is the correct one.

Problem 7.2   Suppose that an asset generates cash flows of $100, $200, and $300 at the end of years one, two, and three, respectively. If the discount rate is 10 percent, which of the following answers is the only one that can be correct?

    a. The PV = $600, FV_3 = $600.

    b. PV ≤ $600, FV_3 ≥ $600.

    c. PV = $481.59, FV_3 = $641.00.

Which answer did you circle? Clearly now that the discount rate is greater than zero, (a) is incorrect. What about (b)? Were you tempted to say it is correct? It is, however, not correct. Because the discount rate is greater than zero, the present value is strictly less than, not less than or equal to as in the answer, the sum of cash flows, and FV_3 > $600 and not ≥ $600. In answer (c), the values of PV and FV_3 are as they should be and, therefore, it can be the only correct answer.

Problem 7.3   Suppose that the discount rate is 10 percent. Asset A generates cash flows of $100, $200, and $300 at the end of the first three years, respectively. Asset B generates cash flows of $300, $200, and $100 at the end of the first three years, respectively. Which is the only one of the following statements that is correct?

    a. PV_A > PV_B and FV_A > FV_B.

    b. PV_A < PV_B and FV_A > FV_B.

    c. PV_A > PV_B and FV_A < FV_B.

    d. PV_A < PV_B and FV_A < FV_B.

Choosing the correct answer is little tricky here. Let us first consider the present values of the two assets. If the discount rate were zero, the present values of the two assets would be the same, that is, $600. However, the discount rate is not zero. In that case, the asset that generates the higher cash flows sooner should have the higher PV. Why? Because we know that

$$\frac{1}{(1+r)} > \frac{1}{(1+r)^2} > \frac{1}{(1+r)^3}.$$

In other words, the PV of $300 received at $t = 1$ is greater than the PV of $300 received at $t = 3$. Thus asset B should have the higher PV or $PV_A < PV_B$. Once we know this, answers (a) and (c) can be ruled out. Next consider the case of the future values of the two assets. The $300 received at $t = 1$ will have a greater FV at $t = 3$ than $300 received at $t = 3$. The former will be compounded by a factor of $(1+r)^2$ and the latter by $(1+r)^0$ (which equals 1). Thus, again the asset that generates the higher cash flows sooner will have the higher future value; that is, $FV_A < FV_B$. Thus, the only correct answer is (d).

    Let us actually calculate the present and future values of the two assets A and B.

$$PV_A = \frac{100}{1.1} + \frac{200}{(1.1)^2} + \frac{300}{(1.1)^3} = \$481.59$$

$$FV_A = 100\,(1.1)^2 + 200\,(1.1) + 300 = \$641.00$$

$$PV_B = \frac{300}{1.1} + \frac{200}{(1.1)^2} + \frac{100}{(1.1)^3} = \$513.15$$

$$FV_B = 300\,(1.1)^2 + 200\,(1.1) + 100 = \$683.00$$

These answers confirm our answer to Problem 7.3. In addition, notice the following:

$$PV_A (1.1)^3 = \$481.59 \, (1.1)^3 = \$641.00 = FV_A, \text{ and}$$

$$PV_B (1.1)^3 = \$513.15 \, (1.1)^3 = \$683.00 = FV_B.$$

The above calculations point out another relation worth remembering. As long as the same (positive) discount rate is used for both the assets, and the assets generate cash flows for the same number of periods, the asset that has the higher present value will also have the higher future value at the end of the last period. Think about this. Does this statement seem intuitive? As long as discount (interest) rates are the same, anything that has more value today will be more valuable also in the future.

7.3 The Present Value of a Perpetuity

In the preceding section, we considered the general case when the cash flows occur over n periods. Here, we want to consider the very special and very important case when n is infinity (usually denoted by ∞) and the cash flows are the same in each period. In other words, what would be the present value of a stream of equal cash flows (C) that occur at the end of each period and go on forever? This special stream of cash flows is called a *perpetuity*. We can always write the general equation for this as follows

$$PV \text{ (perpetuity)} = \sum_{t=1}^{\infty} \frac{C}{(1+r)^t}.$$

The above equation seems impossible to solve and, consequently, useless. However, our friends (?) in mathematics have made life very simple for us. They have **proved** that the above summation **exactly** equals a very simple expression and, therefore, we have the following

$$PV \text{ (perpetuity)} = \frac{C}{r}.$$

Do you think this expression is still of any use? Are there any assets that generate equal cash flows forever? It turns out that there are. For example, in the United Kingdom, there are some bonds that have no maturity (that is, maturity is infinity) and pay a fixed coupon every period. You can see that the cash flows from owning this bond are exactly described by a perpetuity. Additionally, we will use this expression several times in the future for valuing stocks and annuities.

Let us consider an example of an asset that generates a cash flow of \$1,000 per year forever, in other words, a perpetuity of \$1,000. If the discount rate is 8 percent, the present value of this perpetuity will be

$$PV \text{ (perpetuity)} = \frac{1,000}{0.08} = \$12,500.$$

Now do the following simple problems in the space provided and see if you obtain the given answers.

Problem 7.4 Suppose the value of a perpetuity is \$38,900 and the discount rate is 12 percent p.a. What must be the annual cash flow from this perpetuity?

$$(0.12)38,900 = \frac{x}{0.12}(0.12)$$
$$x = 4,668$$

Answer: \$4,668.

Problem 7.5 An asset that generates $890 per year forever is priced at $6,000. What is the required rate of return?

$$(x)6000 = \frac{890}{x}(x) = \frac{6000x}{6000} = \frac{890}{6000} = 14.8333\%$$

Answer: 14.833 percent.

7.4 The Present Value of an Annuity ....

In the previous section, we considered a cash flow stream where a fixed amount was received every year forever. An *annuity* is a cash flow stream where a fixed amount is received every year (period) for a fixed number of years or periods. Examples of this should be quite easy to conceive. For example, if you rent out a property at a rent of $12,000 per year for ten years, then you are going to receive a ten-year annuity of $12,000.

A little later in this chapter we are going to start using a financial calculator, which will make finding the present value of an annuity very simple. However, let us first look at an annuity in a conceptual framework. We can find the present value of an annuity using three of the concepts we have studied so far: (i) present value of a single future cash flow, (ii) the present value of a perpetuity, and (iii) value additivity.

Consider an asset A that generates cash flows that are a perpetuity of $100 per year and let the discount rate be 10 percent. The time line for this is as below

	$100	$100	$100	$100	$100	forever
t = 0	t = 1	t = 2	t = 3	t = 4	t = 5	to infinity

Then the present value of this asset is:

$$PV_A = \frac{100}{0.1} = \$1,000.$$

Now consider another asset B that also generates a perpetual cash flow of $100 per year except that the first cash flow occurs at t = 4, that is, at the end of year 4. There are no cash flows at the end of the first three years. Let us draw the time line as below for this asset

	0	0	0	$100	$100	forever
t = 0	t = 1	t = 2	t = 3	t = 4	t = 5	to infinity

What is the present value of this stream of cash flows. Note that from t = 4 onwards, the cash flow stream is a perpetuity. Therefore, we can find the value of this perpetuity at t = 3 by using the formula for the present value of a perpetuity as follows:

$$PV_3 = \frac{100}{0.1} = \$1,000.$$

We are, however, interested in finding out the value of this stream at t = 0. We know that the value of this stream at t = 3 is $1,000. Therefore, the value of this stream at t = 0 must be the present value of the $1,000 at t = 3. That is,

$$PV_B = \frac{1,000}{(1.1)^3} = \$751.31.$$

$$1000 = \frac{\$751.31}{(1.1)^3}$$

Now suppose that you buy Asset A. You will receive the cash flows from this asset which are $100 per year forever with the first cash flow received at t = 1. In addition, now suppose that you sell asset B. In other words, to the person that buys Asset b from you, you will have to pay $100 per year forever with the first payment of $100 to be made to the buyer at t = 4.

Let us look at the cash flows that result to you from these transactions.

	t = 1	t = 2	t = 3	t = 4	t = 5	each later period
Buying Asset A	$100	$100	$100	$100	$100	$100
Selling Asset B	$ 0	$ 0	$ 0	−$100	−$100	−$100
Total	$100	$100	$100	$ 0	$ 0	$ 0

The last row gives the net cash flow to you from these transactions and the entries in the row are simply the sums of the entries in the two rows above it.

How would you describe the cash flow stream in the last row of the table above. It is an annuity of $100 per year for three years. What would be the present value of this annuity? Recall the principle of value additivity. Because this annuity is obtained by subtracting the cash flows of perpetuity B from those of perpetuity A, the value of this annuity must be the difference between the present values of perpetuities A and B. That is,

$$\text{PV (annuity of \$100 per year for 3 years)} = PV_A - PV_B$$

$$= \$1,000 - \$751.31 = \$248.69.$$

Let us check if the answer is correct. We can do this as follows:

$$PV = \frac{100}{1.1} + \frac{100}{(1.1)^2} + \frac{100}{(1.1)^3} = \$248.69.$$

Thus, we have discovered a method for computing the present value of an annuity. The present value of an annuity of $C per year for n years equals the difference between the present values of two perpetuities, one that begins paying $C per year from t = 1 and another that begins paying $C per year from t = n + 1.

This gives the following formula:

$$\text{PV (annuity of \$C per year for n years)} = \frac{C}{r} - \frac{C}{r} \times \frac{1}{(1+r)^n}.$$

In the above, the first term on the right hand side is the present value of the perpetuity that begins at t = 1 and the second is the present (t = 0) value of the perpetuity that begins at t = 4. By rearranging terms, we can express the above formula also the following way

$$\text{PV (annuity of \$C per year for n years)} = \frac{C}{r}\left[1 - \frac{1}{(1+r)^n}\right].$$

Again, we introduced this formula only to provide an intuitive understanding of how the present value of an annuity is computed. Shortly, we will simply be punching buttons on a financial calculator. However, to cement this understanding, solve the following problems to see if you can obtain the given answer.

Problem 7.6 What is the present value of a three-year annuity of $700 per year? The discount rate is 8 percent p.a.

$$PV = 700 \times \left[\frac{1 - \frac{1}{(1+.08)^3}}{.08} \right] \qquad PV = \$1,803.97$$

Answer: $1,803.97.

Problem 7.7 What is the present value of an annuity of $1,800 per year for four years? The discount rate is 12 percent p. a. $PV = 1800 \times \left[\dfrac{1 - \frac{1}{(1+.12)^4}}{.12} \right] = \$5,467.23$

Answer: $5467.23.

Problem 7.8 You want to replicate the cash flow streams from a four-year annuity of $3,000 per year. Show how two perpetuities will allow you to do this as we did earlier, in a table?

Answer: $PV = \left(\dfrac{3000}{r} \right) - \left(\dfrac{3000}{r} \right) \left(\dfrac{1}{1+r} \right)^3$.

Problem 7.9 You decide to invest in two investments A and B. The cash flows from these two investments are as follows:

	t = 1	t = 2	t = 3	t = 4
Inv. A	$475	$381	$533	$291
Inv. B	$325	$419	$267	$509

What is the present value of your total investment if the required rate of return is 11 percent?

$PV = 800 \left[\dfrac{1 - \frac{1}{(1+.11)^4}}{.11} \right] = \$2,481.96$

Answer: $2,481.96.

How did you do this problem? One is the long way where you find the present value of each of the two investments and then sum the two present values. The other is the shorter way. Notice that if you sum the cash flows from the two investments in each year, you will obtain $800 every year. Then the solution is to find the present value of a 4-year $800 annuity.

7.5 Time Value Calculations with a Financial Calculator ....

Several excellent financial calculators are available in the market. All of them are pretty similar in their method of usage. There are, however, some differences in the operating procedures. To illustrate the use of a financial calculator, we are going to use the model **BAII PLUS** from **Texas Instruments.** If you are using a different financial calculator, you can still work through this material as long as you now the basic operations of your model. Finally, this section is meant to be an introduction to some of the uses of this very powerful machine. We strongly urge you to study the manual that comes with the machine, to derive the full benefit of owning this instrument.

7.5.1 The Basics

Study the keys on the calculator. Most of the keys have notation on the key and above it. For example, the 'N' key has 'xP/Y' written above it. To access the function written above the key, first press the key that has '2nd' written on it. In what follows, the notation on the key is written in single quotes and the one above the key is written in brackets. For example, 'PV' and [Amort].

Let us first set the calculator.

1. Press '2nd' and [Format]. The screen will display the number of decimal places that the calculator will display. If it is not eight, press '8' and then press 'Enter'. Although we do not really need so many places after the decimal, there is no harm.

2. Press '2nd' and then press [P/Y]. If the display does not show one, press '1' and then 'Enter'. [P/Y] stands for the number of payments per year. As a rule, we want to ensure that this number is always one unless we specifically need it to be different. This says that the frequency of payment is once a year. Many times, the cause of your not obtaining the correct answer is that the [P/Y] is set at something other than one.

3. Press '2nd' and [BGN]. If the display is not END, that is, if it says BGN, press '2nd' and then [SET]. The display will read END. This tells the calculator to assume that all the payments are at the end of the period. This is something that we have always assumed thus far. In case payments occur at the beginning of the period, this setting may be changed. For now, set it at END.

Now that the basic setting is done, we can begin doing some problems.

7.6 Present and Future Values of Single Cash Flows ....

For these computations, we will need to use the following special keys in addition to the standard calculator keys:

N: Number of years (periods)

I/Y: Interest rate or the discounting or compounding rate p.a.

PV: Present value

PMT: The periodic fixed cash flow in an annuity

FV: Future value

CPT: Compute

We will now do a few time value problems on the calculator.

1. Find the present value of $6,000 that occurs at t = 6 when the discount rate is 14 percent.

   a. 6,000 and then 'FV'.

   b. 6 and then 'N'.

   c. 14 and then 'I/Y'.

   d. 0 (zero) and then 'PMT'. (This is necessary to avoid the possibility that the calculator uses a value from an earlier calculation in which there was some value for 'PMT'.)

   e. Finally, press 'CPT' and then 'PV'.

   The number −2,733.519286 will be in the display. The answer is $2,733.52. You might wonder about the minus sign before the number. If the future value is entered as a positive number, the present value will appear as a negative number. As a rule (as in the time line) any amount you receive should be positive, and any amount that leaves your pocket should be negative. Thus, to receive $6,000 at t = 6 you need to spend $2,733.52 at t = 0. Or, receive $2,733.52 at t = 0 and pay $6,000 at t = 6. If you want to convert a number from positive to negative or the other way round, use the key '+/−' on the calculator.

2. Suppose you deposit $150 in an account today and the interest rate is 6 percent p.a. How much will you have in the account at the end of 33 (why not, its a calculator anyway) years?

   a. 150 then '+/−' and then 'PV'.

   b. 33 then 'N'.

   c. 6 then 'I/Y'.

d. zero then 'PMT'.

e. 'CPT' then 'FV'.

Answer: $1,026.09.

Now that you are familiar with how to enter values, in the following problems, we will simply give you the values for each of the keys. A question mark, '?', after a key means that is the value to be computed.

3. You deposited $15,000 in an account twenty-two years ago and now the account has $50,000 in it. What was the annual rate of return that you received on this investment?

$$PV = -15,000, \quad N = 22, \quad PMT = 0, \quad FV = 50,000, \quad I/Y = ? \quad 5\cdot625\,I$$

Answer: 5.625 percent

4. You currently have $38,000 in an account that has been paying 5.75 percent p.a. You remember that you had opened this account quite some years ago with an initial deposit of $19,000. You forget when the initial deposit was made. How many years (in fractions) ago did you make the initial deposit?

$$PV = -19,000, \quad PMT = 0, \quad FV = 38,000, \quad I/Y = 5.75, \quad N = ? \quad 12\cdot3981 \text{ yrs}$$

Answer: 12.398 years

As you can see, the financial calculator makes time value calculations quite simple. Now try the following problems in the space provided and see if you obtain the given answer.

Problem 7.11 A friend wants to borrow $15,000 from you today. He promises to repay the loan by paying you $20,000 after five years. What is the promised interest rate?

$$PV = 15,000 \qquad n = 5 \qquad I/Y = ?\ 5.9224\ \%$$
$$FV = 20,000 \qquad pymt = 0$$

Answer: 5.922 percent.

Problem 7.12 Your friendly neighbor has come up with an investment opportunity for you that (he claims) will double your investment in six years. What is the yearly rate of return from this investment?

$$PV = 15,000 \qquad n = 6 \qquad I/Y = ?\ 12.2462\ \%$$
$$PV = 30,000 \qquad pymt = 0$$

Answer: 12.246 percent.

Problem 7.13 You have decided to buy some furniture. The total price of the furniture is $19,350. The store has a special deal, which is as follows. If you pay cash today, you will obtain a 15 percent discount off the total price. Otherwise, you have to pay the full amount at the end of three years. If your required rate of return is 5 percent, which payment alternative would you choose?

$$PV = ? \qquad pymt = 0 \qquad PV = 16,447.50\ w/15\%\ disc.$$
$$FV = 19,350$$
$$n = 3 \qquad PV = 16,715.26 \qquad \text{Take } 15\%\ disc. \text{ today}$$
$$I/Y = 5\%$$

Answer: Take the 15 percent discount and pay cash today.

Problem 7.14 You notice that the sales of a firm were $31 million in 1988 and $63 million in 1995. What has been the annual growth rate in sales over this period? Assume that all sales occur at the end of the year.

$$PV = 31 \qquad n = 7$$
$$FV = 63 \qquad PYMT = 0$$
$$I/Y = ? \qquad 10.6616\%$$

Answer: 10.662 percent.

The purpose of the above problem is to illustrate that the kind of calculations we have been making in solving time value problems are not restricted to finance. The calculator does not know that you are dealing with interest rates. The calculator just computes the compound growth rate. Thus, to solve the above problem, you need only to enter PV = −31, FV 63, N = 7, PMT = 0, I/Y = ? to obtain the answer.

A **common mistake** that some people make (not you, of course) is to do the following in computing the growth rate

$$\frac{\$63 \text{ m.} - \$31 \text{ m.}}{31 \text{ m.}} = 1.032 \text{ or } 103.2 \text{ percent in seven years}$$

$$\text{or } \frac{103.2}{7} = 14.743 \text{ percent per year.}$$

This is **incorrect.** It ignores the compounding effect.

7.7 Present and Future Values of Annuities ....

Recall that when we did some problems on annuities earlier where we used the formula for computing the present value of an annuity, we made the calculations simple by considering annuities of just a few years. With the financial calculator, we no longer need to restrict ourselves to short time periods. Additionally, we can compute some things, such as future value of an annuity or the interest or discount rate implied by an annuity, that we (conveniently) omitted in the earlier section. We will illustrate many of the possibilities with the help of problems.

1. Suppose an investment promises to yield annual cash flows of $13,000 per year for eleven years. If your required rate of return is 13 percent, what is the maximum price that you would be willing to pay for this investment?

   The maximum price that you would be willing to pay is the present value of this annuity using your required rate of return as the discount rate. To compute the PV, do the following on your calculator.

   $$N = 11, \quad I/Y = 13, \quad PMT = 13,000, \quad FV = 0, \quad PV = ?$$

   Answer: $73,930.23

   The fixed cash flow from the annuity is entered as the PMT. Also, you will notice that the PV displayed has a minus sign. The reason for the minus sign is the same as the one we had discussed earlier.

2. An asset promises the following stream of cash flows. It will pay you $80 per year for twenty years and, in addition, at the end of the twentieth year, you will be paid $1,000. If your required rate of return is 9 percent, what is the maximum price that you would pay for this asset?

   $$PYMT = 80 \qquad FV = 1000$$
   $$n = 20 \qquad I/Y = 9\%?$$
   $$PV = ? \qquad \$908.71 \text{ max}$$

Again you have to find the PV of all these cash flows. With the calculator, enter the following.

$$N = 20, \quad PMT = 80, \quad FV = 1{,}000, \quad I/Y = 9, \quad PV = ?$$

Answer: $908.71

The only difference between this and the previous problem is the entry for FV. If you draw the time line for the above problem, you will see why 1000 is entered as the FV. By the way, you have just found the price of an 8 percent fixed-coupon bond with twenty years to maturity when the market interest rates are 9 percent. We will do bond valuation in greater detail later.

3. You have $1,000,000 that you want to use for the first fifteen years of your retirement. You need equal yearly withdrawals at the end of each year (that is, the first withdrawal will be one year from now), and at the end of the fifteen years, you do not want any of the original amount left over. You could deposit the money in the bank today at 9 percent p.a. and make fifteen equal yearly withdrawals. A retirement planner offers the following alternative. Buy an annuity of $125,000 per year for fifteen years with the million. Which alternative would you choose?

$PV = 1mil$ $pymt = ?$
$i/y = 9$ $n = 15$ ANN of $124,058.88$
$Fv = 0$

You can look at it in two different ways.

a. Find the equal withdrawals that you can make from the bank account and compare them to the annuity of $125,000. To do this,

$$N = 15, \quad PV = -1{,}000{,}000, \quad FV = 0, \quad I/Y = 9, \quad PMT = ?$$

$$PMT = \$124{,}058.88 \text{ per year for 15 years}$$

Since this is lower than that promised in the annuity, choose the annuity.

b. Find the interest rate of the annuity and compare it to the bank's 9 percent. That is

$$N = 15, \quad PV = -1{,}000{,}000, \quad FV = 0, \quad PMT = 125{,}000, \quad I/Y = ?$$

$$I/Y = 9.128 \text{ percent p.a.}$$

This is more than the 9 percent offered by the bank, so choose the annuity.

4. You plan to retire forty years from now. After retirement, you expect that you will need $250,000 per year for twenty years with the first amount required at the end of the forty-first year. You want to start saving for retirement and plan to make forty equal yearly payments into your retirement account, which yields 8 percent. The first payment into this account will be at the end of one year from today. What should these equal payments be to satisfy your retirement needs?

Let X be the amount that you deposit each year, and you have to determine what it should be. For this problem, it is useful to draw a time line.

From the time line, it is clear that there are two annuities, one of $X per year for forty years beginning at t = 1 and the second of $250,000 per year for twenty years, beginning at t = 41. The first one you pay in and the second one you receive. The interest rate for the entire period is 8 percent p.a. The logic is that the initial $X annuity should exactly pay for the later $250,000 annuity. This would be true if the present values of the two annuities, that is t = 0, are the same.

Let us first determine the PV of the second annuity at $t = 0$. To do this, we will first compute its PV at $t = 40$ and then discount that amount to $t = 0$. To determine the PV at $t = 40$, on the calculator enter

$$N = 20, \quad PMT = 250{,}000, \quad FV = 0, \quad I/Y = 8, \quad PV = ?$$

$$PV_{40} = \$2{,}454{,}536.85$$

Next discount PV_{40} to $t = 0$ as follows:

$$FV = 2{,}454{,}536.85, \quad N = 40, \quad I/Y = 8, \quad PMT = 0, \quad PV = ?$$

$$PV_0 = \$112{,}984.62$$

If you deposited \$112,984.62 into the account today you could satisfy your retirement needs. However, you are not going to put this amount in today; instead you are going to make forty equal yearly deposits into the account. In other words, you want to find the annuity payment that has a present value of \$112,984.62. Thus, on your calculator, enter

$$PV = -112{,}984.62, \quad N = 40, \quad I/Y = 8, \quad FV = 0, \quad PMT = ?$$

Answer: \$9,474.91 per year for forty years.

In the above problem, notice how the solution became apparent after the time line was drawn.

Your calculator allows you to find present values of unequal cash flows in one operation. You can have each of the cash flows occur consecutively several times. The use of this operation is illustrated in the following example.

5. An asset promises to yield the following series of cash flows. At the end of each of the first three years, \$5,000. At the end of each of the following four years, \$7,000. And, at the end of each of following five years, \$9,000. If your required rate of return is 10 percent, how much is this asset worth to you?

Let us first draw the time line.

?		5,000	$\longrightarrow$	5,000		7,000	$\longrightarrow$	7,000		9,000	$\longrightarrow$	9,000
$t = 0$		$t = 1$	$\longrightarrow$	$t = 3$		$t = 4$	$\longrightarrow$	$t = 7$		$t = 8$	$\longrightarrow$	$t = 12$

From, the time line, it is apparent that we have to find the $t = 0$ value of three annuities. Notice that you can solve this problem using the methods we have studied earlier. Let us, however, use two new calculator functions 'CF' and 'NPV'.

a. Press CF. Then press [CLR TVM], then [CLR Work]. (Do this clear process each time you begin a new CF problem.) You will see a display $CFo = 0.0$. This asks you for the cash flow at $t = 0$. In our problem, this is zero, so we don't need to enter a different value here. Thus, press '↓'.

b. You will see $C01 = 0.0$. In our case, this is \$5,000. So, enter '5000' and then press 'ENTER'.

c. Press '↓'. You will see $F01 = 1.0$. This asking for the frequency of the first cash flow, that is, how many time this cash flow occurs. In our problem, this cash flow is received three times, at the end of the first three years. So enter '3' and then 'ENTER'.

d. Press '↓'. Enter '7000' for C02 and then press 'ENTER'.

e. Press '↓'. Enter '4' for F02 because the \$7000 cash flow occurs four times. Press 'ENTER'.

f. Press '↓'. Enter '9000' for C03 and then press 'ENTER'.

g. Press '↓'. Enter '5' for F03 because the $9000 cash flow occurs five times. Press 'ENTER'.

h. Press '↓' and make C04 zero if it is not so.

i. Scroll through using the '↓' key to make sure that all the numbers are entered correctly.

j. Press the 'NPV' key. Enter the interest rate as '10' and then press 'ENTER'.

k. Press '↓' and then press 'CPT'. The display will provide the present value as NPV. For our problem, this $46,612.68.

We have covered a lot of material since the last set of problems that you had to solve. So, attempt the following problems in the space provided and see if you obtain the given answer. Get into the habit of drawing a time line. Doing so will eliminate many possible errors.

Problem 7.15   You are considering buying some rental property. The yearly rent from this property is $18,000. You expect that the property will yield this rent for the next twenty years after which you will be able to sell it for $250,000. If your required rate of return is 12 percent p.a., what is the maximum amount that you would pay for this property?

$PV = ?$ $pymt\ 18000$
$1/y = 12\%$ $n = 20$
$FV = 250,000$
$PV = -160,366.67$

Answer: $160,366.67.

Problem 7.16   You own 100 acres of a forest that has timber on it. A paper manufacturing company has made you an offer for it today at $10,000 per acre. You could harvest the timber yourself over the next ten years to obtain $100,000 per year and at the end of the ten years, sell the entire land for $500,000. If your required rate of return is 10 percent, which alternative should you elect?

Answer: Sell today because the PV of harvesting is only $807,228.36 versus the $1,000,000 from selling today.

Problem 7.17   You open an account today with $20,000 and at the end of each of the next fifteen years, you deposit $2,500 in it. At the end of fifteen years, what will be the balance in the account if the interest rate is 7 percent p.a.?

$n = 15$ $FV = ?$ $PV = 20,000$
$1/y = 7\%$ $pymt$
$20,000$ 2500

$\$118,003.19$

Answer: $118,003.19.

Problem 7.18   You plan to retire after thirty years. After that, you need $200,000 per year for ten years (first withdrawal at t = 31). At the end of these ten years, you will enter a retirement home where you will stay for the rest of your life. As soon as you enter the retirement home, you will need to make a single payment of $1,000,000. You want to start saving for your retirement in an account that pays you 9 percent interest p.a. Therefore, beginning from the end of the first year (t = 1), you will make equal yearly deposits into this account for thirty years. You expect to receive $500,000 at t = 30 from a cash value insurance policy that you own. This money will be deposited in your retirement account. What should your yearly deposits into the account be?

$500\ 200,000\ 9\%\ 1,000,000$
0 $30\ 31$ 40

Answer: $8,847.22.

Problem 7.19 See problem number 5 solved above where we used the 'CF' and 'NPV' functions for the first time. Solve this problem without using these functions. You will need to use the PV function of the calculator.

Answer: $46,612.68.

Problem 7.20 An asset is expected to produce cash flows of $33,000 per year for the first two years, $45,000 per year for the next three years, $61,000 per year for the following four years, $54,000 per year for the next two years, and $29,000 per year for the last three years. If the discount rate is 11 percent, what is the present value of this stream of cash flows?

Answer: $316,711.68.

7.8 Special Topics in Time Value ·······································

There are a few "bells and whistles" kind of concepts left for us to consider in this chapter on the time value of money. These are as follows. First, thus far, we have assumed that interest is paid once a year or that discounting or compounding is performed once every year. We will now consider what happens when interest rates are compounded at a frequency of more than once a year. Second, we will also consider the special case when compounding and discounting are continuous. Next, we have thus far assumed that cash flows of annuities occur at the end of the period, we will now compute present and future values of annuities that are paid at the beginning of each period. Finally, we will analyze amortization.

7.8.1 Compounding Period Is Less Than One Year

The effect of increasing the frequency of compounding to more than once per year is best illustrated with the following numerical example. Suppose that your bank "states" that the interest on the account is 8 percent p.a. However, interest is paid semi-annually, that is every six months. The 8 percent is called the *stated interest* rate. However, the bank will pay you 4 percent interest (8 percent divided by two because the interest is paid semi-annually) every six months. In other words, the compounding frequency is two.

Suppose you deposit $100 into this account today. At the end of six months, your account balance will be

$$\$100 \times (1.04) = \$104.$$

At the end of the year, the balance will be

$$\$104 \times (1.04) = \$108.16.$$

If the interest had been paid once a year, the account balance at the end of the year would have been

$$\$100 \times (1.08) = \$108.$$

Thus, with semiannual compounding, you effectively obtain more than the stated interest. The *effective interest rate* is

$$\frac{\$108.16 - \$100}{\$100} = 0.0816 \text{ or } 8.16 \text{ percent.}$$

Viewed another way, your account balance at the end of the year will be

$$\$100 \times (1.04)^2 = \$108.16,$$

and the effective interest rate is

$$(1.04)^2 - 1 = 0.0816 \text{ or } 8.16 \text{ percent.}$$

If the interest had been paid quarterly, you would have received $\frac{8}{4} = 2$ percent interest every quarter. In this case, your end-of-year account balance would be

$$\$100 \times (1.02)^4 = \$108.2432,$$

and the effective interest rate would be

$$(1.02)^4 - 1 = 0.082432 \text{ or } 8.2432 \text{ percent.}$$

Suppose you want to compute your account balance at the end of five years with quarterly compounding. In this case,

$$\text{the number of compounding periods} = 5 \times 4 = 20.$$

Therefore, the account balance at the end of five years would be

$$\$100 \times (1.02)^{20} = \$148.59.$$

You could compute this on the financial calculator as follows:

$$N = 20, \quad PV = -100, \quad I/Y = 2, \quad PMT = 0, \quad FV = ?$$

Answer: FV $= \$148.59$.

In general, let 'n' be the number of years, 'm' be the frequency of compounding every year, and let 'r' be the stated interest rate, then

$$PV = \frac{FV}{\left(1 + \dfrac{r}{m}\right)^{m \times n}}, \text{ and}$$

$$FV = PV \times \left(1 + \dfrac{r}{m}\right)^{m \times n}.$$

Let us solve a problem of this nature with the help of a financial calculator.

Suppose that to buy a house, you need to take on a mortgage of $200,000. The stated interest rate is 8 percent p.a. The mortgage is for thirty years and payments need to be made every month beginning at the end of the first month. What will be your monthly payment?

We could solve this problem by using the [xP/Y] and [P/Y] functions in the calculator. This is, however, not necessary. We can do the following.

First divide 8 by 12 and then press 'I/Y'. In other words, the interest rate we have entered is the monthly interest rate computed from the stated interest rate. Next, multiply 30 by 12 and then press 'N'. In other words, we have computed the number of months in thirty years and entered that as the number of periods. The rest is as before, that is

$$I/Y = 0.66666666667, \quad N = 360, \quad FV = 0, \quad PV = -200{,}000, \quad PMT = ?$$

Answer: $1,467.53.

In the above, make sure to divide 8 by 12 and press 'I/Y'. By doing so, you are ensuring that the monthly interest rate is entered accurately to as many decimal places as the computer handles. Suppose that instead, you compute $\frac{8}{12} = 0.67$ and then enter 0.67 as 'I/Y'. Your answer would be $1,473.11, a fairly substantial error. In fact, the PV is $757.58.

Problem 7.21   Your bank's stated interest rate on a three-month certificate of deposit is 4.68 percent p.a. What is the effective interest rate?

Answer: 4.763 percent p.a.

Problem 7.22   You have decided to buy a car for $45,000. The dealer offers to finance the entire amount and requires 60 monthly payments of $950 per month. What are the yearly stated and effective interest rates for this financing?

Answer: stated $= 9.723$ percent, effective $= 10.168$ percent p.a.

7.8.2 Continuous Compounding

A special case of compounding more often than once a year is continuous compounding. In this case, the compounding frequency is infinity. With continuous compounding, the present and future value expressions are as follows:

$$PV = FV \times e^{-r \times n}, \text{ and}$$
$$FV = PV \times e^{r \times n}.$$

In the above expressions, 'e' is the exponential function (that appears on your financial calculator as [e^x]), r is the stated interest rate, and n is the number of years.

Suppose that the stated interest rate on a bank account is 6 percent p.a. With continuous compounding, a deposit of $100 made today will, after five years, become

$$FV = \$100 \times e^{0.06 \times 5}$$
$$= \$100 \times e^{0.30}$$
$$= \$100 \times 1.3499$$
$$= \$134.99.$$

Similarly, the present value of a cash flow of $1,000 to be received three years from now with stated interest rate equal to 12 percent p.a. is

$$PV = \$1,000 \times e^{-0.12 \times 3}$$
$$= \$1,000 \times e^{-0.36}$$
$$= \$1,000 \times 0.69768$$
$$= \$697.68.$$

Finally, if the stated interest rate is 'r' p.a., the effective interest rate with continuous compounding is given by

$$\text{Effective interest rate} = e^r - 1.$$

Suppose the stated interest rate is 9 percent, then, with continuous compounding, the effective interest rate is

$$e^{.09} - 1 = 1.09417 - 1 = 0.09417 \text{ or } 9.417 \text{ percent.}$$

Now attempt the following problems and see if you obtain the given answers.

Problem 7.23   BNM Bank pays a stated interest of 4 percent per year and uses continuous compounding. You deposit $1,800 into this account. What will be your account balance in eleven years?

$$1800 \times e^{0.04 \times 11}$$

Answer: $2,794.87.

Problem 7.24   ZXC bank pays a stated interest of 5 percent p. a. and uses continuous compounding. How long will it take you to double your money in this account? (Your answer can contain fractional years.)

$$FV = PV \times e^{.05 \times n} \qquad 2 = 1 \times e^{.05n}$$

Answer: 13.862 years.

The above problem might have confused you a little bit. To solve it, you must know the relation between the exponential (e) value and the natural log (ln) value. The following solution to the above problem will illustrate this relationship.

Note that we want the money to double. Therefore, PV = $1, FV = $2, r = 0.05, and n = ?. We know that

$$FV = PV \times e^{r \times n}.$$

Substituting the appropriate values we have

$$2 = 1 \times e^{0.05 \times n}.$$

Next, we take the natural log of both sides of the above equation to obtain

$$\ln(2) = 0.05 \times n.$$

In other words, the natural log of e^z is simply z. Using our calculator, we compute that $\ln(2) = 0.6931$. Then,

$$0.6931 = 0.05 \times n, \text{ implying that}$$
$$n = 13.862 \text{ years.}$$

7.8.3 Annuities Valuation with Payments at the Beginning of the Period

Consider an annuity of $300 per year for three years. When payments are made at the end of the period as before, the time line is as below:

Let us compute the present and future (at t = 3) values of this annuity the long way. Let the discount rate be 10 percent p.a.

$$PV = \frac{300}{1.1} + \frac{300}{(1.1)^2} + \frac{300}{(1.1)^3} = \$746.06, \text{ and}$$

$$FV_3 = 300\,(1.1)^2 + 300\,(1.1) + 300 = \$993.$$

Now suppose that the annuity makes payments at the beginning of the period (also known as *annuity due*). The time line would then be

Let us compute the present and future (at t = 3) values of this annuity the long way.

$$PV = 300 + \frac{300}{1.1} + \frac{300}{(1.1)^2} = \$820.66, \text{ and}$$

$$FV_3 = 300\,(1.1)^3 + 300\,(1.1)^2 + 300\,(1.1) = \$1{,}092.30.$$

Compare the expressions for PV and FV of the two annuities. Notice that if you multiply the right hand side expression for the PV of the regular annuity, you obtain the expression for the present value of the annuity due. Similarly, multiplying the FV expression of the regular annuity yields the expression for the FV of the annuity due. In general

$$PV(\text{annuity due}) = PV\,(\text{regular annuity}) \times (1 + r), \text{ and}$$
$$FV_n(\text{annuity due}) = FV_n\,(\text{regular annuity}) \times (1 + r).$$

Notice that this is true of the values that we have calculated.

Now attempt the following problem and see if you obtain the given answer.

Problem 7.25 You have a rental property that you want to rent for ten years. Prospective tenant A promises to pay you a rent of $12,000 per year with the payments made at the end of each year. Prospective tenant B promises to pay $12,000 per year with payments made at the beginning of each year. Which is a better deal for you if the going discount rate is 10 percent?

Answer: $PV(A) = \$73{,}734.81$, $PV(B) = \$81{,}108.29$. Choose B.

7.8.4 Loan Amortization

Suppose that you borrow $10,000 at 10 percent and plan to repay it in five equal yearly installments. Your yearly repayment will be computed as

$$N = 5, \quad PV = 10{,}000, \quad I/Y = 10, \quad FV = 0, \quad PMT = ?$$

Answer: $2,637.97.

In other words, you will pay $2,637.97 at the end of each of the next five years.

This payment goes toward interest payment and toward repayment of principal. At $t = 0$, your loan balance or principal is $10,000. At $t = 1$, just before you make your first payment, you have had a loan of $10,000 for one year. Given an interest rate of 10 percent, you need to pay interest of

$$\$10{,}000 \times 0.10 = \$1{,}000.$$

Thus, from your $t = 1$ payment of $2,637.97, $1,000 is towards interest and the rest

$$\$2{,}637.97 - \$1{,}000 = \$1{,}637.97$$

is towards principal repayment. Therefore, just after your $t = 1$ payment, your principal balance is

$$\$10{,}000 - \$1{,}637.97 = \$8{,}362.03.$$

Then, from your $t = 2$ payment of $2,637.97,

$$\$8{,}362.03 \times 0.10 = \$836.20$$

is towards interest and

$$\$2{,}637.97 - \$836.20 = \$1{,}801.77$$

is towards principal repayment.

This process is known as loan amortization and the entire amortization schedule for this loan is presented in the table below.

Year	Beginning balance	Payment	Interest	Principal	Ending balance
$t = 0$					$10,000.00
$t = 1$	$10,000.00	$2,637.97	$1,000.00	$1,637.97	$ 8,362.03
$t = 2$	$ 8,362.03	$2,637.97	$ 836.20	$1,801.77	$ 6,560.26
$t = 3$	$ 6,560.26	$2,637.97	$ 656.03	$1,981.94	$ 4,578.32
$t = 4$	$ 4,578.32	$2,637.97	$ 457.83	$2,180.14	$ 2,398.18
$t = 5$	$ 2,398.18	$2,637.97	$ 239.82	$2,398.15	0

Now attempt the following (extremely tedious) problem. For obvious reasons, no answer is given.

Problem 7.26   You have borrowed $8,000 from a bank and have promised to return it in five equal years' payments. The first payment is at the end of the first year. The interest rate is 10 percent. Draw up the amortization schedule for this loan.

Students often ask us how it is possible to remember how to do all that is presented in this chapter to solve time value of money problems. The answer is simple. Work many, many time value of money problems. The more you work, the easier this will become. We have given you many problems in the text to work with, and there are many at the end of this chapter. Additional time value of money problems can be found on the Internet (try a Google search for the term "time value of money problems"). After a while, you will see that working time value of money problems is like driving a car. At first, it seems impossible to do. There are just so many things going on at the same time that it is difficult to focus on any one thing. Soon, however, driving becomes second nature. As I have witnessed while driving on the Interstate in my home town, people even learn to drive with their knees while putting on makeup, eating, shaving, or talking on their cell phones. Maybe even doing all of these at the same time! (well, perhaps not makeup and shaving—but you never know).

We have by now covered the time value of money concepts necessary to study issues of security valuation and capital budgeting in finance. The remainder of the book will cover these two areas. Once you understand the material on time value of money, you will find the rest of the book to be exceedingly easy as far as solving problems is concerned.

Assignment 7.1 ▪▪▪▪▪▪▪▪▪▪▪

Name:_____   Date:_____

Solve the following problems in the space provided.

1. Investment A requires you to pay $30,000 at t = 0, and you will receive $49,000 after five years. Investment B costs $73,000 and provides a cash flow of $128,000 after seven years. What is the rate of return for each of the two investments?

A: $PV = 30,000$ $n = 5$
      $FV = 49,000$
      $I/Y = ?$ 10.31%

B: $PV = 73,000$
      $FV = 128,000$
      $n = 7$
      $I/Y = ?$ 8.3530%

2. You plan spend the next four summers vacationing abroad. The first summer trip, which is exactly one year away, will cost you $22,000, the second, $27,500, the third, $33,000, and the fourth $35,000. You want to save for these vacations. How much should you deposit in your account today so that you will have exactly enough to finance all the trips? The account pays interest at 6 percent p.a.

6%

```
   ├───┼───┼───┼───┤
   0  22,000 27,500 33,000 35,000
```

$CF_0 = \$100,660.3336$

3. You make the following deposits into an account that pays interest at 8 percent p.a. Open the account today with a deposit of $11,000, then $13,000 at the end of the first year, $17,400 at the end of the second year, $12,800 at the end of the third, $9,600 at the end of the fourth, and $17,200 at the end of the fifth year. How much will you have in your account at the end of ten years?

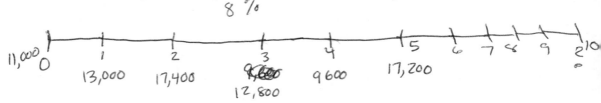

$$NPV = 66,878.1028$$

$$n = 10$$

$$I = 8\%$$

$$FV = 144,384.81$$

Assignment 7.2

Name:_____   Date:_____

Solve the following problems in the space provided.

1. You deposit $28,000 in an account today. You plan to make ten withdrawals from this account with the first withdrawal at the end of the first year. At the end of ten years, you want the account to have a balance of $30,000. If the account pays interest of 6 percent p.a., what will be the size of each of the yearly withdrawals?

2. You deposit $2,500 per year for twenty years in an account that pays 8 percent interest. At $t = 21$, you make the first of the twenty-five equal yearly withdrawals from this account. What can be the maximum amount of these withdrawals?

3. You plan to retire in twenty-five years. When you retire, you will need $150,000 per year for twenty-five years with the first payment needed at t = 26. You expect to receive $25,000 from a trust at t = 14 which you will deposit in your retirement account. At t = 11, you plan to take a world cruise that will cost you $60,000 to be paid out of the retirement account. You open your retirement account today with an initial deposit of $5,000. You plan to make twenty-five equal yearly deposits beginning at the end of the first year into this account. If the account pays interest at 7 percent p.a., what should be these annual deposits?

4. An asset yields the following year-end cash flows. $12,000 per year for years 1–3, $17,000 per year for years 4–7, $21,000 per year for years 8–15, $24,000 per years for years 16–20, and then $30,000 per year from year 21 forever. Use a discount rate of 12 percent to determine the present value of these cash flows.

Assignment 7.3

Name:_____   Date:_____

Solve the following problems in the space provided.

1. The stated interest rate for a bank account is 7 percent and interest is paid semi-annually. How many years will it take you to double your money in this account?

2. Bank A pays interest annually of 10 percent p.a. Bank B has a stated interest of 9.8 percent p.a. and the interest is paid semi-annually. Bank C has a stated interest of 9.6 percent p.a. and pays interest quarterly. Bank D has stated interest of 9.5 percent p.a. and pays interest monthly. Bank E has a stated interest rate of 9.4 percent p.a. and compounds the interest continuously. Compute the effective rate of interest for each bank.

3. You will retire twenty years from now and will need $140,000 per year for ten years beginning at $t = 21$. You plan to make twenty equal yearly deposits into a retirement with the first deposit to be made today. The account pays interest at 9 percent p.a. What should be the size of these deposits?

4. You borrow $40,000 at 8 percent p.a. and promise to repay it in six equal yearly installments. What will be these installments? Present the amortization table for this loan repayment.

Additional Questions and Problems

1. All else constant, for a given nominal interest rate, an increase in the number of compounding periods per year will cause the future value of some current sum of money to:

   a. Increase

   b. Decrease

   c. Remain the same

   d. May increase, decrease, or remain the same depending on the number of years until the money is to be received.

   e. Will increase if compounding occurs more often than twelve times per year and will decrease if compounding occurs less than twelve times per year.

2. Consider three investment alternatives: a perpetuity, an ordinary annuity, and an annuity due. All three have the same payment amount. The annuity due and the ordinary annuity have the same number of payments and the number of payments is greater than one. The interest rate is positive and the same for all three investments. Given this information, which of the following statements is correct?

   a. The present value of the perpetuity is less than the present value of the ordinary annuity.

   b. The future value of the annuity due is less that the future value of the ordinary annuity.

   c. The perpetuity and the ordinary annuity have the same present value.

   d. The ordinary annuity and the annuity due have the same present value.

   e. The present value of the ordinary annuity is less than the present value of the perpetuity.

3. How long does it take for an investment to quadruple in value if the investment yields (that is, pays interest of) 8.5 percent per year?

4. The average price of a movie ticket at the end of 1988 was $5.50 and the average price of a movie ticket at the end of 1990 was $6.00. At what annual rate did ticket prices grow?

5. Suppose that I am trying to borrow money from you to finance my business. And suppose that I promise to repay you in two installments, one payment in two years of $5,000 and one payment in four years for $10,000. If your opportunity cost of funds is 10 percent, how much are you willing to lend me?

6. Consider the problem of calculating a loan amortization schedule. The portion of the payment that goes toward the payment of interest is _____ than the previous period's interest payment, and the portion of the payment that goes toward the repayment of principal is _____ than the previous period's principal payment.

    a. greater; less

    b. lower; less

    c. greater; greater

    d. less; greater

    e. None of the above

7. The number of years it would take $.83 to double, assuming an annual stated rate of 7.9560931 p.a., would be least under which compounding assumption?

    a. Continuous

    b. Daily

    c. Monthly

    d. Quarterly

    e. Annual

8. What is the effective annual rate of interest for a loan that has an 18 percent annual percentage rate, compounded monthly?

9. If I invest $100 today in an account that earns 10 percent per year, compounded semi-annually, how much will I have in this account at the end of twenty years if I make no withdrawals?

10. Which of the following statements is most correct?

    a. A five-year $100 annuity due will have a higher present value than a five-year $100 ordinary annuity.

    b. A fifteen-year mortgage will have larger monthly payments than a thirty-year mortgage of the same amount and same interest rate.

    c. If an investment pays 10 percent interest compounded annually, its effective rate will also be 10 percent.

    d. Statements a and c are correct.

    e. All of the statements above are correct.

11. Frank Lewis has a thirty-year, $100,000 mortgage with a nominal interest rate of 10 percent and monthly compounding. Which of the following statements regarding his mortgage is most correct?

    a. The monthly payments will decline over time.

    b. The proportion of the monthly payment that represents interest will be lower for the last payment than for the first payment on the loan.

    c. The total dollar amount of principal being paid off each month gets larger as the loan approaches maturity.

    d. Statements a and c are correct.

    e. Statements b and c are correct.

12. Compute the present and future values of a ten-year annuity with payments of $5,000 per year using discount rates of 0, 5, 10, 15, 20, 25, 30, 35, 40, 45, and 50 percent p.a. Plot them on the same graph with the discount rates on the horizontal and PV and FV on the vertical axis.

13. If you deposit $650 each year (first deposit made at $t = 1$), into an account that pays 6 percent interest per year, compounded annually, what will be the balance in the account after you have made fifteen payments, assuming that you make no withdrawals from the account?

14. If you deposit $725 each year (first deposit made at $t = 0$) for eighteen years into an account that pays 7.4 percent interest per year, compounded annually, what will be the balance in the account at the end of year 25, assuming you make no withdrawals from the account? (Note that after you stop making deposits, the balance in your account will continue to earn interest until the end of year 25.)

15. If you deposit $1 per month in an account that pays 12 percent interest, compounded monthly, what will be the balance in the account after two years if you make no withdrawals?

16. If you deposit $100 in an account each quarter for two years, beginning next quarter, what will be the balance in the account at the end of two years if interest is 12 percent, compounded quarterly if you make no withdrawals?

17. In 1950, a Jack-in-the-Box hamburger cost 24. In 1994, a Jack-in-the-Box hamburger cost 79. What is the effective annual increase in the price of a Jack-in-the-Box hamburger from 1950 to 1994?

18. In 1955, an order of McDonald's French fries cost 10. If McDonald's had increased the cost of its fries to keep up with inflation, an order of fries would cost 55 in 1994. Given this information on the price of fries, what is the effective annual rate of inflation over the period from 1955 to 1994?

19. Assume that you deposit $2,000 each year for the next twenty years, starting one year from today, in an account that pays 9.6 percent interest per year, compounded annually. If exactly ten years from today you withdraw $5,000 from the account, how much will be in your account on the day you make the last deposit (that is, at the end of year 20)?

20. A security pays you $40 every six months for thirty years and, additionally, at the end of the thirty years, pays you $1,000. The present value of this security is $1,111. What is the stated *p.a.* rate of return? What is the effective *p.a.* rate of return?

21. You loan your friend $100,000 today. She will pay you $10,000 per year for the first five years, and will make five more equal yearly payments. If the interest rate is 12 percent p.a., what should be the size of these payments?

22. You loan your friend $100,000. He will pay you $12,000 per year for ten years and a balloon payment at t = 10 of $50,000. What is the interest rate that you are charging the friend?

23. You have borrowed $35,000 at 12 percent p.a. and plan to repay it in seven years with equal yearly installments. What is the size of these installments. Just after you make the fourth payment, what will be the remaining loan balance?

24. You borrowed some money at 11 percent p.a. You repay the loan by making first six yearly installments of $10,000, then three yearly installments of $12,000, and then four yearly installments of $15,000. How much had you borrowed?

Annuity Due

25. You have just had a second child. You expect that the child will go to college after eighteen years. College will be for four years, and each year will cost you $33,000. The payments are to be made at the beginning of each college year, that is the first payment will be at t = 18. Your first child will go to college after twelve years and college will cost $25,000 per year for four years with the first payment due at t = 12. You had started saving for the first child's education when the child was born six years ago. You have $20,000 in that account today and plan to make ten more equal yearly payments beginning t = 1. To have exactly enough money for education of both children, how much should you deposit each year? The account pays interest at 8 percent p.a.

26. A factory generates $800,000 per year for the next ten years. If the discount rate is 12 percent, what is the factory worth today? What will the factory be worth at the end of five years?

27. If a five-year ordinary annuity has a present value of $1,000 and if the interest rate is 10 percent p.a., what is the amount of each annuity payment?

28. Assume that your required rate of return is 12 percent and you are given the following stream of cash flows:

Year	Cash Flow
1	$10,000
2	$15,000
3	$15,000
4	$15,000
5	$15,000
6	$20,000

If payments are made at the end of each period, what is the present value of the cash flow stream?

29. Suppose you put $100 into a savings account today, the account pays an interest rate of 6 percent p.a. compounded semi-annually, and you withdraw $100 after six months. Thereafter, you make no additional deposits or withdrawals. What would your ending balance be twenty years after the initial $100 deposit was made?

30. The Bushes have asked for your help in planning for the college education of their second child, Jeb. They expect that he will start college fifteen years from today. At that time they would like to have on deposit sufficient funds to make quarterly withdrawals of $2,500 per quarter to pay for college costs. Because college will last four years, there will be a total of sixteen quarterly withdrawals, with the first one to be made on the day Jeb starts college. They plan to accumulate the necessary funds by making quarterly deposits into an account that pays 5 percent, compounded quarterly. There is, however, one complication. Their first child, George, will start college twelve years from today. Due to the generosity of proud grandparents, they already have sufficient funds to pay for most of George's college costs. However, they estimate that they will not be able to make any deposits toward Jeb's education while George is in college due to the high cost of pizza. Thus they will only be able to make a total of forty-eight quarterly deposits into Jeb's college account, with the first deposit one quarter from today and the last deposit on the day George starts college. What should be the amount of these quarterly deposits?

31. You have just taken out an installment loan for $100,000. Assume that the loan will be repaid in twelve equal monthly installments of $9,456, and that the first payment will be due one month from today. How much of your third monthly payment will go toward the repayment of principal?

32. A commercial loan is made for 11 years at a 9 percent interest rate. If equal annual payments are made at the end of each year, what annual payment is required to amortize an initial loan of $6,300,000? (Round your answer to the nearest $1)

33. You plan to deposit money in a savings account that earns 7 percent annually. You will make five equal deposits of $10,000 each. The first deposit will be made today. No deposits will be made after the fifth deposit. What will be the accumulated sum available at the end of ten years? (Round your answer to the nearest $1)

34. Your uncle has agreed to deposit $3,000 into your brokerage account at the beginning of each of the next five years (t = 0, t = 1, t = 2, t = 3, and t = 4). You estimate that you can earn 9 percent a year on your investments. How much will you have in your account four years from now (at t = 4)? (Assume that no money is withdrawn from the account until t = 4.)

35. You are considering buying a new car. The sticker price is $15,000 and you have $2,000 to put toward a down payment. If you can negotiate a nominal annual interest rate of 10 percent and you wish to pay for the car over a five-year period, what are your monthly car payments?

36. You have a $175,000, thirty-year mortgage with a 9 percent nominal rate. You make payments every month. What will be the remaining balance on your mortgage after five years?

37. You bought a new car three years ago. The sticker price was $13,876 and you put $2,000 toward a down payment. The nominal annual interest rate on the loan used to finance the remaining balance was 10 percent and the term of the loan was five years (with monthly payments required). What is your current payoff on the loan (that is, balance immediately after the thirty-sixth payment)?

38. You plan to deposit money in a savings account that earns 7 percent annually. You will make five equal deposits of $7,130 each. The first deposit will be made today. No deposits will be made after the fifth deposit. What will be the accumulated sum available at the end of ten years?

39. You have a $175,000, thirty-year mortgage with a 9 percent nominal rate. You make payments every month. What will be the remaining balance on your mortgage after six years (that is, immediately after the seventy-second payment)?

Annuity Due 40. You will need to pay for your son's private school tuition (first grade through twelfth grade) a sum of $8,000 per year for years 1 through 5, $10,000 per year for years 6 through 8, and $12,500 per year for years 9 through 12. Assume that all payments are made at the beginning of the year, that is, tuition for year 1 is paid now (that is, at t = 0), tuition for year 2 is paid one year from now, and so on. In addition to the tuition payments, you expect to incur graduation expenses of $2,500 at the end of year 12. If a bank account can provide a certain 10 percent p.a. rate of return, how much money do you need to deposit today to be able to pay for the above expenses?

41. John Keene recently invested $5,000 in a project that is promising to return 10.5 percent per year. The cash flows are expected to be as follows:

End of Year	Cash Flow
1	$1,700
2	$1,800
3	???
4	$2,000

Note that the fourth year cash flow is unknown. Assuming that the present value of this cash flow stream is $5,000 (that is, CF0 $= -5000$), what is the missing cash flow value (that is, what is the cash flow at the end of the third year)?

Chapter 8

Financial Securities

After studying Chapter 8, you should be able to:

♦ Describe the basic nature of a financial security.

♦ Understand the difference between a debt security and an equity security.

♦ Define several different types of debt securities.

♦ Describe the basic rights and privileges of shareholders.

♦ Describe different types of financial markets, in particular the primary markets and the secondary markets.

♦ Understand the relationship between risk and return and be able to explain the relationship between risk and return for debt securities and equity securities.

♦ Intuitively explain the Capital Asset Pricing Model.

8.1 Chapter Overview ··

Corporations raise long-term money (that is, capital) by issuing corporate bonds, preferred stock, and common stock. These instruments are referred to as securities, financial securities, or financial assets. Securities trade in financial, or securities, markets. There are many different types of securities markets in the United States, and throughout the world; however, all securities markets provide the same important function. Financial markets are the place where buyers (that is, deficit units) and sellers (that is, surplus units) come together, and where price discovery occurs. For financial securities, the equilibrium price of any security is actually that price that represents an expected rate of return that compensates the investor for the risk inherent in the security.

In this chapter, we describe the properties of the major types of securities issued by most corporations. We then present an overview of the various types of securities markets in the United States. Finally, we discuss the principles of risk and return as these relate to corporate bonds and common stock.

Note that the material in this chapter is presented with the least amount of analytical and mathematical notion possible. Additionally, there are no computational problems within the chapter and a limited number of computational problems at the end of the chapter. This chapter is mainly an informational reading chapter. Nonetheless, we believe that you will find the material presented in this chapter to be very interesting, and important foundational information for chapter 9.

8.2 What Is a Financial Security? ··

Suppose that you are an entrepreneur and have developed an innovative new product that you believe will sell very well in the market. You do not, however, have the financial resources to buy all the assets required to manufacture this product. What do you do? You contact some entity that has the financial resources but not the product idea (for example, a bank or a venture capitalist) and ask it to lend you the money necessary to manufacture the product. If they believe that your idea is good, these financiers will provide you the money.

What do the providers of these funds receive in return? They receive your promise that they will be paid out of the cash flows that your firm will generate. In the financial world, promises have to be written down and the roles and obligations of all the parties under all conceivable scenarios have to be specified. All the parties have to agree to these by affixing their signatures. The promise then becomes a ***contract***. A ***financial security*** is simply a contract between the provider of funds and the user of these funds that clearly specifies the amount of money that has been provided and the terms and conditions of how the user is going to repay the provider.

Let us continue with the example of your firm. Assume that you start your firm by borrowing money, say $7.5 million, from a bank at 8 percent interest p.a. Your contract with the bank stipulates that you will repay the bank in ten equal yearly installments. From the previous chapter, we know that this means that you will have to pay the bank approximately $1.118 million every year. The loan that the bank has given you is a financial security.

> **An Aside**: The bank, on the other hand, by lending you money, has made an investment of $10 million in your firm. In fact, a bank's loans are its assets. Did you know that banks regularly sell these loan assets to other banks and investors?

You will make the required payments on the loan out of the revenues that you generate from your firm. After paying the bank and all the other expenses related to manufacturing and selling your product, whatever is left over is your income from this venture. You are the owner. If the firm does well, there will be a lot of money left over for you and, if the firm does poorly, so will you. In fact, if the firm were to do so poorly that there was no hope that you would ever be able to repay the loan, you would be bankrupt and the assets of your firm would belong to the bank and other persons to whom you owed money. The loan that the bank has given you is a financial security.

Now assume it is ten years since you started the firm. Your original $7.5 million has just been paid off, however, you have just borrowed another $8 million from the bank to buy some new equipment to replace some machines that have worn out. Suppose that your product has done very well and your firm has flourished over the past ten years. You, however, are kept so busy with the work that you have no time to enjoy the fruits of your creation.

Let us suppose that your firm is generating a total of $5 million per year as net cash flow. You expect that it will continue to do so (for convenience in computation) forever. Assuming a discount rate of 10 percent, the present value of this perpetuity is $\frac{\$5\,m.}{0.1}$ = $50 million. In other words, the value of the firm (that is, the market value of the firm's assets) is $50 million. Suppose that all your liabilities, including the new loan to the bank, amount to a total of $10 million (your $8 million long-term loan and $2 million in current liabilities). Because you are the owner of the firm, the difference between what the firm is worth and what you owe, $50 − $10 = $40 million, is your wealth or *equity.*

Is this equity of $40 million in your bank account? No. In fact, this "wealth" is really only "theoretical" wealth—value that exists in theory but which cannot be immediately spent. If you are tired of running the company and would like to ease up, what can you do? You can sell the company in its entirety and if you receive the fair price for it, you will have your $40 million. On the other hand, you might not want to sell off your entire ownership in the firm. In that case, you could sell only a portion of your ownership in the firm. You can do this by either taking on a partner or taking the company public.

Taking the company public requires you to obtain authorization from the Securities Exchange Commission (SEC) to issue shares to the public. You obtain authorization for, say, four million shares. Because the value of your ownership is $40 million, each of these shares is worth $10. If you wanted to sell, say, half of your equity ownership in the firm, you would sell two million shares to the public and retain the remaining two million. From the sale of the shares, you should receive $20 million. What do the people who buy these shares obtain in return? They are now part owners of the firm. Whatever cash flows are left over after paying all other obligations would now be divided among all shareholders. You would be entitled to half because you owned half of the outstanding shares. Others would receive an amount proportionate to their ownership. Note that the equity shares that you have sold are also contracts, as we have defined above, and, hence, are financial securities.

In general, the securities that a firm issues to investors are contracts with investors that specify the exact nature of the claim that investors owning a specific security have on the cash flows of the firm. As an aside, think of the dealings that firm has with its suppliers, or its customers, or its workers, or its management, or with the government (for taxation). In each case, these dealings are nothing but contracts. In fact, you can think of a firm as a set of several such contracts. A better and more popular description is that a firm is a "nexus" of all such contracts. In this chapter, however, we will focus on only the most common financial securities issued by firms, specifically, corporate bonds, preferred stock, and common stock.

8.3 Common Financial Securities

If you open the business section of the daily newspaper, you will be inundated with a myriad of different financial securities. Some of these securities represent contracts between the firm and investors (for example, stocks and bonds). Others are contracts between two investors and the firm is not involved. For example, a call option on the stock of ABC Corp. is a contract between the buyer and the seller of the option (also the option exchange). ABC Corp., despite the fact that the option is written on its stock, has nothing to do with the option; it is not a party to the option contract.

We are concerned here with only the former types of securities—those that are contracts between the firm and investors. These securities basically represent a contract under which the firm borrows capital from investors and, in return, depending upon the type of contract or security, promises a specific claim on the firm's future cash flows.

The above explanation about what securities are and why corporations issue securities serves a very important purpose. To an *investor* who owns a financial security, the security is nothing but a *stream of expected future cash flows.* Based on what we have studied in the previous chapters, then, the *value* of any security to the investor is the present value of all the *expected future cash flows* from owning the security discounted at the appropriate discount rate, or *required rate of return.* We will next describe the commonly observed securities in terms of the cash flows that these securities promise. Then, after describing the markets in which these securities trade, we will investigate the main issues concerning determining the required rate of return for individual securities.

There are two basic classifications for the securities that a firm issues to raise capital—*debt* and *equity.* Securities in the debt category usually promise fixed payments to the investor. These payments have to be made to the investors before anything can be paid to owners of equity securities. If the cash flows of the firm are very high, owners of debt securities still receive only the amount that was promised to them. They do not share in the cash flows over and above these fixed payments. In other words, debt investors are not the owners of the firm. However, if the cash flows to firms are so low that the firm is unable to meet its obligatory payments to owners of debt securities, the firm is held to be in default. The extreme case of default is when the value of the firm is so low that there is no possibility of ever satisfying its debt obligations. In this case the firm is bankrupt and the ownership of the assets of the firm goes to the owners of the debt securities.

Equity investors, those who own shares in the firm, are, unlike debt investors, owners of the firm. They receive the cash flow left over after the firm has made all its obligatory payments such as those to debt securities. Note that, by its very design, the cash flows to an equity security are not fixed. The higher the firm's cash flows are, the higher are the cash flows to equity securities. On the other hand, if the cash flow to the firm is less than what the firm owes to its debt securities, the equity investors obtain nothing. The following numerical example will make this clear.

Suppose that a firm has outstanding debt securities on which the obligatory payment is $300,000 per year. The following table provides the cash flows to debt and equity investors for different levels of the firm's cash flow.

Firm cash flow level	$500,000	$300,000	$100,000	$0
Cash flow to debt	$300,000	$300,000	$100,000	$0
Cash flow to equity	$200,000	$ 0	$ 0	$0

Notice that equity obtains a cash flow only when the firm's cash flow is greater than the amount due to debt. If the firm's cash flow is less than the amount due to debt, the entire cash flow goes to debt. Following is a graphical representation of this. In the graph, the horizontal axis represents the level of cash flows to the firm and the vertical axis the cash flows to debt and equity. D denotes the cash flow due to debt. As long as the firm's cash flow is less than D, the entire cash flow goes to debt. When it is greater than D, the debt-owners receive D and the residual cash flow goes to equity. For this reason, equity is commonly known as the *residual claim.* Note also that the cash flow to debt or equity security owners can never be negative. This is due to a legal feature called *limited liability.* According to it, limited liability investors can never lose more than what they have invested.

Now that we have the basic idea about the two types of claims that firms issue, we can specifically describe the securities that a firm issues.

8.3.1 Debt Securities

Recall that owners of debt securities usually have a claim on a firm's cash flows prior to that of equity-holders. Additionally, the payment to debt-holders is fixed beforehand. If the firm does very well in terms of generating cash flows, the debt-holders still obtain only their promised cash flows. Most importantly, debt-holders of a firm are not owners of the firm. They are creditors. Therefore, they do not get to vote on

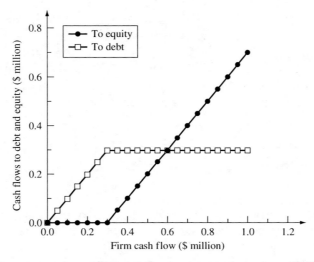

Figure 8.1   Debt and Equity Claims (D = $300,000)

matters pertaining to the operations of the firm. However, if the firm is in financial distress, that is, there is a significant chance that it will go bankrupt in the near future, the debt-holders, as per the usual debt contracts, have more of a say in the day-to-day running of the company. The reason for this is not all that difficult to see. As the cash flows of the firm become low, the cash flows to debt-holders begin to depend more and more on the cash flows of the firm. For example, in the previous numerical illustration, when cash flows to the firm are $300,000 or less, the cash flows to the debt-holders are completely determined by the cash flows to the firm. When this is the case, a firm is in financial trouble (or distress), and it is natural that debt-holders will want a say in the operations of the firm.

Fixed-Coupon Bonds – These are debt securities under which the firm pays a specific (fixed) amount called the *coupon* to the investor every period until the bond matures, and, at maturity, pays the *face value* of the bond. The most common face value, also referred to as par value, for a corporate bond is $1,000, however, bonds with par values other than $1,000 exist.

For example, if a firm issues an 8 percent thirty-year bond with annual coupon payments, the coupon is 8 percent, the maturity is thirty years, the face value is $1,000 (always assumed if no other face value is specifically mentioned), and the coupon is paid annually. The cash flows associated to this bond come in two parts—periodic coupon payments and the repayment of face value at maturity. Coupon payments are computed by multiplying the face value by the coupon rate. The *coupon rate* of a bond is **not** the required rate of return; it simply establishes the amount of the periodic coupon payment. So, from this bond, an investor will receive the following cash flows in the future: an annuity of $80 (8 percent of face value) for thirty years and $1,000 at the end of thirty years.

The coupon payment on the bond need not be annual; it can be paid semi-annually or quarterly. Suppose that the bond described above paid coupons semi-annually, the cash flow stream would be: $40 (0.5 × 8 percent of $1,000) every six months for sixty (thirty years × 2) six-month periods and $1,000 at the end of sixty six-month periods. If it paid quarterly, the cash flow stream would be $20 every three months for 120 three-month periods and $1,000 at the end of 120 three-month periods. Notice that when mentioning the repayment of face value of maturity, I changed the wording from "end of thirty years" to the number of six- or three-month periods depending on how often the coupon is paid. This is an important aspect to note at this time. It will have implications when we value bonds.

Zero-Coupon Bonds – A zero-coupon bond is a debt security that promises only one payment at maturity. This payment is fixed. In other words, a zero-coupon bond is a fixed-coupon bond with a zero coupon rate. Suppose that a firm issues a zero-coupon bond that matures in thirty years. Then the only payment that the firm has promised to the investors who bought these bonds is $1,000 (the face value) at the end of thirty years.

Variable-Rate Bonds – These bonds pay periodic coupons, but the coupon, unlike the fixed-coupon bond, is not fixed. As the name suggests, the coupon is variable. The size of the coupon is usually tied to the level of prevailing interest rates. The interest rate to which the coupon rate is tied to is also specified in the contract.

Consols (that is, Perpetual Bonds) – A consol is a fixed coupon-paying bond that has no maturity. In other words, the issuer of the bond agrees to pay a fixed coupon payment every period forever. If you recall, we had alluded to this security in the previous chapter.

Income Bonds – Income bonds have some features of both fixed-coupon and variable-rate bonds described earlier. On the one hand, income bonds, similar to fixed-coupon bonds, carry a promise to pay a fixed coupon. However, the firm is required to pay the coupon only when its earnings are sufficiently high. In other words, if the firm's earnings are sufficiently low, it can postpone or omit the periodic coupon payment. The omission of this payment does not put the firm in default as it would if it did not make the coupon payment in a fixed-coupon or variable-rate bond.

Convertible Bonds – As the name implies, a convertible debt security allows the security holder to convert it to another security, usually equity, according to some pre-specified terms. For example, ABC Corp. may issue a convertible bond that carries a 7 percent coupon paid annually, has a thirty-year maturity, has a face value of $1,000, and carries the feature that after five years, the owner of the bond can exchange it for fifty shares of ABC stock. Now suppose that after five years, the cash flows from this bond are worth $1,000 and ABC's stock is trading at $30 per share. In this case, the convertible bondholder will have a strong incentive to convert the bond into fifty shares of stock. On the other hand, if the price of the stock is $15 per share, the bondholder will not. As you can see, when you purchase a convertible bond, you are buying a security that is a (sort of) combination of debt and equity.

Callable Bonds – A callable bond is like a fixed-coupon bond except that the issuer of the bond, that is, the firm, has the right to repurchase it at a predetermined price. Suppose that ABC Corp issued a thirty-year bond with a 7 percent coupon paid annually and specified that after five years it, that is, ABC Corp., had the right (that is, it could if it wanted) to call (that is, buy back from the owners of the bond) the bond at $1,100. Whether ABC will call this bond after five years depends primarily on a very simple criterion—what is the market price of the bond at that time? If the price is more than $1,100, it makes sense to call. If it is not, there is no reason to call the bond.

The above is a very selected list of the types of debt securities. U.S. corporations are very creative about designing debt securities, and you will encounter many other types of debt securities. The chances are, however, that those securities will be some combination of two or more of the above debt securities. For example, we described convertible and callable bonds separately. U.S. corporations, however, issue bonds that are usually both convertible and callable. In addition to the above, you will encounter other features of debt contracts. These features include sinking fund provisions, level of security (that is, backed by assets of the firm), level of subordination (that is, between two classes of debt which class has the priority in terms of cash flows of the firm), and others.

8.3.2 Equity Securities

Contrary to debt, equity securities are much more uniform across corporations. As mentioned earlier, equity-holders have "residual" claim on a firm's cash flows. That is, they receive the cash flow that is "left over" after all other payments have been made. Equity-holders are the owners of the firm. As owners, they have a say in the operating decisions of the firm; that is they have *"control"* privileges. Equity-holders have the right to vote on matters of importance facing the firm. These are called equity *voting rights.* Suppose that the management of a company wanted to make an important change, say changing the firm's auditors.

To make this change, the management has to call a **general shareholder meeting** and propose this change and the change is effected only if a majority of the shareholders vote in favor of this change. Attendance at a shareholder meeting might not be required; all shareholders are sent **proxy ballots** before the meeting and shareholders can, thus, vote in absentia.

In practice, for most corporations (think of General Motors, which has millions of shareholders) it is impractical for shareholders to keep tabs on what the manager is doing. Therefore, the control (arising out of ownership) aspect of equity ownership is in the form of a **board of directors** whose responsibility is to ensure that the management takes actions that maximizes the welfare of shareholders. In other words, the board is supposed to look out for the interests of the shareholders. Shareholders elect board members, and the board represents shareholders, similar to the way your local politician is supposed to represent you.

Usually, the only way in which equity securities can differ from company to company is in the level of voting power. For example, voting on a share may be cumulative or may be non-cumulative (or straight). Cumulative voting exists (and is mandated in some states) because it allows minority shareholders to have more of a say in the election of board members. The easiest way to explain this is with the help of an example.

Suppose that a corporation has only two shareholders A and B. A owns twenty shares and B owns eighty shares. The firm has to elect five members to the board. A is a minority shareholder and wants to be on the board of directors. B, however, does not want A to be on the board. Each shareholder nominates five candidates. (Because B does not want A, their list of nominations has to be different by at least one candidate.)

Under non-cumulative or straight voting, A can cast twenty votes per candidate and B can cast eighty votes per candidate. Thus, all of B's candidates will win. In other words, B can freeze out the minority shareholder A. Under cumulative voting, on the other hand, the number of votes per share is determined by the number of directors to be elected. Because five directors are to be elected, each share has five votes. Therefore, A has $20 \times 5 = 100$ votes and B has $80 \times 5 = 400$ votes. Each shareholder can distribute these votes across the candidates as they wish. For example, they can cast all their votes for just one candidate. Thus, with 100 votes, A can be guaranteed election to the board. There is no possible way that B can divide 400 votes over five candidates such that all five have higher votes than A.

The nature of the equity security/contract provisions is fairly uniform across firms. The uniformity is because, as explained below, the owners of equity shares are not guaranteed any cash flows. Additionally equity, being a residual claim, generates cash flows only if all other claims on the firm's cash flow have been met. Thus, there is no question of creating different types of equity claims by structuring different streams of cash flows (as was the case with debt securities).

The owner of a share of stock can expect cash flows of two types. The first is in the form of dividends that the firm pays its shareholders. Recall from your analysis of income statements that dividends to equityholders are paid from net income after tax, that is, after all other payments have been made. Thus **dividends** are a **residual cash flow.** It is also true that the firm is not required to pay a dividend or to keep the level of periodic dividends constant. In other words, to the equity holders, there is no guaranteed cash flow from dividends. The other type of cash flow that equity holders can receive is from the **sale of their shares.** Again note that the price that they receive is the prevailing market price of the stock. In other words, there is no guaranteed cash flow here either.

8.3.3 Preferred Stock gets pd. before C/S.

The debt and equity securities described above account for a very large portion of the corporate financing activity in the U.S. The rest is primarily composed of a security that has some features of both debt and equity. This security is preferred stock. Cash flows to preferred stock are made after the payment to debt holders but before equity holders can be paid. Thus, preferred stock has a claim priority between debt and equity. A typical preferred stock has no maturity and in this sense is similar to equity. Preferred stock has a stated par value and, usually, a stated fixed dividend. These two features make it seem more like a debt security. Even though the level of dividend payments is fixed, non-payment of preferred stock dividends by the firm does not constitute default as it would if coupon on bonds were not paid. Dividend payment on preferred stock is at the discretion of the board of directors. It should, however, be noted that corporations very rarely forgo preferred stock dividend payment. As far as the control and ownership aspect is concerned, preferred stock is usually non-voting.

8.4 Overview of Financial Securities Markets ....

In Chapter 1 we noted that in the most basic sense, finance is concerned with the process through which funds are transferred from savers to borrowers. In general, savers are households and borrowers are corporations. Households provide cash to corporations to commence operations, cover seasonality, fund growth and cover losses during economic, industry, or company downturns. In exchange for this cash, corporations issue financial securities, the most common of which are corporate bonds, preferred stock, and common stock. The markets in which these financial securities trade are called financial markets or securities markets.

8.4.1 Types of Markets

There are actually many different types of markets in a financial market system associated with an economy such as ours. For example, there are *money markets* and *capital markets.* Money markets are the markets where financial assets trade that are close substitutes for cash and mature in one year or less. Money market securities include Treasury bills, negotiated certificates of deposit (CDs), bankers' acceptances, and commercial paper. Capital markets, on the other hand, are the markets for intermediate-term and long-term debt and corporate stocks. Capital market securities include Treasury notes and bonds, mortgages, municipal bonds, corporate bonds, preferred stock, and common stock. To a financial manager of a corporation, the last three capital market securities are of greatest interest.

Other types of markets are *spot markets* and *futures markets.* In spot markets, securities are bought and sold for "on-the-spot" delivery. For example, if you purchase 100 shares of GM stock through a broker, you have made a spot market transaction. As soon as the transaction is complete, money changes hands and 100 shares of GM stock are credited to your account. In futures markets, full payment for and delivery of the asset takes place at some future date, such as six months or one year. A particularly interesting futures market concerns the sale and delivery of agricultural products, such as corn. In the corn futures market, a farmer can actually sell bushels of corn at a pre-determined price before he even plants the seeds. This "futures contract" to sell corn at a set price will allow him to borrow money for his seeds and other planting needs. Futures contracts are usually used as insurance against some unforeseen event, but they can be used for speculative purposes. When used as insurance, futures are referred to as a *hedge.* Financial managers can use futures contracts to hedge against unfavorable interest rate or foreign exchange movements.

The financial markets that are of greatest interest to a financial manager are *primary markets* and *secondary markets.* Primary markets are the markets in which companies raise money. In a primary market transaction, one participant is a company and the other is an investor. Every security sells only once in the primary market. A subset of the primary markets is the *initial public offering* (or IPO) market. In this market, firms "go public" by issuing shares to investors for the first time. Secondary markets are where already issued securities that is, seasoned issues) trade among investors. Trading in the secondary markets does not specifically involve the company whose security is traded, in that the company does not receive any money from the transactions. Investors merely trade securities back and forth among themselves.

Secondary market trading, however, is extremely important to a company. First of all, if secondary market trading did not exist, few investors would buy securities from companies (that is, in the primary market) in the first place. Without secondary markets, investors would be "stuck" with the original security until it matured. In the case of corporate bonds, this is usually thirty years from issue, and common stock never matures. Investors would not be able to liquidate their securities regardless of personal needs. Would you buy a share of Cisco Systems stock, a stock that currently pays no dividends, for $18.00 per share if you knew that you would never able to sell the stock? We wouldn't, and we are sure you wouldn't either. Thus, without secondary markets, companies would not be able to raise money in the primary market. Second, secondary markets set prices for primary market transactions. If GM decided that it wanted to sell 10 million shares in the primary market, how would GM know what price these shares would probably sell for? The answer is whatever shares of GM stock are currently selling for in the secondary market, assuming that GM will spend the money raised wisely. New shares of GM are essentially the same as seasoned shares that are already actively trading. (Note that IPO shares do not yet have a secondary market, so determining what these shares will sell for is extremely difficult.) Finally, secondary markets provide instant evaluation and feedback to a financial manager. Recall that the goal of a financial manager is to maximize shareholder wealth and that shareholder wealth is represented by the market value of a firm's equity (which is merely price per share times the number of shares outstanding). If, all else constant, the price per share of a company's stock is declining while other company stock prices are rising, the financial manager is receiving a bad evaluation from the market. Likewise, if a firm's manager announces some change in policy that, all else constant, causes the company's stock price to rise, the new policy is probably a good idea.

Because the primary and secondary markets for stocks and bonds are of significant importance to financial managers, we will describe these markets in greater detail. We will also explain some of the measures that are used to describe the performance of the overall market.

8.4.2 How Companies Issue New Securities in the Primary Market

There are two ways that a company can issue new securities and thereby raise capital in the primary market: *private placement* and through the *investment banking process.* Private placement, as the name implies, is the direct sale of new securities by the issuing company usually to individual investors, commercial banks, mutual funds, pension funds, or insurance companies. The company merely prints up new securities and sells them to the public. Corporations often allow employees to purchase stock directly from the company, allow current shareholders to purchase additional stock, and offer dividend reinvestment plans, all often at a reduced price or without transaction fees. These are all examples of private placements of stock to individual investors. Larger private placements of securities usually involve a financial institution.

Investment banking is another way that companies can issue new securities. Most large issues involve investment bankers. An investment banker is a financing specialist. Many large brokerage firms, such as Merrill Lynch, have an investment banking division, as do most commercial banks.

When a company wishes to raise new long-term funds, they contact an investment banker who will assist the company in designing and pricing the issue. The investment banker will assess the merits of the issue, advise the company on whether it should issue corporate bonds or new shares of stock, tailor the issue (if necessary) to match the market's desire for new and different securities, and estimate the price at which the new issue will sell. If the company agrees to go forward with the investment bankers' recommendations, the investment banker will purchase the entire new issue from the company. This purchase is known as *underwriting* the issue.

For especially large issues, the investment banker may form a syndicate of several investment bankers, each taking a part of the new issue. After the purchase, the investment banker must then sell the purchased shares to the public. This is usually done through the company's brokerage department. Via the investment banking process, the issuing company gets its funds in a relatively short period of time and the company leaves the actual issuance of the security to the public in the hands of those who specialize in that area.

Investment bankers take on a substantial amount of risk when they purchase such large blocks of shares from the company. If a sudden, unforeseen downturn occurs in the price of the company's stock after the primary market transaction, the investment banker might have bought the shares for a price greater than what they can be sold. For example, if the investment banker purchases 10 million shares for $50 per share and subsequently the share price falls to $40 per share, the investment banker will face possible losses of $100 million.

To compensate for potential losses, investment bankers typically charge a fee of up to 10 percent of the value of the entire issue. In practice, once the sale price is identified, the investment banker actually purchases the new issue from the company at a discount. In the example above, the investment banker may actually purchase the new stock for $45 per share. If they can sell the stock to the public at an average price of $50 per share, the investment banker will record revenue of $50 million on the transaction. Of course, should the price of the stock subsequently rise to $60 per share, the investment banker will earn an even greater return.

8.4.3 How Securities Trade in the Secondary Market

The trading of securities in the secondary market typically takes place in an organized exchange, such as the New York Stock Exchange. Public trading of stock on organized exchanges is much more common than trading of bonds. Most bond trading tends to take place chiefly among large institutional investors. The largest and best known exchange in the world is the New York Stock Exchange (NYSE). The NYSE is located on Wall Street in New York City. The other major national exchange is the American Stock Exchange (AMEX). Regional markets include the Boston, Chicago, Cincinnati, Pacific and Philadelphia exchanges. The process of trading on all exchanges is basically the same, hence the description of trading on the NYSE below applies to all exchanges.

All major brokerage firms are members of the NYSE, and they route buy and sell orders from their clients to the floor of the exchange. There the trading process is somewhat complicated and varied, however, the main purpose of the exchange is to guarantee that demand exists for every sell order and supply exists for every buy order at a fair price. Every stock *listed* on the exchange has a *specialist* assigned to it who, when matching outside orders do not exist, guarantees this corresponding supply or demand.

Not all companies are listed on the NYSE. A company must meet strict listing requirements based on size, financial performance, and the distribution of its shares. Currently about 3,000 companies have their common stock listed on the NYSE. These tend to be older, well established companies. Other companies that wish to have their stock listed on an exchange but do not qualify for NYSE listing, can choose to list their stock on the AMEX or on any of the regional exchanges, based on the company's size, location, and market.

The other major market for trading securities is the *over-the-counter* (OTC) market. This market has no physical location; instead it consists of an automated quotation system, called the NASDAQ, that links dealers together to buy and sell securities from the public. A dealer is similar to a specialist, however, whereas there is only one specialist for most stocks that trade on the NYSE, there are many dealers for most stocks that trade on the OTC. Dealers are referred to as market makers. They list bid and ask prices at which they are willing to buy and sell a specific security on NASDAQ. NASDAQ then identifies the highest bid price and the lowest ask price. If an investor wishes to buy a security, he will buy it from the dealer with the lowest ask price. Conversely, if an investor wishes to sell a security, she will sell it to the dealer with the highest bid price. When the inventory of the specific security held by a dealer reaches the maximum or minimum that the dealer wishes to hold, the dealer will change his bid or ask prices. Most bonds trade in the OTC bond market. The OTC stock market has most recently become the favorite trading location for technology firms.

8.4.4 Market Indices

How did the market do yesterday? What is the average annual rate of return on an unmanaged portfolio of stocks? These questions are often answered by computing an index that represents the entire market or some subset of the market. Actually, there are numerous indices that are used to measure the performance of the different markets in the U.S. All differ from one another in the number of securities used to compute the index and in the manner in which the different stocks in the index are weighted. The two most popular indices used to describe the NYSE are the Dow Jones Industrial Average (DJIA) and the S&P 500 Index.

The DJIA is price-weighted average of thirty stocks. These stocks span the major non-financial industries in the U.S. economy. Most are the dominant companies in their respective industry. To compute the closing average for a given day, the daily prices of the thirty stocks are added together and divided by some divisor. Originally, the divisor was set equal to the number of stocks in the DJIA (thus, the DJIA represented the average stock price). Now the divisor is much smaller (you can look up the current divisor in the financial pages of the Wall Street Journal). To maintain consistency through time, the divisor must be changed whenever a company splits its stock or when a company is removed from the DJIA and replaced with another company. A *stock split* occurs when a company increases (or decreases) every investor's holdings by some multiple. For example, in a two-for-one stock split, if you owned 100 shares before the split, you would own 200 shares after the split. At least theoretically, a two-for-one stock split should merely reduce the price of the stock by 50 percent—the number of shares change but the market value of the company's equity remains the same. Movement on and off the DJIA, though rare, does in fact occur from time to time. Companies go bankrupt, are acquired by other companies, or are no longer representative of their industry—or their industry is no longer considered in the mainstream.

The S&P 500 Index is a value-weighted index of 500 stocks. These are the 500 most dominant and influential stocks on the NYSE. To compute the closing index for a given day, the market values (that is, price per share times number of shares outstanding) of all 500 stocks are added together. This value is then compared to the prior day's value to compute the percentage change from one day to the next. The percentage change is then applied to an index that many years ago was set equal to 100. Thus, if yesterday the S&P 500 Index was equal to 250 and today the percentage change in the market values of the 500 stocks increased by 2 percent, the S&P 500 Index at today's close would be $(250)(1.02) = 255$.

Value-weighted indices are theoretically more accurate than price-weighted indices and many stocks in an index should produce a more reflective index than few stocks. For this reason, traders, analysts, and those who study the market should use more comprehensive measures such as the S&P 500 Index or the New York Composite Index (which is value-weighted and includes all stocks on the NYSE). Nonetheless, the DJIA is the most widely reported index in the press. Though not the best, following the DJIA is at least acceptable to most investors in that financial studies show that the DJIA is at least highly (though not perfectly) correlated with the S&P 500 Index.

8.5 The Principles of Risk and Return

As we noted earlier in this chapter, the major purpose of a financial market is to establish equilibrium prices of the securities that trade in the market. Security prices, which can easily be observed, are actually the end product of a more fundamental purpose, which is the association of risk and return. In trading securities, investors are actually attaching a required rate of return to the perceived risk level inherent in the security. This required rate of return (often referred to as the appropriate discount rate in the previous two chapters) then determines the price of the security.

For example, consider a two-period security that promises to pay $100 per year at the end of each of the next two years. Assume that the required rate of return for this security is 10 percent. What is the value (that is, the equilibrium price) of this security? It is the present value of these cash flows discounted at 10 percent, which is equal to $173.55. What would happen to the equilibrium value of this security if investors changed the required rate of return to 9.6 percent? The present value of $100 per year for two years discounted at 9.6 percent is $174.49; thus, the price of the security would increase. And, if investors changed the required rate of return to 10.25 percent, the price of the security would decrease to $172.97. That is, the required rate of return (applied to the expected future cash flow stream) determines the price of the security. Thus, the main issue concerning price discovery is determining the precise relationship between risk and return.

8.5.1 Risk and Return

Suppose that your instructor walks into your classroom today and announces a pop quiz covering all of the material in this chapter. (You are probably in trouble since you have yet to finish reading this chapter unless, of course, you are reading this for the second time). Assume that the weight of a single quiz in your overall grade is 1 percent. Though not terribly significant in the grand scheme of your final grade, doing better on the quiz is preferred to doing worse.

Now assume that your instructor also offers you the following game opportunity. You may come to the front of class and flip a coin (assume it is a fair coin). If your toss produces a "head" you are exempt from the quiz and you will automatically get a 100 for your quiz score. If your toss produces a "tail," however, you will have to take the quiz and whatever grade you receive on the quiz will be your quiz score. Would you play this game? You should! The expected return of the game is a 50 percent of a 100 plus 50 percent of what you will receive if you take the quiz (presumably less than 100 percent, perhaps even zero). The risk of playing the game is actually nothing. There is no cost and no possibility of loss.

Now assume that your instructor makes a simple change to the offer. It costs $50 to play the game and you only get one chance. Would you still play the game? Probably not! The expected return is the same, but the cost of the game (that is, the risk of playing the game) is $50. Unless the value of the expected return is worth more to you than $50, you should not play the game. Given that a quiz counts as only 1 percent of your grade, the risk is probably too steep.

Now assume another change. Your instructor offers the same game (for a cost of $50) but the 100 score will be on the next exam that you take instead of on a quiz. Also assume that exams count as 25 percent of your final course average. Would you play the game for this return? Most of you probably would (assuming you have $50 to spend and assuming that, as most students, you are more interested in your final grade than you are in what you learn—an ominous fact of education to most instructors).

What has this game taught us about risk and return? Two facts. First, there is a positive relationship between risk and return. When your instructor increased the risk to $50 for a quiz score, most people chose not to play the game. When the return was raised to an exam score (with a higher overall weight, and therefore a higher expected return), many again chose to play the game. All else constant, the higher the risk, the higher the expected return must be to keep people in the game. Would you play the game for an exam score if the cost were $250? What if the cost was $250, but you were playing for an automatic A in the course instead of for an exam score. Pay $250, flip a head and you get an A—no more exams, no more reading, no more attending class!!!

Second, the relationship between risk and return is not a finance issue only. In fact, most of us make risk-return tradeoff decisions every day. Should you major in finance or marketing? Should you speed to make an appointment on time, or should you be late? Should you sit next to this person in class or on the bus? Should you eat that stuff that they call meatloaf in the school cafeteria? Decisions concerning these issues are all based on some perceived risk-return tradeoff.

In finance, we want to go further than merely associating risk and return. In fact, we want to quantify both measures and try to find a specific mathematical relationship between them. The basic relationship between risk and return for securities is fairly easy to identify. Assume that you own a security that you believe will pay you $100 one year from today. What are the main risk factors inherent in this cash flow stream for which you must be compensated? In fact, there are three factors, or components of interest rates.

First, any security cash flow must return to the investor some return for giving up current consumption in favor of future consumption. Assume that the cost of the one-year security above was $100. You will have to give up $100 today to receive $100 one year from today. That is, you will give to the seller of the security the ability to purchase $100 worth of merchandise today and you yourself will have to wait one full year to purchase and consume the exact same merchandise. This makes no sense. Investors must be compensated for giving up current consumption. This component of return is called the real rate of interest or the real return. In fact, we discussed this component of rates in chapter 6.

Second, any security cash flow must return to the investor a return equal to the expected inflation rate. If you believed that prices over the next twelve months were going to increase by 10 percent, than the return on this investment must be at least 10 percent. Otherwise you would lose to inflation by making an investment. Again, that would make no sense. This component of return, the expected inflation rate, was also discussed in chapter 6.

Recall from chapter 6 that we defined the following relationship:

$$r_{nominal} = r_{real} + i + (r_{real} \times i),$$

where, "$r_{nominal}$" was the nominal rate, "r_{real}" was the real rate, and "i" was the expected inflation rate. We then noted that if the real interest rate and the inflation rate are fairly small, one could say that the nominal rate is approximately equal to the sum of the real rate and the rate of inflation. That is,

$$r_{nominal} = r_{real} + i.$$

The sum of the real rate and the expected inflation rate is also called the ***risk free interest rate,*** the risk-free rate, or r_f. It is the rate of return that reflects economic conditions only. The risk-free rate is independent of the risk inherent in the cash flows of any particular security. In addition to r_f then, any security must generate a return to the investor to compensate for the risk inherent in the expected future cash flows associated with the security. This component of interest rates is called the ***risk premium.***

Thus, the three components of the required rate of return for any security are: the real rate, the expected inflation rate, and the risk premium specifically associated with the security's expected future cash flows. The first two components represent the risk-free rate, and therefore:

Required rate of return = r_f + Risk premium.

Because fixed income securities (that is, debt) and equity securities have different factors that determine their risk premiums, we will briefly explore the risk premium of each type of security below.

8.5.2 Risk Premium for Fixed Income Securities

Recall that a fixed income security, for example a corporate bond, is actually a contract between a lender and a borrower that specifies the exact payment stream and the term required to repay the debt. For example, a bond with a $1,000 par value, an 8 percent coupon rate and a term to maturity of five years, promises to pay to the investor the following cash flow stream:

Year	Cash Flow
1	$ 80
2	$ 80
3	$ 80
4	$ 80
5	$1,080

Due to the exact contractual nature of a bond, the only risk inherent in this cash flow stream is the probability that the issuer might default on the payments. That is, that a specific payment or payments might be made late or may not be made at all. The return associated with the probability of default for a bond is called a bond's ***default risk premium.***

Fortunately for investors, several independent companies (for example, Standard and Poor's) rate, or grade, bonds according to their default risk. A typical grading scheme is:

AAA	—	Lowest probability of default
AA	—	↓
A	—	
BBB	—	Higher probability of default
BB	—	↓
B	—	
CCC	—	Highest probability of default
CC	—	Currently in default of some or all terms of the contract

A particularly important segment of the bond market is called the junk bond market. Junk bonds are bonds that are rated BB and below. These are highly speculative bonds with high default risk premiums. All else constant, corporate bonds with the same grade should have about the same default risk premium.

A second risk factor for fixed income securities has to do with the term, or length, of the loan. There is more risk inherent in lending long term than short term. This relationship is mainly a function of the difficulty associated with forecasting long-term versus short-term default risk and inflation rates. The return associated with this second risk factor is known as the *maturity risk premium.* The maturity risk premium is higher for ten-year bonds than for two-year bonds. In fact, the maturity risk premium is easy to observe. Which interest rate is higher: a fifteen-year mortgage or a thirty-year mortgage? A three-year car loan or a six-year car loan? If you look these up, you will find that the shorter term security has a lower interest rate.

If we denote the default risk premium as DP and the maturity risk premium as MP, we find that (for actively traded securities) the:

$$\text{Required rate of return for fixed income securities} = r_f + DP + MP.$$

This is a mathematical relationship that relates risk to return. In an efficient market (we will assume that the U.S. financial markets are efficient), the required rate of return is also the expected rate of return. For corporate bonds, this rate is also called the appropriate discount rate or the bond's yield to maturity.

Note that the required rate of return is not a constant over the life of a security. Investors alter their view of expected inflation almost every time that new economic data is reported in the press. A company's default risk can change with movements in the economy from recession to boom or with changes in characteristics specific to the industry or the company (for example, a newly announced major suit against the company). And maturity risk changes as the security term naturally alters towards maturity, and with changes in the general level of uncertainty concerning all economic factors (for example, with the election of a new president or with a war in some strategic location in the world).

8.5.3 Risk Premium for Equity Securities

The risk premium for equity securities is much more difficult to define. This is because whereas the expected future cash flows for a bond are explicitly stated in the bond contract and non-payment results in company default, the expected future cash flows to equity are completely uncertain. Recall that equity is a residual claim. Equity holders get what is "left over" after all creditors have been paid. In a particularly bad year for a firm when revenues are low, the cash flows to equity holders can be zero. In a good sales year, the cash flows might be very big.

Another reason for the difficulty in defining the risk premium for equity is due to the effect of diversification on the volatility of expected future cash flows. If an investor creates a portfolio of stocks, the volatility in the return for the portfolio as a whole is less than the sum of the volatilities of the individual stocks. The effect of diversification on equity risk is an extremely important concept in finance. Although developing the complete mathematical model concerning risk and return for equity is beyond the scope of this book, it is important that you understand the basic intuition behind this idea. To do so, we must define a few mathematical and statistical measures, which hopefully, you are already familiar with.

The expected return for a stock has two components: a *dividend yield* and a *capital gain (or loss) yield.* The dividend yield is simply defined as D_1/P_0, where D_1 is the dividend expected to be paid one period (assume one year) from today and P_0 is the current price. The capital gain yield is defined as $(P_1 - P_0)/P_0$, where P_1 is the expected price of the stock one year from today. Thus, the total expected return for a stock is defined as $[D_1 + (P_1 - P_0)]/P_0$. For example, if you purchase a share of stock today for $100 and you expect that the stock will pay a dividend of $4 one year from today and that the price of the stock one year from today will be $108, then the expected return on your stock will be $[(\$4 + (\$108 - \$100)]/100 = 12/100 = 12\%$.

Expected returns are difficult to estimate in practice because the expected future dividend and the expected future stock price are unknown (they will occur in the future and residual cash flows are highly uncertain). In practice, investors estimate expected returns by computing past returns and using these as a guide for the future. For example, if for the past five years, a particular security has generated the following returns:

Year	Return
1	10%
2	4%
3	(8%)
4	7%
5	12%

then it would be reasonable to assume that the average annual return over this five-year period will be the expected return next year. The average return of a series of historical returns is simply equal to the sum of the returns divided by the number of returns. Thus, for this series:

Average Annual Return = (10% + 4% − 8% + 7% + 12%)/5 = 5%.

More recent information or the current state of the economy can be factored into this computation by weighting the returns differently. In the above computation, each observed return is weighted by 1/5. Perhaps more recent returns are more reflective of the future than distant past returns. In this case, we might place a greater weight on the year 5 return (for example, 3/10) and a smaller weight on the year 1 return (perhaps 1/10). Obviously, regardless of the weighting scheme, the sum of all weights must be 1.

For simplicity, assume that we use the simple average to forecast the future. Now that we have a measure of expected return, we must compute a measure of risk. In the most basic sense, risk reflects the level of certainty (or, uncertainty) that an investor has about his expectation. For this example, we expect a 5 percent return. How certain is the investor that this will be the actual return? If you look at the historical data, your answer would probably be not very certain. Over the past five years, the highest return on this stock has been 12 percent and the lowest return has been negative 8 percent. Assume that instead the stock had behaved as follows over the past five years:

Year	Return
1	6%
2	4%
3	5%
4	4%
5	6%

This series of historical returns has the same average return (5 percent), but the returns are significantly less volatile than before. An investor should feel more confident about her 5 percent expected return figure for this second set than for the first set. Thus, the higher the volatility of returns, the higher the risk.

In statistics, the most common measure of volatility is a standard deviation (SD). A standard deviation for equally weighted historical data is computed as follows:

1. Compute the average return of the historical series of returns.
2. Find the deviation from the average for each observation.
3. Square each of these deviations.
4. Add the squared deviations.
5. Divide this sum by the total number of historical returns. Then compute the square root of this sum.

For our first example:

1. Average return $= 5\%$

2. $(10\% - 5\%) = 5\%$
   $(4\% - 5\%) = -1\%$
   $(-8\% - 5\%) = -13\%$
   $(7\% - 5\%) = 2\%$
   $(12\% - 5\%) = 7\%$

3. $5^2 = 25$
   $-1^2 = 1$
   $-13^2 = 169$
   $2^2 = 4$
   $7^2 = 49$

4. $(25 + 1 + 169 + 4 + 49) = 248$.

5. $248/5 = 49.6$ and the square root of $49.6 = 7.04$.

Thus, the standard deviation of the first series of historical returns above equals 7.04 percent. Now, repeat these steps yourself to prove that the standard deviation of the second series of historical returns is 0.89 percent.

As noted above, the higher the standard deviation, the higher the risk. So, as proved by standard deviation, the first series of returns is more risky than the second set of returns. An investor will be more certain about his expectation of a 5 percent return for the second series than for the first series.

Now we will consider the effects of diversification on standard deviation. Consider two stocks, A and B. The historical returns for each stock are shown in the first two return columns in the table below. The third return column in this table represents the returns on a portfolio made up of 50 percent of stock A and 50 percent of stock B. For example, if we assume the investor has $10,000 to invest, we assume that she purchased $5,000 of Stock A and $5,000 of Stock B. Note that for each year, the return to the portfolio is simply 50 percent of the return for Stock A plus 50 percent of the return for Stock B.

Year	Returns for Stock A	Returns for Stock B	Returns for Portfolio
1	14%	6%	10%
2	5%	7%	6%
3	-4%	10%	3%
4	12%	-8%	2%
5	16%	0%	8%
6	-3%	21%	9%

As you can probably tell without even computing standard deviations, the standard deviation of the portfolio is significantly less than the standard deviation of the two individual stocks. Nonetheless, you should prove to yourself that the standard deviation of Stock A is 8.7 percent, the standard deviation of Stock B is 9.7 percent, and the standard deviation of a portfolio composed of 50 percent of Stock A and 50 percent of Stock B is 3.3 percent.

The reason why diversification reduces the standard deviation and risk is easy to understand. Many factors affect a stock price and therefore stock returns. For example, a strike against a company might cause the stock of the company to decrease. The introduction of a successful new product might cause the price to increase. An increase in the general level of interest rates in the economy, a recession, or a war might cause the price to decrease. In fact, this list could go on and on. Most important, however, these factors do not affect all stocks in the same way. A strike against a company might cause that company's stock price to fall but it might also cause the price of companies in the same industry not facing a strike to rise. If a report is released today that proves that chicken causes cancer, companies in the chicken industry will probably suffer, but companies in the beef, pork, and seafood industries might benefit. Other companies not related in any way to the chicken market (for example, companies in the automobile industry) might experience no effect whatsoever from this announcement.

Diversification causes some factors that affect some stocks to cancel out (chicken and beef) and other factors to be isolated to only a few stocks in the portfolio (chicken and automobiles). The larger the portfolio, the greater the effect of diversification. Risk, however, can never be completely eliminated because there are some factors that affect nearly every stock in the same way. For example, a recession causes nearly all stocks to decrease in value. Passage of a tax cut will generally cause nearly all stocks to increase in value.

Thus, total risk actually has two components: diversifiable risk and non-diversifiable risk. An investor can eliminate diversifiable risk by creating a very large portfolio of stocks (for example, the S&P 500 portfolio or the New York Composite portfolio). What is still left in the portfolio is non-diversifiable risk. In practice, diversifiable risk is called *specific risk* and non-diversifiable risk is called *market risk.* Because specific risk can be eliminated by creating a portfolio, the only measure of risk that is important to determine the risk premium for equity is the market risk of an individual security.

In finance, there is a statistical way to compute an index of the market risk inherent in an individual stock. This measure is called *beta.* There is also a model in finance that relates beta to the risk premium on equity. This model is called the Capital Asset Pricing Model, or CAPM (pronounced "cap M"). The CAPM is one of the most significant contributions of academic finance to the business world. The model has limitations and alternative models exist; however, the CAPM is intuitively appealing and still extremely popular. Nearly all businesses and investment companies estimate and use betas and the CAPM. Explaining the theory and developing the CAPM is left to a more advanced course and text. Here we will merely state the equation and illustrate some of its uses and implications.

The CAPM shows that the risk premium on equity can be defined as:

$$\beta(r_m - r_f),$$

where β is a stock's estimated beta, r_m is the expected rate of return on a large, diversified portfolio, called the market portfolio (the S&P 500 or the New York Composite can be thought of as proxies for the market portfolio), and r_f is the risk-free interest rate. Thus, according to the CAPM, the

Required rate of return on equity (or RR_e) = $r_f + \beta(r_m - r_f)$.

Applying the CAPM is very simple. If for a given stock, $\beta = 1.2$, $r_m = 12\%$, and $r_f = 4\%$, then the required rate of return on this stock (that is, that rate that will compensate the investor for the risk inherent in the security) is:

$4\% + 1.2\,(12\% - 4\%) = 13.6\%.$

Similarly (proof left up to you) if $\beta = 1.0$ (assume the same r_m and r_f), $RR_e = 12\%$, and $\beta = 0.8$, $RR_e = 10.4\%$.

Beta is an index of market risk and β's can be computed for individual stocks or for portfolios of stocks. The β of the market portfolio is 1.0. If an individual stock or a portfolio has a β of 1.0, it is said to have risk that is equal to the risk of the market, or average risk. The return on a stock with $\beta = 1.0$, will have an expected return that is the same as the expected return on the market portfolio. Note above, that when $\beta = 1.0$, $RR_e = 12\% = r_m$. If $\beta > 1.0$, the market risk of the individual stock or portfolio is greater than average (hence, $RR_e > r_m$) and vice versa for $\beta < 1.0$.

Beta actually measures the relationship between the volatility of a particular stock and the volatility of the entire market. Because the market is highly correlated with the business cycle, an intuitive way to think of β is to the answer to the following question. For a given company, if the economy goes into a recession, what will happen to the demand for that company's product? If the decline in demand is average, $\beta = 1.0$. If greater than average, $\beta > 1.0$ and if less than average, $\beta < 1.0$. Given this intuitive definition, it is easy to understand why utility companies have betas that are less than one and why automobile, durable goods (such as refrigerators) and luxury goods producers and sellers have betas that are usually greater than 1.0.

There is one final point that needs to be made concerning the relationship between the *required* rate of return and the *expected* rate of return for a security. Consider two stocks, A and B. Assume that the β of both stocks equals 1.2. Also assume that the expected return (defined as $[D_1 + (P_1 - P_0)]/P_0$) for Stock A equals 10 percent and that the expected return for Stock B equals 12 percent.

According to CAPM, two stocks with the same β have the same required rate of return. Assume that CAPM shows that the required rate of return for a stock with $\beta = 1.2$ is 12 percent. What will happen to Stock A? No one should buy it. As long as they can freely choose stock B over stock A, stock B is clearly preferred to stock A. Stock B produces a higher expected return for the same level of risk. Now if no one buys stock A, its price should fall. And if stock A's price falls (that is, P_0 decreases), then (all else constant) the expected return on stock A will increase. For example, if for stock A, originally $D_1 = \$2$, $P_1 = \$108$ and $P_0 = \$100$, then the original expected return on stock A is 10 percent. But if no one will buy stock A at this return level, P_0 will decrease. Assume that P_0 decreases to $98.21. This will increase the expected return on Stock A to:

$$[\$2 + (\$108 - \$98.21)]/\$98.21 = 12\%.$$

The two stocks with the same β will have the same expected return—both are now equally attractive and there will be no pressure on the price of either security to change. This means that the market is in equilibrium. Also, the expected rate of return will be equal to the required rate of return. These two returns will always be equal as long as financial markets are efficient.

Although this might seem to be a minor point, it is actually very important. This result is what guarantees that the present value of a stock is equal to the price that the stock trades for in the market. The same is true for bonds. In the next chapter, when you learn specifically how to determine the value of bonds and stocks, we will merely assume this relationship (price = present value) to be true.

In this chapter we have discussed the major types of securities that firms issue and the markets in which these securities trade, and we have provided insight into how expected returns are determined. In chapter 9, we will show you how to value these securities. Throughout the following chapter we will assume that for any given security we are trying to value, the appropriate discount rate, the required rate of return, the yield to maturity, or the expected rate of return is given. From this chapter you now know that these terms are all one and the same, and therefore can be used interchangeably.

Additional Questions and Problems

1. Describe a *financial security* in terms that a friend who is majoring in history could understand.

2. Assume that you own 100 percent of a private company that has no debt and an equity value of $1,000,000. Describe two ways that you could "extract" some of the equity (say, $500,000) from your company.

3. Complete the following sentences:

   • "To an investor who owns a financial security, the security represents a stream of _____."

   • "The value of any security to an investor is the _____ of the _____ from owning the security discounted at the _____."

4. What are the two basic classifications for the securities that firms issue to raise capital? In what way(s) are these types of securities similar? In what way(s) are these types of securities different?

5. Suppose a firm has outstanding debt securities of $100 million with an obligatory payment of $8 million per year. What is the cash flow to debt and the cash flow to equity if the firm cash flow level is:

   a. $40 million   b. $20 million

   c, $10 million   d. $5 million

   e. $0

6. The shareholders of Filbun, Inc. are about to vote for 5 new board members. The company has 10,000,000 shares of stock outstanding. Assume that 90 percent of Filbun's shareholders support candidates A, B, C, D and E and the rest of Filbun's shareholders support candidate F. Show how, under cumulative voting, the minority shareholders will be able to elect candidate F to the board.

7. Define each of the following types of markets in the U.S. financial market system:

   a. Money markets   b. Capital markets

   c. Spot markets   d. Futures markets

   e. Primary markets   f. Secondary markets

8. Compare and contrast the trading of securities on the NYSE to the trading of securities on the OTC market.

9. Consider the following data for stocks A through E.

Stock	Beginning of Year Price	End of Year Price	Number of Shares Outstanding
A	$ 10.00	$ 18.00	150,000,000
B	$ 2.00	$ 4.00	200,000,000
C	$ 60.00	$ 72.00	100,000,000
D	$110.00	$100.00	80,000,000
E	$ 28.00	$ 36.00	60,000,000

a, Compute the price-weighted average price (that is, add the five prices and divide by 5) of the five stocks at the beginning of the year. Compute the simple average price of the five stocks at the end of the year. Compute the percentage change in the price-weighted average price of the stocks from the beginning of the year to the end of the year.

b. Compute the value-weighted average price (that is, multiply number of shares outstanding times the price for each stock, sum and divide by 5) of the five stocks at the beginning of the year. Compute the value-weighted average price of the five stocks at the end of the year. Compute the percentage change in the value weighted average price of the stocks from the beginning of the year to the end of the year.

c. Note that the price-weighted average is analogous to the DJIA and the value-weighted average is analogous to the S&P 500 Index. Compare/contrast these two measures.

10. Assume that the risk-free interest rate is 4.5 percent. Assume that the default risk premium (DP) on AAA rated fixed income securities is 3.5 percent, on AA rated fixed income securities is 3.8 percent, on BB rated fixed income securities is 4.4 percent and on BBB rated fixed income securities is 4.7 percent. Finally, assume that the maturity risk premium (MP) for fixed income securities is given by $.1(t - 1)$, where t is the term of the security. Thus, for a 10 year fixed income security, $MP = (.1)(10 - 1) = .9$ percent. Given these relationships, compute the required rate of return for each of the following fixed income securities:

a. AAA rated fixed income securities that mature in 8 years.

b. BBB rated fixed income securities that mature in 3 years.

c. AA rated fixed income securities that mature in 18 years.

d. BB rated fixed income securities that mature in 26 years.

11. The annual returns for Stock X for the past 10 years are shown in the table below:

Year	Return
1	12%
2	−8%
3	30%
4	9%
5	−6%
6	0%
7	−3%
8	24%
9	38%
10	8%

a. Compute the average annual rate of return over this ten-year period.

b. Compute the standard deviation of returns over this ten-year period.

12. The annual returns for Stock A and Stock B for the past 5 years are shown in the table below.

Year	Stock A Return	Stock B Return	Portfolio Return
1	18%	8%	_____
2	0%	32%	_____
3	−10%	−4%	_____
4	14%	16%	_____
5	44%	8%	_____
6	−2%	26%	_____

a. Fill in the last column by computing the returns on a portfolio made up of 40 percent of Stock A and 60 percent of Stock B.

b. Compute the average return and the standard deviation of returns for Stock A.

c. Compute the average return and the standard deviation of returns for Stock B.

d. Compute the average return and the standard deviation of returns of the portfolio made up of 40 percent of Stock A and 60 percent of Stock B.

e. Compare the standard deviation of the portfolio to the weighted average of the standard deviations of Stock A and Stock B. Explain, in terms that your friend who is a sociology major would understand, why is the standard deviation of the portfolio less than 40 percent of Stock A's standard deviation plus 60 percent of Stock B's standard deviation?

Chapter 9

Valuation of Bonds and Stocks and the Cost of Capital

After studying Chapter 9, you should be able to:

- Describe the concepts that underlie the cost of capital.
- Explain the key features of bonds.
- Distinguish between different kinds of bonds.
- Estimate the value of a bond and compute a bondholder's expected rate of return.
- Identify the basic characteristics and features of preferred stock.
- Value preferred stock.
- Identify the basic characteristics and features of common stock.
- Value common stock.
- Calculate a stock's expected rate of return.

9.1 Chapter Overview ....

In the previous chapter, we studied financial securities in a descriptive and intuitive manner. In this chapter, we will focus on applying the valuation techniques that we have studied to the cash flows from many of the securities described in the previous chapter. In addition to valuing securities, we shall also consider the concept of the cost of capital.

9.2 The Cost of Capital ....

Recall the concept of the required rate of return from the earlier chapter on time value of money. We described an investor's required rate of return as the minimum return that investors would require for giving up the use of their money. How do investors determine this rate? One possibility is that investors look at the market to determine this rate. The market tells investors what they could earn on a comparable investment. Therefore, if a firm wants investors' capital, the investors will locate another investment in the market that is comparable to the firm seeking their funds. The return on that comparable investment would be the *minimum* that investors would require from their investment in this firm. In other words, investors' required rate of return is determined as the *opportunity cost* of their funds. Recall also the fact that, this required rate of return for investors was used as the discount rate in determining the value that investors place on an asset.

Suppose that for a particular investment, investors determine that the required rate of return is 15 percent. One can think of this 15 percent as the minimum "price" that investors are charging for their capital. Anyone who wants these investors' capital must pay a "price" of at least 15 percent. Now consider the situation from the point of view of the firm that wants the investors' capital. To obtain these investors' capital, the firm will have to pay the investors a "price." The price that the firm pays to the investors is the "cost" of the capital to the firm. What is the relation then between the investors' "price" for their capital (investors' required rate of return) and the "cost" of these investors' capital to the firm (firm's cost of capital)? The answer is very simple. Lending capital to the firm is similar to "selling" the capital and when the firm takes the investors' capital, it is akin to "buying;" thus, the investor is the "seller" and the firm is the "buyer."

From earlier discussions we know how prices are set in a competitive market. The seller will accept a price no less than the minimum price of 15 percent. The buyer, knowing this, will not pay a price greater than 15 percent. Therefore, the price for the transaction between the investor and the firm is 15 percent, which was the investor's required rate of return. Therefore, *the firm's cost of capital is equal to the investor's required rate of return.* Taking this further, the investor's required rate of a return from a firm's debt issue would be the firm's *cost of debt* and the investor's required rate of return from the firm's equity would be the firm's *cost of equity.* In the case of debt, the cost of debt or the debt investors' required rate of return is also called the *yield-to-maturity* of the bond.

9.3 Bond Valuation ....

We will now discuss the valuation of different types of debt securities. Additionally, having now seen the conceptual relation between the required rate of return and the cost of capital, we will also present methods for determining the cost of each of these debt securities.

9.3.1 Valuation of Consols

A consol or perpetual debt is a bond that pays coupon every period forever. Thus, an investor who buys a consol is buying the perpetuity of the fixed coupon. If the coupon is C dollars, the price of the consol is simply the present value of the perpetuity. In other words,

$$P_{consol} = \frac{C}{r_d^{consol}},$$

where r_d^{consol} is the cost of capital, d denotes the fact that a consol is a debt security, and the superscript tells us the type of the security.

Rearranging the above equation, we obtain the equation for the cost of a consol or perpetual debt as follows:

$$r_d^{consol} = \frac{C}{P_{consol}}.$$

Suppose that in 1990, a firm issued consols that promised a coupon of $100 per year paid annually. If the investor's required rate of return is 10 percent, what is the price of the consol? The answer is pretty straightforward to compute.

$$P_{consol} = \frac{100}{0.10} = \$1,000$$

Now suppose that five years have passed since the issuing of these consols. The market price of these consols is now $960. What is the investor's required rate of return from such consols today? If the firm wanted to issue debt in the form of consols today, what would be its cost of capital? We compute the investor's required rate of return as follows:

$$r_d^{consol} = \frac{100}{960} = 0.1042 \text{ or } 10.42 \text{ percent.}$$

Additionally, if the firm wanted to issue such consols today, it would have to ensure that investors received their required rate of return of 10.42 percent. Thus the firm's cost of debt capital would be 10.42 percent.

How would the firm go about doing this? It would have two obvious choices. One, it could promise a coupon of $100 per year and receive a price of $960 per consol. Or, it could promise a coupon of $104.20 per year and obtain a price of $1,000 per bond. Usually, firms like to sell bonds at their par or face value, which is generally $1,000. Therefore, we suspect that the firm would be more likely to choose the second alternative.

Now attempt the following problems and try to obtain the given answers.

Problem 9.1 A firm's perpetual debt promises a coupon of $80 per year forever. If the investor's required rate of return is 12 percent, what is the price of this bond?

$$P_{un} = \frac{80}{.12} = 666.6667$$

Answer: $666.67.

Problem 9.2 ABC Corp. wants to issue perpetual debt to raise capital. It plans to pay a coupon of $90 per year on each bond with face value of $1,000. Consols of a comparable firm with a coupon of $100 per year are selling at $1,050. What is the cost of debt capital for ABC? What will be the price at which it will issue its consols?

$$\frac{100}{1050} = .0952 \qquad \frac{90}{.0952} = 945.3782$$

Answer: cost of capital = 9.52 percent and price = $945.38.

Problem 9.3   If ABC (from the previous problem) wanted to raise $100 million dollars in debt, how many such consols would it have to issue?

$$P_{con} = \frac{C}{r_{d\,con\,consul}}$$

$$\frac{100,000,000}{945.3782} = 105,777.7723$$

Answer: 105,778 consols.

Problem 9.4   If ABC wanted to issue its consols at par, that is, at a price of $1,000, what coupon must it pay?

$$1000 \times .0952 = \$95.20$$

Answer: $95.20 per year.

Problem 9.5   What would be the price of a *comparable* consol that has a face value of $1,000 and a coupon rate of 8 percent?

$$1000 \times .08 = \frac{\$80}{95.20} = \$840.3361$$

Answer: $840.34.

9.3.2 Valuation of Zero-Coupon Bonds

Recall that a zero-coupon bond (ZCB), as the name implies, pays no periodic coupon. The only cash flow that investors receive is the face value (usually $1,000) at maturity. Then, it is easy to see that the price of a ZCB will be the present value of the face value of the bond. In other words,

$$P_{ZCB} = \frac{F}{\left(1 + \boxed{r_d^{ZCB}}\right)^N},$$

where F is the face value of the bond, r_d^{ZCB} is the cost of ZCB debt capital, and N is the number of years to maturity.

Suppose that ABC Corp. wanted to issue a ZCB with a maturity period of twenty years. If the investor's required rate of return is 8 percent, the price that ABC will receive for this bond is $214.55. This is obtained with the help of the financial calculator (N = 20, I/Y = 8, FV = 1000, PMT = 0, PV = ?). Given the price of a ZCB and the maturity period, it is also possible to determine r_d^{ZCB}, the cost of debt capital. Suppose that a ZCB with fifteen years to maturity is trading at a price of $400. To compute the r_d^{ZCB}, we enter into the financial calculator PV = −400, FV = 1000, N = 15, PMT = 0, I/Y = ? to obtain 6.30 percent as the cost of capital for this ZCB. Now attempt the following problem and see if you obtain the given answer.

Problem 9.6   Find the price of a ZCB with 25 years to maturity and r_d^{ZCB} of 14 percent.

$$\frac{1000}{1.14^{25}} = 37.79$$

Answer: $37.79.

Problem 9.7   The ZCB of XCorp. is trading in the market at a price of $332. The bond has seventeen years to maturity. What is XCorp's cost of ZCB's debt capital?

$$\frac{332}{1000} = \frac{1000}{1+r^{17}}$$

$$.3320 = 1+r^{12}$$

$$1/_N = 6.7010$$

Answer: 6.70 percent.

Can the price of a ZCB ever be greater than the face value? The answer is no, as long as the discount rate is positive. The reason for this is pretty straightforward. A ZCB gives you a single cash flow (the face value) in the future. For all positive discount rates, the present value of this cash flow must be less than the cash flow itself.

To illustrate this property, consider the graph in Figure 9.1. In this graph, we have plotted the price of a ZCB using a discount rate of 10 percent for periods to maturity varying from thirty to zero years. Or, you can interpret this graph as the price path over time of a ZCB that is issued with a maturity of thirty years.

Note from the graph below that as the ZCB approaches maturity (read graph from right to left), that is, zero years, the price becomes closer and closer to the face value. That is the way it should be. Consider how much you would pay now for receiving $1,000 next second. An amount extremely close to $1,000, we are sure.

9.3.3 Valuation of Fixed-Coupon Bonds

The fixed-coupon bond (FCB) is the most common bond issued by U.S. corporations. As you may recall, this bond promises fixed periodic coupon payments and the face value at maturity. The price of this bond is, therefore, given by

$$P_{FCB} = \boxed{\sum_{t=1}^{N}\frac{C}{(1+r_d)^t} + \frac{F}{(1+r_d)^N}},$$

where C is the periodic coupon, F is the face value, N is the number of periods to maturity, and r_d is the cost of debt capital.

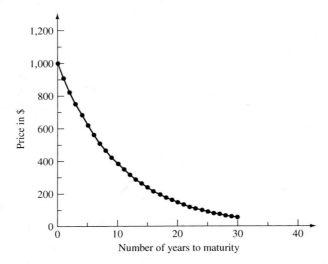

Figure 9.1   **The Price of a Zero-Coupon Bond and the Time to Maturity** (FV = 1,000 and r = 10%)

For example, a typical bond description may be "8 percent coupon paid annually and twenty years to maturity." As before, unless otherwise stated, the face value is $1,000. Thus, this bond will provide an annuity (because coupon is paid annually) of $80 (8 percent of the face value) for twenty years and will pay the face value of $1,000 at the end of twenty years. If the investor's required rate of return (cost of capital) is 10 percent, the price of this bond can be computed as follows: I/Y = 10, FV = 1,000, PMT = 80, N = 20, PV = ? to obtain $829.73.

On the other hand, a firm can compute its cost of debt capital by observing the price of its bonds. Suppose that a firm has some FCBs outstanding that pay a coupon of 6 percent annually, have twelve years left to maturity, and have a market price of $830. This firm's cost of debt capital can be computed as FV = 1,000, PV = – 830, N = 12, PMT = 60, I/Y = ? to obtain 8.29 percent. This is the firm's cost of debt capital. It is also the bond's yield-to-maturity (YTM).

Let us suppose that the Qco. is considering issuing debt (FCB). The firm has estimated that its cost of debt capital is 8 percent. It has decided to issue thirty-year FCBs. However, it is deciding on the coupon rate. The choices for the coupon rate are (a) 5 percent, (b) 8 percent, and (c) 11 percent. If the coupons are paid annually, the price of the bonds under the three alternatives would be:

a. *Coupon of 5 percent:* I/Y = 8, FV = 1,000, PMT = 50, N = 30, PV = ? to obtain *$662.27* as the price.

b. *Coupon of 8 percent:* I/Y = 8, FV = 1,000, PMT = 80, N = 30, PV = ? to obtain *$1,000.00* as the price.

c. *Coupon of 11 percent:* I/Y = 8, FV = 1,000, PMT = 110, N = 30, PV = ? to obtain *$1,337.73* as the price.

Notice that the higher the coupon, the higher is the price. That should not be surprising; the higher the cash flow that investors receive, the higher will be the price that they will be willing to pay. The above numbers illustrate another interesting property of FCBs. Note that **when the coupon rate** is 5 percent, that is, **lower than the discount rate, the price is lower than the face value** ($1,000). **When the coupon rate is the same as the discount rate** (8 percent), **the price is the same as the face value.** Finally, **when the coupon rate is greater than the discount rate** (as in the case of the 11 percent coupon), the **price of the bond is greater than the face value.** In fact, this is always true. When the price of the bond is less than the face value, the bond is said to be **selling at a discount.** When the bond sells at a price that equals the face value, the bond is said to **sell at par.** Finally, when the price of the bond is greater than the face value, the bond is said to **selling at a premium.** As a general rule, corporations like to issue debt at par, that is, the coupon rate is set equal to the prevailing rate on comparable debt securities.

Finally, the coupon on the bond is not always paid once a year or annually. It is common to see firms paying coupons semi-annually or quarterly. Suppose that you want to find the price of a ten-year bond that pays a coupon of 8 percent paid semi-annually and the market interest rate (another way of saying the investor's required rate of return) is 10 percent. This bond gives you a cash flow of $40 (half of 8 percent of 1,000) every six months. That is, in ten years it will give you $10 \times 2 = 20$ such cash flows. Additionally, at the end of these twenty six-month periods, you will receive $1,000. The price of this bond is given by

$$P = \left[\sum_{t=1}^{20} \frac{40}{(1.05)^t} + \frac{1,000}{(1.05)^{20}} \right].$$

The first term of the above pricing equation is the present value of the twenty periodic (once every six months) payments of $40 discounted, as we did in the past with semi-annual compounding, at half the discount rate, that is, $0.5 \times 10 = 5$ percent. The second term is the present value of the $1,000 that is to be received at maturity. Notice that we have discounted this future cash flow also for twenty periods at a discount rate of 5 percent. You might wonder why we should use semi-annual compounding for this cash flow because it is received as a lump sum at the end of ten years. The reason is consistency. You receive two cash flows at the end of ten years. One is the (last) coupon payment of $40 and the other is the face value of the bond of $1,000. At what rate are you discounting the $40 cash flow? At a rate of 5 percent for twenty periods. Then the other cash flow of $1,000 from the same bond at the same time should also be discounted at the same rate, that is, at 5 percent for twenty periods. The price of this bond, is therefore (FV = 1,000, PMT = 40, I/Y = 5, N = 20, PV = ?) $875.38.

If the coupon had been paid quarterly, the price could be obtained by entering FV = 1,000, PMT = 20, I/Y = 2.5, N = 40, PV = ? in your calculator to yield $874.49. In this case the bond makes forty (the number of quarters in ten years) payments of $20 (quarter of 8 percent of 1,000) and a final payment of $1,000. The discount rate is $0.25 \times 10 = 2.5$ percent.

If a bond pays coupon semi-annually or quarterly, you must remember the following in computing the cost of debt. You must multiply the value you obtain for I/Y by two if the coupon is semi-annual and by four if it is quarterly. For example, suppose that a 10 percent coupon bond with fourteen years to maturity pays coupon semi-annually and is trading at $1,050 in the market. To compute the cost of capital or investor's required rate of return, you would enter the following in your calculator FV = 1,000, PMT = 50, PV = −1,050, N = 28, I/Y = ? and obtain I/Y to be 4.676 percent. The cost of debt capital is therefore $4.676 \times 2 = 9.352$ percent.

Now try the following problems and see if you obtain the given answers.

Problem 9.8 A firm is planning to issue $50 million of fixed-coupon debt. Each bond will have a face value of $1,000, a coupon of 9 percent paid annually, and maturity period of twenty-five years. If the market rate for such debt is 12 percent, what will be the market price of such a bond and how many bonds will the firm have to issue?

$$CB = 90$$
$$N = 25$$
$$r = 12\%$$

$$P_0 = 764.7058$$

$$\frac{50,000,000}{764.7058} = 65,384.6202$$

Answer: price of bond = $764.71, # of bonds = 65,385.

Problem 9.9 A firm is trying to determine its cost of debt capital. It has some bonds outstanding. These bonds pay a coupon of 7 percent annually and have eleven years to maturity. The market price of these bonds is $821.50. What is the firm's cost of debt?

$$1000 \times .07 = 70$$
$$11 \text{ yt m}$$
$$P_0 = 821.50$$

$$Yy = 9.7119$$

Answer: 9.71 percent.

Problem 9.10 The market interest rate is 12 percent. What is the price of a fifteen-year, 9 percent coupon bond, which pays coupon semi-annually?

$$1000 \times .09 = 90/2 = 45$$
$$15 \times 2 = 30 \text{ yrs}$$
$$\frac{12}{2} = 6\%$$

$$45 \left[1 - \frac{\frac{1}{1.06^{30}}}{.06} \right] + \frac{1000}{1.06^{30}}$$

$$619.4174 + 174.1101 = 793.5275$$

Answer: $793.53.

Problem 9.11 Suppose that the coupon of the bond in the previous problem is paid quarterly. What would be the price of the bond?

$$1000 \times .09 = 90/4 = 22.50$$
$$15 \times 4 = 60$$

$$22.50 \left[\frac{1 - \frac{1}{1.03^{60}}}{.03} \right] + \frac{1000}{1.03^{60}}$$

Answer: $792.43.

$$622.7002 + 169.7331 = 792.4333$$

Problem 9.12 Find the firm's cost of capital for the following two bonds that it has outstanding. (a) 8 percent coupon bond with thirteen years to maturity, semi-annual coupon, and market price of $980. (b) 12 percent coupon bond with six years to maturity, quarterly coupon, market price $1,180.

a) $1000 \times .08 = 80/2 = 40$
$N = 26$
$1/4 = 8.25\%$

b. $1000 \times .12 = 120/4 = \$30$
$N = 24$
$1/y = 8.1744$

Answer: (a) 8.25 percent, (b) 8.17 percent.

Problem 9.13 Suppose that a bond is trading at a price of $940. This bond has twenty years to maturity and pays coupon interest annually. The market rate of interest for such a bond is 11 percent. What is the coupon rate for this bond?

$$940 + \frac{1000}{1.11^{20}}$$

$P_0 = 940$
$N = 20$
$r = 11\%$

$$940 = X \left[\frac{1 - \frac{1}{1.11^{20}}}{.11} \right] + \frac{100}{1.11^2}$$

Answer: 10.2465 percent.

$$10.2466\%$$

$$940 = 7.9633x + 124.034$$

Problem 9.14 A bond has coupon rate of 10 percent and the coupon is paid quarterly. The price of this bond is $1,075 and the market rate is 9 percent. How many years does this bond have until it matures?

$$1000 \times .10 = 100/4 = 25$$
$P_0 = 1075$
$1/y = 9/4 = 2.25\%$ $N = 12.1145\,yrs$

Answer: 12.63 years.

9.4 Preferred Stock Valuation ....

The owner of preferred stock receives a fixed dividend forever. Therefore, the price of preferred stock is simply the present value of a perpetuity. In other words,

$$P_{ps} = \frac{D\ (Dividend)}{r_p\ (firm\ cost\ of\ capital\ P/s)}$$
$$r/return$$

where D is the periodic dividend on the preferred stock and r_p is the firm's cost of capital for preferred stock or, equivalently, the investor's required rate of return. Rearranging the above relation yields the following simple relation for the cost of preferred stock:

$$r_p = \frac{D}{P_{ps}}.$$

Applying the above relations to numbers is simple. The price of a preferred stock that pays a dividend of $3 per year when the cost of capital is 12 percent is:

$$\frac{3}{.12} = \$25.$$

Similarly, if a preferred stock with a dividend of $2.80 is selling at a price of $22, the cost of capital is:

$$\frac{2.80}{22} = .1273 \text{ or } 12.73 \text{ percent.}$$

9.5 Valuation of Common Stock

Besides fixed-coupon debt, equity is the preferred mode of financing for most U.S. corporations. Unfortunately, valuation of equity is significantly more difficult than the pricing of bonds. In the case of bonds, the future cash flows are generally known—a stream of coupon payments and the face value at maturity. In the case of common stock, because equity is a residual claim, the future cash flows (dividends or selling price) are not fixed. Thus, it is necessary to make several assumptions to derive frameworks for valuing equity. In what follows, we shall begin with very strong (unrealistic) assumptions and obtain fairly simple formulae. As we progress, the assumptions will become more realistic but the valuation technique will become more complex.

9.5.1 Assuming a Constant Dividend Stream

The easiest scenario is when we assume that the dividends to the stock are constant. Under this assumption, the pricing technique for equity will be identical to that for preferred stock. In other words,

$$P_e = \frac{D}{r_e},$$

where D is the constant dividend per period and r_E is the cost of equity capital. In this case, the cost of equity can be computed as follows:

$$r_e = \frac{D}{P_e}.$$

As you can see, when we make the unrealistic assumption that the dividends from a stock will remain constant forever, we obtain a simple valuation formula.

9.5.2 Assuming That Dividends Grow At a Constant Growth Rate

Let us add a small dose of realism to the previous scenario. Instead of assuming that dividends will be constant forever into the future, let us assume that dividends will grow at a constant rate of g per period. Let D_t denote the dividend in time t and let D_0 be the dividend that the firm has just paid, that is, at $t = 0$. Then

$$D_1 = D_0(1 + g),$$
$$D_2 = D_1(1 + g) = D_0(1 + g) \times (1 + g) = D_0(1 + g)^2,$$
$$D_3 = D_2(1 + g) = D_0(1 + g)^2 \times (1 + g) = D_0(1 + g)^3,$$
$$\text{and} \quad D_t = D_{t-1}(1 + g) = D_0(1 + g)^{t-1} \times (1 + g) = D_0(1 + g)^t.$$

Then the price of the stock, that is, the PV of future cash flows is:

$$P_e = \sum_{t=1}^{\infty} \frac{D_t}{(1+r_e)^t} = \sum_{t=1}^{\infty} \frac{D_0(1+g)^t}{(1+r_e)^t}.$$

The expression seems impossible to solve. However, as in the past, our friends in the mathematics field have proved that the above summation is exactly equal to:

$$P_e = \sum_{t=1}^{\infty} \frac{D_0(1+g)^t}{(1+r_e)^t} = \frac{D_0(1+g)}{r_e - g} = \frac{D_1}{r_e - g}.$$

Thus, when dividends are assumed to grow at a constant rate of g, the price of a share of common stock can be found by the above (fairly easy) formula. Rearranging the above yields the following relation for the cost of equity capital:

$$r_e = \frac{D_1}{P_e} + g.$$

In the above relation, the first term, $\frac{D_1}{P_e}$, is also known as the **dividend yield** or the dividends per share and the second term, g, is the **capital gains yield.** The required rate of return from a stock r_e **is,** therefore, **the sum of the dividend yield and the capital gains yield.**

Suppose that a stock is expected to pay a dividend of $2. This dividend is expected to grow at the rate of 5 percent forever. The investor's required rate of return is 15 percent. The price of this stock should then be:

$$\frac{2}{0.15 - 0.05} = \$20.00.$$

Notice that when the firm is **expected** to pay the dividend, that value becomes D_1. Suppose we change this problem by assuming that a firm has just paid a dividend of $2 and everything else is the same as before. In this case, $2 is D_0 and $D_1 = \$2 \times (1 + 0.05) = \$2.10$, and the price of the stock is:

$$\frac{2.10}{0.15 - 0.05} = \$21.00.$$

Take a look at the pricing formula, $\frac{D_1}{r_e - g}$, again. In this formula, if g is greater than r_e, the denominator will be negative and the price will be negative too. We know that prices cannot be negative. Thus, for this formula to work, the growth rate, in addition to being constant, must be less than r_e, the investor's required rate of return. Can the growth rate be greater than r_e? Sure it can. However, it can never be greater than r_e forever. Suppose that r_e for a particular stock is 15 percent. Can this stock's dividend grow at, say, 20 percent forever? If it did, the investors would be strange people. Even though the cash flow grows at a rate of 20 percent, they require a return of only 15 percent. It doesn't make sense. Thus, the growth rate can be greater than r_e for some periods but in the long run, it has to be the case that either g decreases or r_e increases so that g is less than r_e.

We have computed the price of a stock whose dividends grow at a constant rate forever. If you look at the expression with which we began the derivation of the formula, you will notice that the price of the stock is the present value of all future dividends. In that case, what happens if you sell the stock after a few years? Does it affect our ability to use the formula? The answer is that it does not. Intuitively you can see why it does not. Suppose that there are two investors, one of whom plans to hold a stock forever and the other for only five years. Will the market price be different for these two persons? Clearly not! We can see why with some numbers equally easily.

Consider a stock that pays a constant dividend of $2 per year forever. Assuming a discount rate of 10 percent, we know that the price of this stock should be:

$$\frac{2}{0.1} = \$20.00.$$

Now suppose that you plan to buy this stock today and then sell it after five years. What will be the cash flows to you? For the first five years ($t = 1$ through $t = 5$) you will receive the yearly dividend of $2. At the end of five years, that is, at $t = 5$, you will sell the stock and receive the selling price. How much will you obtain for this stock? Well, the person who buys it from you will pay a price, which is the present value of all the future cash flows that the buyer will receive from this stock. What are they? Again, $2 per year forever. Therefore, the price that you receive at $t = 5$ will the present value of the dividends from $t = 6$ onward forever. In other words, whether you hold the stock or sell it after five years, the cash flows that you receive are identical. Therefore, the price does not depend upon whether you sell the stock or not.

Now attempt the following problems and see if you obtain the given answers.

Problem 9.15 What is the price of a stock that is expected to pay a dividend of $3.50 next year and this dividend is expected to grow at a rate of 6 percent per year forever? The appropriate discount rate is 12 percent.

$$P_0 = \frac{3.50}{.12 - .06} = 58.33$$

Answer: $58.33.

Problem 9.16 The price of a stock in the market is $40. You know that the firm has just paid a dividend of $4.00. The dividend growth rate is expected to be 7 percent. What is the investor's required rate of return from this stock?

$$r = \frac{4(1.07)}{40} = 10.70\% + .07$$

$$17.70\%$$

Answer: 0.1770 or 17.70 percent.

Problem 9.17 A firm is expected to pay a dividend of $3.25 on its stock next year. The price of this stock is $45 and the investor's required rate of return is 15 percent. What is the growth rate expected by the market in the dividend stream?

$$45 = \frac{3.25}{.15 - g} \left(\frac{1}{3.225} \right) = 13.8462 + g =$$

$$P(g) = \frac{D_1}{P} + r$$

Answer: 0.0778 or 7.78 percent.

Did you obtain the answer for the above question? Note that you have to compute g, the growth rate. You can rearrange the formula $r_e = \frac{D_1}{P_e} = g$ as follows:

$$g = r_e - \frac{D_1}{P_e} = 0.15 - \frac{3.25}{45} = 0.0778.$$

9.5.3 Non-Constant Dividend Growth

Suppose that you had to value a stock. To do so, you would have to forecast the future dividend stream from the stock. It is natural that you will be able to forecast dividends in the near future (say the next three years) more confidently than the later stream of dividends. One possibility is to forecast specific values for the dividends expected in the first three or so years and then assume a constant growth rate for subsequent dividends. For example, in valuing the stock of ABC Corp., suppose that you forecast that dividends will be $2, $3, and $3.50 in the next three years, respectively. After that you expect dividends to grow at a rate of 5 percent per year forever. Let us suppose that the appropriate discount rate for ABC's stock is 15 percent. The projected future dividends are: $D_1 = \$2.00$, $D_2 = \$3.00$, $D_3 = \$3.50$, $D_4 = \$3.50 \times (1.05) = \$3.675$, and so on. On a time line, it would be:

Consider the dividend stream from $t = 4$ onwards. It is a stream with constant growth. Therefore, if one were at $t = 3$, the future dividend stream from this stock would be as follows: $3.675 the next year ($t = 4$) and a constant growth thereafter of 5 percent per year. Thus, the price of this stock at $t = 3$, denoted by P_3, can be determined with the constant growth formula as follows:

$$P_3 = \frac{D_4}{r_E - g} = \frac{3.675}{0.15 - 0.05} = \$36.75.$$

Note that the price at $t = 3$, P_3, is the present value of all dividends after $t = 3$. To determine the price of the stock today, that is at $t = 0$, we can therefore, rewrite the future cash flows to the stock as follows:

$$
\begin{array}{ccccc}
 & \$2.00 & \$3.00 & (\$3.50 + \$36.75) \\
\vdash & + & + & + \\
t = 0 & t = 1 & t = 2 & t = 3
\end{array}
$$

You can think of the above as keeping the stock for three years and selling it for $36.75. Recall from our earlier discussion that, in valuing a stock, it does not matter whether you sell the stock or not. Therefore, the price of the stock at $t = 0$, denoted by P_0, is:

$$P_0 = \frac{2}{1.15} + \frac{3}{(1.15)^2} + \frac{40.25}{(1.15)^3} = \$30.47.$$

Another possible scenario in stock valuation is as follows. Suppose firm A has just paid a dividend of $1. You expect the dividend to grow by 20 percent per year for the first two years, by 15 percent per year in years three and four, and then settle down to a constant growth rate of 6 percent per year. If the appropriate discount rate is 12 percent, what is the current price of the stock?

Again we estimate the future dividend stream as follows: $D_0 = \$1.00$, $D_1 = D_0 \times (1 + g_1) = 1 \times (1.20) = \$1.20$, $D_2 = D_1 \times (1 + g_2) = 1.20 \times (1.20) = \$1.44$, $D_3 = D_2 \times (1 + g_3) = 1.44 \times (1.15) = \$1.656$, $D_4 = D_3 \times (1 + g_4) = 1.656 \times (1.15) = \$1.9044$, $D_5 = D_4 \times (1 + g_5) = 1.9044 \times (1.06) = \$2.0187$ and keeps increasing at 6 percent per year for ever. Note that from $t = 5$ *onward,* the stock dividend has a constant growth rate. Therefore, the *price of the stock at $t = 4$* can be computed by the formula as follows:

$$P_4 = \frac{D_5}{r_e - g} = \frac{2.0187}{0.12 - 0.06} = \$33.645.$$

To find P_0, the price at t = 0, we then have the following time line:

```
            $1.20        $1.44       $1.656     ($1.9044 + $33.645)
    |---------+-----------+-----------+-----------|
  t = 0     t = 1       t = 2       t = 3       t = 4
```

The price of the stock at t = 0 is then computed as follows:

$$P_0 = \frac{1.20}{1.12} + \frac{1.44}{(1.12)^2} + \frac{1.656}{(1.12)^3} + \frac{35.5494}{(1.12)^4} = \$25.99.$$

Now attempt the following problems and see if you obtain the given answer. In solving these problems, drawing a cash flow time line may prove to be extremely useful.

Problem 9.18 ABC Corp. is expected to pay the following dividends in the future. In the first year, $1.50, $2.00 in the second year, and after that the dividend is expected to grow at a constant rate of 4 percent. Assuming a discount rate of 10 percent, compute the current price of ABC stock.

Answer: $31.67.

Problem 9.19 XYZ Corp. is expected to have dividend growth rates of 25 percent in the first two years and after that the dividend is expected to remain constant forever. The company just paid a dividend of $1.00. Assuming a discount rate of 11 percent, compute the current price of XYZ stock.

Answer: $13.92.

Problem 9.20 PQR Co. is not expected to pay any dividend for the next three years. At t = 4, it will pay a dividend of $3.00, and the dividend is expected to grow at a constant rate of 5 percent forever after that. If the appropriate discount rate is 10 percent for this stock, what is the current stock price?

Answer: $45.08.

Problem 9.21 You expect EXRON Corp. to pay no dividends for the next two years. In years three and four, the dividend will be $4 per year. After that, the dividend will grow at a constant rate of 7 percent per year. If the appropriate discount rate is 10 percent, what is the price of EXRON stock today?

Answer: $103.18.

In this chapter, we applied the "discounted cash flow valuation concept to the pricing of common securities such as bonds, preferred stocks, and equity. As you must have noticed, the important thing is to be able to determine the stream of future cash flows and the appropriate discount rate. Having done that, the pricing of a security is a fairly simple matter of computing present values. If security valuation were so simple, the stock market and other financial markets would not hold such mystique. Note that everywhere in this chapter, the future cash flows and the discount rates were always assumed to be known. Determining these two things is a matter of great skill, and the ability to estimate them separates the winners from the losers in the financial markets.

Assignment 9.1 ∎∎∎∎∎∎∎∎∎∎

Name:_____   Date:_____

Solve the following problems in the space provided.

1. Using a discount rate of 8 percent, value the following bonds: (a) a consol that pays a coupon of $82.50 per year, (b) a zero-coupon bond with fifteen years to maturity, and (c) a 7 percent coupon bond that has twenty years to maturity with coupon paid annually.

2. Value the following bonds assuming a discount rate of 9 percent: (a) a 7 percent coupon bond that pays coupon semi-annually and has thirty years to maturity, (b) a 10 percent coupon bond that pays coupon quarterly and has twenty years to maturity.

3. ABC Co. has 9 percent coupon bonds outstanding (coupon is paid annually) that have fourteen years to maturity. These bonds are currently trading at $978 per bond. What is ABC's cost of debt?

4. STU Co. has 8 percent bonds outstanding (coupon paid quarterly) that have seventeen years to maturity. These bonds are trading at $1,020 per bond. What is STU's cost of debt?

Assignment 9.2

Name:_____   Date:_____

Solve the following problems in the space provided.

1. QWE Co. plans to issue preferred stock that pays a dividend of $2.25 per year. The company has estimated that the investors' required rate of return is 11 percent. What is the price that QWE expects to receive for this preferred stock? Suppose that after issuing the preferred stock, QWE finds that the preferred stock is trading at $24 per share. What can you say about QWE's estimate of the investors' required rate of return? What is the actual required rate of return?

2. The common stock of WER Co. is expected to pay a dividend of $1.50 per share forever. If the appropriate discount rate is 9 percent, what should be the price of the stock?

3. The common stock of ERT Co. is expected to pay a dividend of $2.50 per share next year. The dividend is expected to grow at the rate of 3 percent per year for ever. If the appropriate discount rate is 10 percent, what should be the price of the stock?

4. The common stock of RTY Co. is expected to pay a dividend of $1.00 per share for the next five years. After that, the dividend will grow at a rate of 5 percent per year forever. If the appropriate discount rate is 12 percent, what should be the price of the stock?

Assignment 9.3

Name:_____   Date:_____

Solve the following problems in the space provided.

1. The stock of TYU Co. is trading at $38 per share. The company just paid a dividend of $2 per share. The growth rate in dividends is projected to be 4 percent per year forever. What is TYU's cost of equity capital?

2. YUI Co. will pay dividends of $2, $1, and $3 in the next three years, respectively. Then the dividend is expected to grow at a constant rate of 6 percent per year. If the cost of equity is 14 percent, what is the current price of the stock?

3. UIO Co. just paid a dividend of 1.75. The company is expected to experience abnormally high growth in the next five years: 50 percent in the first two years, 30 percent in the next two years, and 20 percent in year 5. After that the growth is expected to settle down to 7 percent per year forever. Assuming a discount rate of 15 percent, compute the current price of the stock.

4. IOP Co. just paid a dividend of $1.00. For the next three years, its growth rate is expected to be 35 percent. In the three years after that the growth rate in dividends is expected to be 20 percent. After that the dividends will remain constant. Assuming a discount rate of 15 percent, compute the current price of the stock.

Additional Questions and Problems

1. OPA Co. issued thirty-year bonds five years ago at par. At that time, the market rate for such bonds was 9 percent. Today, these bonds are trading at a 10 percent premium. What is the market interest for these bonds today?

2. PAS Co. has issued a bond that carries a coupon of 8 percent (paid annually) and has thirty years to maturity. Suppose that this bond can be "called" for $75 over face value at the end of the fifth year. What must the interest rate be for PAS to be indifferent between calling or non-calling the bond?

3. ASD Co. issued an 8 percent coupon (paid annually) twenty-year bond twenty years ago ($t = 0$). The company had issued the bond at par. For the first five years after the issue, the interest rate remained the same as that at the issue date. For the next five years, the appropriate interest rate was 7 percent. In the subsequent five years the interest rate rose to 11 percent and in the last five years of the bond, the interest rates were at 9 percent. Compute the price of the bond at (a) $t = 4$, (b) $t = 6$, (c) $t = 14$, (d) $t = 17$, and (e) $t = 19$?

4. A $1,000 par value bond sells for $1,092. It matures in twenty years, has a 10 percent coupon rate, and pays interest semi-annually. What is the bond's yield to maturity?

5. Zeta Corporation has issued a $1,000 face value zero-coupon bond. Which of the following values is closest to the correct price for the bond if the appropriate discount rate is 4 percent and the bond matures in eight years?

6. A $1,000 par value, fixed coupon bond has seventeen years remaining until maturity. The bond has a coupon rate of 8 percent and it pays semi-annual coupon payments. If the market rate for this bond is 7.25 percent, what is the price of the bond?

7. Bounty Inc. has outstanding a fixed coupon, $1,000 par value bond with fifteen years remaining until maturity. The bond makes semi-annual coupon payments and the coupon rate is 7 percent. If the bond currently sells at a price of $825 per bond, what is the yield to maturity of the bond?

8. Compute the yield to maturity of Arundel bonds based on the following information: Arundel bonds have a $1,000 par value, twenty-five years remaining until maturity, an 11 percent coupon rate, paid semi-annually, and a current market price of $1,187.

9. Calculate the current market price for a Potemkin bond based on the following information: currently, a Potemkin bond matures in sixteen years, has a par value of $1,000, a coupon rate of 10 percent paid semi-annually and a required rate of return of 12 percent.

10. The Johnson Company needs to raise $100,000,000 for an expansion project. The CFO is debating whether to issue zero-coupon bonds or semi-annual coupon bonds. In either case the bonds would have the same nominal required rate of return, a thirty-year maturity and a par value of $1,000. If he issues the zero-coupon bonds, they would sell for $99.38. If he issues the semi-annual coupon bonds, they would sell for $886.88. What coupon rate is the Johnson Company planning to offer on the coupon bonds?

11. SDF Co. wants to raise $20,000,000 through issuing preferred stock. The cost of preferred stock is estimated to be 11 percent. If the company wants to issue 1,000,000 shares of the preferred stock, how much should be the promised dividend per stock?

12. The common stock of Hyperion Inc. just paid an annual dividend of $1.50. Its dividends are expected to grow at a constant rate of 4 percent per year forever. If the required rate of return for this stock is 12 percent, what is the price of the stock?

13. FGH Co. is in a declining industry. It has just paid a dividend of $4.00 per share. The dividend is expected to *decline* at a rate of 5 percent in the future. Assuming a discount rate of 20 percent, what is the current stock price?

14. The common stock of Darkover Inc. just paid an annual dividend of $1.00. The dividend is expected to grow at a constant rate forever. The required rate of return for this stock is 12 percent. If the current price of the stock is $15.00, what is the expected growth rate of the dividends?

15. The stock of Wabbit, Incorporated is trading at $72.25 per share. The company just paid a dividend of $5.12 per share. The growth rate in dividends is projected to be 6 percent per year forever. What is Wabbit's cost of equity capital?

16. A firm expects to pay dividends at the end of each of the next four years of $2.00, $1.50, $2.50, and $3.50. If growth is then expected to level off at 8 percent, and if you require a 14 percent rate of return, how much should you be willing to pay for this stock?

17. The common stock DFG Co. is trading at $24 per share. In the past the company has paid a constant dividend of $3 per share. However, the company has just announced new investments that the market did not know about. The market expects that with these new investments, the dividends should grow at 3 percent per year forever. Assuming that the discount rate remains the same, what will be the price of the stock after the announcement?

18. Baxter Company just paid a dividend of $2.00 per share and is expected to pay a dividend one year from today of $2.14 per share. The future growth rate in dividends is expected to remain equal to the growth rate in Year 1 forever. Baxter stock has a required rate of return of 26 percent. Baxter's dividend payout ratio is 40 percent and the company's debt ratio is 62 percent. Given the information above, compute the current market price of Baxter Company stock.

19. The stock of Takone, Inc. currently sells for $15.00 per share. The company just paid a dividend of $2.10 per share and the current market price per share (that is, $15.00) is based on investor belief that the dividends of the company will remain constant forever. The market, does not know, however, that Takone is about to announce the introduction of a modified product line that will cause the future earnings and therefore dividends of the company to grow at a rate of 4 percent per year forever, starting today. This new growth rate will begin with the dividend to be paid one year from today. The modified product line will not in any way affect the required rate of return for the stock of Takone, Incorporated. Assuming that the market reacts rationally, what will be the new stock price of Takone, Incorporated after the announcement?

20. The Frenall Company just paid a common stock dividend of $4.00 per share. The required rate of return on Frenall stock is 18.4 percent. Due to a major restructuring of the company's production process, Frenall's dividends are expected to decline by 25 percent in year 1, 14 percent in year 2, and 6 percent in year 3. From that point on, the company's dividends are expected to grow at a rate of 4.4 percent per year forever. Given these expectations, compute the current equilibrium market price of Frenall's stock.

Chapter **10**

Basics of Capital Budgeting

After studying Chapter 10, you should be able to:

- ◆ Explain the purpose and importance of capital budgeting.

- ◆ Determine whether a new project should be accepted using the net present value.

- ◆ Determine whether a new project should be accepted using the profitability index.

- ◆ Determine whether a new project should be accepted using the internal rate of return.

- ◆ Determine whether a new project should be accepted using the payback period.

- ◆ Explain which decision criterion should be used to maximize shareholder wealth.

- ◆ Compute the cost of capital for a company and project.

10.1 Chapter Overview ···

In the previous chapter, we used the concept of discounted cash flows to value debt and equity securities. The purpose of this chapter is to use similar valuation techniques for evaluating the investment by a firm in real assets. These investments in real assets, which we will call projects, can be of several types; the common ones being investments in new plant and machinery, cost saving technologies, and such. A project, as far as we are concerned, is any firm decision that involves cash outflows (costs) made to receive cash inflows (benefits). The decision that we will consider here is a pretty straightforward one. Given the cash flow stream (outflows and inflows), is the project a worthwhile investment? Decisions of this sort are commonly termed as capital budgeting decisions. In this chapter, we shall consider several capital budgeting techniques and evaluate the validity of each of them.

10.2 The Basic Rationale for Capital Budgeting ·····························

Consider a typical decision that you may have to make in your day-to-day life. Suppose that you are deciding whether to replace your existing automobile. What is the standard framework for your decision-making? You will first determine the costs of replacing your car and also the benefits of owning the new car. You will then compare the two and if the benefits outweigh the costs, you will replace the car. If not, you will keep the old car. You, and most other individuals, probably follow this rule in making decisions of an economic nature. Calling such a decision a project, we can state the rule as follows: ***Accept the project if the benefits from the project are greater than the cost of the project.***

10.3 Capital Budgeting Techniques ···

Well, why shouldn't firm managers follow the same rule? In fact, for making capital budgeting decisions, that is, investments in projects, you will see that the same rule applies. It turns out that this rule takes on different forms. Instead of describing these seemingly different methods first, let us begin with the rule that we stipulated as the logically most suitable rule.

Let C denote the cost associated with the project and let B denote the benefits, and let us, for the time being, not worry about how B and C are calculated. According to our rule, then, we should ***accept the project if benefits are greater than cost.*** That is $B > C$. This rule can be restated a few different ways. ***Accept the project if the difference between benefits and costs is positive.*** Or, ***accept the project if the ratio of benefits to cost is greater than one.*** In other words, we can rewrite the basic rule above in the following equivalent ways:

    a. **Accept if $B - C > 0$**, or

    b. **Accept if $\dfrac{B}{C} > 1$.**

According to (a) above, accept the project if the benefits net of costs are positive. This rule is one of the most famous finance rules and is called the ***net present value (NPV)*** rule. It states that, ***accept the project if the NPV is positive*** where NPV is defined as $B - C$. The second rule (b) is called the ***profitability index (PI)*** rule. It states that, ***accept the project if the profitability index is greater than one,*** where PI is defined as the ratio $\frac{B}{C}$.

An important thing to note is that whenever the NPV of a project is positive ($B - C > 0$), the PI for the project must also be greater than one ($\frac{B}{C} > 1$). In other words, ***when the decision is about accepting or rejecting a project, the NPV and the PI rule give the same answer.*** If the NPV rule says accept, so will the PI rule, and if the NPV rule says reject, so will the PI rule.

So far, we have not said anything about how B, the benefits, and C, the costs of the project, are to be determined. We are sure that you have a pretty good idea about how to do this already. Recall that a project is nothing but a stream of cash flows that occur over a period of time. From our earlier discussions, we know that money has time value and we know how to compare cash flows that occur at different points in time. Applying these concepts to capital budgeting, we have the following. *The benefit (B) of a project is the present value of all future cash inflows and project cost (C) is the present value of all future cash outflows.* We can now restate our NPV and PI relations more precisely as follows:

$$\text{Net Present Value (NPV)} = B - C = \sum_{t=0}^{N} \frac{CIF_t}{(1+r)^t} - \sum_{t=0}^{N} \frac{COF_t}{(1+r)^t}, \text{ and}$$

$$PI = \frac{B}{C} = \frac{\displaystyle\sum_{t=0}^{N} \frac{CIF_t}{(1+r)^t}}{\displaystyle\sum_{t=0}^{N} \frac{COF_t}{(1+r)^t}},$$

where

CIF_t = the cash inflow at the end of period t,
COF_t = the cash outflow at the end of period t,
r = the appropriate discount rate for the project's cash flows,
N = the number of years in a project's economic life.

By *appropriate discount rate* we mean that it is the rate of return that investors require from the project or, equivalently, the firm's *cost of capital* for the project.

The above relations are the most general ones for NPV and PI. In most projects, the costs occur at the beginning, that is, at $t = 0$ and the cash inflows occur in the future. Following is an example of a typical project cash flow stream.

−5,000	3,000	3,000	3,000
t = 0	t = 1	t = 2	t = 3

The project depicted above costs (or requires an investment of) $5,000 in the beginning ($t = 0$) and then generates cash flows of $3,000 per year for three years. Assuming a discount rate of 10 percent, the NPV of this project is:

$$NPV = \frac{3,000}{1.1} + \frac{3,000}{(1.1)^2} + \frac{3,000}{(1.1)^3} - 5,000$$

$$= 7,460.56 - 5,000$$

$$= 2,460.56.$$

And the PI is:

$$PI = \frac{7,460.56}{5,000} = 1.4921.$$

According to our rules, because NPV > 0 and PI > 1, the project should be accepted.

In the above example, we used a discount rate of 10 percent. Suppose we use a higher discount rate. What will happen to the NPV and the PI? Both will decrease. In fact, if we increase the discount rate sufficiently, the NPV will become negative and the PI will become less than one. For example, when the discount rate is

30 percent, the NPV is barely positive at $448.39 and if a discount rate of 40 percent is used, the NPV of the project becomes −$233.24. Thus, at 30 percent, the NPV is positive and at 40 percent, the NPV is negative. Then, it must be the case that at some rate between thirty and 40 percent, the NPV must be zero. It turns out that this rate is 36.31 percent. At this rate, the NPV of the project is zero. That is,

$$\frac{3,000}{1.3631} + \frac{3,000}{(1.3631)^2} + \frac{3,000}{(1.3631)^3} - 5,000 = 0.$$

In other words, at the discount rate of 36.31 percent B = C, or the present value of future cash inflows equals the cost of the project. The discount rate at which the NPV of the project is zero is called the *internal rate of return (IRR)* of the project.

Recall that in the relationship between the discount rate and NPV, lowering the discount rate increases the NPV and increasing the discount rate lowers the NPV. The IRR is the discount rate at which NPV is zero. Then, if we used a discount rate that is less than the IRR, what will be the NPV? Positive. On the other hand, if we use the discount rate greater than the IRR, the NPV will be negative. In computing the NPV, recall that we have to use the firm's cost of capital (investor's required rate of return) as the discount rate. Then, if IRR is greater than the cost of capital (r), the project has a positive NPV, implying that benefits are greater than costs and, therefore that the project is acceptable. On the other hand, if the project's IRR is less than the cost of capital, the benefits are less than the cost, or, equivalently, the NPV is negative, implying that the project should be rejected. We, thus, have a third capital budgeting technique, the IRR. The decision rule is to accept the project if IRR is greater than the cost of capital.

Intuitively, one can think of the IRR as the return from the project. Then the project should be accepted if the return is greater than the required rate of return.

Let us state again the three equivalent capital budgeting decision criteria:

1. **NPV > 0, accept the project; NPV < 0, reject.**
2. **PI > 1, accept the project; PI < 1, reject.**
3. **IRR > r, accept the project; IRR < r, reject.**

NPV and IRR are the two most important capital budgeting techniques. The relation between them may become clearer with the following graph (Figure 10.1).

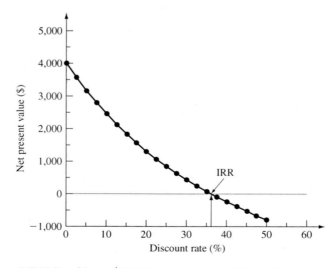

Figure 10.1   Project NPV Profile, −$5,000 at t = 0 and Three Future Cash Flows of $3,000

The graph in Figure 10.1 plots the NPV of the project on the vertical axis for different discount rates. When the discount rate is zero, the NPV is 4000. As the discount rate increases, the NPV decreases. The graph showing the NPV values for different discount rates is called the project's NPV profile. The discount rate at which the NPV profile intersects the horizontal axis, that is, when the NPV is zero, is the IRR.

10.4 Using the Financial Calculator for NPV and IRR ·······························

For the project in the problem in the previous section, we could have computed NPV and IRR with the calculator the following way.

NPV – First, compute the present value of a three-year annuity of $3,000 using a discount rate of 10 percent. That is, in the financial calculator enter, $N = 3$, $I/Y = 10$, $PMT = 3,000$, $FV = 0$, $PV = ?$ to obtain a present value of $PV = \$7,460.56$. Then, subtract the cost of the project, $5,000, from this value to obtain the NPV as follows:

$$NPV = \$7,460.56 - \$5,000 = \$2,460.56.$$

The NPV is positive, therefore the project should be accepted.

IRR – To compute the IRR, we must find the discount rate that gives a zero NPV, that is $B - C = 0$. In other words, we need to find a discount rate such that $B = C$. That is we need to find a discount rate which will make the present value of the three-year $3,000 annuity equal the cost of $5,000. To do this, enter in the calculator $N = 3$, $PV = -5000$, $PMT = 3,000$, $FV = 0$, $I/Y = ?$ to obtain 36.31 percent as the IRR. This use of the calculator is not new. We did the same thing to determine the cost of debt in the previous chapter.

Apart from the above method for computing NPV/IRR, the financial calculator has special functions to compute NPV and IRR. Note the keys NPV and IRR in the second row of your calculator. Let us illustrate their use with following example. In this example, unlike the previous one, we will make the cash inflows from the project uneven. In this case, it becomes harder to compute the NPV in the way outlined above. As far as IRR computation is concerned, it becomes impossible to do it the way we did when cash inflows were in the form of an annuity.

Problem 10.1   A firm is considering investment in a project that costs $1,200 and yields cash flows of $500 in the first year, $600 in the second year, and $700 in the third year. Compute the NPV and IRR of this project. The appropriate discount rate for this project is 10 percent.

Let us first draw the time line for this project.

NPV – Press CF, press −1200 and then press ENTER for CF0. Next press "↓" and enter 500 for C01. Press "↓" and enter 1 for F01. Similarly enter the C02 = 600, F02 = 1, C03 = 700, and F03 = 1. Make sure that all the cash flows later than C03 are zero.

Press NPV. Enter the discount rate of 10 percent by pressing 10 and then ENTER. The display will show that I = 10.0000. Next press the "↓" and press CPT. The calculator will display the NPV of 276.33.

IRR – To compute the IRR, follow the same steps as above for entering the cash flows. Then instead of pressing NPV, press the IRR button and then press CPT. The calculator will display the IRR as 21.92 percent.

Because the NPV > 0 and IRR > 10 percent, the project is acceptable.

Problem 10.2 Without any other time value calculations, compute the PI for the project in Problem 10.1.

The NPV is $276.33, so we know that

$$B - C = \$276.33.$$

Because the cost is $1,200, we know C. Substituting this value for C, we obtain

$$B - 1,200 = 276.33, \quad \text{or}$$

$$B = 276.33 + 1,200 = 1,476.33.$$

Therefore,

$$PI = \frac{B}{C} = \frac{1,476.33}{1,200} = 1.2303.$$

Now attempt the following problems in the space provided and see if you obtain the given answers.

Problem 10.3 Compute the NPV, IRR, and PI of the following project that a firm is considering. The firm's cost of capital for this project is 12 percent. The project will require an initial investment of $6 million and it will generate cash flows $750,000 per year forever.

$P_o = \frac{CF}{r} \qquad P_o = \frac{750,000}{.12} = 6,250,000$

$r = 120\%$
$C = 6,000,000$

$6,250,000 = B - 6,000,000$
$B = 6,250,000 - 6,000,000$
$NPV = 250,000$

$IRR =$

$PI = \frac{6,250,000}{6,000,000} = 1.0417$

$r = \frac{P}{P_o}$

$\frac{750,000}{6,000,000}$

Answer: NPV = $250,000, IRR = 12.50 percent, PI = 1.0417.

Problem 10.4 Assuming a discount rate of fourteen percent, compute the NPV, IRR, and PI of a project that costs $8 million and generates cash flows of $1 million per year for ten years.

$r = 14\%$ $PV = 5,216,115.646$ $IRR = 4.2775$
$C = 8,000,000$ $NPV = -2,783,884.354$
$CF = 1,000,000$ $PI = \frac{5,216,115.646}{8,000,000} = .6520$
$N = 10$

Answer: NPV = −$2,783,884.35, IRR = 4.2775 percent, PI = 0.652.

The above project should not be undertaken (should be rejected) because NPV < 0, IRR < r, and PI < 1.

Problem 10.5 The cost of capital for a firm is 15 percent. Should it invest in the following project? Use all the three methods: NPV, IRR, and PI.

$r = 15\%$ $NPV = 261,229.8785$ $PI = \frac{2,561,2}{2,3\alpha}$
$B = 2,561,229.875$
$PI = 1.113$

$IRR = 20.0439$

Year	Cash flow
0	−$2,300,000
1	$ 700,000
2	$ 850,000
3	$1,200,000
4	$ 650,000
5	$ 300,000

Answer: NPV = $261,229.88, IRR = 20.0439 percent, PI = 1.1136. Thus, accept the project.

10.5 Some Warnings on the Use of the IRR Criterion ....

You must have noticed that in all the examples that we did above, in determining whether a project is acceptable, all the three capital budgeting criteria, NPV, IRR, and PI, gave the same accept or reject answer. However, this not always the case, particularly for NPV and IRR. We will discuss some situations where either NPV and IRR yield different accept/reject decisions or IRR yields peculiar answers. In either case, you will notice that *the NPV criterion always leads to the correct decision.*

In the projects we have considered so far, the cost of the project occurred in the beginning and the cash inflows occurred later. Is it possible to have a project where the cash inflows occur first and the outflow occurs later? The answer is yes. (Can you think of an example?) Consider the project that yields a cash flow of $120 at t = 0 and requires a cost of $100 to be paid at t = 1. Let us first calculate the NPV of this project with r = 10 percent.

$$\text{NPV} = 120 - \frac{100}{1.1} = \$29.09$$

Because NPV is positive, the project is acceptable. Now let us compute the IRR. Enter N = 1, PV = 120, PMT = 0, FV = −100, I/Y = ? in the calculator. We obtain an IRR of −16.667 percent. Does this seem strange? Let us see if using this discount rate yields a zero NPV.

$$120 - \frac{100}{1 + \text{IRR}} = 120 - \frac{100}{1 - 0.16667}$$

$$= 120 - \frac{100}{0.83333} = 0$$

Thus, the IRR is indeed negative. According to our decision rule, we accept the project if the IRR is greater than the cost of capital. In this case the IRR is less than the r of 10 percent. Thus, according to the IRR rule, the project should be rejected.

Would you reject this project, a project that gives you $120 today and requires you to pay $100 one year later? Certainly not! What is happening here? Let us draw an NPV profile of this project. This is given in Figure 10.2. Do you see a difference between this NPV profile and the one in Figure 10.1 for the normal project? The previous one was declining and this one is increasing in the discount rate. Think about it. If you have a project that requires the cash outflow later, the higher the discount rate the better off you are. Why? Think of it like this. Suppose you wanted to guarantee that you had the $100 that is required to be

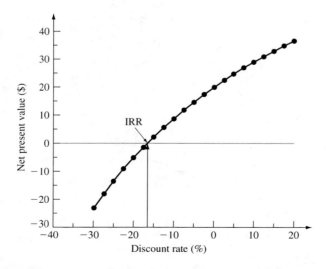

Figure 10.2   Project NPV Profile, CF at t = 0 is 120 and at t = 1, is −100

paid at t = 1. What would you do? You would deposit the present value of $100 in a bank account. Note, however, that the higher the interest rate that the bank pays you, the less that you would need to deposit. In other words, the higher the discount rate the less the amount that you have to put aside. Or, the higher the discount rate the lower the present value of the cost of the project. Thus higher the NPV.

For projects of this type, the IRR method does not fit. The NPV method, however, gives the correct accept/reject decision. We had asked you to think of a project of this type. Did you? A project that involves borrowing money for later repayment fits the description.

There is another scenario in which NPV and IRR give different answers. Think of a project that yields a cash inflow of $100 at t = 0 and a cash outflow of $121 at t = 1. The NPV of this project at a r = 10 percent is −10, which implies that the project should be rejected. The IRR of this project is, however, 21 percent, which implies that the project should be accepted. You can see that it is not a particularly desirable project. The reason that IRR gives the peculiar answer is similar to the one given earlier. Note that NPV is again appropriate.

Finally, consider the following project cash flows: at t = 0, −$400, at t = 1, $2,500, and t = 2, −$3,000. Suppose that the discount rate is 70 percent. Then,

$$NPV = -400 + \frac{2,500}{1.7} - \frac{3,000}{(1.7)^2} = \$32.53.$$

The project is, therefore, acceptable. Let us now draw the NPV profile of this project. This is shown in Figure 10.3.

What is the IRR for this project? If you enter the cash flows into the calculator and compute the IRR using the IRR function, you will obtain an IRR of 61.98 percent. However, from the NPV profile in the above Figure, you know that this IRR is the first discount rate at which NPV is zero. You see that the NPV is zero also when the discount rate is approximately 363 percent. So what is the IRR for this project? Well it has two, approximately 62 percent and 363 percent. Is one more correct than the other? No. Both give zero NPV and hence are IRRs. Is the project acceptable? On the basis of the IRR criterion, it is difficult to say because the discount rate is greater than one IRR and less than the other. In such cases when there are multiple IRRs, the IRR method loses meaning. Note, however, that the NPV method is still valid.

The question then arises, when do we have multiple IRRs? It turns out that this is pretty easy to figure out. Count the number of sign changes in the cash flow stream of the project. If there is just one sign change, there is just one IRR. On the other hand, if there are more than one sign changes, the number of IRRs may

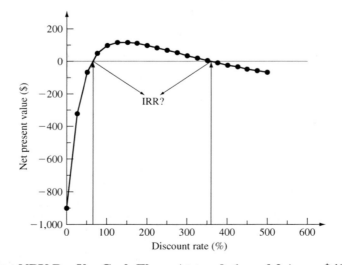

Figure 10.3 Project NPV Profile, Cash Flows At t = 0, 1, and 2 Are −$400, $2,500, −$3,000

equal the number of sign changes. For example, in the project above, there are two sign changes and there are two IRRs.

In view of the above, you must be wondering about which capital budgeting criterion to use. For most projects, it does not matter, because all the three methods give you the same answer. In fact, when the NPV profile is smoothly declining in the discount rate, both NPV and IRR give identical answers. However, in some cases the IRR criterion causes confusion. This occurs when the NPV profile is not smoothly declining. If it is increasing in the discount rate, then the IRR criterion will reject acceptable projects. If the NPV profile crosses the horizontal zero-axis more than once, we have multiple IRRs and it is better to stay away from the use of the IRR criterion.

10.6 The Payback Period Criterion ....

As we saw in the previous section, the NPV, IRR, and PI techniques for capital budgeting utilize the concept of discounted cash flows. Therefore, the use of these methods, the NPV method in particular, is consistent with the concept of the time value of money. There is another project selection criteria that does not use these concepts. This criterion is known as *the payback period* criterion.

Simply stated, the payback period is the number of periods it takes the cash inflows from a project to recover the original cost of the project. For example, suppose that a project costs $10,000 and generates cash flows of $2,000 per year for ten years. How long will it take for this project to recover the original investment of $10,000. The answer is pretty easy—five years. Then five years is the payback period of this project. On the basis of the payback period of five years, should this project be accepted? The answer here is not clear.

Recall that the NPV, IRR, and PI criteria had very clearly defined rules for accepting or rejecting projects. The payback period criterion, however, does not. A firm chooses an arbitrary number of years as the critical number. If the payback period is less than this number, the project is accepted, else it is rejected. Thus, the project with a payback period of five years will be accepted if the critical number is greater than five years and rejected if it is less than five years. Thus, the accept/reject rule for the payback period method is arbitrary.

Problem 10.6   Compute the payback periods for the following two projects.

Project	C_0	C_1	C_2	C_3	C_4	C_5
A	−9,000	2,000	3,000	4,000	5,000	6,000
B	−11,000	2,000	3,000	4,000	5,000	6,000

Answers: Payback period for A = 3 years, B = 3.4 years.

In the above problem, computing the payback period for project A is straightforward. However, for B, we need to make an assumption. Note that at the end of three years, 9,000 of the cost of the project (11,000) is recovered, leaving 2,000 to be recovered. In the fourth year, the cash inflow is 5,000. Thus it would take the first $\frac{2000}{5000} = 0.4$ fraction of the year to recover the remaining cost of the project. The payback period is, therefore, 3.4 years. The assumption is that cash flows are received evenly throughout the year. Suppose that, on the other hand, cash flows from the project were received only at the end of each year. In this case, the payback period for project B would not be 3.4 years but 4 years. Unless otherwise stated, in payback period calculations, assume that cash flows are received evenly throughout the year.

It is easy to see the shortcomings of using the payback period criterion for project selection. First, it is an arbitrary decision rule because the critical number is arbitrarily chosen. Second, it ignores the time value of money. Third, it ignores the cash flows that occur after the critical number. Let us illustrate the third shortcoming as follows. A firm uses two years as the critical number for the payback period. This firm is faced with two projects whose cash flows are as follows:

Project	C_0	C_1	C_2	C_3
A	−1,000	500	510	10
B	−1,000	0	0	99,000,000

According to the payback rule, given the critical number of two years, project A will be accepted and B will be rejected.

The second shortcoming of the payback period criterion, that it ignores the time value of money, can be rectified by using discounted values of the cash flows. However, the other two shortcomings are inherent in the rule and cannot be rectified. If the discount rate is 10 percent, then the discounted payback period of the following project is computed as:

Project	C_0	C_1	C_2	C_3	C_4	C_5
A	−9,000	2,000	3,000	4,000	5,000	6,000
Discounted cash flows		1,818	2,479	3,005	3,415	3,726
Cumulative discounted cash flows		1,818	4,297	7,302	10,717	14,443

The discounted payback period is computed using the discounted values of the cash flows. For example, the discounted value of the cash flow of 4,000 at t = 3 is:

$$\frac{4,000}{(1.1)^3} = 3,005.$$

The last row in the table above is the cumulative discounted cash flows, $1,818 + 2,479 = 4,297$ and so on. The **discounted payback period** is, therefore,

$$3 + \frac{9,000 - 7,302}{10,717 - 7,302} = 3 + \frac{1,698}{3,415} = 3.497 \text{ years.}$$

Despite the obvious shortcomings that the payback period rule has, corporations use it quite widely. It is, however, used primarily as a secondary project selection criterion. For example, a firm may require a project to have positive NPV first and also satisfy some payback criterion. The primary reason for its popularity is that it could serve as a control on errant managerial behavior. In your later finance courses, you will spend enough time on this aspect of finance.

10.7 Estimating the Cost of Capital ....

The cost of capital is integral to each of the capital budgeting evaluation techniques discussed in this chapter that use the concept of time value of money. To compute an NPV, we discount all cash flows by the cost of capital. To determine whether a project's IRR is sufficient, we compare it to the cost of capital. To derive a profitability index, cash inflows and outflows must first be discounted by the cost of capital.

In the previous chapter, we mentioned that the cost of capital is the price that a company must pay to investors for the funds that the investors provide. That is, the cost of capital is the return that the project must generate to adequately compensate all investors for the money given to the firm to fund the project. In this chapter, we show that companies use money provided by investors to fund capital budgeting projects. More specifically, companies use money provided by investors to buy new plant and equipment, to pay for research and development, to finance the development of new products or markets, and so on.

Investors provide funds to a company in two basic forms: debt and equity. For long-term capital budgeting projects, the main sources of funds provided are through corporate bonds and common stock. If 40 percent of a project is financed with debt and 60 percent of a project is financed with equity, then the cost of capital (which equals the return on the project) is just the weighted average of the cost of debt and the cost of equity, or:

$$(.40)(\text{Cost of debt*}) + (.60)(\text{Cost of equity}).$$

This overall return will provide all investors with their individual requirements. For example, assume that debt investors require a return of 10 percent and equity investors require a return of 20 percent. Assume that a company raises $10,000,000 to finance a one-year project. The funds come from debt and equity investors, with $4,000,000 coming from the issuance of new corporate bonds and $6,000,000 coming from either the new issuance of common stock or from retained earnings (the equity cost of both of these are the same, though proving this fact is well beyond the scope of this book—just trust us on this one for now). To give these investors their required returns, the overall return on the project must be:

$$(.40)(10\%) + (.60)(20\%) = 16\%.$$

A 16 percent project return will mean that the project will generate a return of $1,600,000. Thus, the $10,000,000 will generate a cash flow in one year of $11,600,000. Of this return, $4,400,000 will be returned to the bondholders (representing their required return of 10 percent on their initial $4,000,000 investment) and the remaining $7,200,000 will go to stockholders (representing their required return of 20 percent on their initial $6,000,000 investment).

Thus, in general, for any percentages of debt and equity (commonly referred to as the weight of debt and the weight of equity, where the sum of the weights must equal 1),

$$\text{Cost of Capital} = (\text{Weight of Debt}) \times (\text{Cost of Debt*}) + (\text{Weight of Equity}) \times (\text{Cost of Equity}).$$

Entire courses are devoted to the estimation of the cost of capital, and there are many theoretical and estimation nuances and refinements to consider to properly estimate a firm or project's cost of capital. One particular nuance is that the cost of debt should be the "after tax" cost of debt. Because interest on debt is deductible for a firm (but returns to equity are not), as long as the project returns:

$$(1 - T) \times (\text{Required Return to Bondholders}),$$

where T is the company's tax rate, then the company will earn enough to pay bondholders what they require. This is the reason for the "*" after Cost of Debt in the equation above. Specifically,

$$\text{Cost of Debt*} = (1 - T) \times (\text{Required Return to Bondholders}).$$

So, to estimate the cost of capital for a firm, we need to know the following: the weight of debt, the weight of equity, the required return to bondholders, the company tax rate, and the cost of equity. Estimating the first two measures involves issues concerning a firm's "optimal capital structure." For simplicity, we will just assume that we know the appropriate weights for debt and equity for problems that we will consider in this book. The company's tax rate is easy to find from tax laws. The average corporate tax rate in the U.S. is about 30 percent, so we will use this rate for most of the problems we consider. Finally, the required return to debt and the cost of equity are items that we discussed in the previous chapter. Specifically, we showed in the previous chapter that the *cost of debt is just the yield to maturity on a company's currently outstanding bonds* and that the *cost of equity is the discount rate in the constant growth stock formula.*

To see how to compute the cost of capital for a firm, consider the following example. Fillips, Inc. is trying to estimate its current cost of capital. Fillips believes that the appropriate weight of debt is 35 percent and the appropriate weight of equity is 65 percent. Fillips has a tax rate of 30 percent. Fillips' bonds currently trade in the market for a price of $835. These $1,000 par value bonds have a coupon rate of 10 percent (annual coupon payments) and they mature in twenty-eight years. Fillips' common stock trades for $22 per share. The dividend just paid by Fillips was $3.15 (that is, $D_0 = 3.15$) and future dividends are expected to grow at a rate of 4 percent per year forever.

- First, we compute the yield to maturity for Fillips' debt. FV = 1,000, PMT = 100, PV = −835, N = 28, CPT I/Y = 12.1%

- Second, find the after tax cost of debt as:

$$\text{Cost of Debt*} = (1 - .30) \times (\text{YTM}) = (.70)(12.1\%)$$

$$= 8.47\%$$

- Next, we compute the cost of equity using the constant growth stock price equation, solving for r_e,

$$r_e = \frac{D_1}{P_e} + g,$$

where, as shown in chapter 9, D_1 is the dividend expected to be paid in year 1, P_e is the current market price of the firm's stock, and g is the growth rate, that is, the expected perpetual growth rate in dividends. Thus, we have:

$$r_e = (3.15)(1.04)/22 + .04$$

$$= .189$$

$$= 18.9\%$$

- Finally, solve the equation for cost of capital:

$$\text{Cost of Capital} = (\text{Weight of Debt}) \times (\text{Cost of Debt*}) + (\text{Weight of Equity}) \\ \times (\text{Cost of Equity})$$

$$= (.35)(8.47\%) + (.65)(18.9\%) = 15.25\%$$

Thus, the cost of capital that Fillips should use to compute the NPV or PI of a project is 15.25% and the rate that IRR should be compared to is 15.25%.

Problem 10.7   KimKups, Inc. is trying to estimate its current cost of capital. KimKups believes that the appropriate weight of debt is 55 percent and the appropriate weight of equity is 45 percent. KimKups has a tax rate of 30 percent. KimKups' bonds currently trade in the market for a price of $1,210. These $1,000 par value bonds have a coupon rate of 8.5 percent (semi-annual coupon payments) and they mature in twenty-six years. KimKups' common stock trades for $52 per share. The dividend just paid by KimKups was $5.00 (that is, $D_0 = 5.00$) and future dividends are expected to grow at a rate of 6 percent per year forever. Compute KimKups' cost of capital.

Answer: Cost of capital $= (.55)(4.7\%) + (.45)(16.2\%) = 9.9\%$

10.8 Recap ....

We discussed four capital budgeting techniques in this chapter. They are the net present value (NPV), internal rate of return (IRR), profitability index (PI), and payback period criteria. The first three use the concept of the time value of money, and have clear-cut decision rules for accepting or rejecting a project. The payback period requires an arbitrary decision rule.

The decision rule for the three discounted cash flow methods are:

1. **NPV > 0, accept the project; NPV < 0, reject.**
2. **PI > 1, accept the project; PI < 1, reject.**
3. **IRR > r, accept the project; IRR < r, reject.**

There are instances where the IRR criterion creates problems. When the benefits of a project occur before the costs, that is, when the NPV profile is upward-sloping, the IRR is lower for better projects. When the number of sign changes in a project's cash flow stream is greater than one, it is possible to have multiple values for the IRR. In this case, the use of the IRR method is not possible. Except in these cases, the three methods, NPV, IRR, and PI always give the same accept/reject decision for a project.

Assignment 10.1 ....

Name:_____   Date:_____

Solve the following problems in the space provided.

1. Compute the NPV, IRR, PI, the payback periods, and the discounted payback periods for the following projects. Assume a discount rate of 9 percent.

Project	C_0	C_1	C_2	C_3	C_4	C_5
A	−9,000	2,200	3,300	4,400	5,100	1,000
B	−11,000	2,500	3,500	4,500	5,500	3,500
C	−23,000	11,000	6,800	3,600	14,100	
D	−13,000	0	6,100	0	0	8,200

2. MNB Corp. is considering the purchase of another company called NBV Corp. The owners of NBV are asking for $200 million in cash. The managers of MNB estimate that the assets of NBV will generate cash flows of $26 million per year for ten years and can then be resold as scrap for $20 million. The appropriate discount rate is 12 percent. Compute the NPV, IRR, and PI for this investment.

3. BVC Co. is considering the purchase of VCX Co. The managers of BVC estimate that the assets of VCX will generate $10 million in cash flows next year and that these cash flows will grow forever at a rate of 5 percent per year. The appropriate discount rate is 14 percent and the purchase price is $100 million. Compute the NPV, IRR, and PI for this investment.

Assignment 10.2

Name:_____   Date:_____

Solve the following problems in the space provided.

1. Compute the NPV of the following project using discount rates of 0, 10, 20, 30, 40, 50, 60, 70, and 80 percent.

Project	C_0	C_1	C_2
A	−7,500	19,800	−12,600

2. Draw the NPV profile of Project A and estimate the IRRs from the graph.

Assignment 10.3

Name:_____   Date:_____

Solve the following problems in the space provided.

1. You are contemplating the purchase of a rental property. The property consists of twelve apartment units, each of which fetches a rent of $600 per month. The cost of maintaining the entire property is $1,800 per month. The appropriate discount rate is 1 percent per month. If the property has an economic life of ten years and can be sold for $500,000 at the end of its economic life, what is the maximum that you would pay for this property?

2. You own a rental property. This property consists of twenty dwelling units, each of which is rented out for $6,000 per year. The maintenance cost is $33,000 per year. The economic life of the property is twelve years, at the end of which it can be sold for $400,000. The appropriate discount rate is 12 percent. For this property, you have just received an offer from a potential buyer of $675,000 to be paid now. How will you determine whether you should sell or not?

3. Gargets, Inc. is trying to estimate its current cost of capital. Gargets believes that the appropriate weight of debt is twenty-five and the appropriate weight of equity is 75 percent. Gargets has a tax rate of 30 percent. Gargets' bonds currently trade in the market for a price of $1,000. These $1,000 par value bonds have a coupon rate of 8.5 percent (annual coupon payments) and they mature in twenty-six years. Gargets' common stock trades for $20 per share. The dividend just paid by Gargets was $1.50 (that is, $D_0 = 1.50$) and future dividends are expected to grow at a rate of 5 percent per year forever. Compute Gargets' cost of capital.

4. Melvyn, Inc. is trying to estimate its current cost of capital. Melvyn believes that the appropriate weight of debt is 60 percent and the appropriate weight of equity is 40 percent. Melvyn has a tax rate of 30 percent. Melvyn's bonds currently trade in the market for a price of $695. These $1,000 par value bonds have a coupon rate of 5.5 percent (semi-annual coupon payments) and they mature in twenty-five years. Melvyn's common stock trades for $26.50 per share. The dividend just paid by Melvyn was $2.10 (that is, $D_0 = 2.10$) and future dividends are expected to grow at a rate of 5.5 percent per year forever. Compute Melvyn's cost of capital.

Additional Questions and Problems ■■■■■■■■■■■■■■■■■■■

1. Compute the NPV, IRR, PI, the payback periods, and the discounted payback periods for the following projects. Assume a discount rate of 11 percent.

Project	C_0	C_1	C_2	C_3	C_4	C_5
A	−1,000	400	400	400	500	500
B	−6,000	1,500	1,500	1,500	1,500	1,500
C	−29,000	0	0	14,100	22,340	
D	−17,000	0	0	0	24,200	8,200

2. Consider a project that has the following cash flows: −1,010 at $t = 0$, 1,996 at $t = 1$, and −740 at $t = 2$. How many IRRs does this project have? Compute them. If the cost of capital is 20 percent, should this project be accepted?

3. Consider the project with the following expected cash flows:

Year	Cash flow
0	−$200,000
1	50,000
2	50,000
3	$200,000

   a. If the discount rate is 0 percent, what is the project's net present value?

   b. If the discount rate is 5 percent, what is the project's net present value?

   c. What is this project's internal rate of return?

4. A project has an NPV of $6,900. This project requires a cash outflow of $15,000 in the beginning and then from $t = 1$ onwards, it generates cash flows $4,500 per year for eight years. Compute the IRR, PI, and the cost of capital for this project.

5. A project requiring a $1 million investment has a profitability index of 0.96. What is its net present value?

6. Which one of the following is true about the internal rate of return rule of capital budgeting:

   a. When it leads to an acceptance decision, NPV is always greater than one.

   b. When evaluating a single independent normal project, it leads the same decision as the decision based on profitability index

   c. It gives multiple answers if the cash flows don't change signs.

   d. It should be preferred over NPV when the two result in conflicting decisions.

   e. It ignores cash flows that are expected to occur in the far future.

7. Which statement is always correct? (Note: PI stands for Profitability Index.)

   a. If the NPV of the project is positive, then the IRR is smaller than 1.

   b. If the NPV of the project is positive, then the IRR is greater than 1.

   c. If the NPV of the project is negative, then the PI is greater than 1.

   d. If the NPV of the project is negative, then the PI is greater than discount rate.

   e. If the NPV of the project is positive, then the PI is greater than 1.

8. For a normal project (that is, a single negative cash (out)flow in year 0 followed by positive cash (in)flows in all future years), if you increase all cash inflows of any project by an inflation rate and do not change the discount rate, then the NPV of the project will

   a. increase.

   b. decrease.

   c. stay the same.

   d. decrease if the project has a single IRR and increase if the project has multiple IRRs.

   e. increase if the NPV of the project was originally positive and decrease if the NPV of the project was originally negative.

9. A five-year project—if taken—will require an initial investment of $80,000. The expected end-of-the-year cash inflows are as follows:

Year 1	$10,000
Year 2	$42,000
Year 3	$42,000
Year 4	$18,000
Year 5	$22,000

Given that the appropriate discount rate for this project is 15 percent, compute the NPV, IRR, and PI. Should this project be accepted or rejected? Why?

10. The following table lists the capital budgeting analysis of four different *mutually exclusive* projects with an equal life:

Project	NPV	IRR	Discount rate
A	$3,000	10.5% and 17%	11%
B	$5,050	13.4%	12%
C	$4,800	14.4%	13%
D	$3,100	21.5%	14%

Which project would you choose?

11. You have the following information on four *independent* projects with an equal life:

Project	IRR	NPV	Initial cost
A	10%	$3,500	$ 8,000
B	13%	$5,000	$20,000
C	15%	$4,000	$ 500
D	25%	$4,500	$ 1,000

Which project(s) would you choose?

12. Your required rate of return is 8 percent. If you invest $150 today you will receive the following cash flows:

At the end of Year 1	$70
At the end of Year 2	$80
At the end of Year 3	$90

What is the NPV of the project?

13. Pickens, Inc. is trying to estimate its current cost of capital. Pickens believes that the appropriate weight of debt is 50 percent and the appropriate weight of equity is 50 percent. Pickens has a tax rate of 30 percent. Pickens' bonds currently trade in the market for a price of $1,095. These $1,000 par value bonds have a coupon rate of 11.6 percent (annual coupon payments) and they mature in twenty-four years. Pickens' common stock trades for $68.25 per share. The dividend just paid by Pickens was $5.25 (that is, $D_0 = 5.25$) and future dividends are expected to grow at a rate of 7 percent per year forever. Compute Pickens' cost of capital.

14. Zubee, Inc. is trying to estimate its current cost of capital. Zubee believes that the appropriate weight of debt is 80 percent and the appropriate weight of equity is 20 percent. Zubee has a tax rate of 30 percent. Zubee's bonds currently trade in the market for a price of $8785. These $10,000 par value bonds have a coupon rate of 7.8 percent (semi-annual coupon payments) and they mature in thirty years. Zubee's common stock trades for $33.75 per share. The dividend just paid by Zubee was $2.90 (that is, $D_0 = 2.90$) and future dividends are expected to grow at a rate of 3.75 percent per year forever. Compute Zubee's cost of capital.

Chapter **11**

Advanced Topics in Capital Budgeting

After studying Chapter 11, you should be able to:

◆ Identify the guidelines by which cash flows should be measured.

◆ Explain how a project's benefits and costs—that is, its incremental after-tax cash flows—are calculated.

◆ Describe the difference between independent and mutually exclusive projects.

◆ Compare projects with different lives using the equivalent annual series technique.

11.1 Chapter Overview ....

In the previous chapter, we discussed the basic techniques for determining whether a project should be accepted or rejected. Specifically, we discussed three discounted cash flow methods, NPV, IRR, and PI. We also discussed the payback period criterion. Given the obvious shortcomings of the payback period criterion, we will now focus our attention on the three discounted cash flow methods of NPV, IRR, and PI. We will apply these methods to more complicated (than in the previous chapter) situations in capital budgeting. By the end of this chapter, you will notice that of these three, the NPV method is the most consistent evaluation technique for capital budgeting.

11.2 Project Cash Flows ....

Imo Sherman owns and operates a delivery business in Atlanta, Georgia. Sherman's company, Imo's Immediate Delivery (referred to by most clients as IID), delivers business packages and letters throughout a 50-mile radius of the center of the city. IID has an excellent reputation, has few legitimate competitors, and is highly profitable. The company currently has a fleet of twenty delivery vehicles (trucks) and employs thirty-two drivers and support personnel. Imo Sherman is the sole owner/manager of the business.

IID guarantees pickup and delivery within two hours of placement of an order. Interestingly, this full money-back guarantee is easy to meet for pickups and deliveries outside of the main downtown area. Within the five-mile radius of the heart of the city, however, traffic and limited parking make it extremely difficult to fulfill the guarantee. In fact, nearly 30 percent of all orders in this area end up being fulfilled free of charge.

Accordingly, Imo is contemplating adding a fleet of bicycles to his business. He is thinking about purchasing thirty bicycles and hiring twenty riders (ten additional riders will double as vehicle drivers and bicycle riders as demand dictates). He will also need to purchase a piece of land adjacent to the main downtown area (about five miles from the heart of the city) and construct a garage to store the bicycles and to use as a hub to connect bicycles with vehicles for pickups and deliveries that span the downtown area and outside the downtown area.

Imo estimates that the bicycles and associated equipment will cost $25,000, the land will cost $75,000, and construction of the garage will cost $100,000. Should Imo spend $200,000 to expand this part of his business? This is a capital budgeting problem, and therefore answering this question requires application of the techniques that you learned in the previous chapter; specifically, computation of the project's NPV, IRR, or PI. What are we missing to compute these values? The project cash inflows and the appropriate discount rate.

In the earlier chapters, these items, the cash flows, and the discount rates applicable to the project, were provided. In fact, estimating the relevant cash flows and the appropriate discount rate for individual projects is one of the most difficult tasks of capital budgeting. For large projects, companies spend weeks, and even months, estimating these variables.

Estimating relevant cash flows actually involves many of the activities that were covered in the first half of this book. Pro forma income statements and corresponding balance sheets for each year of the life of the project must first be constructed. This also involves estimating all related working capital requirements and changes in these requirements associated with any forecasted annual changes in sales. These issues were covered in chapters 4 and 5. Then, the pro forma statements must be converted into cash flow statements. This procedure was the basis of Chapter 3. Finally, relevant cash flows must be identified and separated from non-relevant cash flows. In this chapter, we will discuss several important items and issues to remember when determining a firm's or a project's relevant cash flows. The procedures outlined in this chapter are purposely limited in scope. Complete details concerning cash flow estimation are left to advanced finance books and courses. Our goal here is to provide a basic understanding of and appreciation for the process of determining whether a capital project should be accepted or rejected.

With regard to the appropriate project discount rate, we completely relegate determining and estimating this variable to a later course in finance. The primary reason for this is that to determine the appropriate discount rate, we must study the area of "risk" in much greater detail than was covered in chapter 8. Additionally, it is necessary to cover the topics of optimal capital structure, and to understand the identification and valuation of options, to determine appropriate individual project discount rates. These topics, though interesting, are beyond the scope of any introductory finance course.

Once relevant cash flows and an appropriate discount rate have been estimated, however, the computation of a project's NPV, IRR, and PI is a fairly simple task. Assume that Imo estimates that the annual net cash flows from adding the bicycle fleet will be as follows:

Year	Estimated Net Cash Flow
1	$50,000
2	$60,000
3	$75,000
4	$80,000
5	$90,000

For simplicity, we will assume that the project will only last five years and that Imo has included the salvage value in the fifth year estimated cash flow figure of $90,000. Imo also has estimated that the appropriate discount rate for this project (that is, the projects cost of capital) is 18 percent.

Problem 11.1   Compute the bicycle project's NPV, IRR, and PI.

NPV = 11,714.2021
IRR = 20.3037
PI = 1.0586

Answers: NPV = 11,714.20; IRR = 20.30%; PI = 1.06.

Problem 11.2   Should IID accept or reject this project?

Accept b/c NPV is positive, PI>1 & IRR>r

Answers: Accept, because the NPV > 0, the IRR > project's cost of capital and PI > 1.

In the next several sections to this chapter, we note several items that must be considered when estimating project cash flows. As you will see, the main issue involves identifying and including all possible relevant cash flows and identifying and excluding all possible non-relevant cash flows.

11.2.1 Cash Flows Must Be "Cash" Flows

The first, and the most important, thing to note about determining a project's cash flows is that *cash flows should be cash.* This statement may sound a little silly, but nonetheless is extremely important. From your study of financial statements in the earlier part of this course, you undoubtedly recall the basic outline of a firm's income statement. Let us consider the following simple income statement for ASD Corp.

Income Statement
ASD Corp.
For the Year Ending December 31, 2003

Net sales	$125,000
Cost of goods sold	80,000
Depreciation	15,000
EBIT	**30,000**
Tax at 30 percent	9,000
Net income	**$ 21,000**

What is the cash flow to ASD in 2003? Is it equal to the net income of $21,000? The answer is no. To see this, let us suppose that there is a person Ms. X in ASD whose job is to keep track of the cash. All the cash that comes in goes into Ms. X's pocket and all the cash that goes out is from Ms. X's pocket. Then, assuming that all sales are cash sales, $125,000 will go into Ms. X's pocket from sales. Again assuming that costs of goods sold are paid in cash, an amount of $80,000 will leave Ms. X's pocket leaving $125,000 − $80,000 = $45,000 in Ms. X's pocket. Will the $15,000 for depreciation leave Ms. X's pocket? No, because depreciation, as we all know, is not a cash expense. How about the $9,000 for tax? Like it or not, this amount will certainly leave Ms. X's pocket, leaving $36,000 in it. There are no other inflows or outflows of cash from Ms. X's pocket. Therefore, in 2003, we know that ASD Corp. had a *cash flow* of $36,000. This is *not* the same as the net income from the income statement. The cash flow is higher than the net income by $15,000, and this amount is the same as the depreciation expense.

The fact that the difference between the net income and the cash flow is exactly equal to the depreciation expense is not a coincidence. Depreciation is not a cash expense. The only reason that it enters an income statement is because it can be deducted for income tax purposes. Therefore, a common method for estimating the cash flow from the income statement is to add the depreciation back to the net income.

cash flow = net income + depreciation expense

As you might recall from the first section of the book, net income plus depreciation expense is commonly referred to as free cash flow.

Let us view this idea another way. Suppose that depreciation expense were not tax deductible. In this case, ASD's income statement would be as follows:

Income Statement
ASD Corp.
For the Year Ending December 31, 2003

Net sales	$125,000
Cost of goods sold	80,000
EBIT	**45,000**
Tax at 30 percent	13,500
Net income	**$ 31,500**

Here, the cash flow and the net income would be identical (assuming that all sales are cash sales and that all expenses are paid immediately in cash). The difference between the cash flows when depreciation is tax deductible and when it is not is $36,000 − $31,500 = $4,500. Note that this difference is equal to the depreciation expense multiplied by the tax rate. In other words, under the existing tax system, depreciation provides a tax shield. The depreciation non-cash expense of $15,000 reduces taxable income and therefore reduces taxes, which is a cash expense, by $15,000 × 0.30 = $4,500. Therefore, we have the following alternative way of writing the cash flow equation:

Cash flow = (Revenue − Costs) × (1 − t_c) + (t_c × Depreciation).

where, t_c is the corporate tax rate and

$$(t_c \times \text{Depreciation}) = \text{Depreciation tax shield.}$$

Depreciation is just one of the reasons why the net income from a firm's financial statement might not represent the cash flow. There are other reasons, too. The most common reason is the accrual method used in accounting. Sales are entered as such even if the cash from those sales is not received. Thus, the sales number from the income statement might not reflect the actual cash received by the firm. The same may be true for the expenses of the firm.

In fact, we covered this concept in chapter 3. Recall that cash flow from operating activities is generally not the same as net income. To convert accrual accounting net income to cash flow from operations, we first added depreciation to net income and then added or subtracted changes in balance sheet accounts that were related to income statement variables (specifically, changes in accounts receivable, inventory, accounts payable, and accruals). This same procedure is required to find the cash flows associated with a given project. That is why it is necessary to construct pro forma income statements and balance sheets for each year of the projected life of the project. From these, we can determine cash flow from operating activities, which are essentially equal to total project cash flows. We are not done, however, because we must still separate relevant from non-relevant cash flows.

11.2.2 Ignore Interest Expenses

Note that in the income statement of ASD Corp. there was no interest expense. Is it a cash expense? Most certainly! Do we take it into account when we determine a project's cash flow? The answer is no. The reason for this is somewhat complex and will require studying other topics in corporate finance such as capital structure. However, for the time being, let us simply state that in determining the NPV of a project, we must ignore how a project is financed. In other words, we do not consider whether the firm issued debt or equity to finance (pay for) the project.

Intuitively, the reason for this can be illustrated with the following examples. Suppose you are buying a car from a dealer. You also own a significant amount of equity in your home. You can borrow the money for the car either by taking a car loan from your bank or you can raise it by selling a part of your ownership in your house to another person. Will the dealer charge you a different price if the cash you gave him was from a loan from a bank or from your sale of a part of the house? The dealer doesn't care. In other words, the price of the car will not be affected by how you have raised the money to pay for it.

On the other hand, suppose that you have decided the model of the car that you are going to buy but have not yet agreed to the price. A respected consumer magazine gives a scathing report on the quality of this model. According to this report, the quality of this car is so poor that the resale value is expected to be a lot lower than what was earlier expected. Irrespective of how you finance the automobile purchase, will the price that you will pay be affected? Most certainly, you will now pay a lower price.

The point made by these examples is that, in a simple world, the value of a project is determined by the cash flows that the project's assets generate and not by how the project is financed. Note that in the above statement we included the phrase: "in a simple world." This phrase is actually much more important than it might appear. When the world is not simple or not perfect, additional items begin to matter and project evaluation becomes more complicated. But, as we stated in the beginning of this chapter, such intricate details are here relegated to more advanced courses in corporate finance.

11.2.3 All Project Cash Flows Must Be Incremental

Consider a soft drink company called Quoqua Quola. Currently this company manufactures and sells a soft drink called QuoquaQuola. It sells ten million units of this drink per year and, to keep matters simple, suppose that from each unit it earns $10 in cash. Thus, currently, its cash flow is $100 million per year. This company is considering the project of introducing a diet drink, DietQuoque, to the market. The marketing people of the company estimate that this new product will have sales of five million units per year. Assume that this product will also generate $10 per unit and that it will require an investment of $400 million. What are the cash inflows for the DietQuoque project? Can you come up with a number? Is it $50 million per year?

Let us think about this for a minute. Look at the kind of product we are considering here. It is highly likely that a significant portion of the sales of DietQuoque will be to persons who are switching from the regular QuoquaQuola. Therefore, the introduction of this product will reduce the sales of the regular drink. Is that a relevant factor to consider for the diet drink project? It certainly is. Now suppose that of the five million units of the diet drink sales, one million are to those who have switched from the company's regular drink. Can you determine the appropriate per year cash inflow for the diet drink project? The answer is $40 million per year. Of the $50 million of the diet drink sales, $10 million are due to the reduction in the regular drink sales. Therefore, as far as the firm is concerned, the net cash inflow from the project is only $40 million. If you believe this, then you have understood the concept of incremental cash flows. In capital budgeting, only *incremental cash flows* are relevant.

How do you determine incremental cash flows? The answer is simple. Look at the cash flows to the firm without the project and then consider the cash flows to the firm with the project. The difference is the incremental cash flow. For example, without the diet drink project, the company in our example was generating a cash flow of $100 million per year from ten million units of the regular drink sale. With the project, it will generate $90 million from the sale of nine million units of the regular drink and $50 million from the sale of five million units of DietQuoque. The total with the project is, therefore, $140 million per year. The incremental cash flow, therefore, is $140 − $100 = $40 million per year.

In reality, estimating incremental cash flows is actually more complicated than it appears. The capital budgeting analyst must actually construct pro forma income statements and balance sheets for the entire company for every year of the project assuming that the project is *not* undertaken, and then construct corresponding pro forma income statements and balance sheets for every year of the project assuming that the project *is* undertaken. Net cash flows from operating activities are then determined for each scenario and these are subtracted to find annual incremental cash flows.

11.2.4 Allocated Costs, Sunk Costs and Opportunity Costs

Suppose that a firm is evaluating a project. This project will use the firm's mainframe computer. The firm's current operations use approximately 40 percent of this computer's capacity and even with the project, will use only 50 percent of the capacity. The firm's accounting department has allocated $30,000 per year as computer usage costs for this project. Is this $30,000 a relevant cash flow for the project? If you think within the framework of the cash flows of the firm with and without the project, you will notice that the firm's computer costs with the project are the same as what they are without the project. Therefore, this $30,000 is not an incremental cash flow.

There are many instances of such allocated costs that might not be incremental, and hence would be irrelevant from the point of view of the project's cash flows. These allocated costs could include several types of expenses such as rent, supervisory salaries, administrative costs, and many other overhead expenses that you can think of. Remember that these costs are not always incremental. The best litmus test for determining whether a cost is incremental or not is the comparison of the cost category to the firm with and without the project.

Suppose that your firm has paid $100,000 to a consulting firm for conducting some market research. On the basis of the consultant's recommendations, your firm has decided to undertake a project. Should the $100,000 paid to the consultant be considered as a cost of the project? The normal temptation is to say yes. But think about it a little more. Suppose you do not take on the project. Will you get this $100,000 back? Certainly not! Thus, the $100,000 is gone whether you do or do not undertake the project. Hence, this amount should not be considered as a part of the cost of the project. Such costs are called *sunk costs,* and should not be included in the cost of the project. Examples of this include R&D expenses, consultant fees, and others. Sunk costs are by definition irrecoverable and, therefore, should not be considered relevant to the project.

A common situation where the above logic becomes important is when someone makes the following type of statement: "Unless we spend an additional million dollars, we will have wasted the ten million that we have already spent." By now you can see the fallacy of this type of an argument. The only reason that you would spend the additional million dollars would be if the additional cash inflow that it generated had a present value of greater than a million dollars. The fact that ten million dollars are already invested is no reason to spend another million dollars. You might not be immediately convinced of the logic of this argument. Think about it for a while and hopefully you will realize that it does indeed make sense. You will also then begin to notice how often and how much money firms (or individuals) and, even more often governments, spend based on such arguments. It's scary.

Suppose that your firm is deciding whether it should build a new factory. The factory will be built on a piece of land that the firm already owns. The market value of this piece of land is $500,000. Should the value of the land be included in the cost of the project? The answer is yes. The argument for its inclusion is a subtle variation of the incremental argument and is called the *opportunity cost* argument. If the firm did not take on the project, it could sell the land for a half a million dollars. By taking on the project, the firm is forgoing the opportunity of selling the land. Therefore, the value of the land, and other such opportunity costs *should* be included in the cost of the project.

Including opportunity costs as relevant costs is akin to the notion that there is no such thing as a "free" asset. Everything has some cost, whether implicit or explicit. Buying a new machine for $1,000,000 has an explicit cost that can easily be identified. Using a piece of land that the company already owns has no explicit cost, because the company does not have to actually put out money to buy the land—they already own it! The land, however, has an implicit cost. As noted above, if the company uses the land for a given project, the land cannot be sold. The land is not "free" to this project, and therefore its cost must be estimated. The most accurate estimated, or implicit, cost, is what the land would return if it were sold.

11.2.5 Net Working Capital

As noted before, annual changes in forecasted net working capital (that is, changes in accounts receivable, inventory, accounts payable, and accruals) must be considered when computing annual net cash flows. This requires generating annual pro forma balance sheets for every year of the project. Although realistic, such detail is again beyond the scope of any introductory finance course. It can easily be avoided by merely assuming that annual net working capital changes will be zero. For simplicity, we will make this assumption for all problems in this chapter. Thus, it will not be necessary to construct annual pro forma balance sheets. To determine annual net cash flow, all that will be required will be to add depreciation to net income.

We will, however, assume that most projects will require an initial increase in net working capital. For example, suppose that by taking on the project, the inventory of the firm will rise by two million dollars and all other components of working capital will remain the same. Thus, there is a net increase of two million dollars in the net working capital of the firm because of the project. Is this relevant? Absolutely! If you take on the project, you will have to maintain the higher level of inventory. This additional $2 million, the increase in the net working capital, should, therefore, be added to the cost of the project. What happens to this inventory at the end of the life of the project? As a matter of convention (mostly convenience), it is assumed that this additional working capital is liquidated at the end of the project's life. Therefore, the increase in working capital is added to the project's initial cost and also is considered a cash inflow in the last period. By the same logic, if the taking on of a project reduces the net working capital, then the magnitude of this decrease in working capital should be subtracted from the project's initial cost and also for the last period cash inflow.

Problem 11.3   After reading the last section of this chapter, Imo Sherman, owner/manager of Imo's Immediate Delivery (IID), realizes that he has forgotten to include the initial net working capital change in his cash flow estimates. Recall that Imo estimated that the bicycles, land, and building would cost $200,000. He now figures that the project will also require a $8,000 increase in inventory, the firm's minimum cash balance will need to increase by $3,500, higher sales will cause accounts receivable to increase by $18,000, accounts payable will increase by $2,500, and accruals are estimated to increase by $500. This change in net working capital will need to be funded immediately. The total amount will be recovered at the end of the life of the project. Compute the initial change in net working capital.

Answers: Change in Net Working Capital = $8,000 + $3,500 + $18,000 − $2,500 − $500 = $26,500.

An increase in net working capital must be funded; therefore this amount represents a required cash outflow. Including this figure in the project cash flows will cause the initial cash outflow (that is, the total cost of the project) to increase to $226,500. Because we will assume that this expenditure will be recovered at the end of the life of the project, we will have a non-operating cash inflow of $26,500 in year 5. This will make the total cash inflow in year 5 equal to $90,000 + $26,500 = 116,500. In summary, the cash flows from the bicycle project are expected to be:

Year	Estimated Net Cash Flow
0	($226,500)
1	$ 50,000
2	$ 60,000
3	$ 75,000
4	$ 80,000
5	$116,500

Problem 11.4   Given the new cash flow estimates in the chart above, compute the NPV, IRR, and PI of the bicycle project assuming an appropriate discount rate of 18 percent.

Answers: NPV = −3,202.40; IRR = 17.45%; PI = 0.99.

Problem 11.5   Should IID accept or reject this project?

Answers: Reject, because the NPV < 0, the IRR < project's cost of capital and PI < 1.

Obviously, inclusion of the initial net working capital effect is important. By ignoring this relevant cost, IDD would have accepted a project that in fact should have been rejected. This in turn would have reduced the value of the company, and therefore would have reduced the shareholder's (that is, Imo Sherman's) wealth.

11.2.6 Treatment of Inflation

When we began the study of the time value of money, we considered the effect of inflation on interest rates (that is, on investors' required rates of return). We noted that the relation between the nominal and real returns with inflation at i was given by

$$(1 + r_{nominal}) = (1 + r_{real}) \times (1 + i).$$

Let us consider a single-period project that costs C_0 and generates a cash flow of C_1 at the end of the first year. Consider first the case when we use the real values for all variables. Then the real NPV of this project will be given by

$$NPV_{real} = \frac{C_1}{(1 + r_{real})} - C_0.$$

Now consider the case when there is inflation and we want to use the nominal values for all variables. We know the relation between the nominal and real interest rates. Thus, the denominator of the NPV expression is easy to adjust. Because inflation implies a general rise in prices, suppose that we assume that the cash inflow also increases by i percent. Then the NPV with nominal values becomes

$$NPV_{nominal} = \frac{C_1 \times (1 + i)}{(1 + r_{nominal})} - C_0.$$

Substituting for $r_{nominal}$, we obtain

$$= \frac{C_1 \times (1 + i)}{(1 + r_{real}) \times (1 + i)} - C_0.$$

You will notice that the $(1 + i)$ terms in the numerator and the denominator cancel each other and we are left with the expression for the real NPV. Does this mean that inflation has no effect on project valuation or selection? What is your gut feel? I am sure that you are not convinced of the validity of this result. And you shouldn't be. There is no mathematical error in the above analysis. There is, however, a conceptual error. When we multiply C_1 by $(1 + i)$ to determine the nominal cash inflow, we are implicitly assuming that all components of the firm's operations that result in this cash inflow are affected by the same amount of inflation. This is clearly not the case. The sales will increase at a different rate than will costs. In particular, labor costs move at different rates than the rate of inflation. Also, because the depreciation expense is not affected by inflation, the tax expenses are affected by an amount that is not proportionate to the inflation rate of i. In summary, it is not correct to adjust the cash flows by simply multiplying them by $(1 + i)$. In an inflationary environment, each component of the income statement has to be individually adjusted to account for inflation.

11.3 A Capital Budgeting Example ....

We have discussed quite a few concepts in this chapter so far. Let us illustrate these with the help of the following (extremely) comprehensive problem.

Problem 11.6   You are given the responsibility of conducting the project selection analysis in your firm. You have to calculate the NPV of a given project. The appropriate cost of capital is 12 percent and the firm is in the 30 percent tax bracket. You are provided the following pieces of information regarding the project:

   a. The project will be built on a piece of land that the firm already owns. The market value of the land is $1 million.

b. If the project is undertaken, prior to construction, an amount of $100,000 would have to be spent to make the land usable for construction purposes.

c. To come up with the project concept, the company had hired a marketing research firm for $200,000.

d. The firm has spent another $250,000 on R&D for this project.

e. The project will require an initial outlay of $20 million for plant and machinery.

f. The sales from this project will be $15 million per year, of which 20 percent will be from lost sales of existing products.

g. The variable costs of manufacturing for this level of sales will be $9 million per year.

h. The company uses straight-line depreciation. The project has an economic life of ten years and will have a salvage value of $3 million at the end.

i. Because of the project, the company will need additional working capital of $1 million, which can be liquidated at the end of ten years.

j. The project will require additional supervisory and managerial manpower that will cost $200,000 per year.

k. The accounting department has allocated $350,000 as allocated overhead cost for supervisory and managerial salaries.

In solving the above problem, the first thing to note is that the computations are not going to be particularly difficult but we have to figure out which information is relevant and which is not.

a. $1,000,000 for the land should be included in the cost of the project (opportunity cost).

b. $100,000 for land improvement should be included in the cost of the project (incremental cost).

c. $200,000 to the marketing research firm are sunk costs and should be ignored.

d. $250,000 on R&D are sunk costs and should be ignored.

e. $20 million for plant and machinery should be included in the cost of the project.

f. The *incremental* sales from the project are only $15,000,000 \times 0.8 = $12,000,000.

g. The variable costs of $9 million are relevant for the project.

h. Straight line depreciation, along with ten-year economic life and $3 million salvage value, implies that the depreciation expense will be

$$\frac{20,000,000 - 3,000,000}{10} = \$1,700,000 \text{ per year.}$$

The $3 million in salvage value will be added to the cash flow at t = 10.

i. The additional working capital of $1 million implies that the initial outlay will be higher by $1 million and $1 million will be added to the cash flow at t = 10.

j. The $200,000 for *additional* managerial manpower is an incremental cash outflow and is relevant to the project.

k. The allocated expense should be ignored.

Having analyzed each piece of information, we can now evaluate the project as follows:

Initial investment = land + land improvement + plant and machinery
+ incremental net working capital

= $1,000,000 + $100,000 + $20,000,000 + $1,000,000

= $22,100,000.

To determine the cash flow each year, let us draw up the *incremental* income statement as follows. Each entry in the statement is incremental.

Incremental sales	$12,000,000
Incremental variable costs	$ 9,000,000
Incremental managerial salaries	$ 200,000
Incremental depreciation	$ 1,700,000
Incremental taxable income	$ 1,100,000
Incremental taxes (@ 30%)	$ 330,000
Incremental net income	$ 770,000
Add back incr. depreciation	$ 1,700,000
Incremental cash flow	$ 2,470,000

Thus the project will generate an annuity of $2,470,000 per year for ten years. In addition to this annuity, we have to consider some other cash flows at t = 10.

Additional cash flows at the end of the project = recovery of incremental net working capital
+ salvage value of plant and machinery

= $1,000,000 + $3,000,000

= $4,000,000

Finally, we compute the NPV using a discount rate of 12 percent.

NPV = −$22,100,000 + PV of annuity of $2,470,000 for ten years
+ PV of $4,000,000 cash inflow at t = 10

= −$6,656,056.17

Given that the NPV is negative, the project should not be accepted.

Note two things here. First, if we had not recognized that 20 percent of the sales were from lost sales of existing products, the annual cash flow would have been $4,570,000 and the NPV would have been positive and the project would have been accepted. Thus, a single mistake would have ended up in the firm investing $22 million in a bad project.

The second cautionary note is in the use of the calculator's NPV function. *A common mistake* would have been to enter CF0 = −22,100,000, C01 = 2,470,000, **F01 = 10, C02 = 4,000,000,** and F01 = 1. Why would entering 10 for the frequency of C01 be incorrect? If we enter the values as above, the calculator assumes that the cash inflow of $4,000,000 entered for C02 occurs at t = 11 and not at t = 10 as it should. The correct procedure here would be to enter the following in the calculator with the CF-NPV functions: CF0 = −22,100,000, C01 = 2,470,000, F01 = 9, C02 = 6,470,000, and F01 = 1. Now you will obtain the correct answer.

11.4 Mutually Exclusive Projects

Thus far, we have the rule that a project that has positive NPV should be accepted. There are, however, many situations where one might have to choose one of several positive NPV projects. This occurs when projects are **mutually exclusive.** Two projects are said to be mutually exclusive if accepting one necessarily implies that the other will have to be forgone. For example, if you have a piece of land on which you can either build a house or a store, but not both, then the house and the store will be two mutually exclusive projects. The interesting aspect of this analysis is that with two mutually exclusive projects, you have to rank the projects. It is possible that each of the mutually exclusive projects has a positive NPV, but because you can choose only one, you have to determine which is the best. It is this determination of the ranking of mutually exclusive projects that we shall spend some time on now.

Consider the following two mutually exclusive projects and assume that the discount rate for each is 10 percent.

Project	C_0	C_1	C_2	C_3	NPV	IRR
A	−10,000	5,000	5,000	5,000	2,434.26	23.3752
B	−10,000	4,800	4,800	4,800	1,936.89	20.7084

Which of the two projects would you choose? Irrespective of whether you use the NPV or the IRR method, project A is better.

The above problem was too simple. Now consider the following two mutually exclusive projects and assume that the discount rate for each is 10 percent.

Project	C_0	C_1	NPV	IRR
X	−1,000	1,500	363.64	50
Y	−10,000	12,000	909.09	20

Now which project would you select? X has the higher IRR and Y has the higher NPV. The correct choice would be project Y. The conflict in ranking here occurs because the two projects have different scales. Thus, in comparing the two projects you must take into account what you would do with the $9,000 left over if you invest in project X. The implicit assumption is that you would earn your required rate of return (remember opportunity cost) of 10 percent. Thus, investment in X actually means that you invest $1,000 in X and $9,000 at 10 percent. Let us call this project X*. X* costs $1,000 + $9,000 = $10,000 and yields t = 1 cash flow of $1,500 (from X) + $9,900 (from investing $9,000 at 10 percent) = $11,400. The NPV of this properly defined project X* is $363.64 and the IRR is 11.4 percent. Now project Y is better with the NPV and with the IRR criterion.

Can you figure out why the NPVs of X and X* are the same? They have to be. Project X* is nothing but the combination (or portfolio) of project X and another project that has a return exactly equal to the discount rate and thus an NPV of zero. Then by value additivity (remember that) the NPV of X* is the sum of the NPVs of the two projects, that is, $363,64 + $0 = $363.64. This also illustrates the fact that when two mutually exclusive projects have different scales, choosing the project with the higher NPV is *always* correct.

Here's another problem of two mutually exclusive projects. The discount rate is 10 percent.

Project	C_0	C_1	C_2	C_3	NPV	IRR
P	−3,000	1,000	2,000	3,000	1,815.93	36.194
Q	−3,000	1,900	1,900	1,900	1,725.02	40.497

Here the NPV is higher for P and IRR is higher for Q. This conflict in ranking cannot be explained with scale differences because both projects cost the same. In this case, the conflict occurs because of the differences in the *implicit reinvestment rate assumptions* in the NPV and IRR frameworks. In the IRR framework, the assumption is that all intermediate cash flows are reinvested at the IRR. In the case of the NPV method, the assumption is that all intermediate cash flows are reinvested at the discount rate used in calculating the NPV.

The above explanation probably does not make much sense. Think about the reinvestment assumption in the following sense. Let us consider the project Q again. Under the IRR scenario, you would have to put $3,000 in a bank account that pays 40.497 percent (the IRR of Q) interest to obtain the $1,900 per year for three years as you would in project Q. On the other hand, what is the value of project Q? It is the present value of future cash flows, that is, $4,725.02. If you invested this amount at 10 percent (the discount rate), you would obtain $1,900 per year for three years. Now, which of the two investment scenarios seems more reasonable? Clearly the latter! Remember that the discount rate is the investor's required rate of return and is, by definition, the return that one could earn on similar investments in the market. Thus, the discount rate is a much better estimate of the reinvestment rate than the IRR of a project.

Because the reinvestment rate assumption in the NPV method is more reasonable, the NPV method gives the more appropriate ranking in the above two projects. Project P is preferable because it has the higher NPV. Note that the reinvestment rate assumption matters in this case because the two projects differ in the manner in which they generate cash flows. Project P generates the higher cash flows later, whereas Q gives constant cash flows. Irrespective of the explanations, it is true that choosing between two mutually exclusive projects on the basis of their NPVs is always correct. The exception to this rule is when the two mutually exclusive projects have unequal lives. We will consider this in the next section.

11.5 Equivalent Annual Series ··

Suppose you have to choose between the following two mutually exclusive projects. The discount rate is 10 percent. Because we know that NPV is the better method for ranking projects than the IRR, we will consider only the NPV.

Project	C_0	C_1	C_2	C_3	C_4	NPV
L	−1,000	500	500	500	500	584.93
S	−600	500	500			267.77

Even though the NPV of L is higher, we should not rush to rank it higher than S. The reason is that the two projects have different lives, and comparing their NPVs would be equivalent to the proverbial comparison of apples and oranges. If we take on project L, we are locked in for four years. However, if we choose S, we can do something after two years. Therefore, to compare the two projects, we must consider what we can do in years three and four if we choose project S. The easiest assumption is that a firm's investment opportunities will remain the same in the future. Then, we can assume that at the end of the second year, the firm invests again in project S. In other words, it spends $600 at t = 2 and generates $500 in each of the next two years, three and four. This is called a *replacement chain.* For notational simplicity, we will call the replacement chain for S as the project S_{RC}. We will consider the two projects again.

Project	C_0	C_1	C_2	C_3	C_4	NPV
L	−1,000	500	500	500	500	584.93
S	−600	500	500			267.77
Second S			−600	500	500	220.66
S_{RC}	−600	500	−100	500	500	488.43

We now compare L with S_{RC} and determine that L is in fact the better project; its NPV is higher than that of the replacement chain of S, denoted by S_{RC}.

Attempt the following problems in the space provided and see if you obtain the given answer.

Problem 11.7 Assume a discount rate of 12 percent. Which of the two mutually exclusive projects will you choose? Project A costs $12,000 and generates cash flows of $4,000 per year for eight years. Project B costs $8,000 and generates cash flows of $4,000 for four years.

Answers: NPV(A) = $7,870.56, NPV(B) = $4,149.40, NPV_{RC}(B) = $6,786.42.
Because NPV(A) > NPV_{RC}(B), choose A.

Problem 11.8 The two projects G and H are mutually exclusive. The appropriate discount rate for both the projects is 14 percent. Project G costs $100,000 and generates cash flows of $50,000 per year for three years. Project H costs $53,000 and generates cash flows of $40,000 per year for two years.

Answers: NPV(G) = $16,081.60, NPV(H) = $12,866.42,
NPV_{RC}(G) = $26,936.22, NPV_{RC}(H) = $30,384.66
Because NPV_{RC}(H) > NPV_{RC}(G), choose H.

In the above problem, the lives of the two projects were three and two years, respectively, so you will have to form replacement chains for both the projects. The common number of years for the two is six and therefore, you will invest in G once more and in H twice more to form the replacement chains.

The aspect of the replacement chain method that is depicted in the above problem makes its use extremely tedious. When the lives of the two projects were three and two years, the process was tedious enough. Imagine how boring it would be if the lives of the two projects were eleven and nine years, respectively. You would have to form replacement chains of the two projects for ninety-nine years.

Fortunately, there is a better way. The whole idea behind forming replacement chains was to ensure that we compared two projects with equal lives. Another way to do the same thing would be to figure out a way to express NPV on a "per year" basis for any project and compare these values for projects. The project that has a higher per year NPV is the better project. This is achieved by constructing *equivalent annual series (EAS)*.

Suppose that we are trying to rank two mutually exclusive projects. Project J costs $12,000 and generates cash flows of $6,000 per year for three years. Project K costs $18,000 and generates cash flows of $7,000 for four years. The first step in constructing the EAS is to compute the NPV of each project. Assuming a discount rate of 10 percent, we find that

$$NPV(J) = \$2,921.11, \quad NPV(K) = \$4,189.06.$$

The next step is to compute the EAS for each project. The EAS of a project is the payment on an annuity whose life is the same as that of the project and whose present value, using the discount rate of the project, is equal to the NPV of the project. The EAC for project J, denoted by EASJ, then is the payment on the three-year (life of project J) annuity whose PV, using 10 percent as the discount rate, is equal to $2,921.11. In other words, we enter the following values in the calculator: $N = 3$, $I/Y = 10$, $PV = -2921.11$, $FV = 0$, $PMT = ?$. This yields $EAS_J = \$1,174.62$. To compute EAS_K, we enter the following values in the calculator: $N = 4$, $I/Y = 10$, $PV = -4,189.06$, $FV = 0$, $PMT = ?$. This yields $EAS_K = \$1,321.53$. Because $EAS_K > EAS_J$, K is the better project.

A very useful application of the EAS concept is in choosing between two machines that do the same job but have different costs and different lives.

Problem 11.9   Suppose that your firm is trying to decide between two machines, say lathes, that will do the same job. Lathe A costs $90,000, will last for ten years, and will require operating costs of $5,000 per year. At the end of ten years it will be scrapped for $10,000. Lathe B costs $60,000, will last for seven years, and will require operating costs of $6,000 per year. At the end of seven years it will be scrapped for $5,000. Which is a better machine? (The discount rate is 10 percent.)

Note that here there is no question of computing the NPV. Because both machines do the same job, we must choose the one with the least cost. Note, however, that their lives are different and therefore, we will need to use an adjustment similar to the EAS. The first step is to compute the present value of the costs for each of the two lathes.

PV of costs (A) = $90,000 + PV of $5,000 annuity for ten years
     − PV of the scrap (at t = 10) value of $10,000
   = $90,000 + $30,722.84 − 3,855.43
   = $116,867.41

PV of costs (B) = $60,000 + PV of $6,000 annuity for seven years
     − PV of the scrap (at t = 7) value of $5,000
   = $60,000 + $29,210.51 − $2,565.79
   = $86,644.72

The next step is to compute the **equivalent annual cost series (EAC)** for each of the two projects. This involves finding the annuity that has the same present value as the PV of the costs of each of the machines. To compute EAC_A, we enter the following values in the calculator: $N = 10$, $I/Y = 10$, $PV = -116,867.41$, $FV = 0$, $PMT = ?$. This yields $EAC_A = \$19,019.63$. To compute EAC_B, we enter the following values in the calculator: $N = 7$, $I/Y = 10$, $PV = -86,644.72$, $FV = 0$, $PMT = ?$. This yields $EAC_B = \$17,797.30$. Therefore, lathe B is better. Remember, we are dealing with costs here and we want to choose the machine with the lower cost. In this case, it is Lathe B.

Problem 11.10   Assume the same decision as in the problem above. However, now assume that the firm pays tax at a rate of 30 percent and uses straight-line depreciation for tax purposes.

The problem is now somewhat more complicated because we have to consider everything on an after-tax basis. The depreciation expenses for the two machines are:

$$\text{Depreciation Expense (A)} = \frac{90,000 - 10,000}{10} = \$8,000 \text{ per year}$$

$$\text{Depreciation Expense (B)} = \frac{60,000 - 5,000}{7} = \$7,857.14 \text{ per year.}$$

Next, note that the operating expense of the machines is a tax-deductible expense and we will have to take the after-tax value of the cost. Then,

$$\text{PV of cost (A)} = \$90{,}000 + \text{PV of } \$3{,}500 \ (\$5{,}000 \times (1 - 0.30)) \text{ annuity for ten years}$$
$$- \text{ PV of the scrap (at } t = 10) \text{ value of } \$10{,}000$$
$$- \text{ PV of } \$2{,}400 \ (\$8{,}000 \times 0.30) \text{ annuity for ten years}$$
$$= \$90{,}000 + \$21{,}505.98 - \$3{,}855.43 - \$14{,}746.96$$
$$= \$92{,}903.59$$
$$\text{EAC}_A = \$15{,}119.63$$

$$\text{PV of cost (B)} = \$60{,}000 + \text{PV of } \$4{,}200 \ (\$6{,}000 \times (1 - 0.30)) \text{ annuity for seven years}$$
$$- \text{ PV of the scrap (at } t = 7) \text{ value of } \$5{,}000$$
$$- \text{ PV of } \$2{,}357.14 \ (\$7{,}857.14 \times 0.30) \text{ annuity for seven years}$$
$$= \$60{,}000 + \$20{,}447.36.97 - \$2{,}565.79 - \$11{,}475.54$$
$$= \$66{,}406.03$$
$$\text{EAC}_B = \$13{,}640.16$$

Since the EAC of B is lower, Lathe B is better.

11.6 Concluding Thoughts and Remarks

You have now completed the final chapter in the book. It is our sincere desire that you have enjoyed your experience and have learned a great deal about the world of finance. As professionals in the field, we appreciate the fact that finance is a central function of any successful business. Hopefully we have conveyed this fact throughout the book.

If you choose to continue your studies in finance, the material and lessons contained in this book will provide you with a solid foundation. If instead this is the only finance book that you ever read, we believe you will find that the knowledge about the field of finance you now possess will be useful in your career, regardless of your profession, and in your life. Because most of you will work for a company (or perhaps even own and operate your own company), you will undoubtedly interact with individuals from the finance department. Hopefully you will be able to understand what they are talking about and why they are concerned about certain issues.

Finally, finance major or not, most of you will someday own stocks and bonds, probably in a retirement account. The knowledge about valuation, financial reporting, efficient financial management, and risk that you have learned from this book will help you to make educated investment decisions. Although we cannot guarantee that this knowledge will lead to great riches, we *know* that educated decisions are much more likely to lead to favorable results than uneducated ones. Perhaps that is why we have chosen education as our career field—it most certainly is not because of great riches!

Good luck in whatever you do, and thank you for reading our book.

Assignment 11.1

Name:_____   Date:_____

Solve the following problems in the space provided.

1. FGH Corp. is considering investment in a project. The project involves an expenditure of $10 million in plant and equipment. These assets will generate $2 million per year for ten years. The company uses straight-line depreciation to zero salvage value for tax purposes. The tax rate is 30 percent and the appropriate discount rate is 13 percent. Compute the NPV of the project.

2. A and B are mutually exclusive projects. Project A requires an initial outlay of $80,000 and generates cash flows of $18,000 per year for eight years. Project B requires an outlay of $40,000 and generates cash flows of $10,000 per year for eight years. Compute the NPV and IRR for each of the two projects. Assume that the discount rate is 10 percent. Which project would you select and why?

3. Two projects, A and B, are mutually exclusive and have the following cash flows. The appropriate discount rate is 13 percent.

Project	C_0	C_1	C_2	C_3	C_4
A	−28,000	6,000	10,000	12,000	18,000
B	−28,000	18,000	12,000	10,000	6,000

Compute the NPV and IRR of each project. Determine which is the better project.

4. P and Q are two mutually exclusive projects. Compute their NPVs for discount rates of 0, 5, 10, 15, 20, 25, 30, 35, 40, 45, and 50 percent. Plot the NPV profiles of the two projects on the same graph. From the graph, answer the following questions. At what cost of capital would you prefer P to Q? At what cost of capital would you choose project Q over P?

Project	C_0	C_1	C_2	C_3
P	−3,000	1,000	2,000	3,000
Q	−3,000	1,900	1,900	1,900

Assignment 11.2

Name:_____   Date:_____

Solve the following problems in the space provided.

1. RTY Co. is deciding between two machines to do a particular job. Machine X100 costs $45,000 to install, has operating costs of $5,000 per year, will last for five years, and has a salvage value of $6,000. Machine Y1300 costs $65,000 to install, has operating costs of $2,000 per year, will last for seven years, and has a salvage value of $10,000. If the firm's cost of capital is 12 percent, which machine will be better?

2. A company is deciding to introduce a new product to the market. In deciding on the product concept, the company spent $300,000 last year on a marketing research study. Once the product concept was decided upon, the company spent another $500,000 on the design of a new manufacturing process. The company is now ready to launch the product on a full scale. To do this, the company will have to invest $31 million in plant and machinery. This has an economic life of twenty years and will have a scrap value of $3 million at the end. The project is expected to generate sales of $5 million per year for the twenty years. Of these, 10 percent are due to lost sales of the existing products of the company. The variable cost of producing the product is 60 percent of sales. Other costs are $600,000 per year. Existing managerial manpower will be able to handle the project quite easily. The company's accountants have allocated $300,000 in supervisory salaries to this project. Investing in the project will result in a decrease of $2 million in the company's working capital. At the end of the project, working capital levels will go back to what they are without the project today. The company uses straight-line depreciation method for tax purposes and is in the 30 percent tax bracket. Assuming a discount rate of 11 percent, compute the NPV of the project.

Assignment 11.3

Name:_____   Date:_____

Solve the following problems in the space provided.

1. A firm is faced with the prospect of deciding between two manufacturing technologies. Technology Q36 will require machinery and equipment worth $3 million. This technology will result in operating cost savings of $600,000 per year for eight years. Technology Z96 will require an initial outlay of $4 million and will result in cost savings of $700,000 for ten years. Assume straight-line depreciation, a 10 percent discount rate, and zero salvage values for both the technologies. The firm pays no taxes. Which technology would you recommend?

2. Assume the same number as in the previous problem. Assume, however, that the firm pays taxes at the 30 percent rate. Which technology would you now recommend?

Additional ■■■■■■■■■■■■■■■■■■■■■■■
Questions and
Problems

1. Rank the following mutually exclusive projects. Assume that the discount rate is 10 percent.

Project	C_0	C_1	C_2	C_3	C_4	C_5
A	−1,000	1,200				
B	−6,000	1,500	1,500	1,500	1,500	1,500
C	−29,000	14,100	22,340			
D	−17,000	0	0	24,200	8,200	

2. Determine which of the following is a relevant cash flow and which is not relevant for capital budgeting purposes. Also, where appropriate, determine whether the item is a sunk cost or an opportunity cost.

- The building will be built on land already owned by the company with a market value of $2 million. If the company does not accept the project, the land will be sold for $2 million.

- $100,000 in preliminary grading work has been done to prepare the site.

- The building will cost $10.5 million and equipment will cost $4.5 million.

- The company paid a $1 million royalty to obtain rights to a production process.

- Additional royalty payments of 1 percent of gross revenues from the product will be required.

- Last year the company signed a non-cancelable ten-year lease on the building, requiring payments of $150,000 per year.

- The product is expected to generate sales of $2 million per year. Of these sales, 7 percent are expected to come from existing products, 30 percent are expected to come from a major competitor, and the rest will be entirely new sales to the industry.

- The plant and equipment will be depreciated for tax purposes on a straight-line basis to zero salvage value over a ten-year period. The tax rate is 36 percent.

- The variable costs of production will be $500,000 per year.

- Accounting plans to allocate supervisory and management costs of $25,000 per year to the project. No new supervisory or management personnel will be required.

- Accounting plans to allocate electricity costs of $1,000 per month to the project due to the energy demands of the new equipment.

- The inventor of the product left the company last year. She will receive non-compete payments of $50,000 per year for the next three years.

- The project will require additional working capital of $2 million. The working capital can be recovered at the end of the life of the project.

- The plant and equipment are expected to last for fifteen years, at which time it is expected that they can be sold for $3.5 million.

3. An automobile company is deciding whether to manufacture the radiators that it uses in its cars or to buy them from a supplier. The annual requirement is for 100,000 radiators. The supplier is willing to sell these at a cost of $120 per radiator. If the company were to manufacture these radiators, it would need to invest in machinery worth $5 million. The manufacturing cost would be $80 per radiator. The economic life of the machinery is ten years and the company uses straight-line depreciation for tax purposes. The tax rate is 30 percent and the discount rate is 9 percent for both projects. Assume that the life of both projects is ten years. Should the company make or buy the radiators?

4. A and B are two mutually exclusive projects. Project A requires an initial outlay of $9,000 and generates a net cash flow of $4,000 per year for four years. Project B requires an initial outlay of $25,000, and will generate cash flows of $6,500 per year for eight years. Which project would you choose? Assume that the discount rate for both projects is 10 percent.

5. Hi Grade Tool Company is faced with the prospect of having to replace a large stamping machine. Two machines currently being marketed will do the job satisfactorily. The Superior Stamping machine costs $50,000 and will require cash operating expenses of $20,000 per year. The Peerless machine costs $75,000, and the operating expenses are $15,000 per year. Both machines have a ten-year useful life with no salvage value and would be depreciated on a straight-line basis. If the company pays a 30 percent tax rate and has a 12 percent after-tax required rate of return, which machine should be purchased?

6. Two mutually exclusive projects have projected cash flows as follows:

PERIOD	0	1	2	3	4
A	−$10,000	$5,000	$5,000	$5,000	$ 5,000
B	−$10,000	0	0	0	$30,000

a. Determine the internal rate of return for each project.

b. Assuming a required rate of return of 10 percent, determine the net present value for each project.

c. Which project would you select? Why?

7. The cash flows of two mutually exclusive projects X and Y are as follows:

YEAR	0	1	2	3	4
PROJ. X	(50,000)	25,000	20,000	15,000	5,000
PROJ. Y	(50,000)	5,000	15,000	20,000	30,000

a. At what discount rate do the NPV profiles of the two projects cross?

b. What is the NPV of the projects at this discount rate?

8. Which of the following items should be included in an incremental cash flow analysis when computing the NPV of an investment? For each item, why or why not?

a. The reduction in the sales of the company's other products caused by the new product.

b. The cost of R&D undertaken in the past year directly attributable to the product.

c. Dividend payments that come from the cash flow to be generated from this product.

d. The cost of additional consulting needed after the new project is launched.

e. Variable costs associated with producing the product.

9. The president of White Star Line has asked you to evaluate the proposed construction of a new passenger ship, to be called the Titanic. White Star is expected to use the vessel for ten years. The vessel's estimated construction cost is $4,000,000 and it is classified as an asset to be depreciated straight line over ten years to a zero salvage value. The operation of the vessel would require an increase in net working capital of $120,000—this amount would be recovered at the end of the life of the project. The vessel would increase the firm's incremental net income by $300,000 per year. The firm's marginal tax rate is 30 percent and the project's cost of capital is 10 percent. Calculate the IRR of the proposed construction project.

10. After you discovered that a State University chemistry professor is planning to illegally produce liquor in his lab, you reported him to the police. He admitted to the police that he spent $12,500 to modify the lab's hot water boiler for this purpose, and that he expected to earn an annual net income of $6,000 on the black market for liquor. He did not plan to pay any taxes. Because he already had tenure, he estimated that he would be able to use the equipment until his retirement, that is, twenty years from now. Then he would sell the equipment for $2,500 to his son. Because of the enormous risk associated with this activity, he estimated a required rate of return of 37 percent p.a. What was the expected **NPV** of the project?

11. Albatros, Inc. is considering buying a piece of equipment (a cyclotron) from an unnamed Finance 3300 instructor for $47 million. By reducing Albatros's expenses for Proton-spectroscopy, the equipment will increase the company's **net income** by $4.3 million per year for the next twenty years. At the end of year 20, the company can sell the cyclotron's magnetic alloys for $2.0 million. The depreciable life of the cyclotron is twenty years and company can use straight-line depreciation to a $2 million salvage value. Albatros, Inc.'s corporate tax rate is 30 percent. The company estimates a discount rate of 15 percent p.a. for this project.

12. Williams Sisters, Inc. is contemplating the purchase of a clothing company to design new clothes for the Williams Sisters company employees. The cost of the clothing company is estimated to be $12,000,000. This entire amount can be depreciated over a ten-year life to a zero salvage value. A financial advisor to Williams Sisters, Inc. has told them that the appropriate cost of capital for such a purchase should be 16 percent, however, the Williams Sisters plan to pay for the clothing company with their own money. Williams Sisters estimates that the new clothing company will generate revenues less costs of $4,000,000 per year for the next ten years. Williams Sisters plans to sell the company to the current owner's father at the end of ten years for $0. Assuming that the tax rate is forty percent, compute the NPV of this purchase.

13. BBB Electronics manufactures a variety of household appliances. The company is considering introducing a new product line. The company's CFO has collected the following information about the proposed product.

- The project has an anticipated economic life of six years.

- R&D costs for development of the new product line were $12 million.

- The company will have to purchase a new machine to manufacture the new product line. The machine will cost the company $20 million to purchase and install, and will be depreciated on a straight-line basis to a $2 million salvage value over its six-year project life.

- If the company goes ahead with the new product line, it will have an effect on the company's net working capital. At the outset (that is, at t = 0), inventory will increase by $1 million and accounts payable will increase by $800,000. At $t = 6$, the net working capital will be recovered after the project is completed.

- The new product line is expected to generate sales revenue of $60 million per for each of the next six years. Operating costs, excluding management salaries, are expected to be $18 million per year. Allocated management salaries will be $2 million per year, although no new managers will be hired for this project.

- Because the new product line is similar to another of BBB's existing products, sales in this other existing product will decrease by $5 million per year, net of cost, once the new product line is on the market. In addition, BBB expects that the product's introduction will cause their competitor's sales to also fall (by $1 million per year).

- The company's interest expense each year will be $1.5 million.

- The company's cost of capital (that is, the required rate of return on this project) is 10 percent.

- The company's tax rate is 30 percent.

Compute the NPV of this proposed new product line.

14. Atlanta Cookie (A Cookie) wishes to purchase a cookie making system that requires the purchase of a mixer costing $42,500 and an oven costing $35,000. This new cookie making system project is expected to meet the firm's growing demand for fabulous, fat-free cookies for the foreseeable future. The firm plans to use a 12 percent cost of capital to evaluate the project. The before tax annual cookie sales revenues over the life the project are shown in the following table:

Year	Estimated Sales Revenue
1	$ 70,000
2	$112,000
3	$160,000
4	$163,000
5	$ 92,000

It is expected that the system will have a zero salvage value and be depreciated straight line over its five-year life. The equipment is not expected to have a market value in five years. The company will get bank financing at a rate of 8 percent effective annual interest rate for the initial investment. After purchasing the new cookie making system, A Cookie will hire Emanuel Jackson to maintain, operate, and train other employees on how to use the new equipment. Emanuel will require a salary and benefits totaling $70,000 per year. Emanuel previously worked for the consulting company that recommended this system to A Cookie. A Cookie paid Emanuel's firm $30,000 to determine which system was ideally suited for them. Flour, sugar, butter, and other ingredients are estimated to cost 20 percent of sales annually. The system is so terrific that it is believed that A Cookie's baking process will become the industry standard and will open new distribution channels. However, the initial cost of setting up these new distribution channels is estimated to be $50,000. The increases in sales from the new customers are incorporated in the estimated sales revenue estimates above. The firm estimates that the project will require an increase in net working capital of $4,000, which will be recovered at the end of the life of the project. The company is in the combined 40 percent state and federal tax brackets.

Given the information above, compute:

a. The initial outlay (at T_0) for Atlanta Cookie to purchase the new cookie making system.

b. Atlanta Cookie's operating cash flow in year 3.

c. The non-operating cash flow in the fifth and final year of the project.

15. Compute the NPV of the following project:

Seinfeld Creative Productions is evaluating the construction of a studio complex. The planned site is currently valued at $400,000, but this parcel would not need to be purchased because Seinfeld already owns it. (If the company does not use the parcel for this project, it will be sold today for its current value.) The studio construction would cost Seinfeld $1 million and would be depreciated for tax purposes using straight-line to a zero salvage value over twenty years. Costanza & Benis, LLP is retained as the creative consultant of this project. George Costanza is due $25,000 in fees next month for services already rendered in the design stage. Another $35,000 in advance fees is expected to be paid at the end of 2000 to Elaine Benis for additional services to be performed if the project is launched.

It is expected that the studio will increase Seinfeld's short-movie production by five new releases every year, with each of them bringing in $90,000 per year in royalty fees. The operation of the studio will necessitate additional marketing expenditures of $100,000 per year and other general expenses of $50,000 per year. Lost fees due to Seinfeld giving up stand-up comedy engagements would run at $50,000 per year. Seinfeld would be expected to increase its net working capital by $20,000 to accommodate increased investment in movies accounts receivable over the life of the studio ownership—this amount would be recovered at the end of the life of the project. Seinfeld Productions intends to sell the site parcel for $400,000 and to sell the studio for an additional $500,000 after ten years.

The marginal tax rate of Seinfeld is 40 percent. For purposes of identifying the timing of cash flows, consider all project-related cash flows to occur at the end of the year. The construction takes place in 2000, the first year of operations is the year 2001, and the last year of operations is the year 2010.

16. Compute the NPV of the following project:

Your instructor, Norman Bates, was considering starting a new business, Finance Consulting, Inc. He had no money, so he contacted you, the richest student in the class, and asked you to finance the project. If you decided to finance the project, all that he wanted was an annual salary of $110,000; the remaining business cash flow, after paying all expenses and taxes, would be yours to keep.

He would immediately need to spend $8,000 for furniture and $10,000 for computers and software. He estimated that he could handle 1,000 appointments per year. His average fee would be $160 per appointment. He also would need to pay an annual rent of $40,000 for the office space and $2,500 each year for utilities. But he warned you that he would retire in six years to run the Bates motel (a family business for many years).

Because this was going to be your first business decision since learning about capital budgeting techniques in class, you were not sure whether Norman's estimates (given above) were realistic. (Even worse, you did not trust your instructor's estimates after all that he had done to you in FI3300). Therefore, you paid $500 to your more experienced marketing classmate, Mr. Sellitall, to double-check whether Norman's estimates were correct. Mr. Sellitall confirmed that the instructor's estimates were correct. However, you and Mr. Sellitall decided that you would not buy the new furniture, but would furnish Norman's office with the old junk from your basement. You thought that it was good enough for Norman, and that he did not deserve any better than that. You estimated that the market price of the old furniture at a flee market would be $2,000.

You also paid $1,000 to your accounting classmate, Ms. Smartgirl, for tax accounting advice. She estimated that your average business tax rate would be 40 percent. You could depreciate the computer equipment, software, and furniture on a straight-line basis for six years, and that at the end of year 6 the salvage value of the computer equipment and software would be $3,000 and the salvage value of the furniture would be zero. To run the business smoothly, however, you would need to provide Norman with working capital of $4,000 (cash) immediately. This amount would be returned to you at the termination of the business. You would not need to do any work. You just would give the cash needed at time zero to Norman, and he would send you checks equal to net business annual cash flow amounts at the end of each year. At the end of the first year you were planning on taking a tax deduction for the amount of $250 that you spent at the beginning of last semester for FI3300 tuition on your personal Federal Schedule A, "Itemized Deductions." However, Ms. Smartgirl suggested that you could allocate this cost to the business at the end of the first year.

Your required rate of return is 15 percent.

Index